SECOND EDITION

SPECIAL EDUCATION LAW

Nikki L. Murdick
Saint Louis University

Barbara C. Gartin
University of Arkansas

Terry Crabtree
Judge, Arkansas Court of Appeals
Little Rock, Arkansas

PEARSON
Merrill
Prentice Hall

Upper Saddle River, New Jersey
Columbus, Ohio

Library of Congress Cataloging in Publication Data

Murdick, Nikki L.
    Special education law / Nikki Murdick, Barbara Gartin, Terry Crabtree.—2nd ed.
        p. cm.
    Includes bibliographical references and index.
    ISBN 0-13-117571-8
    1. Special education—Law and legislation—United States.   I. Gartin, Barbara C.
        II. Crabtree, Terry.   III. Title.
    KF4210.M87 2007
    344.78'0791—dc22

                                                                        2005034715

Vice President and Executive Publisher: Jeffery W. Johnston
Senior Acquisitions Editor: Allyson P. Sharp
Editorial Assistant: Kathleen S. Burk
Senior Production Editor: Linda Hillis Bayma
Production Coordination: Penny Walker, TechBooks/GTS
Design Coordinator: Diane C. Lorenzo
Cover Designer: Ali Mohrman
Cover Image: Images.com
Production Manager: Laura Messerly
Director of Marketing: Ann Castel Davis
Marketing Manager: Autumn Purdy
Marketing Coordinator: Brian Mounts

This book was set in Garamond by TechBooks/GTS. It was printed and bound by R.R. Donnelley & Sons Company. The cover was printed by R.R. Donnelley & Sons Company.

Pearson Education Ltd.
Pearson Education Singapore Pte. Ltd.
Pearson Education Canada, Ltd.
Pearson Education—Japan

Pearson Education Australia Pty. Limited
Pearson Education North Asia Ltd.
Pearson Educación de Mexico, S.A. de C.V.
Pearson Education Malaysia Pte. Ltd.

10 9 8 7 6 5 4 3 2 1
ISBN: 0-13-117571-8

A Word to Our Readers

In the first edition of this text, we described the reasoning for our choice of organization, specific cases, and so forth to provide a background as to why we focused on certain aspects of the law or cited certain cases. On reflection, we decided that this information is appropriate for inclusion in the second edition of this text.

From a historical perspective, the Individuals with Disabilities Education Act (IDEA) was a response, in part, to issues raised by advocacy groups and court decisions. IDEA is, in fact, rooted in the social and philosophical fabric of the ideals of equality in the United States. These ideals have led the nation to review possible injustices and loss of personal rights through litigation at the state and national levels. The results of this litigation are catalogued and known as "case law." This information provides a historical, and often relevant, body of knowledge that is cited as "precedent" or *stare decisis* when issues are addressed through litigation or legislation at a later date. The study of law is, in part, the study of history.

Therefore, as we prepared this text, we cited and discussed cases that were brought before the courts at all levels to illustrate the points being examined in each chapter. Lower court decisions have a limited effect and only officially influence the state, district, or specific federal circuit in which they are heard (see Appendix A). However, as Judge Crabtree says: "What is law? I prefer to think of it as based on prior cases as applied to the facts. The law is what a court states it is at a given time."

Until a case is heard at the highest tier (the U.S. Supreme Court), the decision at the lower levels (district or circuit) provides the legal mandate for that issue in that specific area of the nation. Such decisions are used by attorneys, advocates, and legislators as a convenient compilation of information concerning a particular issue. It is important to note here that any opinions that are unpublished may be used for educational purposes only. They have no influence or effect on future court decisions, and they cannot be used as supporting citations.

When we discuss issues in the text, we also use other forms of supporting information to assist in clarifying our viewpoint on the topic (see Appendix B). For instance, the United States Code is cited with accompanying federal regulations whenever we discuss the specific section of IDEA that has resulted in controversy. Along with the legislation and litigation, where available, we have used Office of Special Education Programs, Office of Special Education and Rehabilitation Services, and letters and memos to the various state education agencies to provide you with the interpretation of IDEA and its regulations concerning an issue as it has been communicated to the states. Although these letters and memos are not considered to be law, they are given deference by the various courts when preparing an opinion.

In the second edition of this text, we address the changes in the legislation that affect the education of students with disabilities and their families. These changes include the most recent reauthorization of the Individuals with Disabilities Education Improvement Act of 2004, as well as information concerning other relevant legislation, including the No Child Left Behind Act, the Americans with Disabilities Act, the Family Educational Rights and Privacy Act, and the Health Insurance Portability and Accountability Act. For those using the book for teacher preparation, the standards and principles from the Council for Exceptional Children (CEC), Interstate New Teacher Assessment and Support Consortium (INTASC), and PRAXIS™ (special education knowledge base core principles) are referenced to reflect the connection between content and the standards and principles of the organization.

Of course, the selection of cases was a personal decision by the authors. We selected pertinent cases that we believed you, as readers, would find both interesting and informative. Cases were also chosen that have been recognized as historical underpinnings for IDEA. Although our philosophical preferences are exhibited throughout the text, we guarded against reinterpretation of the legal opinions. The briefings at the end of the chapters are provided to acquaint our readers with the methods used to examine disputed points of law. We urge you to review additional cases using that methodology, thereby obtaining firsthand knowledge of the reasoning of the court.

As you read this text, we hope you will remember that IDEA is the result of a reaffirmation of the beliefs of our society that *all* citizens should be provided an education. Beliefs enacted into legislation usually result in controversy. Legislative controversy is resolved by the judicial system.

Acknowledgments

We want to thank our families, who tolerated our preoccupation with this project, supported us with food and encouragement as needed, carried on with the responsibilities of life while we wrote, and read and reread numerous revisions. Our special thanks and love are extended, therefore, to Mike Reynierse, Tammy Rhomberg, Lynn Esteban, Jason Murdick, Ed and Meredith Gartin, and Diane Crabtree.

Our thanks to Andrew Brulle, Wheaton College, and Kristine Jolivette, University of Kentucky, for their comments on the manuscript.

Finally, we want to thank Wayne Spohr, retired special education representative, for his encouragement to submit the original manuscript to Prentice Hall. Our sincere thanks also go to Allyson Sharp, acquisitions editor at Merrill/Prentice Hall, who provided us with support and encouragement to not only write, but also to complete, this second edition of the book.

Discover the Merrill Resources for Special Education Website

Technology is a constantly growing and changing aspect of our field that is creating a need for new content and resources. To address this emerging need, Merrill Education has developed an online learning environment for students, teachers, and professors alike to complement our products—the *Merrill Resources for Special Education* Website. This content-rich website provides additional resources specific to this book's topic and will help you—professors, classroom teachers, and students—augment your teaching, learning, and professional development.

Our goal with this partnership and initiative is to build on and enhance what our products already offer. For this reason, the content for our user-friendly website is organized by topic and provides teachers, professors, and students with a variety of meaningful resources all in one location. With this website, we bring together the best of what Merrill has to offer: text resources, video clips, web links, tutorials, and a wide variety of information on topics of interest to general and special educators alike. Rich content, applications, and competencies further enhance the learning process.

The *Merrill Resources for Special Education* Website includes:

- Video clips specific to each topic, with questions to help you evaluate the content and make crucial theory-to-practice connections.

- Thought-provoking critical analysis questions that students can answer and turn in for evaluation or that can serve as a basis for class discussions and lectures.

- Access to a wide variety of resources related to classroom strategies and methods, including lesson planning and classroom management.
- Information on all the most current relevant topics related to special and general education, including CEC and Praxis standards, IEPs, portfolios, and professional development.
- Extensive web resources and overviews on each topic addressed on the website.
- A search feature to help access specific information quickly.

To take advantage of these and other resources, please visit the *Merrill Resources for Special Education* Website at

http://www.prenhall.com/murdick

TEACHER PREP

**MERRILL
PRENTICE HALL**

Teacher Preparation Classroom

Your Class. Their Careers. Our Future. Will your students be prepared?

We invite you to explore our new, innovative and engaging website and all that it has to offer you, your course, and tomorrow's educators! Organized around the major courses pre-service teachers take, the Teacher Preparation site provides media, student/teacher artifacts, strategies, research articles, and other resources to equip your students with the quality tools needed to excel in their courses and prepare them for their first classroom.

This ultimate on-line education resource is available at no cost, when packaged with a Merrill text, and will provide you and your students access to:

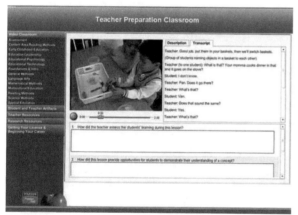

Online Video Library. More than 150 video clips—each tied to a course topic and framed by learning goals and Praxis-type questions—capture real teachers and students working in real classrooms, as well as in-depth interviews with both students and educators.

Student and Teacher Artifacts. More than 200 student and teacher classroom artifacts—each tied to a course topic and framed by learning goals and application questions—provide a wealth of materials and experiences to help make your study to become a professional teacher more concrete and hands-on.

Research Articles. Over 500 articles from ASCD's renowned journal *Educational Leadership.* The site also includes Research Navigator, a searchable database of additional educational journals.

Teaching Strategies. Over 500 strategies and lesson plans for you to use when you become a practicing professional.

Licensure and Career Tools. Resources devoted to helping you pass your licensure exam; learn standards, law, and public policies; plan a teaching portfolio; and succeed in your first year of teaching.

How to ORDER *Teacher Prep* for you and your students:

For students to receive a *Teacher Prep* Access Code with this text, instructors **must** provide a special value pack ISBN number on their textbook order form. To receive this special ISBN, please email: **Merrill.marketing@pearsoned.com** and provide the following information:

- Name and Affiliation
- Author/Title/Edition of Merrill text

Upon ordering *Teacher Prep* for their students, instructors will be given a lifetime *Teacher Prep* Access Code.

CONTENTS

CHAPTER FOUR

Nondiscriminatory Evaluation   66

CHAPTER FIVE

Program Development   90

CHAPTER SIX

Least Restrictive Environment   118

CHAPTER SEVEN

Procedural Due Process   142

CHAPTER EIGHT

Parental Participation   **164**

PART III

Remedies   **179**

CHAPTER NINE

Enforcement of Special Education Law   **180**

CHAPTER TEN

Discipline Issues   202

CHAPTER ELEVEN

Mediation and Impartial Due Process Hearing   218

CHAPTER TWELVE — Ethics and the Special Education Professional — 242

APPENDIX A — The American Legal System — 253

APPENDIX B — Reading and Researching Case Law — 259

NOTE: Every effort has been made to provide accurate and current Internet information in this book. However, the Internet and information posted on it are constantly changing, and it is inevitable that some of the Internet addresses listed in this textbook will change.

PART I

The Bases for Special Education

CHAPTER 1
Historical Overview of Special Education

CHAPTER 2
A New Foundation for Special Education Services

CHAPTER ONE

Historical Overview of Special Education

GUIDING QUESTIONS

1. What is the importance of the deinstitutionalization movement and the philosophy of normalization in the development of today's special education services?

2. Why did advocacy groups feel the necessity for a "bill of rights" for persons with developmental disabilities?

3. How did the Civil Rights movement impact the provision of services for persons with disabilities?

4. How did President Kennedy's charge to Congress in 1963 change the direction of services for persons with disabilities for the next 20 years? *Neglect of MR was too long – develop programs*

5. What was the litigative base for the provision of educational services for persons with disabilities?

6. What was the legislative basis that provided the early civil rights guarantees for persons with disabilities?

Knowledge of the past helps one understand the forces that influence the development and provision of today's educational services for individuals with disabilities. The past will continue to influence the development and provision of services in the future. One must realize that all programs, practices, and facilities reflect the prevailing social climate. As attitudes have changed, so have the types of services provided. Changes in attitudes are also reflected in the legislative and regulatory bases for the provision of those services. Therefore, four significant factors (deinstitutionalization and normalization, advocacy, the Civil Rights movement, and the Kennedy era) are discussed briefly to frame the legislative and judicial actions that have influenced the education of individuals with disabilities.

Deinstitutionalization and Normalization

In the early 1900s, the service options available for individuals with disabilities were private and/or state institutions because most public schools would not accept such identified students. These residential facilities were originally developed to provide appropriate educational training for individuals with mental and physical disabilities. For example, in 1848, Dr. Samuel Howe persuaded the Massachusetts legislature to appropriate public funds to establish the first state school in the United States for the education of persons with mental retardation (Vitello & Soskin, 1985, p. 25). According to Fernald (1883), this school was organized according to a "family plan" where training and care were provided, and only a "relatively small number of inmates could successfully be cared for in one institution" (p. 206). However, by the turn of the 20th century, institutions began to function less as schools for training persons to return to the community and more as institutions for controlling persons in order to protect the community. By the time this attitude of fear had passed, institutions had become firmly established (Vitello & Soskin, 1985, pp. 26–27).

As a result, by the mid-1900s, all states had built publicly supported state institutions. Because individuals with disabilities were excluded from the public schools and public life, the institutions became custodial, with a focus on lifelong care. The result was an overcrowding of the facilities. Hence, throughout the United States, professionals, as well as the public, became concerned that many institutions were not providing the level of services, or quality of life, that should be available to all individuals. This concern was expanded and

Standards and the Law

CEC Standard 1: Foundations
INTASC Standard 1: Subject Matter
PRAXIS Standard: Legal and Societal Issues
PRAXIS Standard: Delivery of Services to Students with Disabilities

substantiated by the report of the President's Panel on Mental Retardation (1962) when it stated that

> The quality of care furnished by State institutions varies widely, . . . but the general level must be regarded as low. In large State institutions, the normal problems of administration and care are compounded by overcrowding, staff shortages, and frequently by inadequate budgets. (pp. 132–133)

Overcrowding, inadequate funding, and quality of care were not the only concerns expressed by the Panel. It also addressed the need for significant changes in attitudes of the residential facilities staff toward their patients, the types and amount of available programming, and administrative practices that led to widespread abuses of the system. In its report, the Panel supported the residential facility concept and advocated building additional facilities to meet the needs of the more than 50,000 children and adults who had been placed on waiting lists for services. In addition, the Panel recommended a maximum bed capacity of 500 per facility, significantly less than the 1,500 maximum policy adopted by the Board of Directors of the National Association of Retarded Citizens in 1958 (Scheerenberger, 1987).

However, conditions in institutions were slow to change. In December 1965, Burton Blatt and Fred Kaplan toured five unidentified institutions in four eastern states and took undercover photos of the back wards in an attempt to facilitate the changes suggested by the President's Panel. According to Seymour Sarason in his foreword to *Christmas in Purgatory,* Blatt and Kaplan's work resulted in "a simple, easily grasped, compelling, upsetting visual document which stood as a reminder of what existed in our society, and as a criterion by which to judge any derivative of our propensity to segregate people who are or look 'different'" (Blatt & Kaplan, 1974, p. iv). However, in 1971, the American Association on Mental Deficiency (AAMD) reported the results of a national study involving 134 public institutions caring for persons with mental retardation that indicated changes were still needed because

1. Sixty percent of the institutions were overcrowded.

2. Fifty percent of the institutions rated below minimum safety standards.

3. Eighty-nine percent of the institutions did not meet acceptable attendant/resident ratios, and 83 percent did not meet professional staffing requirements.

4. Sixty percent of the institutions provided insufficient space for programming (e.g., education, recreation).

5. Sixty-four percent of the institutions used residents to maintain the institution, and only 23 percent compensated residents. (Vitello & Soskin, 1985, pp. 28–29)

In fact, conditions in many institutions were no different than when Blatt and Kaplan made their famous tour. In 1972, Geraldo Rivera published another exposé documenting the conditions in institutions for persons with mental retardation. In his book *Willowbrook*, Rivera (1972) reported that the call for change had resulted in temporary improvement only, and that

> what is necessary in the Willowbrooks of America is not just cleaner wards and better clothing that continued scrutiny would bring. Change is necessary, and it must be massive and fundamental. . . . Change is difficult, but change is necessary. We've got to close that goddamned place down. (pp. 146–147)

Responses to the reports and exposés during this time supported the search for alternatives to institutionalization, to relieve the overcrowding of institutions and to reduce the expanding costs of providing institutional care. One response was to develop agricultural colonies where residents engaged in domestic and agricultural tasks to defray the cost of their care. In addition, the removal of these persons from institutions reduced the resident populations. A second method developed that led to the establishment of community-based services was to "parole" the resident to the community. The movement that evolved in support of these actions was called "deinstitutionalization" and was based on the philosophy of normalization. Normalization had been a well-recognized principle in Scandinavian countries for some time but was not introduced into the United States until the late 1960s by Neils Bank-Mikkelson and Bengt Nirje. The original purpose of this principle was to reform the services and environments provided for individuals with mental retardation so their lives were "normalized," or more like those of persons not residing in institutions. Wolf Wolfensberger (1972), the major contributor to the philosophy in the United States, expanded this theory to include "normalizing" the behavior of the individual with a disability and using cultural mores to identify *normal* behaviors. As the 20th century progressed, this concept was further expanded and clarified by Wolfensberger (1983) to include the idea of "social valorization," which placed an emphasis on valuing the person even when the person could not participate fully in society because of a disability. It affirmed not only the right of an individual to be both valued and different, but also the right of an individual to a life with dignity.

Although the principle of normalization was a major factor in the deinstitutionalization movement, it was seen by many as an inadequate approach to meeting the needs of persons with disabilities. During the late 1960s and early 1970s, some consumers, professionals, and parents were dissatisfied with prevailing philosophies and service delivery options. For example, a group founded in 1973, known as People First International, noted that the principle of normalization did not truly meet the goal of inclusion into the social fabric of society for persons with disabilities, but actually fostered social isolation. They disagreed with the principle of normalization because they believed it ignored the view that persons with a disability could be seen and valued as a minority group within society as a whole. The People First International group believed persons with disabilities would have more opportunities for inclusion into society and subsequent relationships if they were seen as a "minority community." This sense of belonging to a community was seen as an essential factor in meeting the special needs of its members. In contrast, "normalization" called for the rejection of minority group designation, as well as the cultivation of relationships with the "normal," or the nondisabled, community (Scheerenberger, 1987).

These actions (i.e., the acceptance of the philosophy of normalization, the deinstitutionalization movement, the report from the President's Panel, and exposés of institutional abuses) were essential factors in the subsequent case law decisions, known as the "Right to Treatment" cases, which would then provide the cornerstone for the legal principle of least restrictive environment. Two major "Right to Treatment" cases (*Halderman v. Pennhurst State School and Hospital,* 1979; *Wyatt v. Stickney,* 1971) focused on the issue of removal of the individual's constitutional right to "liberty" through involuntary institutionalization and whether this removal created a presumptive right to receive treatment for the characteristic that precipitated the institutionalization. In *Wyatt v. Stickney,* the aunt and guardian of Ricky Wyatt, a resident of Partlow State School and Hospital in Alabama, brought suit against Stickney, superintendent of the institution, alleging that the residents were not receiving proper treatment and habilitation, the primary purpose for their involuntary commitment. The Court agreed with this premise and held that a person with mental retardation who was committed involuntarily to a public institution possessed "an inviolable constitutional right to habilitation" and that the Partlow State School and Hospital in Alabama was "a warehousing institution incapable of furnishing habilitation to the mentally retarded and conducive only to the deterioration and debilitation of the residents" (Vitello & Soskin, 1985, p. 33). This judgment not only upheld the constitutional rights of individuals with mental retardation, but also set forth minimum treatment standards that covered "admission policies, right to treatment and habilitation, staffing patterns, records and review, physical plant and environment, medication, and resident labor" (Scheerenberger, 1987, p. 229).

This holding was further supported in *Halderman v. Pennhurst State School and Hospital* (1979), wherein the Court stated that

> the retarded at Pennhurst [were] not receiving minimally adequate habilitation [and] such minimally adequate habilitation cannot be provided at Pennhurst because it does not provide an atmosphere conducive to normalization, which experts all agree is vital to the minimally adequate habilitation of the retarded. (Scheerenberger, 1987, p. 123)

After reviewing the issues surrounding the provision of adequate services for those who are involuntarily committed to an institution, the District Court held that individuals placed in residential settings must receive treatment developed to enable them to acquire the skills necessary for their survival in life. This concept was later supported by the holding in *Romeo v. Youngberg* (1982), wherein the Supreme Court noted that persons with mental retardation who were institutionalized still had liberty interests protected by the U.S. Constitution.

Advocacy and a "Bill of Rights"

At the same time that social forces were changing national philosophies (e.g., deinstitutionalization, normalization), they were affecting another group of individuals. Parents of children with mental retardation were becoming more frustrated

Standards and the Law

CEC Standard 9: Professional and Ethical Practices
PRAXIS Standard: Legal and Societal Issues

with the exclusion of their children from tax-supported public schools and the scarcity of available services in state residential facilities. As a result of these problems, parents formed local support groups, which later combined into national groups. The most well-known group is the National Association for Retarded Children (ARC), now known as The Arc. This group was, and continues to be, a significant lobbying force for changes in funding availability and for the provision of appropriate preservice and in-service personnel preparation at the state and national levels (Kirk, 1978).

During this time, a number of advocacy and professional groups (the International League of Societies for the Mentally Handicapped, the American Association on Mental Retardation, and the Joint Commission on Mental Health of Children) developed a basic rights statement for individuals with mental retardation and other disabilities, which was accepted in 1971 by the United Nations General Assembly. The Declaration stated

Article I
The mentally retarded person has the same basic rights as other citizens of the same country and same age.

Article II
The mentally retarded person has a right to proper medical care and physical restoration and to such education, training, habilitation, and guidance as will enable him to develop his ability and potential to the fullest possible extent, no matter how severe his degree of disability. No mentally handicapped person should be deprived of such services by reason of the costs involved.

Article III
The mentally retarded person has a right to economic security and to a decent standard of living. He has a right to productive work or to other meaningful occupation.

Article IV
The mentally retarded person has a right to live with his own family or with foster parents, to participate in all aspects of community life, and to be provided with appropriate leisure time activities. If care in an institution becomes necessary, it should be in surroundings and other circumstance as close to normal living as possible.

Article V
The mentally retarded person has a right to a qualified guardian when this is required to protect his personal well-being and interest. No person rendering direct services to the mentally retarded should also serve as his guardian.

Article VI

The mentally retarded person has a right to protection from exploitation, abuse, and degrading treatment. If accused, he has a right to a fair trial with full recognition being given to his degree of responsibility.

Article VII

Some mentally retarded persons may be unable, due to the severity of their handicap, to exercise for themselves all of their rights in a meaningful way. For others, modification of some or all of these rights is appropriate. The procedure used for modification or denial of rights, must be based on an evaluation of the social capability of the mentally retarded person by qualified experts, and must be subject to periodic reviews and to the rightful appeal to higher authorities. (United Nations General Assembly, 1971)

These statements, a reaffirmation of beliefs held by society, were used by lobbying groups in their drive to initiate reforms in service delivery for individuals with disabilities. As a result of these efforts, a rights statement was also included in the Developmental Disabilities Assistance and Bill of Rights Act of 1975 (P.L. 94–103):

(1) Persons with developmental disabilities have a right to appropriate treatment, services, and habilitation for such disabilities.

(2) The treatment, services, and habilitation for a person with developmental disabilities should be designed to maximize the developmental potential of the person and should be provided in the setting that is least restrictive of the person's personal liberty.

(3) The Federal Government and the States both have an obligation to assure public funds are not provided to any institution or other residential program for persons with developmental disabilities that—

(A) Does not provide treatment, services, and habilitation which is appropriate to the needs of such persons; or

(B) Does not meet the following minimum standards:

(i) Provision of a nourishing, well-balanced daily diet to the persons with developmental disabilities being served by the program.

(ii) Provision to such persons of appropriate and sufficient medical and dental services.

(iii) Prohibition of the use of physical restraint on such persons unless absolutely necessary and prohibition of the use of such restraint as a punishment or as a substitute for a habilitation program. (*Rehabilitation and Developmental Legislation,* 1976, p. 53)

These statements provided the philosophical base for later legislation such as the Education for All Handicapped Children Act of 1975 (P.L. 94–142), as well as the report from the U.S. Commission on Civil Rights (1983).

The Civil Rights Movement and Its Impact on Educational Services

During the 1960s and the early 1970s, there was a pervasive national concern with the rights of the individual, especially the rights of persons who had previously been disenfranchised by the government. This era of expanding civil rights for

Standards and the Law

CEC Standard 2: Development and Characteristics of Learners
INTASC Standard 3: Diverse Learners
PRAXIS Standard: Delivery of Services to Students with Disabilities

persons of differing ethnic and racial backgrounds also impacted the provision of services and the rights of persons with disabilities. In fact, the rights of persons with disabilities became a significant part of the larger social issue of the time. The major civil rights issue of exclusion and segregation of students based on race was expanded to include students with disabilities. Exclusion from schools based on disability was included in state statutes throughout the United States and had been supported in the courts. For instance, the Supreme Judicial Court of Massachusetts had upheld the exclusion of a student with mental retardation based on his mental and physical disabilities (*Watson v. City of Cambridge,* 1893), and the Wisconsin Supreme Court had upheld a school's decision to exclude a student with normal mental abilities based on his physical appearance, his inability to physically care for himself, and the amount of time a teacher was required to assist him (*State ex rel. Beattie v. Board of Education of Antigo,* 1919). However, in the landmark case of the Civil Rights movement (*Brown v. Board of Education of Topeka, Kansas,* 1954), Chief Justice Warren supported education as one of the most important activities of the government. *Brown* was used by advocates for persons with disabilities in opposition to the exclusion of students with disabilities from the public schools. It also provided the basic tenet for later federal legislation guaranteeing educational and civil rights for persons with disabilities. In fact, the *Brown* case has been the seminal case in the development of legislation and litigation in the field of special education.

The Kennedy Era and a Change of Direction

The election of John F. Kennedy in 1960 signified a new focus in the federal government's involvement in the provision of services to persons with disabilities. As a result of lobbying groups and his own personal experiences with the mental retardation of his sister, Kennedy formed the President's Panel on Mental Retardation to study ways to improve the quality of life for persons with disabilities. When addressing this committee, Kennedy challenged them by saying,

> Although we have made considerable progress in the treatment of physical handicaps, although we have attacked on a broad front the problems of mental illness, although we have made great strides in the battle against disease, we as a Nation have too long postponed an intensive search for solutions to the problems of the mentally retarded. That failure should be corrected. (President's Panel, 1962, p. 196)

The report of the Panel provided the basis for Kennedy's charge to Congress, in which he stated,

> We as a nation have long neglected the mentally ill and the mentally retarded. This neglect must end, if our nation is to live up to its own standards of compassion and dignity and achieve the maximum of its manpower.
>
> The tradition of neglect must be replaced by forceful and far-reaching programs carried out at all levels of government, by private individuals and by State and local agencies in every part of the Union. (1963, p. 13)

The Panel's report, containing 112 recommendations, outlined the basic charge for future legislation affecting persons with disabilities. On the basis of the Panel's recommendations, two major pieces of legislation (the Maternal and Child Health and Mental Retardation Planning Amendments of 1963 and the Mental Retardation Facilities and Community Mental Health Centers Construction Act of 1963) were passed within the year, and the legislative future of disability law was projected for the next 20 years.

Litigative Base for Educational Services

The advocates of civil rights and social equality sought justice through the courts, as well as through advocacy within the political and legislative arena. The resulting court decisions provided a new direction for the provision of educational services to individuals with disabilities, as well as an affirmation of basic rights and guarantees that would be expanded and confirmed through legislation as the 20th century progressed. Six court decisions, ranging from federal District Court consent decrees to a Supreme Court decision, provided the basis for later litigation and subsequent legislation. These cases are briefly described.

Brown v. Board of Education of Topeka, Kansas (1954)

In 1954, the U.S. Supreme Court heard a case that has significantly impacted the social and educational fabric in the United States since that time. This case had been consolidated from lawsuits in four states (Kansas, South Carolina, Virginia, and Delaware), which alleged that African American children who were required to attend segregated schools were denied their constitutional rights under the Fourteenth Amendment. The lower courts had relied on a previous holding in *Plessy v. Ferguson* (1896), which

> ### *Standards and the Law*
>
> **CEC Standard 1:** Foundations
> **INTASC Standard 1:** Subject Matter
> **PRAXIS Standard:** Delivery of Services to Students with Disabilities

upheld segregated schools as constitutional because they were seen as substantially equal. The justices did not agree with this "separate but equal" doctrine and held that

> In these days, it is doubtful that any child may reasonably be expected to succeed in life if he is denied the opportunity of an education. Such an opportunity, where the state has undertaken to provide it, is a right which must be made available to all on equal terms. (*Brown v. Board of Education of Topeka, Kansas,* 1954)

This decision by the U.S. Supreme Court to end the White "separate but equal" schools provided the basis for the future rulings that children with disabilities cannot be excluded from public school. In the *Brown* decision, the Court found that segregated facilities were not equal as previously supported in *Plessy* and, in fact, that segregated facilities resulted in diminished educational opportunities and reduced interaction with peers of other backgrounds and ethnicity. The Court stated that segregation based on unalterable characteristics with the result being inequitable opportunities could not be upheld in the United States and demanded that such segregation end with "all deliberate speed" (*Brown v. Board of Education of Topeka, Kansas,* 1954). This support for integrated educational opportunities was later used by advocates for persons with disabilities in both their lobbying efforts for federal legislation that mandated equal educational opportunities for students with disabilities and in their appeals to the judicial system.

Hobson v. Hansen (1967)

The discussion and subsequent holding in *Hobson* expanded the basic issue beyond that of physical exclusion from public school. The plaintiffs in this case were Black students who were placed in disproportionate numbers into the lower tracks in the educational tracking system used by the public school system in Washington, DC. The issue, therefore, was whether the tracking system discriminated against students who were from lower socioeconomic areas or from minority groups. The students were included in the public schools; however, as a result of "biased" assessments using group tests that were standardized primarily on White middle-class students, the Black students were inaccurately labeled and placed in segregated classes. The Court found that through mislabeling and segregation, the school system violated its public responsibilities because of

> ... the degree to which the poor and the Negro must rely on the public schools in rescuing themselves from their depressed cultural and economic condition, and also our common need of the schools to serve as the public agency for neutralizing and normalizing race relations in this country. With these interests at stake, the Court must ask whether the virtues stemming from the Board of Education's pupil assignment policy (here the neighborhood policy) are *compelling* or *adequate justification* for the considerable evils of *de facto* segregation which adherence to this policy breeds. (*Hobson v. Hansen,* 1967)

The placement of mislabeled students into segregated classes resulted in the students being provided a curriculum significantly different from students in the

Standards and the Law

CEC Standard 2: Development and Characteristics of Learners
INTASC Standard 3: Diverse Learners
PRAXIS Standard: Delivery of Services to Students with Disabilities

"mainstream" of the school and lowered their educational opportunities. Because the tracking system was based on the students' unalterable characteristics, as in *Brown,* and "discriminated against the socially and/or economically disadvantaged" (*Hobson v. Hansen,* 1967), the Court required the school district to discontinue the practice and to provide compensatory education to those students who had been hampered in their educational opportunities by previous placement through the tracking system.

PARC v. Commonwealth of Pennsylvania (1972)

In 1971, the Pennsylvania Association for Retarded Children's (PARC's) case against the state resulted in a legal decision that is considered to be the second indicator of the new period in special education services. This case resulted in a consent decree that enjoined the State of Pennsylvania from denying educational opportunities to children with mental retardation who reside in the state. The case had been brought by parents of children with mental retardation who had been excluded from the public schools as a result of their disability. This case was based on two basic tenets of the U.S. Constitution: equal protection and due process. In 1972, the order of the Court stated that

> [A] free, public program of education and training appropriate to the child's capacity, within the context of the general educational policy that, among the alternative programs of education and training required by statute to be available, placement in a regular public school class is preferable to placement in a special public school class [i.e., a class for "disabled" children] and placement in a special school class is preferable to placement in any other type of program of education and training. (*PARC v. Commonwealth of Pennsylvania,* 1972, p. 307)

This landmark decision was supported by a second court-ordered consent decree (*Mills*), which expanded the rights it had guaranteed to all children with disabilities.

Mills v. Board of Education of the District of Columbia (1972)

In *Mills,* the plaintiffs, children labeled as "exceptional," brought a class action suit against the District of Columbia on behalf of students who had been labeled as having behavioral problems, or being mentally retarded, emotionally disturbed, and/or hyperactive. These children had been excluded, suspended, expelled, reassigned, and transferred from regular public schools without due process of law; thus, they were denied the opportunity for an education. This litigation ended in a consent decree that extended the right for special education guaranteed in *PARC* to all children with disabilities and reinforced the right to a free public education:

> No child eligible for a publicly supported education in the District of Columbia public schools shall be excluded from a regular public school assignment by rule, policy, or practice of the Board or its agents . . .
>
> The District of Columbia shall provide to each child of school age a free and suitable publicly supported education regardless of the degree of the child's mental, physical, or emotional disability or impairment. Insufficient resources may not be a basis for exclusion. (*Mills v. Board of Education of the District of Columbia*, 1972)

This case and the previous one served as the impetus for the proliferation of similar cases in other states. At the same time, the decision delineated a set of due process requirements related to assessment, labeling, and placement of children in special education by the public schools, providing the outline for federal and state legislation that would be enacted in the 1970s.

Diana v. State Board of Education (1970)

In 1970, the issue of the use of standardized tests to classify minority students was specifically addressed when a suit was filed on behalf of nine Mexican American students who had been assigned to special education classes in California (*Diana v. State Board of Education*, 1970). The Hispanic students had been assigned to special education classes on the basis of intelligence tests given in the English language and standardized on a White, native-born American population with items that were later determined to be culturally biased. In the agreement, it was stipulated that the performance of minority students be compared with their peer group and not with nonminority groups. This requirement was later included in the regulations of the Education of All Handicapped Children Act to ensure "nonbiased" testing.

Larry P. v. Riles (1972, 1974, 1979, 1984)

The issue in this case was similar to that in *Diana*, except that it focused on a student who was African American. As in the previous case, the plaintiffs stated that the assessment was biased and subsequent placement was discriminatory because both used intelligence tests as the basis for the decisions. In *Larry P.*, the basis for discrimination was not the language difference of the tests but that the tests had not been validated on an appropriate population. The result of the biased evaluation was that a disproportionate number of minority students were placed in special education classes. The courts agreed with this argument and held that students of minority groups could not be placed in special education classes until nonbiased assessments had been developed. In addition, the Court directed the State to retest all students in special education programs and, when necessary, to provide appropriate compensatory education.

Civil Rights Legislation Protecting Persons with Disabilities

During this period of change and intense furor within the field of special education concerning the provision of appropriate services to persons with disabilities, advocacy groups continued their efforts to reaffirm the basic rights for persons with disabilities through their lobbying for the enactment of national legislation. Congress, influenced by these advocacy efforts and the results of recent court decisions, enacted legislation to codify and expand the foundation of civil rights guarantees being developed.

The Rehabilitation Act of 1973

The Rehabilitation Act of 1973 (P.L. 93–112) included a section considered to be the first piece of civil rights legislation specifically providing guarantees of rights to persons with disabilities. Section 504 stated that

> No otherwise qualified individual with a disability in the United States . . . shall, solely by reason of her or his disability, be excluded from the participation in, be denied the benefits of, or be subjected to discrimination under any program or activity receiving Federal financial assistance or under any program or activity conducted by any Executive agency or by the United States Postal Service. (29 U.S.C. § 794)

This provision supported the rights of individuals with disabilities to be included in those programs supported by federal funds, thus extending the rights granted previously to persons of different races and ethnicity to persons with disabilities.

The Rehabilitation Act does not provide funding but only a guarantee of rights. It does, however, include two remedies that can be accessed when individuals believe schools have discriminated against children with disabilities. First, individuals can file a complaint with the Department of Education (DOE). If the DOE finds a violation, it can order (and has ordered) a termination of federal funds to the offending school subject to judicial review (34 C.F.R. §§ 100.8–.10, 600.1–.41, 1991). Second, individuals may also sue offending school districts directly. The successful complainant can be awarded damages and attorney fees.

Developmental Disabilities Assistance and Bill of Rights Act of 1975

The legislative basis for the Developmental Disabilities Assistance and Bill of Rights Act of 1975 (known as the DD Act) was the Mental Retardation Facilities and Community Mental Health Centers Construction Act of 1963. The 1963 Act was enacted by Congress to implement recommendations of the President's Panel on Mental Retardation. It contained funding for the development of research centers, university-affiliated facilities, and community facilities whose purposes were to expand the knowledge and services available for persons with mental retardation.

As the field of special education grew and changed, so did the Act. In 1975, the 1963 Act was amended to include a Bill of Rights for Persons with Disabilities. Subsequent amendments expanded the scope of the act to include a functional definition of disability, development of state plans that included provisions for deinstitutionalization, state grants for services, and development of State Developmental Disabilities Councils to provide each governmental entity with input from consumers of the services being planned. As with the Rehabilitation Act of 1973, language from this act has been incorporated into later legislation, such as the Americans with Disabilities Act of 1990 (P.L. 101–336).

Summary

When reviewing the chapter, one finds that today's legislation reflects the past. For example, the preference for deinstitutionalization and normalization is reflected legally in provision of the continuum of alternative placements and in the mandate for the provision of educational services in the least restrictive environment. Both deinstitutionalization and normalization are efforts to reduce segregation and isolation and encourage the inclusion of all people into the community. When isolation and segregation occur, often abuse and poor quality services are also present. The ideas of community as a place for all people and of inclusion in schools and classrooms for all children are direct descendents of deinstitutionalization and the philosophy of normalization.

Because of the continuing exclusion of persons with disabilities from public services and the denial of their state-sanctioned rights, advocacy groups sought a "bill of rights" for persons with developmental disabilities. This document included in the DD Act outlined the rights of persons with developmental disabilities, and affirmed that the rights of persons with developmental disabilities were the same rights as persons without disabilities who were citizens of the same country and of the same age. The Civil Rights movement, therefore, focused national concern on the rights of individuals who had been previously disenfranchised. Exclusion and segregation based on inalterable characteristics were determined to be illegal. In opening the schools to those with differences in race and ethnicity, those persons with disabilities were also allowed to enter.

President Kennedy challenged Congress to focus resources on finding a solution for the problems of those with mental retardation. The legislation that was passed at that time was a forecast of the course of disability legislation for the next 20 years.

Beginning in the 1950s with *Brown* and then following the actions of President Kennedy, there were six court decisions that provided additional direction for future legislation. In 1954, *Brown* established that separate was unequal. In 1967, *Hobson* stated that denial of services through mislabeling and tracking equated to functional exclusion. In 1972, *PARC* expanded the Constitutional guarantees of due process and equal protection rights to include public education of children with mental retardation. Later in 1972, *Mills* expanded *PARC* to include children with all types of disabilities.

In 1970, *Diana* revisited standardized testing in terms of culturally biased testing where Mexican American children were assigned to special education classes based on test results from English-only tests using nonminority norms.

From 1972 to 1984, *Larry P.* examined a similar issue as *Diana,* except it focused on discriminatory placement of an African American student. The findings of these cases were later used as a basis for educational legislation governing the education of children with disabilities.

The result of these political advocacy and judicial actions was an awareness of a need for civil rights legislation for persons with disabilities. Legislation was passed that codified and expanded the foundation for civil rights of persons with disabilities, including the Rehabilitation Act of 1973 and the Developmental Disabilities Assistance and Bill of Rights Act of 1975. Section 504 of the Rehabilitation Act specifically guaranteed the right of persons with disabilities to be included in programs receiving federal funds. The language from both acts has been incorporated into later legislation.

In summary, throughout the 20th century, the United States has gradually become aware of the needs of individuals with disabilities and the inequity of the services provided. Initially, attention was given to the provision of residential services. However, as changes in the political and social climates led to the rejection of segregated services, the focus became the provision of services within the community. Institutional practices were challenged, and public schools were forced to serve persons with disabilities. The Supreme Court affirmed the right to a free appropriate education for all citizens through its stance on civil rights, whereas the federal government expanded its interests in the provision of education through funding legislation.

Questions for Discussion

1. How did the philosophy of normalization and its follow-up concept of deinstitutionalization impact the provision of services for persons with mental retardation?
2. Explain the impact of advocacy civil rights legislation and the involvement of a national political figure such as President Kennedy on the future of services for persons with exceptionalities?
3. What is the litigative base for special education legislation and programs?
4. What is the legislative base?
5. Based on your understanding of the bases for special education services, how will future services be affected?

Websites for Further Exploration

Deinstitutionalization and Normalization
www.disabilitymuseum.org/lib/docs/1941.htm
soeweb.syr.edu/thechp/dsbiblio.htm
www.socialrolevalorization.com/resource/Bookflyr.htm
www.thearclink.org/news/article.asp?ID=390
www.equipforequality.org/cippreport.html

History of Services (Advocacy, Civil Rights Movement, The Kennedy Era)
www.awesomelibrary.org/Library/Special_Education/Developmental_Disabilities/
    Developmental_Disabilities.html
www.dddcec.org/Links.htm
www.acf.hhs.gov/programs/pcpid/pcpid_history.html
www.usccr.gov

Legislative Base
www.acf.hhs.gov/programs/add/
www.usdoj.gov/crt/ada/cguide.htm
www.nau.edu/~ihd/aztap/factsheets/ddabra.shtml
www.access-board.gov/sec508/guide/act.htm
www.hhs.gov/ocr/504.html
www.usdoj.gov/crt/ada/adahom1.htm
www.eeoc.gov/facts/fs-ada.html

ILLUSTRATING THE LAW

Briefing of:
Oliver BROWN et al., Appellants, v. BOARD OF EDUCATION OF TOPEKA,
Shawnee County, Kansas, et al.
United States Supreme Court
347 U.S. 438, 98 L.Ed. 873, 74 S.Ct. 686
Argued December 8–11, 1952
Reargued December 7–9, 1953
Decided May 17, 1954

FACTS: This case was a consolidated appeal of four separate groups of plaintiffs in Kansas, South Carolina, Virginia, and Delaware. The Court summarized why the four cases were treated together, "In each of the cases, minors of the Negro race, through their legal representatives, seek the aid of the Courts in obtaining admission to the public schools of their community on a nonsegregated basis." The plaintiffs alleged that such segregation denied them their right of equal protection of the laws under the Fourteenth Amendment. The Courts each relied on the holding in *Plessy v. Ferguson* (163 U.S. 537, 41 L.Ed. 256, 16 S.Ct. 1138) for the proposition that "equality of treatment is accorded when the races are provided substantially equal facilities, even though those facilities be separate." The plaintiffs argued that segregated public schools could not be made "equal," thus depriving them of their equal protection rights.

ISSUE: The Court summarized the major issue as follows: "Does segregation of children in public schools solely on the basis of race, even though the physical facilities and other 'tangible' factors may be equal, deprive the children of the minority group of equal educational opportunities?"

HOLDING: The Court rejected the "separate but equal" doctrine of *Plessy v. Ferguson*. In doing so, the Court held that in the field of public education, "separate but equal" has no place.

RATIONALE: The Court's holding was based on the history of the post-Civil War amendments affecting slavery and racial segregation. The Court also looked to modern theories of psychology, accepting the idea that segrega-

tion, especially among school-age children, fostered lifelong feelings of inferiority. Furthermore, the Court used its holding in *Sweat v. Painter* (339 U.S. 629, 94 L.Ed. 1117, 70 S.Ct. 848) to support the notion that qualities that are incapable of objective measurement, such as the ability to engage in discussions and exchange views with other students, made the "separate but equal" doctrine inadequate for assuring equal educational opportunities for children.

EFFECTS: The effects of the *Brown* decision are far reaching in the areas of constitutional law, education, civil rights, and race relations. The specific holding only addressed the constitutionality of the segregated education systems of four school districts, but the decision effectively began the slow process of desegregating schools across the United States. Although the Court specifically overruled *Plessy v. Ferguson* in only the public education context, the *Brown* decision was an important catalyst in the Court's later decisions affecting all facets of American society.

ILLUSTRATING THE LAW THROUGH DISCUSSION

1. Prior to *Brown v. Board of Education,* segregation was "the way things are done." As a result of the Court's ruling, what changes occurred in your state in
   a. Elementary and secondary public school?
   b. Vocational education?
   c. Higher education?
   d. Teacher training programs?
   e. The provision of education to persons with disabilities?

2. How did the decision in *Brown v. Board of Education* support each of the following:
   a. The deinstitutionalization movement?
   b. The advocacy movement?
   c. Civil rights activism?
   d. Governmental involvement in education?

References

Americans with Disabilities Act, 42 U.S.C. § 12101 *et seq.* (1990).

Blatt, B., & Kaplan, F. (1974). *Christmas in purgatory: A photographic essay on mental retardation.* Syracuse, NY: Human Policy Press.

Brown v. Board of Education of Topeka, Kansas, 347 U.S. 483 (1954).

Developmental Disabilities Assistance and Bill of Rights Act, 42 U.S.C. § 6000 *et seq.* (1975).

Diana v. State Board of Education, Civ. Act. No. C-70-37 RFP (N.D.Cal. 1970) *further order* (1973) (unpublished opinion).

Education for All Handicapped Children Act, 20 U.S.C. § 1471 *et seq.* (1975).

Fernald, W. E. (1883). The history of the treatment of the feeble-minded. In *Proceedings of the National Conference for Charities and Correction* (pp. 203–221). New York: Columbia University.

Halderman v. Pennhurst State School and Hospital, 612 F.2d 84 (3rd Cir. 1979).

Hobson v. Hansen, 269 F. Supp. 401 (D.D.C. 1967), *aff'd sub nom.,* Smuck v. Hobson, 408 F.2d 175 (D.C. Cir. 1969).

Kennedy, J. (1963). *Message from the president of the United States.* Washington, DC: House of Representatives (88th Congress), Document number 58.

Kirk, S. A. (1978). The federal role in special education: Historical perspectives. Reprinted in G. A. Harris & W. D. Kirk (Eds.). (1993). *The foundations of special education: The selected papers and speeches of Samuel A. Kirk* (pp. 284–285). Reston, VA: The Council for Exceptional Children.

Larry P. v. Riles, 343 F. Supp. 1306 (N.D.Cal. 1972), *aff'd,* 502 F.2d 963 (9th Cir. 1974), *further proceedings,* 495 F. Supp. 926 (N.D.Cal. 1979), *aff'd in part, rev'd in part,* 793 F.2d 969 (9th Cir. 1984).

Maternal and Child Health and Mental Retardation Planning Amendments, 42 U.S.C. § 1305 *et seq.* (1963).

Mental Retardation Facilities and Community Mental Health Centers Construction Act, 42 U.S.C. § 295 *et seq.* (1963).

Mills v. Board of Education of the District of Columbia, 348 F. Supp. 866 (D.D.C. 1972).

PARC v. Commonwealth of Pennsylvania, 343 F. Supp. 297 (E.D. Pa. 1972).

Plessy v. Ferguson, 163 U.S. 537 (1896).

President's Panel on Mental Retardation. (1962). *A proposed program for national action to combat mental retardation.* Washington, DC: Superintendent of Documents.

Rehabilitation Act, 29 U.S.C. § 794 *et seq.* (1973).

Rehabilitation and developmental legislation [A compilation prepared for the Subcommittee of the Handicapped of the Committee on Labor and Public Welfare, United States Senate]. (1976). Washington, DC: U.S. Government Printing Office.

Rivera, G. (1972). *Willowbrook: A report on how it is and why it doesn't have to be that way.* New York: Random House.

Romeo v. Youngberg, 457 U.S. 307 (1982).

Scheerenberger, R. C. (1987). *A history of mental retardation: A quarter century of promise.* Baltimore: Paul H. Brookes.

State ex rel. Beattie v. Board of Education of Antigo, 169 Wis. 231 (Wis. 1919).

United Nations General Assembly. (1971). *Declaration of general and special rights of the mentally retarded.* New York: Author.

U.S. Commission on Civil Rights. (1983). *Accommodating the spectrum of individual abilities.* Washington, DC: Author.

Vitello, S. J., & Soskin, R. M. (1985). *Mental retardation: Its social and legal context.* Upper Saddle River, NJ: Prentice Hall.

Watson v. City of Cambridge, 157 Mass. 561 (1893).

Wolfensberger, W. (1972). *The principle of normalization in human services.* Toronto, Ontario, Canada: National Institute on Mental Retardation.

Wolfensberger, W. (1983). Social role valorization: A proposed new term for the principle of normalization. *Mental Retardation, 21,* 234–239.

Wyatt v. Stickney, 325 F. Supp. 781 (M.D. Ala. 1971), *aff'd in part, rev'd in part,* Wyatt v. Aderholt, 503 F.2d 1305 (5th Cir. 1974).

CHAPTER TWO

A New Foundation for
Special Education Services

GUIDING
QUESTIONS

1. What were the findings of Congress that led to the passage of the Education for All Handicapped Children Act of 1975 (P.L. 94–142)?

2. How did the Elementary and Secondary Education Act of 1965 and its subsequent amendments impact the passage of P.L. 94–142?

3. What are the six basic principles of P.L. 94–142, and how did they change the educational services provided to children and youth with disabilities?

4. What were the significant changes the 1990 Amendments made to P.L. 94–142, and how did these changes impact the delivery of services to children and youth with disabilities?

5. What were the changes enacted in 1997 under the Individuals with Disabilities Education Act (IDEA) Amendments of 1997?

6. What were the changes enacted with the passage of the Individuals with Disabilities Education Improvement Act of 2004?

7. What other federal statutes support IDEA, and how do they guarantee the rights of persons with disabilities?

The question often arises as to why federal legislation that would mandate services for children with exceptionalities was needed. This is especially true because by the early 1970s, nearly 70% of the states had adopted mandatory legislation requiring educational services for students with disabilities (Abeson, 1972; Weintraub & Ballard, 1982; Zettel & Ballard, 1979). Although 70% represented a significant number of states, no laws or regulations existed that codified the educational responsibilities across state and local entities (Zettel & Ballard, 1979). The result was an uneven access to, and quality of, educational services for children with disabilities (Horn & Tynan, 2001). In fact, some states continued to exclude students with disabilities through enactment of statutes that allowed this exclusion. When children had disabilities, cognitive or behavioral, that were severe in nature, this exclusion occurred more often (Yell, 1998). As Turnbull and Turnbull (1998) stated, "as a general rule, the nation's public schools were ingenious and successful in denying educational opportunities, equal or otherwise, to children with disabilities" (p. 15).

As noted in Chapter 1, a variety of factors provided the basis for the increased involvement of the federal government through the enactment of the landmark legislation, the Education for All Handicapped Children Act (EAHCA) of 1975 (P.L. 94–142). These factors included the emergence of advocacy groups and parental activism, political activism arising from the Civil Rights movement, and litigation concerning the issues surrounding the exclusion of individuals with disabilities from schools, either actual or through inappropriate educational services. As a result of the strength of the arguments put forth by advocacy and parent groups, and subsequent litigation, Congress scheduled hearings throughout the United States to gather information concerning the need for further federal intervention. This fourth factor, congressional findings, supported that concern and the need for expanded federal involvement in the education of students with disabilities. These findings indicated to Congress that excessive numbers of students were being excluded from public education, too many students were receiving inappropriate educational services, and too many students were being inappropriately placed in segregated settings because of misclassification (Tucker & Goldstein, 1996). Indeed, in 1975, Congress listed the following nine specific reasons for the passage of the Act:

(1) there are more than eight million handicapped children in the United States today;

(2) the special educational needs of such children are not being fully met;

(3) more than half of the handicapped children in the United States do not receive appropriate educational services which would enable them to have full equality of opportunity;

(4) one million of the handicapped children in the United States are excluded entirely from the public school system and will not go through the educational process with their peers;

(5) there are many handicapped children throughout the United States participating in regular school programs whose handicaps prevent them from having a successful educational experience because their handicaps are undetected;

(6) because of the lack of adequate services within the public school system, families are often forced to find services outside the public school system, often at great distance from their residence and at their own expense;

(7) developments in the training of teachers and in diagnostic and instructional procedures and methods have advanced to the point that, given appropriate funding, State and local educational agencies can and will provide effective special education and related services to meet the needs of handicapped children;

(8) State and local educational agencies have a responsibility to provide education for all handicapped children, but present financial resources are inadequate to meet the special educational needs of handicapped children; and

(9) it is in the national interest that the Federal Government assist State and local efforts to provide programs to meet the educational needs of handicapped children in order to assure equal protection of the law. (20 U.S.C. § 1401[b][1–9])

The Federal Base for Special Education Services

In 1975, EAHCA was enacted as a means of addressing these concerns. EAHCA was a unique piece of legislation as a result of three features: (a) a mandatory requirement that any state electing to receive federal funding was to follow the federal requirements, (b) a procedural section of the law that was permanent legislation (i.e., not requiring reauthorization), and (c) an existing statutory base.

Standards and the Law

CEC Standard 1: Foundations
INTASC Standard 1: Subject Matter
PRAXIS Standard: Legal and Societal Issues

Elementary and Secondary Education Act of 1965 (P.L. 89–10)

To understand EAHCA, it is necessary to review other pieces of legislation that were its precursors. The first federal legislation generally considered as a statutory base for EAHCA is the Elementary and Secondary Education Act (ESEA) of 1965 (P.L. 89–10). ESEA was the original federal commitment to improving education for elementary and secondary-age students identified as "educationally disadvantaged," a group of students having diverse educational needs, which also included children with disabilities. According to Gearheart, Mullen, and Gearheart (1993), ESEA was written to provide "something for everyone" (p. 16). ESEA authorized an initial budget of $1.3 billion for programs to assist disadvantaged children, instructional materials, centers for educational innovation and research, and state educational agencies (Martin, 1968). According to Scheerenberger (1987), the "funding program enabled residential facilities to obtain additional teachers, supplemental personnel, and sorely needed equipment. For many residents, custodial care was replaced by education" (p. 160).

Subsequent amendments to ESEA included P.L. 89–313 (1965) and P.L. 89–750 (1966). These amendments expanded the funding programs and established a federal grants program for the education of children with disabilities. The legislation established the Bureau of Education for the Handicapped (BEH), which was charged with administering all federal programs for children with disabilities. By 1968, ESEA was providing funding for the following: regional resource centers, information dissemination efforts concerning disabilities, centers and services for children with deaf-blindness, media programs for all children with disabilities, assistance for design and implementation of new educational programs, the recruitment and training of educational personnel for students with disabilities, and research and training efforts for children with disabilities.

Education of the Handicapped Act of 1970 (P.L. 91–230)

ESEA Amendments of 1970 (P.L. 91–230) consolidated the existing grant programs related to children with disabilities, including Title VI from ESEA of 1966. The new authorization was renamed the Education of the Handicapped Act (EHA) of 1970 and was the precursor to EAHCA of 1975.

Education of the Handicapped Act Amendments of 1974 (P.L. 93–380)

Four years later, President Ford signed EHA Amendments of 1974 (P.L. 93–380). The 1974 Amendments affected almost all aspects of education because they directed the states to develop state plans. These state plans were to include timetables toward providing full educational opportunities to children with disabilities. Also, EHA required that procedural safeguards be used to protect children during identification, assessment, and placement procedures. Testing and evaluation materials used in evaluation and placement were to be nondiscriminatory in nature. The Act also mandated that placement decisions give preference to placing children into regular classes whenever possible. According to Zettel and Ballard (1979), the Act can be considered "early warning legislation" (p. 15) because it included many of the guarantees of P.L. 94–142.

Education for All Handicapped Children Act of 1975 (P.L. 94–142)

P.L. 94–142, EAHCA, enacted in November 1975, combined a bill of rights for children with disabilities with federal funding for the increased educational responsibility placed on the states to fully educate these children. The stated purpose of this act is as follows:

(a) To ensure that all children with disabilities have available to them a free, appropriate public education that includes special education and related services designed to meet their unique needs;

(b) To ensure that the rights of children with disabilities and their parents are protected;

(c) To assist States and localities to provide for the education of all children with disabilities; and

(d) To assess and ensure the effectiveness of efforts to educate those children. (34 C.F.R. § 300.1)

The Act was developed to meet the needs of a specific class of children who, according to congressional findings, were not receiving the appropriate educational services necessary for success in society. According to the Act, the criteria for receiving services were that school-age children should have

mental retardation, hearing impairments including deafness, speech or language impairments, visual impairments including blindness, serious emotional disturbance, orthopedic impairments, autism, traumatic brain injury, other health impairments, specific learning disabilities, deaf-blindness, or multiple disabilities, and because of these impairments need special education and related services. (34 C.F.R. § 300.7 [a][1])

States may provide services to those children with disabilities who are between the ages of 3 and 5, including those

Who are experiencing developmental delays, as defined by the State and as measured by appropriate diagnostic instruments and procedures, in one or more of the following areas: physical development, cognitive development, communication development, social or emotional development, or adaptive development; and Who, for that reason, need special education and related services. (34 C.F.R. § 300.7 [a][2])

The legislation has eight subchapters, sometimes known as Parts. They provide the basic definitions, requirements, and procedural safeguards for the provision of educational services for children with disabilities. According to Tucker, Goldstein, and Sorenson (1993, p. 1:2), "rather than establishing substantive educational standards for all disabled children, the Act relies heavily on procedural protections to reach its goals." These subchapters have as their underpinnings six basic principles, which continue today in the Individuals with Disabilities Education Improvement Act (IDEA) of 2004 (P.L. 108–446).

Zero Reject. The first principle, Zero Reject, comprises the theoretical nucleus of the Act. This principle is based on the concept that all children with disabilities, regardless of the severity or type of their disability, are entitled to receive a free appropriate public education (FAPE). It includes the belief that *all* children can learn and can be taught. The Zero Reject principle is affirmed in the public schools through a component of EAHCA. FAPE is defined in IDEA 2004 as special education and related services that

    (A) have been provided at public expense, under public supervision and direction, and without charge;

    (B) meet the standards of the State educational agency;

    (C) include an appropriate preschool, elementary school, or secondary school education in the State involved; and

    (D) are provided in conformity with the individualized education program required under section 614(d). (20 U.S.C. § 602[9])

Nondiscriminatory Assessment. The second basic principle is Nondiscriminatory Assessment. After students have been included in the public schools, it is necessary to provide them with an appropriate diagnosis, program plan, and educational placement, which can only be achieved through a nondiscriminatory assessment. According to the Part B Regulations of EAHCA, testing, evaluation materials, and procedures used in the identification and evaluation of children with disabilities are to be selected and administered so as not to be racially or culturally discriminatory (34 C.F.R. § 300.530[b]).

In addition, the evaluation procedures require that tests and other evaluation materials are to be (a) in the child's native language or other appropriate mode of communication, (b) validated for the purpose for which they are being used, and (c) administered by trained personnel. No single procedure or test can be used as the sole criterion for determining the appropriate educational program for the identified child, and the evaluation is to be made by a multidisciplinary team (34 C.F.R. § 300.532).

Standards and the Law

CEC Standard 8: Assessment

NTASC Standard 8: Assessment

PRAXIS Standard: Delivery of Services to Students with Disabilities

In IDEA 2004, the assessment procedures state that the evaluations are

(1)   To include a variety of assessment tools and strategies

(2)   Not to use a single measure or assessment as the sole criterion

(3)   To use technically sound instruments that are selected so as not to be discriminatory on a racial or cultural basis and are used for the purposes for which the assessments or measures are valid and reliable

(4)   To use instruments in the language and form that is most likely to provide accurate information on what the child knows

(5)   To be administered by trained and knowledgeable personnel in accordance with assessment protocols provided by the test provider. (IDEA of 2004, P.L. 108–446, § 614[b], 118 Stat. 2647 [2005])

Procedural Due Process.   The principles of Zero Reject and Nondiscriminatory Assessment are supported by the third principle, Procedural Due Process. Due Process safeguards were developed to both strengthen and guarantee the rights of all persons involved in the provision of educational services for children with disabilities. These safeguards result in educators and parents being equal partners in the educational process by facilitating parental participation in their child's education. In addition, due process procedures protect parents and school districts when disagreements occur related to identification and program development for children with disabilities.

Parental Participation.   Furthermore, the principle of Due Process is interrelated with that of Parental Participation. A parent is defined in IDEA 2004 as

(A)   a natural, adoptive, or foster parent of a child (unless a foster parent is prohibited by State law from serving as a parent);

(B)   a guardian (but not the State if the child is a ward of the State);

(C)   an individual acting in the place of a natural or adoptive parent (including a grandparent, stepparent, or other relative) with whom the child lives, or an individual who is legally responsible for the child's welfare; or

(D)   except as used in Section 615(b)(2) and 639(a)(5), an individual assigned under either of those sections to be a surrogate parent. (IDEA of 2004, P.L. 108–446, § 602[23], 118 Stat. 2647 [2005])

A surrogate parent should be appointed to protect the rights of the infant, toddler, or child when the parents of the child are unknown; when the agency, after reasonable

Standards and the Law

CEC Standard 10: Collaboration
INTASC Standard 10: Collaboration, Ethics, and Relationships

effort, cannot locate the parents; when the child is a ward of the State; or when the child is an unaccompanied homeless youth as defined by the McKinney-Vento Homeless Assistance Act (IDEA of 2004, P.L. 108–446, § 615[b][2][a] and § 639[a][5], 118 Stat. 2647 [2005]). This expansion of the definition was necessary to protect the rights of the child and to guarantee the development and implementation of an appropriate education.

The participation of parents and guardians is considered pivotal in the provision of an appropriate education because IDEA requires parents to be included as part of the Individualized Education Program (IEP) team that develops the child's program. Parental responsibilities include providing written permission for testing and evaluation, participating in the determination of eligibility for services, assisting in the development of the IEP, participating in the annual review process, and advocating for their child. Parents also have the opportunity under IDEA to advocate for all children with disabilities through participation in special education policy development and state advisory panels, and in some cases, local educational advisory panels. It is undeniable that parents play a significant role in the education of the child with disabilities under IDEA.

Least Restrictive Environment.   The fifth principle, Least Restrictive Environment (LRE), is based on the assumption that the preferred placement for students with disabilities is the regular classroom. Other placements on the continuum of alternative placements should only be accessed when success in the regular class cannot be achieved without significant alterations. The principle of LRE as outlined in IDEA 2004 ensures that

> To the maximum extent appropriate, children with disabilities, including children in public or private institutions or other care facilities, are educated with children who are not disabled, and special classes, separate schooling, or other removal of children with disabilities from the regular educational environment occurs only when the nature or severity of the disability is such that education in regular classes with supplementary aids and services cannot be achieved satisfactorily. (IDEA of 2004, P.L. 108–446, § 612[a][5][A], 118 Stat. 2647 [2005])

Individualized Education Program.   The final principle, the IEP or Individualized Family Service Plan (IFSP), is central to the provision of an appropriate education for a child with disabilities. As outlined in IDEA 2004, an IEP is a written statement for a child with a disability that meets the requirement of Section 636(d), and is developed, reviewed, and revised for each child with a disability in accordance with Section 614(d) (IDEA of 2004, P.L. 108–446, § 612[a][4], 118 Stat. 2647 [2005]). It is both a process for developing an appropriate program for a child with a disability and a product/document that directs the education of the child.

The IEP for each child must include

(1) A statement of the child's present levels of academic achievement and functional performance;

(2) A statement of measurable annual goals, including academic and functional goals;

(3) A description of how the child's progress toward meeting the annual goals will be measured and when periodic reports on the progress will be reported;

(4) A statement of the special education and related services and supplemental aids and services and of program modifications or supports to be provided;

(5) An explanation of the extent, if any, to which the child will not participate with nondisabled children in regular class and extracurricular and nonacademic activities;

(6) A statement of any individual appropriate accommodations that are necessary to measure the academic achievement and functional performance of the child on State and districtwide assessments;

(7) The projected date for the beginning of services and modifications and the anticipated frequency, location, and duration of those services and modifications, and;

(8) Beginning no later than the first IEP in effect when the child is 16, and updated annually, a statement of appropriate measurable postsecondary goals based upon age appropriate transition assessments related to training, education, employment, and, where appropriate, independent living skills. (IDEA of 2004, P.L. 108–446, § 614 [d][1][A], 118 Stat. 2647 [2005])

For each infant or toddler with a disability served under IDEA 2004, a written IFSP must be developed by a multidisciplinary team that includes the family. The IFSP must include

(1) A statement of the infant's or toddler's present levels of development based on objective criteria;

(2) A statement of family resources, priorities, and concerns related to the development of the family's infant or toddler with a disability;

(3) A statement of measurable results or outcomes expected to be achieved for the infant or toddler and the family;

(4) A statement of specific early intervention services needed to meet the unique needs of the infant or toddler and the family including frequency, intensity, and method of delivering services;

(5) A statement of the natural environments in which early interventions will, or will not, be provided;

(6) The projected dates for the initiation of services and the anticipated length, duration, and frequency of the services;

(7) The identification of the service coordinator from the profession most immediately relevant to the infant's or toddler's or family's needs who will be responsible for the implementation and coordination of the plan including transition services;

(8) The steps to be taken to support the transition of the toddler with a disability to preschool or other appropriate services. (IDEA of 2004, P.L. 108–446, § 636[d], 118 Stat. 2647 [2005])

As a process, the IEP is to be developed collaboratively by parents and school personnel. During the IEP process, which includes referral of the child for evaluation, identification of the child as eligible for special education and related services, and development of the IEP document designating the individualized program and subsequent placement, collaboration between the school personnel and parents is vital. In fact, the IEP is a document that supports parental participation and shared decision making within the educational process. It is also a process that provides a method for holding schools accountable to the parents in the provision of an appropriate education for children with disabilities.

Subsequent Reauthorizations and Amendments to EAHCA

As previously indicated, EAHCA contained eight subchapters also known as parts. The most well-known section, Part B, is considered the central section of the Act and does not require reauthorization. Part B sets forth the procedural safeguards and the state formula grant program that funds the state special education programs. The other parts of the Act include Part A, the general provisions of the Act containing the definitions and administrative provisions; Part C, authorization for regional resource and federal centers; Part D, grants for personnel training and national clearinghouses; Part E, research and demonstration projects; Part F, instructional media; and Part G, technology, educational media, and material development and dissemination for individuals with disabilities. Unlike Part B, these sections require reauthorization. Thus, in November 1978 (P.L. 95–561) and again in December 1983 (P.L. 98–199), reauthorizations did occur.

Handicapped Children's Protection Act of 1986 (P.L. 99–372)

In 1986, a significant amendment to EAHCA was enacted as a result of a Supreme Court case, *Smith v. Robinson* (1984). Prior to the decision in this case, prevailing parties in litigation under EAHCA often sought the reimbursement of attorneys' fees by relying on Section 505 of the Rehabilitation Act or Section 1988 of the Civil Rights Attorney's Fees Award Act. The holding in *Smith* stated that those who prevailed in EAHCA claims could only use the statutory remedies provided under that Act, and EAHCA did not provide for the awarding of attorneys' fees (Tucker et al., 1993). The amendment, known as the Handicapped Children's Protection Act of 1986 (P.L. 99–372), was enacted to void this decision by providing for the award of attorneys' fees to prevailing parties according to the Court's discretion.

Education of the Handicapped Act Amendments of 1986 (P.L. 99–457)

In October, EHA Amendments of 1986 (P.L. 99–457) were enacted, providing an expansion of the original legislation. Part B was expanded to include services to children with disabilities ages 3 through 5. At that time a new subchapter was created, commonly called Part H, which provided funding for the planning and implementation of early intervention programs for young children with special needs.

Standards and the Law

CEC Standard 1: Foundations
PRAXIS Standard: Legal and Societal Issues

Individuals with Disabilities Education Act of 1990 (P.L. 101–476)

During the reauthorization of 1990, the title of the law was changed from the Education of the Handicapped Children's Act to the Individuals with Disabilities Education Act (P.L. 101–476), now known as IDEA. This change reflected the use of "people first" language, which is the accepted language when referring to persons with disabilities. Part B was also expanded to include services to children with disabilities ages 18 through 21. The law added under special education services both transition services and assistive technology, and under related services, it added rehabilitation counseling and social work services. Services and rights under the law were also expanded to include children with autism and traumatic brain injury.

Individuals with Disabilities Education Act Amendments of 1991 (P.L. 102–119)

In October 1991, IDEA Amendments (P.L. 102–119) were passed by Congress. The primary purpose of these amendments was to reauthorize the Part H program. The name of the reauthorized Part H program was changed to the Early Intervention Program for Infants and Toddlers with Disabilities. Significant changes were made to assist in the transition of children from the Part H programs to preschool services. Federal funds were authorized at that time to assist states in the education of infants, toddlers, preschoolers, children, and youth with disabilities. Instead of requiring an IEP for children age birth to 3, the amendments required an IFSP. An IFSP must include the following: (a) information about the child's status, (b) family information, (c) outcomes, (d) early intervention services, (e) other services, (f) dates, (g) duration of services, (h) service coordinator, and (i) transition from Part H services (34 C.F.R. § 303.344).

Individuals with Disabilities Education Act Amendments of 1997 (P.L. 105–17)

In a unique occurrence, a joint committee of the House and Senate developed the 1997 Amendments to IDEA. According to Gorn (1997), the basic structure, major provisions, and core concepts of the original bill (P.L. 94–142) remain intact (ERIC, 1999), but "modifications to improve educational results and promote school safety" and "to increase parental participation and reverse the trend of increasingly antagonistic parent-school relationships" have been added (p. i). Most of the changes, the most wide ranging since the 1990 Amendments, became effective on signing, with regulations developed in 1999. According to *CEC Today* ("IDEA sails through Congress!," 1997)

> The law protects the educational rights of students with disabilities who are violent or dangerous while enabling educators to more easily remove such students from their current educational placement. The bill also requires schools to include students with disabilities in local, state, and district assessments, thus ensuring accountability for students with special needs, and increases the amount of information to be included in the Individualized Education Program (IEP). In another change from the previous legislation, the bill requires states to provide mediation for parents and schools to more easily resolve differences about a child's placement.

To address the cost of special education, the new legislation revamps the way schools receive federal funding. Rather than using a child count formula as the basis for special education funding, the new bill will gradually base new federal aid on census data and account more accurately for poverty. In addition, the legislation makes provisions to reduce the financial burden of special education on local districts by permitting them to share the costs of services such as assistive technology devices, supplementary aids and services, related services, and transition services with other agencies. (p. 1)

Although Part B of IDEA is permanently authorized, the other parts of the legislation are considered to be discretionary or support programs and, thus, are to be reauthorized every 4 to 5 years (Yell, 1998). When legislation is permanently authorized, funding continues unless the legislation is amended or repealed. The other portions of the legislation expire unless reauthorization occurs. During reauthorization, bills are prepared and processed through committees in both the House and the Senate. After negotiation, a final bill is compiled and voted on by the House and the Senate, and finally approved by the president. After the legislation has been signed, then the U.S. Department of Education is directed to issue regulations for developing regulations (Wright & Wright, 2000).

Individuals with Disabilities Education Improvement Act of 2004 (P.L. 108–445)   *NCLB*

On December 3, 2004, President George W. Bush signed the reauthorization and major revision of IDEA, the Individuals with Disabilities Education Improvement Act (P.L. 108-446). Most of the provisions of the new law go into effect on July 1, 2005. The new law preserved the basic principles underpinning IDEA and its civil rights guarantees, but also made some significant changes. These include

- Definition of highly qualified special education teachers and the requirement that all special education teachers be highly qualified
- Provisions for reducing paperwork and other noneducational activities, including a pilot paperwork reduction program
- Revised state performance goals and requirements for children's participation in state and local assessments aligning the requirements with those of ESEA of 1965. *Ever since they tried fixing what wasn't broken we've spiraled down*
- Major changes in compliance monitoring to focus on student performance, not just compliance with procedures
- Provisions aimed at ensuring children with disabilities who need special education services and related services, and who are homeless or members of highly mobile populations, will receive an appropriate education
- Changes in procedural safeguards, including
  - Requirement of a resolution session prior to a due process hearing to encourage the parties to resolve their disputes
  - Revision of the test for manifestation determination
  - Addition of a new category (where a child has inflicted serious bodily harm on another person) allowing the school to place a child with a disability into an interim alternative educational setting

- Modifications to requirements for parents who unilaterally place their children with disabilities in private schools
- Authority for Local Education Agencies (LEAs) to use local IDEA grant monies for early intervening services aimed at reducing or eliminating the future need for special education for children with educational needs who do not currently qualify for IDEA
- Extension of Part C to include infant and toddler services beyond the age of 2

The changes to IDEA may be seen as an attempt to reduce the conflict between IDEA and the No Child Left Behind Act (NCLB) of 2001 (P.L. 107–110). The emphasis of the amendments of 2004 focused on the promise of paperwork reduction, monitoring of student's academic performance, and aligning IDEA requirements with the requirements of ESEA.

Federal Statutes Relating to IDEA

IDEA is the best known of the disability-related legislation affecting the provision of education in the public schools. Two other laws that expand on the protection of and provide support for IDEA are P.L. 93–112 (the Rehabilitation Act of 1973) and P.L. 101–336 (the Americans with Disabilities Act [ADA] of 1990). In contrast to IDEA, which is a federal grant program, both of these laws are federal antidiscrimination legislation.

Rehabilitation Act of 1973 (P.L. 93–112)

In the early 1900s, through the enactment of the Vocational Rehabilitation Act (1920), the federal government established a system of vocational rehabilitation agencies in each state. The Act was revised significantly in 1954 (the Vocational Rehabilitation Act) and then completely rewritten in 1973 to become the Rehabilitation Act (P.L. 93–112). This act authorized federal support for the rehabilitation and training of persons with mental and physical disabilities. The goal of these services was to assist the individual with disabilities in obtaining employment and full participation in society (OSERS, 1992). Section 504 is considered a nondiscrimination regulation and, as such, impacts all recipients of federal funding. Section 504 states that

> No otherwise qualified individual with a disability . . . shall solely by reason of her or his disability, be excluded from the participation in, be denied the benefits of, or be subjected to discrimination under any program or activity receiving federal financial assistance. (29 U.S.C. § 794)

By virtue of this section, all individuals regardless of age within the schools (students, staff, faculty, parents, etc.) receive a guarantee prohibiting discrimination on the basis of disability. This nondiscrimination guarantee covers both programmatic and physical accessibility for individuals with disabilities.

Although the federal regulations for Section 504, finalized in 1978, closely parallel the regulations promulgated for IDEA, there are significant differences. For example, in defining which persons with disabilities are eligible for services, IDEA outlines specific categories of disability and notes that the eligibility for services is based on the lack of educational success that is related to the impact of the individual's disability. However, Section 504 has no such requirement, and eligibility is determined solely on the existence of a disability. Therefore, Section 504 includes persons eligible for services under IDEA, as well as persons with disabilities who are not eligible for the specialized programming and services required under IDEA.

Three other sections of this legislation are considered important support for IDEA (Sections 501, 503, and 505). Section 501 established a federal Interagency Committee on Employees with Disabilities. According to Tucker (1994), "Congress' purpose in enacting Section 501 was to require the federal government to act as the model employer of disabled persons and to take affirmative action to hire and promote disabled persons" (p. 49). Thus, Section 501 required the submission of affirmative action plans but did not specifically provide individuals with a private right of action. Section 503 is also not considered to provide a private right of action, although, according to Tucker (1994), it

> extends the non-discrimination mandates of Section 504 (as applied to recipients of federal financial assistance) and Section 501 (as applied to federal agencies) to persons or companies having existing contracts (or subcontracts) of $10,000 or more with the federal government. (p. 55)

To ensure benefits are received and discrimination has not occurred in their delivery, Section 504 relies on the U.S. Office of Civil Rights (OCR). If a violation of Section 504 is found, OCR may issue an order to terminate federal funds. Also, there has been a consensus developing within the federal circuit courts that an individual has the right to initiate litigation under Section 504, that is, a private right of action (*School Board of Nassau County v. Arline*, 1987; *Southeast Community College v. Davis*, 1979).

Americans with Disabilities Act of 1990 (P.L. 101–336)

After passage of the Rehabilitation Act in 1973, Congress continued to enact various pieces of legislation to expand protections for persons with disabilities. Subsequently, a concern developed among persons with disabilities, their families, and others that these statutes were too fragmented and too limited to provide adequate protection. In 1990, ADA was passed to address this issue. This Act is viewed as one of the most comprehensive pieces of legislation enacted since the passage of EAHCA in 1975. According to First and Curcio (1993), the intent of ADA was "to provide a clear and comprehensive national mandate for the elimination of discrimination against individuals with disabilities" (p. 5).

Through its five titles (sections), the Act defined those who are covered by its guarantees, prohibited discriminatory employment practices and discrimination in both public and private services, required the installation of telecommunication relay services, and addressed numerous other issues. All areas of employment, education, and recreation services are covered by this Act. Title II relates to the operation of elementary and secondary public schools and institutions of postsecondary training. ADA mandates reasonable accommodations be provided for individuals with disabilities within the public and work environment. Thus, ADA, like Section 504, prohibits discrimination based on disability by schools and requires that reasonable accommodations be developed and implemented throughout all aspects of the educational program.

In 1990, the majority of the ADA requirements for the schools already existed through Section 504 of the Rehabilitation Act. However, in some cases, ADA clarified issues in question. For example, the original provision of rights to individuals with contagious diseases under Section 504 was unclear. ADA clearly established that individuals with contagious diseases are protected from discrimination as long as they do not directly threaten the health or safety of others. In addition, ADA extended protection to individuals who are associated with someone with a disability. For example, a child could not be prevented from enrolling in school because his or her mother has a communicable disease such as AIDS.

ADA is more far reaching than Section 504 because it prohibits discrimination on the basis of disability by not only private entities, but also by state and local governments. A significant aspect was that ADA modified the interpretation of the Eleventh Amendment concerning immunity of governmental agencies, thus making it possible for state and local governments and even Congress to be subjected to litigation.

ADA is also significant because it brought the enforcement powers of the federal government to the process. Through ADA, a variety of remedies, including injunctive relief, monetary damages, attorneys' fees, and costs, became available. The selection of the appropriate remedies, as well as that of the appropriate enforcement agency, depends on the requirements of the particular title of the act under which the complaint is made. For example, enforcement under Title II is through Section 504 procedures, whereas Title III enforcement includes the remedies and procedures of the Civil Rights Act of 1964 through the Attorney General.

No Child Left Behind Act of 2001 (P.L. 107–110)

The NCLB signed by President Bush in 2003 is considered to be "one of the most sweeping changes to education in a generation" (ISBE, 2004, p. 1). This latest piece of federal education legislation has as its purpose

> that all children have a fair, equal, and significant opportunity to obtain a high-quality education and reach, at a minimum, proficiency on challenging State academic achievement standards and state academic assessments. (20 U.S.C. § 6301)

The act contains 10 sections labeled Titles. Title 1 provides funding through grants for the improvement of academic achievement of students who are disadvantaged, including the improvement of basic programs operated by the school districts; the improvement of student reading skills; the improvement of education of migratory children; the improvement of prevention and intervention programs for neglected, delinquent, or at-risk children; and funds for comprehensive school reform, advanced placement programs, and school dropout prevention. Title II is a controversial section that focuses on the preparation, training, and recruiting of high-quality teachers and principals. It includes funds for teacher and principal training, as well as recruitment, mathematics and science partnerships, innovation programs to improve teacher quality, and the enhancement of education through technology. Title III focuses on language instruction for Limited English Proficiency and Immigrant Students and provides funding for the improvement of language instruction educational programs. Title IV is entitled "21st-Century Schools," and has as its purposes the creation of safe, orderly, drug-free schools. The promotion of parental choice and innovative programs is the focus of Title V, whereas Title VI focuses on the expansion of the flexibility of states and school districts to use federal funds, and in fact, encourages local solutions of local problems. Included in this section is funding for the educational needs of rural areas. Title VII addressed Indian Education, Native Hawaiian Education, and Alaska Native Education program needs and curricular issues. The last three sections address the loss of funding as a result of parents living on federal property (Title VIII) and general provisions, including privacy of assessment results, school prayer, etc. (Title IX). Title X (Repeals, Redesignations, and Amendments) includes three sections that are unique because they are amendments to other statutes: the McKinney-Vento Homeless Education Assistance Act of 2001 (Part C), the Native American Education Improvement Act of 2001 (Part D), and the General Education Provisions Act (Part F).

In essence, as Wright, Wright, and Heath (2004) stated, "'The No Child Left Behind Act' seeks to close the achievement gap by holding states, local school districts, and schools accountable for improving the academic achievement of all children" (p. 21). Although this act has lofty goals, many parents and education professionals are concerned that in the rush to reach these goals and meet the state standards required by this federal initiative, students with disabilities will be placed at risk.

Summary

By the 1970s, nearly 70% of the states had laws requiring educational services for students with disabilities. However, the result was uneven access and an irregular quality of services. Some states continued to exclude students with "severe" disabilities from services. A variety of factors converged to support the enactment of P.L. 94–142. These factors included the emergence of advocacy groups and parental activism, civil rights activism, litigation surrounding the exclusion of children with disabilities from educational services, and congressional findings supporting the need for an expanded federal presence in the schools.

ESEA of 1965 was the predecessor of P.L. 94–142. It was the first federal commitment to improving education for children identified as having special learning needs. The amendments of 1970 renamed the act as EHA. Then, in 1974, EHA Amendments were passed, containing many of the guarantees of the seminal piece of legislation, EAHCA, passed in 1975. The goal of this legislation was to ensure that an FAPE was available to all individuals with disabilities and that the educational rights of children with disabilities and their parents are protected. Thus, it included six basic principles known as (a) zero reject, (b) nondiscriminatory assessment, (c) procedural due process, (d) parental participation, (e) LRE, and (f) IEP.

P.L. 94–142 has been reauthorized several times, but the 1990 Amendments significantly expanded the services and changed the name of the act. The title of the law became IDEA. Services were to be provided to children with autism and traumatic

[Handwritten margin notes: EAHCA / Ed for all handicapped children Act 1975]

brain injury, and to persons 18 to 21 years old. Special education services were also expanded to include both transition services and assistive technology. Related services were expanded to include rehabilitation counseling and social work.

IDEA Amendments of 1997 retained the basic provisions of the bill, but addressed the issue of school safety and reinforced parental participation. Free mediation services were to be made available in every state. The Amendments also made provisions for local districts to share the cost burden of assistive technology and related services, and revamped special education funding.

The latest reauthorization of IDEA, the Individuals with Disabilities Education Improvement Act of 2004, continued the refinements of the basic requirements and included measures to align this act with NCLB. Changes in the act focused on ensuring that all special education teachers are highly qualified, that requisite paperwork be reduced, that state and local assessments be aligned with ESEA, that more emphasis be placed on the education of homeless children, and that more changes be made to the procedural safeguards included in the law. IDEA 2004 continues to support the basic underpinnings of earlier versions of the law and to emphasize its civil rights guarantees for children with disabilities.

Other federal statutes that support IDEA include the Rehabilitation Act of 1973 and ADA. The Rehabilitation Act covers both programmatic and physical access for individuals with disabilities. Later, a concern developed that statutes protecting individuals with disabilities were too fragmented, so ADA was passed to address the issue. ADA provided a national mandate for the elimination of discrimination against individuals with disabilities. These laws are considered to be civil rights legislation that is antidiscriminatory and, as such, relies on the OCR to ensure that discrimination does not occur.

Throughout the 20th century, the federal government has expanded its involvement in disability-related legislation as a result of the actions of professionals, advocates, and consumer groups. In the early 1900s, federal involvement began with the introduction of employment rights through the Vocational Rehabilitation Act. Then, in the 1970s, the involvement advanced to guarantee educational rights through EAHCA, and concluded in the 1990s, with a comprehensive guarantee of civil rights through ADA. Because of this continuing federal role in our lives, it is imperative that professionals recognize the effect of federal legislation on program accessibility in the schools for persons with disabilities.

Questions for Discussion

1. How has federal involvement in the education of individuals with disabilities expanded in the past 30 years?
2. How do the Rehabilitation Act, ADA, and NCLB expand the focus of federal education legislation?
3. Do you believe that this continuing expansion of federal legislation is a movement toward a national education system? Why or why not?

Websites for Further Exploration

Federal Base for Services (ESEA, EHA, Education Act Amendments, EAHCA)
www.weac.org/Capitol/esea.htm
www.signetwork.org/
www.parentsunitedtogether.com/page15.html
www.healthyplace.com/Communities/ADD/judy/terms.htm
www.usdoj.gov/crt/cor/byagency/ed1703.htm

Reauthorizations and Amendments to EAHCA (HCPA, EHA Amendments, IDEA)
caselaw.lp.findlaw.com/casecode/uscodes/20/chapters/33/subchapters/i/sections/
    section_1400.html
www.schwablearning.org/articles.asp?r=551&g=2
www.edpolicy.gwu.edu/resources/enhancing/part_b.html
www.ideapractices.org/

Supporting Statutes (Rehabilitation Act, ADA, NCLB)
www.nea.org/lac/esea/
www2.edtrust.org/edtrust/ESEA
www.ascd.org/cms/index.cfm?TheViewID=567
www.hhs.gov/ocr/504.html
www.usdoj.gov/crt/ada/cguide.htm
www.ed.gov/nclb/landing.jhtml?src=pb

ILLUSTRATING THE LAW

Legislation:
P.L. 108–446: Title and Findings 108th Congress

SECTION 1. SHORT TITLE: This Act may be cited as the "Individuals with Disabilities Education Improvement Act of 2004".

SECTION 2. ORGANIZATION OF THE ACT

Title I—Amendments to the Individuals with Disabilities Education Act

Sec. 101. Amendments to the Individuals with Disabilities Education Act Parts A through D of the Individuals with Disabilities Education Act (20 U.S.C. 1400 *et seq.*) are amended to read as follows:

PART A—GENERAL PROVISIONS: Sec. 601. Short Title; Table of Contents; Findings; Purposes
a. SHORT TITLE.—This Act may be cited as the 'Individuals with Disabilities Education Act'.
b. TABLE OF CONTENTS.—The table of contents for this title is as follows: . . .

c. FINDINGS.—Congress finds the following:

1. Disability is a natural part of the human experience and in no way diminishes the right of individuals to participate in or contribute to society. Improving educational results for children with disabilities is an essential element of our national policy of ensuring equality of opportunity, full participation, independent living, and economic self-sufficiency for individuals with disabilities.

2. Before the date of enactment of the Education for All Handicapped Children Act of 1975 (P.L. 94–142), the educational needs of millions of children with disabilities were not being fully met because—

   (A) the children did not receive appropriate educational services;

   (B) the children were excluded entirely from the public school system and from being educated with their peers;

   (C) undiagnosed disabilities prevented the children from having a successful educational experience or

   (D) a lack of adequate resources within the public school system forced families to find services outside the public school.

3. Since the enactment and implementation of the Education for All Handicapped Children Act of 1975, this title has been successful in ensuring children with disabilities and the families of such children access to a free appropriate public education and in improving educational results for children with disabilities.

4. However, the implementation of this title has been impeded by low expectations, and an insufficient focus on applying replicable research on proven methods of teaching and learning for children with disabilities.

5. Almost 30 years of research and experience has demonstrated that the education of children with disabilities can be made more effective by—

   (A) having high expectations for such children and ensuring their access to the general education curriculum in the regular classroom, to the maximum extent possible, in order to—

      (i) meet developmental goals and, to the maximum extent possible, the challenging expectations that have been established for all children; and

      (ii) be prepared to lead productive and independent adult lives, to the maximum extent possible;

   (B) strengthening the role and responsibility of parents and ensuring that families of such children have meaningful opportunities to participate in the education of their children at school and at home;

   (C) coordinating this title with other local, educational service agency, State, and Federal school improvement efforts, including improvement efforts under the Elementary and Secondary Education Act of 1965, in order to ensure that such children benefit from such efforts and that special education can become a service for such children rather than a place where such children are sent;

   (D) providing appropriate special education and related services, and aids and supports in the regular classroom to such children, whenever appropriate;

   (E) supporting high-quality, intensive preservice preparation and professional development for all personnel who work with children with disabilities in order to ensure that such personnel have the skills and knowledge necessary to improve the academic achievement and functional performance of children with disabilities, including the use of scientifically based instructional practices, to the maximum extent possible;

(F) providing incentives for whole-school approaches scientifically based early reading programs, positive behavioral interventions and supports, and early intervening services to reduce the need to label children as disabled in order to address the learning and behavioral needs of such children;

(G) focusing resources on teaching and learning while reducing paperwork and requirements that do not assist in improving educational results; and

(H) supporting the development and use of technology, including assistive technology devices and assistive technology services, to maximize accessibility for children with disabilities.

6. While States, local educational agencies, and educational service agencies are primarily responsible for providing an education for all children with disabilities, it is in the national interest that the Federal Government have a supporting role in assisting State and local efforts to educate children with disabilities in order to improve results for such children and to ensure equal protection of the law.

7. A more equitable allocation of resources is essential for the Federal Government to meet its responsibility to provide an equal educational opportunity for all individuals.

8. Parents and schools should be given expanded opportunities to resolve their disagreements in positive and constructive ways.

9. Teachers, schools, local educational agencies, and States should be relieved of irrelevant and unnecessary paperwork burdens that do not lead to improved educational outcomes.

10. (A) The Federal Government must be responsive to the growing needs of an increasingly diverse society.

(B) America's ethnic profile is rapidly changing. In 2000, 1 of every 3 persons in the United States was a member of a minority group or was limited English proficient.

(C) Minority children comprise an increasing percentage of public school students.

(D) With such changing demographics, recruitment efforts for special education personnel should focus on increasing the participation of minorities in the teaching profession in order to provide appropriate role models with sufficient knowledge to address the special education needs of these students.

11. (A) The limited English proficient population is the fastest growing in our Nation, and the growth is occurring in many parts of our Nation.

(B) Studies have documented apparent discrepancies in the levels of referral and placement of limited English proficient children in special education.

(C) Such discrepancies pose a special challenge for special education in the referral of, assessment of, and provision of services for, our Nation's students from non-English language backgrounds.

12. (A) Greater efforts are needed to prevent the intensification of problems connected with mislabeling and high dropout rates among minority children with disabilities.

(B) More minority children continue to be served in special education than would be expected from the percentage of minority students in the general school population.

(C) African-American children are identified as having mental retardation and emotional disturbance at rates greater than their White counterparts.

(D) In 1998–1999 school year, African-American children represented just 14.8 percent of the population aged 6 through 21, but comprised 20.2 percent of all children with disabilities.

(E) Studies have found that schools with predominately White students and teachers have placed disproportionately high numbers of their minority students into special education.

13. (A) As the number of minority students in special education increases, the number of minority teachers and related service personnel produced in colleges and universities continues to decrease.

(B) The opportunity for full participation by minority individuals, minority organizations, and Historically Black Colleges and Universities in awards for grants and contracts, boards of organizations receiving assistance under this title, peer review panels, and training of professionals in the area of special education is essential to obtain greater success in the education of minority children with disabilities.

14. As the graduation rates for children with disabilities continue to climb, providing effective transition services to promote successful post-school employment or education is an important measure of accountability for children with disabilities.

d. PURPOSES.—The purposes of this title are—

1. (A) to ensure that all children with disabilities have available to them a free appropriate public education that emphasizes special education and related services designed to meet their unique needs and prepare them for further education, employment, and independent living;

(B) to ensure that the rights of children with disabilities and parents of such children are protected; and

(C) to assist States, localities, educational service agencies, and Federal agencies to provide for the education of all children with disabilities;

2. to assist States in the implementation of a statewide, comprehensive, coordinated, multidisciplinary, interagency system of early intervention services for infants and toddlers with disabilities and their families;

3. to ensure that educators and parents have the necessary tools to improve educational results for children with disabilities by supporting system improvement activities; coordinated research and personnel preparation; coordinated technical assistance, dissemination, and support; and technology development and media services; and

4. to assess, and ensure the effectiveness of, efforts to educate children with disabilities.

ILLUSTRATING THE LAW THROUGH DISCUSSION

1. The 2004 Reauthorization and Amendments to IDEA provided a list of findings influencing the legislation. Which finding do you believe is the most important, and why?

All can learn – Ind. Living
High expectations – M Steven

2. How did the 2004 Amendments to IDEA ensure that each of its four purposes would be met? *Highly qual. teachers, reduced paperwork, assessment aligned, procedural safeguards, homeless children ed, civil rights guarantees*

References

Abeson, A. (1972). Movement and momentum: Government and the education of handicapped children. *Exceptional Children, 39,* 63–66.

Americans with Disabilities Act, 42 U.S.C. § 12101 *et seq.* (1990).

Education for All Handicapped Children Act, 20 U.S.C. § 1400 *et seq.* (1975).

Education of the Handicapped Act, 20 U.S.C. § 1471 *et seq.* (1970).

Education of the Handicapped Act Amendments, 20 U.S.C. § 1400 (1974).

Education of the Handicapped Act Amendments, 20 U.S.C. § 1471 *et seq.* (1986).

Elementary and Secondary Education Act, 20 U.S.C. 2701 *et seq.* (1965).

Elementary and Secondary Education Act Amendments, 20 U.S.C. § 2701 *et seq.* (1970).

ERIC Clearinghouse on Disabilities and Gifted Education. (1999). *An overview of the Individuals with Disabilities Education Act Amendments of 1997 (P.L. 105–17): Update 1999.* Retrieved March 30, 2004, from ericec.org

First, P. F., & Curcio, J. L. (1993). *Individuals with disabilities: Implementing the newest laws.* Newbury Park, CA: Corwin.

Gearheart, B., Mullen, R. C., & Gearheart, C. J. (1993). *Exceptional individuals: An introduction.* Pacific Grove, CA: Brookes/Cole.

Gorn, S. (Ed.). (1997). *1997 IDEA amendments: An overview of key changes.* Horsham, PA: LRP.

Handicapped Children's Protection Act of 1986, 20 U.S.C. § 1415 *et seq.* (West, 1990).

Horn, W. F., & Tynan, D. (2001). Time to make special education "special" again. In C. E. Finn, Jr., A. J. Rotherham, & C. R. Hokanson, Jr. (Eds.), *Rethinking special education for a new century* (pp. 23–51). Washington, DC: Thomas B. Fordham Foundation & Progressive Policy Institute.

IDEA Sails Through Congress! (1997). *CEC Today, 3*(10), 1, 9, 15.

Individuals with Disabilities Education Act, 20 U.S.C. § 1400 *et seq.* (1990).

Individuals with Disabilities Education Act Amendments, 20 U.S.C. § 1400 *et seq.* (1991).

Individuals with Disabilities Education Act Amendments, 20 U.S.C. § 1400 *et seq.* (1997).

Individuals with Disabilities Education Improvement Act of 2004, P.L. 108–446, § 601 *et seq.,* 118 Stat. 2647 (2005).

Illinois State Board of Education (ISBE). (2004). *No Child Left Behind (NCLB).* Retrieved March 9, 2004, from www.isbe.state.il.us/nclb/htmls/news.htm

Martin, E. (1968). Breakthrough for the handicapped: Legislative history. *Exceptional Children, 34,* 493–503.

No Child Left Behind Act, 20 U.S.C. § 6301 *et. seq.* (2001).

Office of Special Education and Rehabilitative Services (OSERS). (1992). *Summary of existing legislation affecting people with disabilities.* Washington, DC: U.S. Department of Education.

Rehabilitation Act, 29 U.S.C. § 794 *et seq.* (1973).

Scheerenberger, R. C. (1987). *A history of mental retardation: A quarter century of promise.* Baltimore: Paul H. Brookes.

School Board of Nassau County v. Arline, 480 U.S. 273 (1987).

Smith v. Robinson, 468 U.S. 992 (1984).

Southeast Community College v. Davis, 442 U.S. 397 (1979).

Tucker, B. P. (1994). *Federal disability law in a nutshell.* St. Paul, MN: West.

Tucker, B. P., & Goldstein, B. A. (1996). *Legal rights of persons with disabilities: An analysis of federal law.* Horsham, PA: LRP.

Tucker, B. P., Goldstein, B. A., & Sorenson, G. (1993). *The educational rights of children with disabilities: Analysis, decisions and commentary.* Horsham, PA: LRP.

Turnbull, H. R., & Turnbull, A. P. (1998). *Free appropriate public education: The law and children with disabilities* (5th ed.). Denver: Love.

Weintraub, F. J., & Ballard, J. (1982). Introduction: Bridging the decades. In J. Ballard, B. A. Ramirez, & F. J. Weintraub (Eds.), *Special education in America: Its legal and governmental foundations* (pp. 1–9). Reston, VA: The Council for Exceptional Children.

Wright, P. W. D., & Wright, P. D. (2000). *Wrightslaw: Special education law.* Hartfield, VA: Harbor House Law Press.

Wright, P. W. D., Wright, P. D., & Heath, S. W. (2004). *No Child Left Behind.* Hartfield, VA: Harbor House Law Press.

Yell, M. L. (1998). *The law and special education.* Upper Saddle River, NJ: Merrill/Prentice Hall.

Zettel, J. J., & Ballard, J. (1979). The Education for All Handicapped Children Act of 1974 (P.L. 94–142): Its history, origins, and concepts. *Journal of Education, 161*(3), 5–22.

PART II

Six Basic Principles of Special Education Legislation

CHAPTER THREE

Free Appropriate
Public Education

GUIDING
QUESTIONS

1. Why is the Fourteenth Amendment interpreted as supporting the provision of a free appropriate public education for children and youth with disabilities? *FAPE*

2. What is meant by the principle of equal protection? *States can't deny privileges given to one person – to any group*

3. How did *PARC* and *Mills* impact the legislation later known as IDEA? *Schools must provide a free, appropriate edu for all; regardless, mental, physical or emotional disability*

4. Why is the meaning of "free appropriate public education" the subject of continuing litigation? *All Free & Approp. are not clearly defined*

5. What are the issues involved when a student with disabilities is suspended or expelled from the public school? *Student a danger to themselves or others. 10 day cooling off to find alt. placement or pursue court intervention if parents disagree. School has to provide a new IEP*

6. If an allegedly dangerous child has a disability, how can public school personnel remove the child from his or her placement without violating the "stay-put" provision in IDEA? *2 Prong test*
   1) child a danger to himself + others
   2) school district has done all it can to reduce risk that child will cause injury
   Parents must be notified + involved.

Every state in the United States has enacted compulsory school attendance laws requiring children to attend schools, at least until they reach a minimum age. Despite this legislation, many children have been barred from schools on the basis of inalterable characteristics such as race, gender, national origin, citizenship, or disability. In resulting litigation, the courts found that states, by assuming the responsibility of providing an education to its citizens, created an entitlement to an education for all its inhabitants, not just a select few. This entitlement was based on the Fourteenth Amendment and is known as the Equal Protection principle.

Equal Protection Doctrine

The Fourteenth Amendment to the U.S. Constitution provided the basis for the equal protection doctrine:

> All persons born or naturalized in the United States and subject to the jurisdiction thereof, are citizens of the United States and of the state wherein they reside. No state shall make or enforce any law which shall abridge the privileges or immunities of citizens of the United States; nor shall any state deprive any person of life, liberty, or property, without due process of law; nor deny to any person within its jurisdiction the equal protection of the laws.

In the early case of *Yick Wo v. Hopkins* (1886), the U.S. Supreme Court applied the Fourteenth Amendment to a discrimination case and found that

> The fact of this discrimination is admitted. No reason for it is shown, and the conclusion cannot be resisted, that no reason for it exists except hostility to the race and nationality to which the petitioners belong, and which in the eye of the law is not justified. The discrimination is, therefore, illegal, and the public administration which enforces it is a denial of the equal protection of the laws and a violation of the Fourteenth Amendment of the Constitution. . . . (p. 374)

The Supreme Court held in the *Yick Wo* case that the ordinance that discriminated against Chinese citizens in the operation and establishment of laundries in San Francisco violated the equal protection clause of the Fourteenth Amendment. The *Yick Wo* case is important in several respects. First, it recognized that there were certain intangible interests that could be considered possessions, such as the right to operate and maintain a business. The Court also stated that the plaintiffs were protected by the Fourteenth Amendment even though they were not U.S. citizens, but rather citizens of China residing within

Standards and the Law

CEC Standard 1: Foundations
INTASC Standard 1: Subject Matter
PRAXIS Standard: Legal and Societal Issues

the boundaries of the United States. The Court stated that the Constitution and its amendments

> are universal in their application, to all persons within the territorial jurisdiction, without regard to any differences of race, of color, or of nationality; and the equal protection of the laws is a pledge of the protection of equal laws. (*Yick Wo v. Hopkins,* 1886, p. 369)

Because the Fourteenth Amendment guaranteed that laws be applied equally to all persons, without special privileges or restrictions applied to any one group, it provided the legal underpinning for the equal protection principle. When a law is enacted that adversely affects a group because of inherent distinctions or classifications, then the principle of equal protection requires that the state must have some "rational" basis for making such distinctions or classifications (see Figure 3.1). In other words, the classification must have some relevance to the purpose or purposes for which the law was made (*Marshall v. United States,* 1974). The principle of equal protection does not prohibit social or economic legislation relating to individual classes as long as the legislation has a rational basis for addressing that class or group in relationship to the legislation (*U.S. Railroad Retirement Board v. Fritz,* 1980).

Until the 1960s, the Supreme Court generally supported the belief that "governmental action alleged to be discriminatory and in violation of the equal protection doctrine was not unconstitutional" (Turnbull, 1993, p. 34). This abdication of judicial review resulted in a failure of the courts to correct abuses of individual rights by government agencies. Subsequently, antidiscrimination law was enacted and constitutional doctrine developed to address this concern. However, the statutory and doctrinal explanation of equal protection was in response to isolated individual and group experiences. It was not developed "as a consistent policy framework on group discrimination" (Valente & Valente, 1998, p. 258). As a result, the Supreme Court, during the Warren era, was called on to address claims from various groups concerning alleged constitutional and statutory rights violations. To address these issues, the Court used a new analysis to evaluate claims under the principle of equal protection (see Figure 3.1). The Court analyzed the answers to three questions. First, who was the complaining party; that is, is that person a member of a suspect classification? A suspect class is a group that has historically been the "victim" of discrimination either by *de jure* or *de facto* legislation. These three groups, called classes, have experienced a long history of discrimination from the majority population as a result of inalterable characteristics—race, national origin, and gender.

Figure 3.1
Equal Protection Tests

Rational Basis Test	Does the state have a rational basis for its actions? Is the state's purpose legitimate with a reasonable relationship between groups and purposes?
	If the answer to the previous question is yes, then the action is not considered to be discriminatory.
Warren Era 3 Question Analysis (Strict Scrutiny Test)	Is the complaining party a member of a suspect class*? Does the rights infringement involve a fundamental interest[†]?
	Can "discriminatory" actions be justified as having a compelling interest[‡]?
	If the answer to question 1 or 2 is yes, courts use the rational basis test for review.
	If the answer to question 1 or 2 is no, then the courts use strict scrutiny test.
	To meet the strict scrutiny review, the answer to question 3 must be yes.
Expanded Warren Analysis (Heightened/Middle-Tier Test)	Does the complaining party meet some of the characteristics as a suspect class?
	If the person meets some of the suspect class criteria (e.g., gender), then use the middle-tier test, which is more rigid than rational, but not as much as strict scrutiny.

*A suspect class is a group that has experienced a history of discrimination based on inalterable characteristics such as race or national origin.
[†]A fundamental interest is one guaranteed by the Constitution such as the right to vote.
[‡]A compelling interest is noted when a government's action is necessary, not just convenient, to achieve its purpose.

Second, the Court asked, what is the nature of his or her interest or what right is being infringed on; that is, is there a fundamental interest (e.g., the right to vote) involved? Since the *Yick Wo* case, the Supreme Court has expanded the equal protection doctrine to include state infringement on other fundamental rights guaranteed by the Constitution. A fundamental interest has been found in several cases, including the right to practice one's religious beliefs (*Fullilove v. Klutznick,* 1980), the right to marry (*Wisconsin v. Yoder,* 1972), the right to procreate (*Loving v. Virginia,* 1967), and the right to travel interstate (*Skinner v. Oklahoma,* 1942).

Moreover, third, the Court asks, can the government justify its allegedly discriminatory action; that is, is the law in question based on a compelling interest by the state, which is required to achieve its legitimate purpose? In other words, the "distinction drawn by the law was necessary, not merely convenient, in order to achieve the government's purpose" (Turnbull, 1993, p. 34).

If the analysis of the answers to the questions listed previously indicated that no fundamental interest or suspect classification was involved in the claim, then the Court used a standard of review known as the "rational basis standard." This standard required only that the state's purposes for the legislation be legitimate and that there be a reasonable relationship between the particular group or classification and the purposes of the legislation. According to *Romer v. Evans* (1996) ". . . if a law neither burdens a fundamental right nor targets a suspect class, we will uphold the legislative classification so long as it bears a rational relation to some legitimate end" (p. 1620).

However, if the review indicated that the legislation alleged to be discriminatory made a distinction based on race, national origin, or a fundamental interest, the Supreme Court applied a more stringent level of review known as "strict scrutiny." Strict scrutiny can only be satisfied when the state demonstrates a compelling state interest and when a statute satisfies that interest without infringement on other fundamental interests. The burden of proving a sufficient compelling state interest to justify an infringement based on race or national origin is almost impossible to meet. Some commentators remark that the strict scrutiny test is actually "fatal scrutiny" because when one of the suspect classes (race, gender, and alienage) is involved, the statute will fail the constitutional analysis.

In the mid-1970s, the Court expanded its approach to analyzing suspected violations of equal protection principles when it became obvious that cases were not receiving strict scrutiny because neither a suspect class nor a fundamental interest was involved. Neither could the Court use rational basis analysis because it was insufficient to address the class discrimination that was asserted. The resultant addition was identified as an intermediate or middle-tier approach (see Figure 3.1). This "heightened" level of scrutiny was developed for use when a group met some, although not all, of the criteria as a suspect class but was entitled to judicial protection. For example the classes of age, gender, and illegitimacy were seen as requiring this heightened level of scrutiny. The middle-tier approach of scrutiny was also to be used with a group of persons such as individuals with disabilities who had a history of discrimination and political powerlessness denying them an important right, but were not considered a "suspect" or "quasisuspect" class.

The case of *Cleburne v. Cleburne Living Center, Inc.* (1985) provided an example of an attempt to include the class of persons with mental retardation in the group with whom the middle-tier scrutiny is to be used. The issue was whether a city could use a zoning ordinance to exclude group homes for persons who are mentally retarded from an area zoned for apartment houses and other congregant living facilities. Although the courts held that persons with mental retardation had a history of discriminatory treatment, they declined to support the inclusion of persons with mental retardation within the "suspect" classes requiring strict scrutiny or within the "quasisuspect" class (e.g., gender) requiring middle-tier scrutiny. However, according to the Respondent's *Amicus Curiae* Brief,

> By means of the language it employed and the precedents it cited, the Court made clear that the "rational basis" test was not to be used in its ordinary, deferential form. Thus the

result is that laws that discriminate against people who are mentally retarded must pass a constitutional test stricter than "ordinary" rational basis, but somewhat more deferential than "heightened" (or "middle tier") scrutiny. (Ellis & Luckasson, 1984, p. 251)

When further considering issues related to equal protection principles and discriminatory actions by government agencies, the question has arisen as to whether education should be considered a "fundamental right," either explicitly or implicitly guaranteed by the Constitution. A response to this question was found in the holding in *San Antonio School District v. Rodriguez* (1973), where it stated that "Education . . . is not among the rights afforded explicit protection under our Federal Constitution. Nor do we find any basis for saying it is implicitly so protected" (p. 35).

Even though education is not considered to be a right guaranteed by the Constitution, courts have found that education is one of the most important duties undertaken by states. In *Brown v. Board of Education* (1954), the Supreme Court stated:

Today, education is perhaps the most important function of state and local governments. . . . In these days, it is doubtful that any child may reasonably be expected to succeed in life if he is denied the opportunity of an education. Such an opportunity, where the state has undertaken to provide it, is a right which must be made available to all on equal terms. (p. 493)

Education, although not a fundamental interest, is considered to be of considerable importance to the future of the United States. Therefore, when educational issues have been raised concerning the principle of equal protection, the courts have elected to use different levels of review depending on the issue and group involved. In cases where a "suspect class" or a "fundamental interest" was involved, the courts have used the strict scrutiny test. If neither were involved, then the courts have used the rational basis test.

In summary, although education is not guaranteed in the Constitution, the fact that the states have undertaken to provide this service has resulted in the need for states to provide the service equally to all its residents. When access to an education is denied a resident based on an inherent characteristic such as disability, then the courts have analyzed the legislation under the rational basis test rather than the strict scrutiny or heightened, or middle-tier, scrutiny test. This changing criteria for review has resulted in the development of legislation, as well as litigation, concerning the application of the equal protection principle in education.

Application of Equal Protection Principle in Education

The result of the move to apply the equal protection principle in public schools, especially for students with disabilities, has resulted in numerous legal challenges. Prior to the enactment of EAHCA in 1975, the litigation focused on the issue of access to public schooling for students with disabilities, whereas later it focused on clarification and implementation of the principle in the public schools for these students.

Pre-EAHCA Litigation

PARC. The District Court in *Pennsylvania Association for Retarded Citizens (PARC) v. Commonwealth of Pennsylvania* (1972) was the first case to address the exclusion of children because of disabilities. In the *PARC* case, expert testimony indicated that persons with mental retardation were capable of benefiting from education and training. Because the Commonwealth of Pennsylvania had undertaken to provide a free, public education to all its children, it could not fail to provide the same to a child who had mental retardation. The state did not dispute that each child had a right to a free, publicly supported education even if the child had mental retardation. Therefore, *PARC* agreed in a consent document to strike down school policies denying children with mental retardation a free, public education.

Mills. A few months after the decision in *PARC,* the District Court for the District of Columbia handed down a similar decision in *Mills v. Board of Education of the District of Columbia* (1972). In *Mills,* however, the suit was brought on behalf of all children who had disabilities. Not only did the Court find a violation of the Fourteenth Amendment (equal protection), but it also found a violation of the due process clause in the Fifth Amendment. The District of Columbia School Board was ordered to provide each school-age child a free, public education regardless of the degree of the child's mental, physical, or emotional disability. The school was also prohibited from suspending a child with a disability for longer than 2 days unless the child was provided a hearing. When a child was suspended, the school was required to continue that child's education.

Legislation Applying Equal Protection Principle

It would appear from these cases that due process and equal protection are both major components in sustaining the right to a public education for children with disabilities. The decisions in *PARC* and *Mills* provided the basis for many of the principles included in later educational legislation for students with disabilities. For example, the concept of equal protection in the educational arena was operationalized as the principle of zero reject and included in the Education for the Handicapped

Standards and the Law

CEC Standard 1: Foundations
PRAXIS Standard: Legal and Societal Issues

Act (EHA) of 1970 as the principle of the right to a free appropriate public education, known as FAPE. This Act later became the more comprehensive EAHCA, and was then amended and renamed the Individuals with Disabilities Education Act (IDEA) of 1990. In its early findings supporting this legislation, Congress determined that there were more than million children with disabilities in the United States and that more than half of them were receiving inappropriate educational services, whereas 1 million children were excluded from public education entirely.

Purpose

The original Act, therefore, clearly defined its purpose as

> to assure that all handicapped children have available to them . . . a free appropriate public education which emphasizes special education and related services designed to meet their unique needs, to assure that the rights of handicapped children and their parents or guardians are protected, to assist States and localities to provide for the education of all handicapped children, and to assess and assure the effectiveness of efforts to educate handicapped children. (EAHCA, 1975, 20 U.S.C. § 602[9])

However, the legislation did not define FAPE and, therefore, the question of "what is a free appropriate public education?" had to be addressed by the courts. We discuss each segment of the phrase "free appropriate public education" in the following sections.

Free Education

The word "free" is not defined in IDEA, although the concept is clearly supported when it states that special education and related services should be "provided at public expense, . . . and without charge" (20 U.S.C. § 1401[a][18]). This supports the definition listed in *Funk & Wagnalls New International Dictionary of the English Language* (1997), wherein the word "free" means "without charge or cost." Thus, parents and families of children with disabilities cannot be charged for services that are to be provided under IDEA and that are needed for the child to benefit from his or her individually developed education plan. Even if a service is costly, a school district cannot refuse to provide such services for that reason. However, school districts can choose the service that is least expensive, if the service selected will meet the "appropriate" requirements of the law. According to Yell (1998), "in enacting the IDEA, Congress specifically rejected limitations of federal funding as justification for denying a FAPE" (p. 147).

There is one instance where students with disabilities may be charged for services. Fees for services may be charged if this is a fee imposed on all students in the school (i.e., "uniformly assessed fees are permissible") (Turnbull & Turnbull, 2000, p. 76). However, schools may not charge fees for either transportation expenses or living expenses for students who are placed in public or private residential programs to meet IDEA requirements.

If the student is covered under Medicaid, the school can collect payment for services provided under IDEA. According to the IDEA regulations, "nothing in this part relieves an insurer or similar third party from an otherwise valid obligation to provide or to pay for services provided to a child with a disability" (30 C.F.R. Section 300.302[b]). In addition, schools may seek third-party payment (i.e., reimbursement) from a parent's private health insurance to offset the cost of expensive related services (Yell, 1998). In a Pennsylvania case (*Chester County Intermediate Unit v. Pennsylvania Blue Shield,* 1990), the issue was whether the cost of physical therapy services required under IDEA were to be borne by the parents' insurance or the schools. The parents, in this instance, had coverage for physical therapy, but the insurer refused to honor the coverage, saying that it did not cover services provided under IDEA. In the 3rd Circuit Court decision, "the court of appeals refused to accept the insurer's position that the IDEA does not authorize the shifting of costs to private insurers when intermediate educational units have a statutory duty to provide an appropriate education for children with disabilities at public expense" (Center for Education and Employment Law, 2004, p. 213) but did not require the insurer to pay for the physical therapy services because "they were provided for free under the IDEA" (p. 213). However, schools cannot request payment from insurers for services if the use of such insurance benefits would result in a financial loss to the parents. This loss can include "(a) depletion or lessening of lifetime benefits or annual coverage; (b) interference with future insurability; (c) an increase in premiums; or (d) termination of coverage" (Yell, 1998, p. 217).

In essence, the inclusion of the term "free" supports the principle of zero reject; that is, all students with disabilities should be provided an appropriate education. This education is to be provided regardless of the cost to the school district. Without the insertion of this term, it is possible that school districts would base their decisions regarding student programs and placement on the basis of cost, not on the appropriateness of the education to meet the child's individual needs.

Appropriate Education

The second word in the acronym FAPE that has resulted in significant controversy is that of "appropriate." As with the word "free," no definition for the word "appropriate" was included in the legislation. This term, however, has been defined by the Supreme Court in the case of *Board of Education of the Hendrick Hudson Central School District v. Rowley* (1982). The following discussion of this case will provide an explanation of the term "appropriate."

The plaintiffs prevailed in the Trial Court on the argument that "Because of this disparity between the child's achievement and her potential . . . she was not receiving a 'free appropriate public education'" (*Board of Education v. Rowley,* 1982, p. 176). The Supreme Court disagreed and stated,

> By passing the Act, Congress sought primarily to make public education available to handicapped children. But in seeking to provide such access to public education, Congress did not impose upon the states any greater substantive educational standard than would be necessary to make such access meaningful. . . . Thus, the intent of the Act was more to open the door of public education to handicapped children on appropriate terms than to guarantee any particular education once inside. (*Board of Education v. Rowley,* 1982, p. 192)

In *Rowley,* the Supreme Court, while supporting educational accessibility for children with disabilities, made it clear that it was not going to establish standards that focused on maximizing a student's potential, but rather that focused on the provision of a "basic floor of opportunity." In this case, the Court also reviewed the issue of a definition for FAPE. In opposition to the lower courts' decisions, the Supreme Court stated that the Act itself defines FAPE as

> *special education* and *related services* which (A) have been provided at public expense, under public supervision and direction, and without charge, (B) meet the standards of the State educational agency, (C) include an appropriate preschool, elementary, or secondary school education in the State involved, and (D) are provided in conformity with the individualized education program. . . . (*Board of Education v. Rowley,* 1982, p. 188)

The question then arose of how does one decide if the child's program is appropriate under the Act's definition. The Court addressed this issue by devising a two-part inquiry, now known as the Rowley test:

> First, has the State complied with the procedures set forth in the Act? And, second, is the individualized educational program developed through the Act's procedures reasonably calculated to enable the child to receive educational benefits? If these requirements are met, the State has complied with the obligations imposed by Congress and the courts can require no more. (*Board of Education v. Rowley,* 1982, pp. 206–207)

When the answer to these two questions is yes, then according to the Act and *Rowley,* the child is receiving an appropriate education.

When the 1997 Amendments to IDEA were developed and implemented, a definition of FAPE was included. This definition, developed to be in compliance with the Rowley test and reiterated in the latest reauthorization of IDEA (2004), states that FAPE means

> special education and related services that—
>
> (A) have been provided at public expense, under public supervision and direction, and without charge;
>
> (B) meet the standards of the State educational agency;
>
> (C) include an appropriate preschool, elementary school, or secondary school education in the State involved; and
>
> (D) are provided in conformity with the individualized education program required under 614(d). (IDEA of 2004, P.L. 108–446, § 602[8], 118 Stat. 2647[2005])

Included in the IDEA definition of FAPE are the terms "special education" and "related services." The Act defines "special education" as

> specially designed instruction, at no cost to parents, to meet the unique needs of a child with a disability, including—
>
> (A) instruction conducted in the classroom, in the home, in hospitals and institutions, and in other settings; and
>
> (B) instruction in physical education. (IDEA of 2004, P.L. 108–446, § 602[29], 118 Stat. 2647[2005])

"Related services" is then defined as

> transportation, and such developmental, corrective, and other supportive services (including speech-language pathology and audiology services, interpreting services, psychological services, physical and occupational therapy, recreation, including therapeutic recreation, social work services, school nurse services designed to enable a child with a disability to receive a free appropriate public education as described in the individualized education program of the child, counseling services, including rehabilitation counseling, orientation and mobility services, and medical services, except that such medical services shall be for diagnostic and evaluation purposes only) as may be required to assist a child with a disability to benefit from special education, and includes the early identification and assessment of disabling conditions in children. . . . The term does not include a medical device that is surgically implanted, or the replacement of such device. (IDEA of 2004, P.L. 108–446, § 602[26], 118 Stat. 2647[2005])

ex. Cochlear implant

The term "related services" has been the focus of a number of court cases wherein the clarification of the services that must be provided is addressed. In only one case, *Irving Independent School District v. Tatro* (*1984*), has the Supreme Court addressed this issue. In *Tatro* (1984), the question was asked whether the provision of clean intermittent catheterization (CIC) of a child by a nurse was included under the Act's rubric of related services as "supportive services" or excluded as "medical services." The concept of supportive services, required to assist the child in receiving benefit from the individualized special education program, is an integral part of the law. Without these supportive services, it is believed that the concept of meaningful access would be a sham. Therefore, in *Tatro* the Court stated,

> The Court of Appeals was clearly correct in holding that CIC is a "supportive servic[e] . . . required to assist a handicapped child to benefit from special education". . . . It is clear on this record that, without having CIC services available during the school day, Amber cannot attend school and thereby "benefit from special education". CIC services therefore fall squarely within the definition of a "supportive service". . . . As we have stated before, "Congress sought primarily to make public education available to handicapped children" and "to make such access meaningful". . . . A service that enables a handicapped child to remain at school during the day is an important means of providing the child with the meaningful access to education that Congress envisioned. (pp. 3376–3377)

Hence, an "appropriate" education is one that

1. Is provided without charge under public direction, supervision, and expense
2. Meets state standards
3. Includes individualized preschool, elementary, and secondary school education
4. Conforms to the procedural requirements set forth in the IDEA

Public Education — *Outside of institutions (not public schools vs private)*

Although the U.S. Constitution does not include education as a guaranteed right, it is considered to be one of the important duties of each state. This concept was supported in the *Brown v. Board of Education* case, wherein education was identified as "the most important function of state and local governments." As a result, IDEA provides a mandate for education and supports funding for services provided in the public educational arena. However, if public schools are not able to provide an appropriate education, then they are required to identify private educational facilities in which these services can be provided. This private service, as noted previously, must be at no cost to the parents or guardians of the student with a disability. For example, in *Wilson County School System v. Clifton* (2000), the school district was required to pay for private placement because the IEP it developed was considered to be inappropriate. In this case, the parents of a child who was deaf objected to the proposed IEP that called for the student being placed in a special education classroom. The parents objected, "on the grounds that it was not suitable for a student with hearing impairments and that the teacher had little experience" (Center for Education and Employment Law, 2004, p. 74). After placement of their child in a private setting, they sought reimbursement from the school district. The Administrative Law Judge (ALJ) ordered the school to provide the requisite related services using qualified professionals, as well as to reimburse the parents for the private school placement. The Tennessee Court of Appeals agreed with the ALJ, "finding that the IEP proposed by the school system was inappropriate for the student and that the private hearing and speech facility represented an appropriate placement" (p. 75). Even though the parents unilaterally placed their child in a private setting, the school was responsible for the cost because "appropriate" services were unavailable in the setting they proposed.

In some instances, the public schools may select a private school to fulfill its obligations toward its students. For example, the St. Johnsbury School District in Vermont did not have a public high school, so students from that district were allowed to choose to attend the St. Johnsbury Academy or a high school outside the district. However, this selection did not abrogate the public school's responsibilities toward the child with a disability who is placed in a private school by the public school district. In the case of *St. Johnsbury Academy v. D.H.* (2001), a student with cerebral palsy, a learning impairment, and a visual impairment chose to apply for admission to St. Johnsbury Academy. The student's IEP required that he be placed in regular classes in English and social studies. The Academy agreed to accept the student, but, they would not place him in their mainstream high school program because they had a requirement that all students must have a fifth-grade ability. The parents refused to send the student under these conditions, so the school district offered to place the student at another high school. The parents rejected this offer, stating that there was a long commute and that vocational programming required by the IEP was not available at the second placement. Both an administrative hearing officer and the District Court held for the student, stating that the Academy must admit the student because the fifth-grade ability requirement violated IDEA. On appeal, the Second Circuit Court reversed this decision concluding that

> there was nothing in the IDEA that warranted its application to private schools. When a public agency places a student with a disability "it does so as a means of providing that child with an educational program that it was unable to provide." Therefore, the public school remains responsible for the education of the child and for ensuring that the child

possesses all the rights of a student with a disability. The IDEA's regulations expressly contemplate that the Act's IEP and LRE requirements will be enforced when a public agency places a student in a private school. However, the obligation to ensure such compliance rests with the appropriate local educational agency, which is, by definition, a public entity, rather than a private one. (*St. Johnsbury v. D.H.*, 2001)

Accessibility of Education for all Children with Disabilities

Central to IDEA is the principle of zero reject. The principle is operationalized in the Act's purpose as a clarification of the belief that *all* children can learn and be taught, and that, regardless of the severity or type of disability, all children are entitled to receive an FAPE. This principle has been questioned in several courts concerning the responsibility of school districts for providing an FAPE for children with "severe" physical or behavioral disabilities.

Timothy W. v. Rochester, N.H. School District (1989)

The issue of the severity of the disability and the child's ability to benefit from an educational program was addressed in *Timothy W. v. Rochester, N.H. School District* (1989). Timothy had profound mental retardation and multiple disabilities, including spastic quadriplegia, cerebral palsy, seizure disorder, and cortical blindness, and was therefore considered to be "severely handicapped." The school district claimed IDEA did not require a school to provide educational services to a child who was alleged to be uneducable. Judge Bownes, writing for a majority of the panel for the First Circuit Court of Appeals, stressed:

> The language of the Act could not be more unequivocal. The statute is permeated with the words "*all* handicapped children" whenever it refers to the target population. It never speaks of any exceptions for severely handicapped children. Indeed, as indicated *supra,* the Act gives priority to the most severely handicapped. Nor is there any language whatsoever which requires as a prerequisite to being covered by the Act, that a handicapped child must demonstrate that he or she will "benefit" from the educational program. Rather, the Act speaks of the *state's* responsibility to design a special education and related services program that will meet the unique "needs" of all handicapped children. The language of the Act, in its entirety, makes clear that a "zero-reject" policy is at the core of the Act, and that no child, regardless of the severity of his or her handicap, is to ever again be subjected to the deplorable state of affairs which existed at the time of the

Standards and the Law

CEC Standard 1: Foundations
PRAXIS Standard: Legal and Societal Issues

Act's passage, in which millions of handicapped children received inadequate education or none at all. In summary, the Act mandates an appropriate public education for all handicapped children, regardless of the level of achievement that such children might attain. (*Timothy W. v. Rochester,* 1989, pp. 960–961)

Accordingly, the states are not given the discretion to determine whether a child is educable, but instead, must provide a free education to every child within its jurisdiction.

The second issue, the legality of suspension and/or expulsion of students with disabilities who are disruptive and/or dangerous to themselves or others, has been addressed in several cases heard by the Supreme Court. Because the purpose of the Act was to ensure all children and youth with disabilities have access to an FAPE, the question has been raised concerning what actions could be taken if the child with disabilities is disruptive in the class. Could children with disabilities qualify for suspension or expulsion from public education, and how can their rights be protected? Prior to the passage of the Act, many minority children were labeled as mentally retarded or severely emotionally disturbed in order to remove them from the public school classroom. The result of these suspension and expulsion practices was a disproportionate number of minority children being denied the right to an education on a false basis.

Goss v. Lopez (1975)

The Supreme Court first addressed the issue of suspension or expulsion of children in *Goss v. Lopez* (1975). The Court in *Goss* did not address special education students, but examined the issue of expulsions without the benefit of due process. The Supreme Court held that suspensions without a hearing violated the due process rights of the students because students have a constitutionally protected property interest in accessing public education. Students also have a liberty interest in that their reputation can be damaged through the act of suspension and, therefore, interfere with future educational and employment opportunities (Zirkel, Richardson, & Goldberg, 1995).

Honig v. Doe (1988)

Yet, the problem remained. Can public schools expel or suspend children who, because of a disability, are a danger to themselves or others? The Supreme Court addressed expulsions and suspensions of special education students in the case of *Honig v. Doe* (1988). In this case, the plaintiff alleged that two students with emotional disabilities were expelled from school in violation of IDEA. In *Honig,* the Court stated:

> The language of § 1415(e)(3) is unequivocal. It states plainly that during the pendency of any proceedings initiated under the Act, unless the state or local educational agency and the parents or guardian of a disabled child otherwise agree, "the child shall remain in the then current educational placement". . . . (p. 604)

In addition, the Court commented that

> Faced with this clear directive, petitioner asks us to read a "dangerousness" exception into the stay-put provision on the basis of either of two essentially inconsistent assumptions: first, that Congress thought the residual authority of school officials to exclude dangerous students from the classroom too obvious for comment; or second, that Congress inadvertently failed to provide such authority and this Court must therefore remedy the oversight. Because we cannot accept either premise, we decline petitioner's invitation to rewrite the statute . . . . (p. 604)

If it is determined that students with disabilities are a danger to themselves or others, the public school was not prevented from employing its standard procedures. Indeed such procedures may include

> the use of study carrels, time-outs, detention, or the restriction of privileges. More drastically, where a student poses an immediate threat to the safety of others, officials may temporarily suspend him or her for up to 10 school days. This authority . . . not only ensures that school administrators can protect the safety of others by promptly removing the most dangerous of students, it also provides a "cooling down" period during which officials can initiate IEP review and seek to persuade the child's parents to agree to an interim placement. And in those cases in which the parents of a truly dangerous child adamantly refuse to permit any change in placement, the 10-day respite gives school officials an opportunity to invoke the aid of the courts . . . . (*Honig v. Doe,* 1988, p. 605)

There are several important aspects of the *Honig* case that need mentioning. First, it adopted the 10-day standard established in the regulations as the maximum time a student may be suspended without considering a new IEP. Second, it required that the stay-put provision be activated before a suspension or expulsion may occur. Third, it did not prevent the use of normal disciplinary procedures with a child with disabilities, but provided guidelines for their utilization.

Light v. Parkway C-2 School District (1994)

The question then becomes, how can the public school personnel remove an allegedly dangerous child with a disability from his or her placement if that child poses an immediate threat to him- or herself or others? The Eighth Circuit Court of Appeals dealt with this issue in *Light v. Parkway C-2 School District* (1994), wherein the Court was presented a case in which a child with disabilities was alleged to be a danger to other students and teachers. The child had multiple mental disabilities and was diagnosed at various times as demonstrating behavioral and conduct disorders, pervasive developmental disorder, mild to moderate mental retardation, autism, language impairment, and organic brain syndrome. She bit, hit, and poked persons, threw objects, and turned over furniture. As a result of her violent and aggressive behaviors, she was suspended from school for 10 days without a due process hearing in compliance with state law. The Court found that she had been denied due process because her parents had not received notice of the hearing.

The Court established a two-prong test to determine if the school had violated the stay-put provision of IDEA. In this test, the Court stated that

> a school district seeking to remove an assertedly dangerous disabled child from her current educational placement must show (1) that maintaining the child in that placement is substantially likely to result in injury either to himself or herself, or to others, and (2) that the school district has done all that it reasonably can to reduce the risk that the child will cause injury. Where injury remains substantially likely to result despite the reasonable efforts of the school district to accommodate the child's disabilities, the district court may issue an injunction ordering that the child's placement be changed pending the outcome of the administrative review process. (*Light v. Parkway C-2 School District,* 1994, p. 1228)

In the *Light* case, the Court left school officials with the responsibility for dealing with dangerous and violent children. However, first the school must demonstrate that the child is a potential danger to him- or herself or others. Then the school district must demonstrate that efforts had been made to reduce the risk of harm to individuals by training teachers and other personnel in behavioral intervention strategies, and through the provision of appropriate special education and related services. In *Light,* both conditions were met. Subsequently, the two-pronged test that was introduced in *Light* did prove manageable and achieved the purpose of ensuring children with disabilities were not expelled or suspended without procedural protection, or in violation of the mandate of the Act that children with disabilities receive FAPE.

Reese v. Board of Education of Bismarck R-V School District (2002)

In a post-*Light* case, the courts expanded the principle of appropriateness to include a review of a unilateral private school placement for a student with severe emotional and behavioral disorders. In *Reese v. Board of Education of Bismarck R-V School District* (2002), the parents of an elementary-age student with emotional disorders unilaterally placed their son in a private school because they disagreed with the school district's decision to place the child in a day treatment program run by the county special education cooperative. The child in question had been placed in the private school previously by the district; after his release, the district had provided homebound services. When these services were terminated because of problems the child was having, the school did not provide any other services for the rest of the school year nor did they offer to review the child's need for extended school year services. The hearing officer panel's decision was that the school district had failed in their responsibilities by not providing services when the homebound placement was terminated and by not considering the need for extended school year (ESY). Thus, compensatory education was ordered. However, the panel also noted that neither the private day program nor the county day treatment program was considered appropriate. On appeal, the Eastern District Court of Missouri supported the hearing panel's decision that the

> private facility was inappropriate. It was overly restrictive; the student experienced numerous outbursts during this time there and had to be physically restrained several times.

The student had no peer role models at the school and rarely engaged in interactive play with classmates. The lack of any inclusion component in the placement made it inappropriate. (Center for Education and Employment Law, 2004, p. 186)

In this case, the courts expanded the view of what is appropriate to consider two factors: (a) the restrictiveness of the educational placement and the ability of the school district to provide activities with nondisabled peers; and (b) the amount of academic, not just behavioral, progress that the child made.

Steinberg v. Weast (2001)

Another District Court decision also considered the restrictiveness of a private school placement, as well as the amount of academic progress the student was making, to decide whether a private school placement was appropriate. In *Steinberg v. Weast* (2001), the school district decided that the public school setting would be more appropriate for a student with significant learning disabilities who had been receiving services in a private school setting for her elementary and middle school years. The proposed IEP, rejected by the parents, focused on a fundamental life skills program in opposition to the diploma-track program offered at the private school. The educators at the private school agreed with the public school's decision "that she needed fundamental skills instruction to prepare her for everyday life and that it would be difficult for her to attend a diploma-track program" (Center for Education and Employment Law, 2004, p. 74). The inability of the student to pass the Maryland basic skills test supported this proposed IEP, along with the belief that a residential placement was too restrictive and that an appropriate education could be provided in the public school district. The District Court upheld this view of appropriateness based on the amount of academic progress that the student had made and gave "due deference" to the viewpoint of the educators at both the public and the private schools concerning the possibility of academic success in a less restrictive environment.

Summary

The Fourteenth Amendment says that no state shall make or enforce any law that denies or limits the rights or privileges of any citizen of the United States; nor shall any state deprive any person of life, liberty, or property, without due process of law; nor deny to any person within its jurisdiction the equal protection of the laws. Therefore, equal protection means that laws are to be applied equally to all persons, without special privileges or restrictions applied to any one group. Using the Fourteenth Amendment, the courts found that when states assumed the responsibility of providing an education to its citizens, then an entitlement to an education was created for all its inhabitants, not just a select few. *PARC* and *Mills* were the first two cases addressing the lack of education and training for persons with disabilities using the Fourteenth Amendment. The decisions in *PARC* and *Mills* provided the basis for many of the principles included in later educational legislation for students with disabilities.

Under the equal protection clause of the Fourteenth Amendment, states were ordered to cease denying to students with disabilities educational opportunities offered to other citizens, that is a "free appropriate public education." The philosophical basis for the concept of an FAPE was the principle that became known as "zero reject." This principle stated that no child should be rejected or denied the opportunity for schooling as a result of an unchangeable characteristic, such as a disability or behavior. This principle was later tested in the courts with children who had been suspended or expelled from public schools. Previously, schools had disagreed that children with behavioral issues were included under the zero reject principle. However, the courts held that states do not have the right to determine whether a child is educable, but instead must provide an FAPE to every child within the jurisdiction, including those children whose disabilities are disruptive and/or dangerous. According to the legislation, and with subsequent support from the courts, the rights of all children must be protected.

Public school personnel can remove a child who is dangerous by following due process procedures that have been outlined in law and regulation. First, the child must be a risk to him- or herself or others. Second, the school district must have done all that is reasonably possible to reduce the risk that the child will cause harm. Third, parents should be notified and involved in the process.

In summary, the concept of FAPE, operationalized by the principle of zero reject, is the essential core of the federal mandate for states to provide educational opportunities for *all* children within their borders. This concept has been supported through constitutional amendments, federal legislation, and litigation. At the local level, this principle is evidenced by school districts in every state being required to provide each child with a disability who is a citizen of the state, regardless of the type or severity of the disability, an education tailored to fit the child's needs. In conjunction with the special education services, supportive services are to be provided if the child will need them to benefit from his or her educational program. These services are to be provided in the public setting if possible. If not, then the school must identify where the child's needs can be met and provide that service to the child. All services, including special education and related services, are to be provided at no expense to the parents and/or guardians of a child with a disability, except for fees uniformly assessed on all students in the public school. In this manner, each child is provided access to an education that is considered to be essential for future success.

Questions for Discussion

1. What impact has the principle of equal protection had on the education of students with disabilities?

FAPE - free, appropriate, public, edu.

2. How have the terms "free," "appropriate," and "public" been defined by the schools, and what impact have they had on the education of children with disabilities?

3. How has recent case law supported the accessibility of educational services for children with disabilities?

Websites for Further Exploration

Equal Protection Doctrine (14th Amendment, Equal Protection Tests)
www.bartleby.com/65/fo/Fourteenth.html
www.thomas.loc.gov
www2.law.cornell.edu/

FAPE
www.fape.org/
www.fapeonline.org/
www.wrightslaw.com/info/fape.index.htm
www.ideapractices.org/
www.ed.gov/pubs/chartdisab/dueproc.html

Application of FAPE
usinfo.state.gov/usa/infousa/facts/democrac/36.htm
www.dredf.org/international/mayerson.html
www.slc.sevier.org/legnlit.htm
www.fapesolutions.com/AboutUs/

ILLUSTRATING THE LAW

Briefing of:
Board of Education of the Hendrick Hudson
Central School District v. Rowley
United States Supreme Court
458 U.S. 176, 73 L.Ed. 2d 690, 102 S.Ct. 3034
Argued March 23, 1982
Decided June 28, 1982

FACTS: Amy Rowley, a deaf student in the Hendrick Hudson Central School District, requested the services of a sign language interpreter as a supplemental service in her IEP, pursuant to the requirements for federal funding of state efforts to educate the students with disabilities under EHA, 84 Stat. 176, as amended, 20 U.S.C. 1010 *et seq.* (1976 ed. and Supp. IV). The school denied the request for an interpreter, and the Rowleys appealed unsuccessfully to an independent examiner and to the New York Commissioner of Education. Pursuant to the Act's provision for judicial review, the Rowleys filed suit in U.S. District Court, alleging the district's denial of an interpreter denied Amy a "free appropriate public education" guaranteed by the Act. The District Court found that Amy was performing better than the average child in her class, even without the aid of an interpreter, but that she was not performing as well as she would without her disability. Based on this unrealized potential, the District Court found she was not receiving a "free appropriate public education." The U.S. Court of Appeals for the Second Circuit affirmed the District Court's decision, and the Supreme Court granted certiorari to review the interpretation of the Act, and answer two questions.

ISSUES: What is meant by the Act's requirement of a "free appropriate public education"?

What is the role of state and federal courts in exercising the review granted by 20 U.S.C. 1415?

HOLDING: The Supreme Court held that the Act is satisfied when the state provides personalized instruction with sufficient support services to permit the child with a disability to benefit educationally from that instruction. The Supreme Court held that under the judicial review provisions of the Act, once a court determines that the state has complied with the statutory procedures, and then determines that the IEP is reasonably calculated to enable the child to receive educational benefits, then the courts can require no more.

RATIONALE: In support of its holding, the Court reasoned that the definitions in the Act did not contain an express substantive standard proscribing the level of education to be afforded children with disabilities, but merely set out procedural requirements and statutory priorities. Furthermore, the Court looked to the legislative history of the Act to determine that the law was intended to open the door to public education for children with disabilities, but not to impose on the states any greater substantive educational standard than is necessary to make such access meaningful. Finally, the Court reasoned that although the Act seeks to help states carry out their constitutional responsibility to provide equal protection under the laws, it did not impose a duty on states to achieve a strict equality of opportunity or services, or to maximize the potential of each child with a disability. In support of its second holding on the limited role the courts should play in reviewing challenges under the Act, the Court reasoned that compliance with the procedural safeguards Congress enacted will, in most cases, ensure substantive content of an IEP. Also, the Court cautioned judges against imposing their own view of preferable educational methods, restating that courts lack the specific knowledge and experience necessary to resolve persistent and difficult problems of educational policy.

EFFECTS: In this case, the Supreme Court held that the courts erred because, in the words of the District Court, Amy was receiving an "adequate" education and the school district had complied with the procedural safeguards. Based on Amy's progress in school and her above-average achievement in relation to other nondisabled students and the school's compliance with the procedural safeguards, she was not entitled to a sign language interpreter under the Act. The Court's broader holding is that schools that carefully follow the Act's procedural safeguards for review, hearings, and appeals of the IEP will be afforded some deference when the way they choose to educate children with disabilities is challenged in court.

ILLUSTRATING THE LAW THROUGH DISCUSSION

1. Amy Rowley was a deaf student denied the assistance of an interpreter by her local school. She was able to perform academically better than the average child in her class, but, because of the limitations imposed by her disability, she was not able to achieve a level commensurate with her full potential. Her parents sought the assistance of an interpreter to reduce these limitations. What is your opinion of the Supreme Court's decision to deny her this opportunity?

2. When examining situations involving the appropriateness of an educational program including related services, why should the Court's decision be based on the educational benefit derived rather than on the student's potential?

References

Board of Education of the Hendrick Hudson Central School District v. Rowley, 458 U.S. 176, 102 S.Ct. 3034, 73 L.Ed. 2d 690 (1982).

Brown v. Board of Education of Topeka, Kansas, 347 U.S. 483, 74 S.Ct. 686, 98 L.Ed. 873, 38 A.L.R. 2d 1180 (1954).

Center for Education and Employment Law. (2004). *Students with disabilities and special education law* (21st ed.). Malvern, PA: Author.

Chester County Intermediate Unit v. Pennsylvania Blue Shield, 896 F.2d 808 (3d Cir. 1990).

Cleburne v. Cleburne Living Center, Inc., 473 U.S. 432, 87 L.Ed. 2d 313, 105 S.Ct. 3249 (1985).

Education for All Handicapped Children Act, 20 U.S.C. § 1400 *et seq.* (1975).

Education for the Handicapped Act, 20 U.S.C. § 1471 *et seq.* (1970).

Ellis, J. W., & Luckasson, R. A. (1984). Respondent's *Amicus Curiae Brief,* City of Cleburne, Texas v. Cleburne Living Center, Inc. 473 U.S. 432 (1984) (No. 84–468).

Fullilove v. Klutznick, 448 U.S. 448, 100 S.Ct. 27, 65 L.Ed. 2d 902 (1980).

Funk & Wagnalls New International Dictionary of the English Language. (1997). Chicago: Ferguson.

Goss v. Lopez, 419 U.S. 565, 95 S.Ct. 729, 42 L.Ed. 2d 725 (1975).

Honig v. Doe, 484 U.S. 305, 108 S.Ct. 592, 98 L.Ed. 2d 686 (1988).

Individuals with Disabilities Education Act, 20 U.S.C. § 1400 *et seq.* (1990).

Individuals with Disabilities Education Act Amendments, 20 U.S.C. § 1400 *et seq.* (1997).

Individuals with Disabilities Education Improvement Act of 2004, P.L. 108–446, § 600 *et seq.,* 118 Stat. 2647 (2005).

Irving Independent School District v. Tatro, 468 U.S. 883, 104 S.Ct. 3371, 82 L.Ed. 2d 664 (1984).

Light v. Parkway C-2 School District, 41 F.3d 1223 (8th Cir. 1994), *cert. denied,* 115 S.Ct. 2557, 132 L.Ed. 2d 811 (1995).

Loving v. Virginia, 388 U.S. 1, 87 S.Ct. 1817, 18 L.Ed. 2d 1010 (1967).

Marshall v. United States, 414 U.S. 417, 94 S.Ct. 700, 38 L.Ed. 2d 618 (1974).

Mills v. Board of Education of the District of Columbia, 348 F.Supp. 866 (D.D.C. 1972).

Pennsylvania Association for Retarded Citizens (PARC) v. Commonwealth of Pennsylvania, 343 F. Supp. 279 (1972).

Reese v. Board of Education of Bismarck R-V School District, 225 F. Supp. 2d 1149 (E.D. Mo. 2002).

Romer v. Evans, 517 U.S. 620, 116 S.Ct. 1620, 134 L.Ed. 2d 855 (1996).

San Antonio School District v. Rodriguez, 411 U.S. 1, 93 S.Ct. 1278, 36 L.Ed. 2d 16 (1973).

Skinner v. Oklahoma, 316 U.S. 535, 62 S.Ct. 1110, 86 L.Ed. 1655 (1942).

St. Johnsbury v. D.H., 240 F.3d 163 (2nd Cir. 2001)

Steinberg v. Weast, 132 F. Supp. 2d 343 (D. Md. 2001).

Timothy W. v. Rochester, N.H. School District, 875 F.2d 954 (1st Cir. 1989), *cert. denied,* 493 U.S. 983, 110 S.Ct. 519 (1989).

Turnbull, H. R. (1993). *Free appropriate public education: The law and children with disabilities* (4th ed.). Denver: Love.

Turnbull, H. R., & Turnbull, A. P. (2000). *Free appropriate public education: The law and children with disabilities* (6th ed.). Denver: Love.

U.S. Railroad Retirement Board v. Fritz, 449 U.S. 166, 101 S.Ct. 453, 66 L.Ed. 2d 368 (1980).

Valente, W. D., & Valente, C. M. (1998). *Law in the schools* (4th ed.). Upper Saddle River, NJ: Merrill/Prentice Hall.

Wilson County School System v. Clifton, 41 S.W.3d 645, 649 (Tenn Ct. App. 2000).

Wisconsin v. Yoder, 406 U.S. 205, 92 S.Ct. 1526, 32 L.Ed. 2d 15 (1972).

Yell, M. L. (1998). *The law and special education.* Upper Saddle River, NJ: Merrill/Prentice Hall.

Yick Wo v. Hopkins, 118 U.S. 356, 6 S.Ct. 1064, 30 L.Ed. 220 (1886).

Zirkel, P. A., Richardson, S. N., & Goldberg, S. S. (1995). *A digest of Supreme Court decisions affecting education* (3rd ed.). Bloomington, IN: Phi Delta Kappa Educational Foundation.

CHAPTER FOUR

Nondiscriminatory Evaluation

GUIDING QUESTIONS

1. What is bias, and how is it evidenced in public schools?

2. Why is nondiscriminatory evaluation essential to the provision of a free appropriate public education?

3. What are the legislative components essential for the provision of a nondiscriminatory evaluation?

4. Because parents are given the right to have independent educational evaluations (IEEs) performed under IDEA, under what circumstances are school districts required to pay for the IEE?

5. Under what circumstances can students receiving special education services be required to pass a minimum competency test in order to receive a high school diploma?

6. What are IDEA requirements for students with disabilities to participate in state- and districtwide assessment programs, and why is the inclusion of students with disabilities in such assessment programs important?

According to Bailey and Harbin (1980), "evidence of bias in our educational system has long been present" (p. 590). Bias, as defined in *Merriam-Webster's Collegiate Dictionary* (1995), is "an inclination of temperament or outlook; esp. a personal and sometimes unreasoned judgment." When individuals are making judgments based on quantitative or observational data, bias can be introduced into the educational process through the misinterpretation of these data or the use of incorrect data that can result in discrimination or misclassification. For example, bias in educational decision making may occur as a result of decisions being inappropriately affected by the child's race, culture, economic background, or disability. Although bias may be present at any time during the educational process, it has been noted most frequently during the evaluation of children for eligibility and placement in special education services. As evidence that bias can influence eligibility and placement decisions, professionals refer to the disproportionately high number of minority and low-income children labeled as mentally retarded and their subsequent placement in special education programs.

During the 1970s, when it was observed that there was an overrepresentation of minority students (Black, non-English speaking, etc.) identified for special education services, a critical examination of the instruments used to determine eligibility was undertaken to discover if test bias existed. Bias in evaluation instruments may be introduced in the selection of the norm groups or through the selection of improper test items. For example, standardized tests may consist of items that penalize linguistically different groups. Or these tests may penalize groups from different cultures or economic background because the tests include items based on White, middle-class experiences; reflect White, middle-class values; and reward cognitive styles congruent with White, middle-class experiences. In addition, the norm group may not adequately reflect the general pool of individuals in the schools, consisting instead predominately of White, middle-class subjects. Although it is unfortunate that an unbiased test currently does not exist, it is essential that those persons involved in the evaluation process attempt to ensure the process be as unbiased and fair as possible through appropriate test selection.

Therefore, test bias, whether from the evaluation instruments or the process itself, may result in the incorrect identification of students as disabled with subsequent placement and educational services based on this misconception. Turnbull and Turnbull (1979) stated that

> misclassifying children as handicapped when they are not, or classifying them inaccurately with respect to their handicaps, can result not only in denying them their rights to an educational opportunity (not to mention their rights to an appropriate education) but also in unjustifiably stigmatizing them. (p. 85)

Standards and the Law

CEC Standard 8: Assessment
INTASC Standard 8: Assessment
PRAXIS Standard: Delivery of Services to Students with Disabilities

Misclassifying a student can result in a stigmatizing label leading to isolation from school experiences; rejection by peers and teachers; assignment of stereotypical expectations, including lowered goals; a self-fulfilling prophesy of differentness; and tainted expectations with the effects of mislabeling persisting even when the label is removed. Indeed, when ADA was enacted in 1990, the legislation defined a person with a disability as any person who has a history of having, or is regarded as having, an impairment. The use of this definition protects persons with only minor disabilities or with no disabilities from being discriminated against because of stereotypical expectations and reactions.

Therefore, there is a conundrum involved in the assignment of a label, whether correct or incorrect. A label may result in a limitation of experiences. However, it may also increase the resources and services available to the student because only children identified through the designated process may be served. Of course, being labeled and then placed in a special education program does not ensure the student will receive educational services to overcome the disadvantages inherent in the classification of "disabled." Hence, nondiscriminatory evaluations are essential in providing an appropriate education to children and youth with disabilities.

Basis for the Principle of Nondiscriminatory Evaluation

The concerns raised regarding possible bias in evaluations were supported in the holdings of three major court cases (*Hobson v. Hansen,* 1967; *Larry P. v. Riles,* 1972, 1979; *Parents in Action on Special Education [PASE] v. Hannon,* 1980). These cases, providing the foundation for subsequent legislation, used the Fifth and Fourteenth Amendments to the U.S. Constitution as their legal basis to question the use of

Standards and the Law

CEC Standard 1: Foundations
PRAXIS Standard: Legal and Societal Issues

allegedly biased evaluation instruments and/or procedures. The Fifth Amendment states that "No person shall be . . . deprived of life, liberty or property, without due process of law." The Fourteenth Amendment states that

> No State shall make or enforce any law which shall abridge the privileges or immunities of citizens of the United States; nor shall any state deprive any person of life, liberty or property, without due process of law; nor deny to any person within its jurisdiction the equal protection of the laws.

Both amendments focus on the denial of property without due process of law. Denying access to education is seen as the denial of right to property and, therefore, a violation of both the Fifth and Fourteenth Amendments. In addition, the Fourteenth Amendment also requires states to treat citizens equally and, in the case of education, provide equal access.

Hobson v. Hansen (1967)

According to Bersoff (1980), in the years following *Brown v. Board of Education of Topeka, Kansas* (1954), many school systems attempted to slow the desegregation process by using standardized tests and testing procedures to place minority children into segregated programs within the public schools. However, in the case of *Hobson v. Hansen* (1967), the federal District Court in Washington, DC, entered the testing controversy by examining the use of standardized tests in assigning public school students to various educational tracks based on ability grouping. The plaintiffs in this case represented Black and poor public school children attending the District of Columbia schools. These students had been placed in disproportionate numbers on the lower-ability track as a result of standardized group IQ test results. In seeking a reason for the disparity within the tracking system, the Court determined that disparities had occurred partially because of the inappropriate use of test scores for assigning students into the track system allegedly based on ability grouping. Therefore, the Court decided that the District of Columbia School System deprived Black and poor school children of their right to equal educational opportunities and stated that

> While the government may classify persons and thereby effect disparities in treatment, those included within or excluded from the respective classes should be those for whom the inclusion or exclusion is appropriate; otherwise the classification risks becoming wholly irrational and thus unconstitutionally discriminatory. It is in this regard that the track system is fatally defective, because for many students placement is based on traits other than those on which the classification purports to be based. (*Hobson v. Hansen*, 1967, p. 513)

Larry P. v. Riles (1972, 1979)

This is the seminal case in the area of nondiscriminatory evaluation. In late 1971, this case, *Larry P. v. Riles* (1972) was filed as a class action suit on behalf of Black, San Francisco elementary school-age children who had been placed in educable mentally retarded (EMR) classes primarily on the basis of an IQ test score. The plaintiffs alleged that the students were not mentally retarded but had been inappropriately classified as EMR on the basis of tests that were biased against the culture and experience of Black children and in violation of their Fourteenth Amendment rights. Accordingly, the plaintiffs contended that as a result of this misdiagnosis, they were subsequently labeled and placed in EMR classes. Allegedly, because of this misdiagnosis and inappropriate placement, the students received an inadequate education because of the minimal curriculum and low teacher expectations present in EMR classes. In addition, the students were subjected to ridicule from other students and developed feelings of inferiority (*Larry P. v. Riles,* 1972, p. 1308).

Statistical data about the San Francisco Unified School District noted that the number of Black children assigned to special education classes for children with mental retardation was disproportionate to the number in the school system. The plaintiffs alleged that this misclassification violated the equal protection clause of the U.S. Constitution and requested that the Court grant an injunction restraining the school district from using IQ tests to identify and place Black children in special education classes until the issue had been resolved. On June 20, 1972, the Court granted an injunction. This injunction enjoined the San Francisco Unified School District from placing Black students in EMR classes on the basis of criteria that relied primarily on the results of IQ tests, if the result was racial imbalance in the composition of such classes (*Larry P. v. Riles,* 1972).

The Court reviewed the alleged discriminatory tests and, in 1979, rendered a decision that

> the state has acted contrary to the law by requiring the use of tests that are racially and culturally discriminatory and have not been validated for labeling Black E.M.R. children . . . and by requiring the use of the I.Q. tests in an I.Q.-centered process which was being used intentionally to perpetuate and legitimate a vast overrepresentation of Black children in those special classes. (*Larry P. v. Riles,* 1979, p. 989)

The Court also found that mislabeling and placing Black students in EMR classes had discriminatory effects and noted that "It doomed large numbers of Black children to E.M.R. status, racially imbalanced classes, an inferior and 'dead-end' education, and the stigma that inevitably comes from the use of the label 'retarded'" (*Larry P. v. Riles,* 1979, p. 980). The Court, then, ordered reevaluations of every Black child identified as EMR using developmental and health histories, adaptive behavior observations, and diagnostic tests that focused on identifying learning needs and pedagogical approaches.

PASE v. Hannon (1980)

In *PASE v. Hannon* (1980), a case similar to *Larry P.* was heard by the U.S. District Court in Illinois. The focus of this case was whether intelligence tests used by the Chicago Board of Education for identification and placement purposes were culturally biased against Black children. The plaintiffs in this case were Black children in the Chicago Public Schools who had been labeled educable mentally handicapped based on scores from standardized IQ tests and placed in special education classes. The Court reviewed three frequently used individual intelligence tests—the Wechsler Intelligence Scale for Children (WISC), the Wechsler Intelligence Scale for Children–Revised Edition (WISC–R), and the Stanford-Binet. Individual test questions were reviewed for biased content. The Court decided that, although a few questions within the tests were biased or suspect, overall the tests were fair. These findings were in contrast to findings in the *Larry P.* (1979) decision. In addition, the Court held that the IQ tests were not being used as the sole basis for placement in special education classes and, therefore, did not discriminate against Black children in the Chicago public schools.

Legislative Basis for Nondiscriminatory Evaluation

Education for All Handicapped Children Act of 1975

The cases previously discussed provided the litigative base for the inclusion of nondiscriminatory evaluation procedures in EAHCA of 1975 (P.L. 94-142). Through EAHCA, Congress attempted to guarantee "nondiscriminatory testing procedures" by requiring that (a) tests and evaluative materials be presented in the child's native language or mode of communication, (b) the material be administered by trained personnel in conformance with the producer's instructions, and (c) the evaluation materials be validated for the purpose for which they are being used. In addition, no single procedure can be used as the sole criterion for determining an appropriate educational program; the evaluation must include assessments of all areas related to the suspected disability, as well as aptitude and achievement levels, and a multidisciplinary team must make the evaluation. All information must be documented, and the final placement decision must be made by a group knowledgeable about the child, evaluative data, and placement options. Although the selection of evaluation materials and specific procedures was left to the individual states or school districts, these conditions had to be met.

IDEA 2004 specified the requisite evaluation guidelines (see Figures 4.1 and 4.2). These guidelines specified for state and local education agencies the criteria for providing a nondiscriminatory evaluation for children with disabilities. When these procedures are followed, then the school district can expect that the possibility of bias in the evaluation, programming, and placement decision-making process will be lessened.

Section 504 of the Rehabilitation Act of 1973

In 1973 the Rehabilitation Act (P.L. 93-112) was enacted. It contained one section (Section 504) that related to nondiscrimination in the provision of programs for individuals with disabilities. The regulations for Section 504 are identical to those in IDEA in regard to nondiscriminatory testing.

In addition, Section 504 specifies the requirement for periodic reevaluations consistent with IDEA requirement for an evaluation at least every 3 years and

Figure 4.1
Evaluation Procedures in IDEA Amendments of 1997

(1) NOTICE.—The local educational agency shall provide notice to the parents of a child with a disability . . . that describes any evaluation procedures such agency proposes to conduct.

(2) CONDUCT OF EVALUATION.—In conducting the evaluation, the local educational agency shall—

(A) use a variety of assessment tools and strategies to gather relevant functional, developmental, and academic information, including information provided by the parent, that may assist in determining—

   (i) whether the child is a child with a disability; and

   (ii) the content of the child's individualized education program, including information related to enabling the child to be involved in and progress in the general education curriculum, or, for preschool children, to participate in appropriate activities;

(B) not use any single measurement or assessment as the sole criterion for determining whether a child is a child with a disability or determining an appropriate educational program for the child; and

(C) use technically sound instruments that may assess the relative contribution of cognitive and behavioral factors, in addition to physical or developmental factors. (IDEA of 2004, P.L. 108–446, § 614 [b], 118 Stat. 2647 [2005])

Figure 4.2
Additional IDEA Evaluation Procedural Requirements

Each local educational agency shall ensure that—

(A) assessments and other evaluation materials used to assess a child under this section—

   (i) are selected and administered so as not to be discriminatory on a racial or cultural basis;

   (ii) are provided and administered in the language and form most likely to yield accurate information on what the child knows and can do academically, developmentally, and functionally, unless it is not feasible to so provide or administer;

   (iii) are used for purposes for which the assessments or measures are valid and reliable;

   (iv) are administered by trained and knowledgeable personnel; and

   (v) are administered in accordance with any instructions provided by the producer of such assessments;

(B) the child is assessed in all areas of suspected disability;

(C) assessment tools and strategies that provide relevant information that directly assists persons in determining the educational needs of the child are provided; and

(D) assessments of children with disabilities who transfer from 1 school district to another school district in the same academic year are coordinated with such children's prior and subsequent schools, as necessary and as expeditiously as possible, to ensure prompt completion of full evaluations. (IDEA of 2004, P.L. 108–446, § 614 [b][3], 118 Stat. 2647 [2005])

Figure 4.3
Nondiscriminatory Evaluation Regulations in Section 504

Tests and all evaluation materials:

(1) have been validated for the specific purpose for which they are used and are administered by trained personnel in conformity with instructions provided by their producer;

(2) include those tailored to assess specific areas of educational need and not merely those which are designed to provide a single intelligence quotient; and

(3) are selected and administered so as best to ensure that, when a test is administered to a student with impaired sensory, manual, or speaking skills, the test results accurately reflect the student's aptitude or achievement level or whatever other factor the test purports to measure, rather than reflecting the student's impaired [abilities] (except where those skills are the factors that the test purports to measure). (34 C.F.R. § 104.35[b], 1977)

guarantees due process protection in evaluation procedures. These regulations, like those in IDEA, provide the criteria for the reduction of possible bias when making decisions that will affect individuals with disabilities (see Figure 4.3).

Americans with Disabilities Act of 1990

In 1990, ADA (P.L. 101-336) was enacted to protect persons with disabilities in both the public and private sectors (ADA, 42 U.S.C. § 12101). Generally, the provisions in ADA paralleled the provisions of the Rehabilitation Act. Case law being brought under the rubric of Section 504 may be used for guidance in interpreting similar questions under ADA. No specific student rights are provided in ADA, and it appears that it will have negligible effect on schools if they are in compliance with IDEA and Section 504.

Protection in Evaluation Procedures

To guarantee that evaluation procedures and results are as nondiscriminatory as possible, IDEA and its concomitant regulations provide specific requirements for each component of the special education process. Litigation has occurred when there is confusion concerning the implementation of these procedures by school districts.

Standards and the Law

CEC Standard 1: Foundations
PRAXIS Standard: Legal and Societal Issues
PRAXIS Standard: Delivery of Services to Students with Disabilities

Preplacement Evaluation

The first component of the process is known as the preplacement evaluation. According to IDEA "a State educational agency, other State agency, or local educational agency shall conduct a full and individual initial evaluation . . . before the initial provision of special education and related services to a child with a disability under this part" (IDEA of 2004, P.L. 108–446, § 614 [a][1][A], 118 Stat. 2647 [2005]).

A preplacement evaluation is required to make a nonbiased decision on the eligibility of the specified child for special education and related services. No provision of services can occur until such an evaluation has been completed. Specifically, IDEA states that

Such initial evaluation shall consist of procedures—

(i)   to determine whether a child is a child with a disability as defined in section 602(3) within 60 days of receiving parental consent for the evaluation, or, if the State establishes a timeframe within which the evaluation must be conducted, within such timeframe; and

(ii) to determine the educational needs of such child. (IDEA of 2004, P.L. 108–446, § 614 [a][1][C], 118 Stat. 2647 [2005])

Parent Consent.   Before any evaluation can be initiated, the parents or guardians of the specified child must consent to this procedure. IDEA has very specific statements concerning the school's acquisition of parental approval prior to evaluation, as well as the right of the parents to refuse the requested evaluation. It states in IDEA that before conducting an initial evaluation the agency ". . . shall obtain informed consent from the parent of such child before conducting the evaluation . . ." and that such consent ". . . shall not be construed as consent for placement for receipt of special education and related services" (IDEA of 2004, P.L. 108–446, § 614 [a][1][D][i], 118 Stat. 2647 [2005]). If the parents do not provide consent or if the parents do not respond when consent is requested, the school may use procedural safeguards guidelines to pursue their request to evaluate (see IDEA of 2004, P.L. 108–446, § 614 [a][1][D][ii], 118 Stat. 2647 [2005]).

An example of a problem with parental consent for evaluation is noted in *Quackenbush v. Johnson City School District* (1983). In this case, the parent requested an evaluation for her son who was suspected of having specific learning disabilities. On receiving the request for preplacement evaluation, a representative of the school district visited the parent to discuss the evaluation process and to elicit parental consent. According to the parent, the school representative told her not to check the consent box but to leave it blank and it would be completed later. According to the parent, the representative later marked the parental refusal box. No evaluation or subsequent program planning occurred. As a result, the child received no special education services from the public school. The parent in her complaint requested damages, and the Court held that the defendant should be required to "respond in punitive damages if, for the purpose of depriving Jason of special education services, he falsely recorded on her form that plaintiff did not consent to an evaluation of Jason" (*Quackenbush v. Johnson City School District,* 1983, p. 149).

Evaluation Timeline. Litigation concerning the preplacement evaluation has also focused on the school district's agreement to evaluate the child and the timeliness of evaluation (*Gerstmyer v. Howard County Public Schools,* 1994). In *Gerstmyer,* the parents requested an evaluation of their kindergarten-age child to assess his strengths and weaknesses, and to determine if there was a need for special education service prior to his entering first grade. Although an official request was made for an evaluation, the school district did not evaluate the child because "it was the summertime, we don't test during the summertime, we have a lot of budget cuts, we are unable to do it" (*Gerstmyer v. Howard County Public Schools,* 1994, p. 362). The court held in this instance that the school district had violated the ". . . IDEA's procedural requirements to such an extent that the violations are serious and detrimentally impact upon the child's right to a free public education . . ." (p. 364). As a result of the district's refusal to initiate and complete a requested evaluation for eligibility for services within a timely manner, no IEP was developed or program implemented that would assist the child in receiving the FAPE to which he was entitled under IDEA.

The question of what is the school district's responsibility to evaluate a child for eligibility for services when the child has been placed in an out-of-state facility was addressed in *Great Valley District. v. Sean* (2001). Because of significant concerns with Sean's mental stability, his emotional issues, and significant self-destructive behavior, his parents unilaterally enrolled him in an out-of-state placement. Prior to that, Sean had received private psychiatric services while attending the local high school. When his behavior problems accelerated, the parents requested an evaluation by the school to verify his need for special education services. The school district sent the Permission to Evaluate Form to the parents, but before they could sign the form, Sean's behavior deteriorated and after his third suicide attempt, Sean received in-patient treatment at a local clinic for a month. Following that, Sean's parents enrolled him in a therapeutic wilderness program in Idaho where he stayed for a month. At the completion of this program, he was enrolled in a private residential school in California for more intensive treatment for his emotional and self-destructive behaviors. These behaviors were so severe that Sean had to be professionally escorted from Idaho to California to the new high school program. During this time, the parents made all arrangements for educational placement without school district input. Once Sean was settled in the residential placement, his parents signed the school district's Permission to Evaluate Form, with a request that this evaluation occur at the California school because Sean's emotional and mental stability was too fragile for him to travel back to Pennsylvania. The school district refused this request, stating that they had no requirement to send staff to California to evaluate a student that had been unilaterally placed out of district. The parents brought suit, asking that the school district be compelled to complete the requested evaluation in California either by sending school staff or by contracting with staff in California. Citing previous cases, the Pennsylvania Court held for the school district:

> that among the burdens initially assumed by those unilaterally enrolling a child in a remote educational institution are burdens associated with the location of that institution. Where a school district has not participated in a placement decision, no burden associated

with the location can be assigned to it. Thus, a school district cannot be compelled to assume any responsibility for evaluating a child while he remains outside Pennsylvania in a unilateral placement.

This case, although heard in a state court, provides another view concerning the responsibilities of school districts when special education eligibility evaluations for students conflict with parent-selected, out-of-state placements.

An additional issue concerning timelines in the evaluation process was addressed in the case of *Baer v. Klagholz* (2001), in which parents brought suit against the state of New Jersey for changes being made in the state's special education law and regulations. The specific questions addressed were "when should the parents receive copies of evaluation reports—during the evaluation meeting or prior to the meeting" and "if the reports are to be provided to the parents prior to the meeting, is there a specific timeline." After reviewing both the federal and state legislation, the Court stated that

> The specific content of an evaluation report is appropriately left by the [IDEA] to State and local discretion. Both the [IDEA] and the regulations require that, upon completing the administration of tests and other evaluation materials, a public agency must provide a copy of the evaluation report and the documentation of determination of eligibility to the parent, but neither establishes a timeline for providing these documents to the parents; rather, this timeline is appropriately left to the State and local discretion. It is, however, important to ensure that parents and other IEP team participants have all the information they need to participate meaningfully in IEP meetings.

The specific amount of time prior to the provision of the reports to the parents, though, was left to the discretion of the school district "as long as the time line adopted results in the report and materials being provided to the parent a reasonable period in advance of the eligibility meeting."

Evaluation Materials and Procedures

Because the evaluation results are the major underpinning of the special education program development, IDEA includes a significant section on the materials and procedures to be used during the evaluation (see Figures 4.1 and 4.4). These requirements are important to fulfill the nondiscriminatory intent of the law. IDEA states that "assessments and other evaluation materials used to assess a child under this section . . . are administered by trained and knowledgeable personnel . . ." (IDEA of 2004, P.L. 108–446, § 614 [b][3][A], 118 Stat. 2647 [2005]).

Examiner Qualifications. The qualification of the examiners is also noted in the legislation. According to Yell (1998, p. 227), "the team's evaluators must be qualified in assessing and evaluating children with disabilities."

Comprehensiveness of Evaluation. The comprehensiveness of the evaluation is also of concern. The required IDEA evaluation procedures (see Figure 4.1) note that no single instrument can be used for eligibility and preplacement determination. In fact, a variety of instruments are required to provide the IEP team with adequate information to develop a program that will provide the student with an appropriate curriculum.

Figure 4.4
IDEA Evaluation Materials

(A) use a variety of assessment tools and strategies to gather relevant functional, developmental, and academic information, including information provided by the parent, that may assist in determining—

(i) whether the child is a child with a disability; and

(ii) the content of the child's individualized education program, including information related to enabling the child to be involved in and progress in the general education curriculum, or, for preschool children, to participate in appropriate activities;

(B) not use any single measure or assessment as the sole criterion for determining whether a child is a child with a disability or determining an appropriate educational program for the child; and

(C) use technically sound instruments that may assess the relative contribution of cognitive and behavioral factors, in addition to physical or developmental factors. (IDEA of 2004, P.L. 108–446, § 614 [b][2], 118 Stat. 2647 [2005])

The issue of appropriate curriculum was addressed in *Bonadonna v. Cooperman* (1985). The question before the Court in *Bonadonna* concerned the identification of the LRE in which the child's educational program could be implemented. Once the review began, the preplacement evaluation was determined inadequate, and it became apparent that the lack of a comprehensive evaluation had a significant impact on the planning. For instance, the planning was based on evaluation results from the beginning of the school year. Further investigation noted that the child's behaviors and abilities had significantly changed during the year, resulting in the previous evaluation providing incorrect information on which to base the next year's program. This nonreliance on current evaluation data resulted in the development of a program that was inappropriate and could negatively impact the child's educational success.

Using the *Rowley* (1982) test, the *Bonadonna* Court reviewed the facts of the case. They addressed whether the State had complied with the procedural requirements of the Act, beginning with the preplacement evaluation. When the Court reviewed the evaluation process documentation, it found that "the defendant's evaluation . . . appears to fall woefully short" (*Bonadonna v. Cooperman*, 1985, p. 409). The Court continued by saying that

> There is no evidence . . . that any validated tests were performed to test Alisa's aptitude rather than her handicap; that all areas of her hearing impairment were assessed; or that anyone on the classification team was an expert in the education of the hearing impaired. Rather, the CST's April, 1983 assessment was based upon observation alone. (*Bonadonna v. Cooperman*, 1985, p. 410)

As a result, it was apparent to the Court that IDEA's procedural requirements had not been fulfilled and that any program that had been developed based on these results should be "rejected on this ground alone" (p. 410). A program developed from a single evaluation instrument would not provide the child with an IEP that meets the requirements of FAPE.

Parental understanding of the type of tests and the procedures to be used is essential if they are to give informed consent. In the case of *Holland v. District of Columbia Public Schools* (1995), the parents refused to consent to an evaluation of their daughter who had been attending a private school for students with emotional problems. The parents claimed that they had requested information concerning "which evaluations are to be conducted," clarification of what constituted a "clinical interview," and whether "this procedure includes tests or other procedures" (p. 418), and that these questions needed to be answered before they could give consent. The lack of resolution of this issue resulted in neither an evaluation being completed nor a program being prepared for Siobhan for nine months. As a result, the parents had an outside evaluation completed, and based on its recommendations, enrolled their daughter in a private residential program. When this case reached the courts, both the parents and the school district were claiming a lack of cooperation as the reason for the stalemate in providing Siobhan with FAPE. The Court held that

> In light of Congress' heavy emphasis on parental involvement and the regulations' various procedural guarantees—that parents receive full notice of any proposed or refused action; that parents receive a full description of each test to be conducted; and that independent assessments must be considered in any decision made with respect to the provision of an education to the child—we find that the Hollands were statutorily entitled to know what procedures were involved in the "clinical interview." (*Holland v. District of Columbia Public Schools*, 1995, p. 425)

The Court then remanded the case to the District Court to determine whether the Hollands had received an answer to their inquiry and, if so, then the ruling in favor of the school district would stand. However, if the Court should determine that the school district "believing the Hollands' request for additional information to be unreasonable, took the parents' inquiry as an excuse to suspend all further action with respect to Siobhan's evaluation and placement" (*Holland v. District of Columbia Public School,* 1995, p. 425), then the holding would be for the Hollands.

Evaluation Team.   An essential component of any evaluation process is the team that will complete the evaluations, in this case the IEP team. According to IDEA, the IEP team will be involved "as part of an initial evaluation (if appropriate) and as part of any reevaluation . . ." (IDEA of 2004, P.L. 108–446, § 614 [c][1], 118 Stat. 2647 [2005]). The membership of the IEP team is also described very clearly in the law (see Figure 4.5). Not only are the members of the team involved in the preplacement evaluation, but they are also intricately involved in the interpretation of the evaluation data and its subsequent utilization for development of the IEP. IDEA specifically describes the responsibilities of the team members in data interpretation, as well as what they should review to make decisions (see Figure 4.6).

Independent Educational Evaluations

When the IEP team is reviewing evaluation or reevaluation data, an issue often arises concerning the request for, or presentation of, a completed, independent educational evaluation (IEE). In the procedural safeguards of IDEA, the parents are

Figure 4.5
Required Membership of the IEP Team

(i) the parents of a child with a disability;

(ii) not less than 1 regular education teacher of such child (if the child is, or may be, participating in the regular education environment);

(iii) not less than 1 special education teacher, or where appropriate, not less than 1 special education provider of such child;

(iv) a representative of the local educational agency who—

    (I) is qualified to provide, or supervise the provision of, specially designed instruction to meet the unique needs of children with disabilities;

    (II) is knowledgeable about the general education curriculum; and

    (III) is knowledgeable about the availability of resources of the local educational agency;

(v) an individual who can interpret the instructional implications of evaluation results, who may be a member of the team . . . ;

(vi) at the discretion of the parent or the agency, other individuals who have knowledge or special expertise regarding the child, including related services personnel as appropriate; and

(vii) whenever appropriate, the child with a disability. (IDEA of 2004, P.L. 108–446, § 614 [d][1][B], 118 Stat. 2647 [2005])

Figure 4.6
Evaluation Responsibilities of IEP Team

(A) review existing evaluation data on the child, including—

    (i) evaluations and information provided by the parents of the child;

    (ii) current classroom-based, local, or State assessments, and classroom-based observations; and

    (iii) observations by teachers and related services providers; and

(B) on the basis of that review, and input from the child's parents, identify what additional data, if any, are needed to determine—

    (i) whether the child is a child with a disability; as described in section 602(3), or, and the educational needs of the child, or, in case of a reevaluation of a child, whether the child continues to have such a disability and such educational needs;

    (ii) the present levels of academic achievement and related developmental needs of the child;

    (iii) whether the child needs special education and related services, or in the case of a reevaluation of a child, whether the child continues to need special education and related services; and

    (iv) whether any additions or modifications to the special education and related services are needed to enable the child to meet the measurable annual goals set out in the individualized education program of the child and to participate, as appropriate, in the general education curriculum. (IDEA of 2004, P.L. 108–446, § 614 [c][1], 118 Stat. 2647 [2005])

given the right to have independent educational evaluations completed and reviewed during the preplacement eligibility phase and in the development of the child's program (see IDEA of 2004, P.L. 108–446, § 615 [d][2], 118 Stat. 2647 [2005]). The question has arisen, though, whether parents may require school districts to pay for the IEE if they did not request it, or if the district can be required to use this IEE in lieu of evaluation by their own personnel. In the case of *W. B. v. Matula* (1995), the parent brought suit based on "the persistent refusal of certain school officials to evaluate, classify and provide necessary educational services" for her child. When the team finally evaluated the child, the mother had grave concerns that the evaluation was not comprehensive and requested an independent evaluation at the school's expense that the school refused. A due process hearing based on the school's refusal resulted in the completion of an independent evaluation, which supported the mother's allegations that "the evaluation by the Mansfield CST did not properly identify E.J.'s problems" (*W. B. v. Matula,* 1995, p. 489). The decision of the administrative proceedings culminated in a 54-page opinion, which ordered the school board to place the child in a private school at its expense, to pay for the child's sessions with the private therapist, to reimburse the parent for the cost of an independent learning disability evaluation, which the board had refused to provide, and to provide a supplementary occupational evaluation. This opinion, appealed to the District Court and then to the Third Circuit Court of Appeals, resulted in a lengthy opinion, which stated that the "student suspected of having [a] qualifying disability must be identified and evaluated within reasonable time; and . . . failure to follow specific federal and statutory schemes violated due process rights" (*W. B. v. Matula,* 1995, p. 484). This case supports the belief that, without a timely evaluation of a child suspected of having a disability, the procedures enacted in IDEA to support the equal protection principle would be useless.

Another issue involved in the IEE controversy is whether parents must exhaust their personal medical insurance to pay for IEEs, even if that payment results in a reduction of their lifetime policy benefits (*Raymond S. v. Ramirez,* 1996; *Seals v. Loftis,* 1985). In the case of *Seals v. Loftis* (1985), the Multidisciplinary Team (MDT) met and recommended to Travis's parents that a medical evaluation be completed because his behaviors had changed since the previous school year. Acting on this request, the parents had Travis evaluated by a pediatrician who then referred him for both a neurological and a psychological evaluation. These evaluations were considered necessary by the pediatrician for him to complete a comprehensive evaluation of Travis's difficulties. The school district refused to pay for the latter two evaluations because it had not specifically requested them. In the report of the due process hearing, it was stated that the school district only needed to pay the previous amounts, that is, those that were paid by the parent's insurance. On bringing this issue to the courts, the parents contended that they had been required erroneously to use their insurance coverage, resulting in a reduction of lifetime benefits, to pay for evaluations that were under the legal purview of the school district. The Court, holding for the parents, concluded that

> parents of a handicapped child cannot be required to utilize their private medical insurance benefits where the utilization of these benefits would cause them to incur a financial

cost. . . . Any other conclusion would be inconsistent with the concept of a free appropriate public education which underlies the EAHCA. (*Seals v. Loftis,* 1985, pp. 305–306)

In *Raymond S. v. Ramirez* (1996), the parents sought reimbursement for an IEE that was not requested by the school district, but that was used by the school district in the child's program development. In this case, the parents had submitted the costs of the IEE to their insurance carrier, which not only paid the majority of the cost, but also reduced the available lifetime benefits on their policy. When the school district refused to pay for the nonrequested IEE, the parents brought suit. The Court held that the parents were entitled to reimbursement because their health insurance policy had a lifetime cap and that a school "may not compel parents to file insurance claim when filing claim would pose realistic threat that parents of handicapped children would suffer financial loss not incurred by similarly situated parents" (*Raymond v. Ramirez,* 1996, p. 1281). The amount awarded them, though, was designated as repayment to the insurance company.

Reevaluation

The special education process delineated in IDEA also requires that school districts have a reevaluation plan for those children receiving special education services. According to IDEA, this reevaluation must occur at least once every 3 years or whenever conditions warrant (IDEA of 2004, P.L. 108–446, § 614 [a][2], 118 Stat. 2647 [2005]). The issues discussed previously under preplacement evaluation are also raised during the reevaluation component of the special education process.

For example, in *Andress v. Cleveland Independent School District* (1995), the parents refused consent for a school district's reevaluation for continuing eligibility for special education services. This refusal was the result of an opinion by Wesley's psychiatrist that he would be traumatized by any additional testing by the district in which he had been "abused" previously by fellow students, resulting in psychiatric hospitalization. The parents acquired independent evaluations, but the school district refused to consider them stating that they did not meet state criteria. The decision of the hearing officer was that the school district could not be compelled to accept independent educational evaluations in lieu of its own reevaluations, and the parents disagreed and appealed the decision. The District Court held for the parents and stated that the school district has a right to use its own personnel for evaluation unless "further testing by school officials would harm the child medically and psychologically," thus suggesting a medical exception to the IEE rule. The Circuit Court disagreed and held that "there is no exception to the rule that a school district has a right to test a student itself in order to evaluate or re-evaluate the student's eligibility under IDEA" (*Andress v. Cleveland Independent School District,* 1985, p. 179). *Doe v. Phillips* (1994) has a similar holding. The *Doe* court found that there is not a medical exception to the school district's right to complete a reevaluation of a student when needed.

Previously, the law stated that reevaluations in conjunction with IDEA requirements did not require additional parental consent. In fact, the question had arisen in the case of *Carroll v. Capalbo* (1983) as to whether a reevaluation that included additional tests required a new parental consent. The *Carroll* court provided that once the parental consent was given for eligibility and placement, no further consent was needed. However, the IDEA Amendments of 1997 changed this decision when it stated that

> Each local educational agency shall obtain informed parental consent . . . prior to conducting any reevaluation of a child with a disability, except that such informed parental consent need not be obtained if the local educational agency can demonstrate that it had taken reasonable measures to obtain such consent and the child's parent has failed to respond. (IDEA of 2004, P.L. 108–446, § 614 [c][3], 118 Stat. 2647 [2005])

Additional Evaluation Issues

There are additional areas of concern about evaluation of students with disabilities that have been, or may be, addressed by the courts. These include the issue of students being required to satisfactorily complete minimum competency tests (MCTs) as a condition of receiving a high school diploma, the inclusion of specialized medical evaluations such as neurological assessments in the evaluation battery, the inclusion of students with disabilities in schoolwide and/or statewide assessments for accountability, and the annual testing required by NCLB.

Minimum Competency Testing.   In the move by school districts to meet the call for reform in education by increasing educational standards for graduation, many states have enacted legislation requiring the satisfactory completion of an MCT to receive a high school diploma. For many students who have been attending special education programs, this has resulted in denial of a diploma indicating satisfactory completion of their school program. A major challenge of this testing movement occurred in *Debra P. v. Turlington* (1981). In *Debra P.,* high school students in Florida filed a class action challenging the constitutionality of the state test under the due process and equal protection clauses of the Fourteenth Amendment. They claimed that the testing program was racially biased and was a device to resegregate the Florida public schools. They based their claim on the results of the test during the 3 previous years of the test's administration. They claimed the results indicated the MCT had a greater impact on Black students than on White students (see Figure 4.7), resulting in a significant number being unable to graduate with their class.

The District Court in 1981 agreed with the plaintiffs' claim, enjoined the defendants from using the test as a requirement for receipt of a high school diploma until the 1982–1983 school year, and stated that

> We recognize that the interests of the State of Florida in both the remediation and diploma denial aspects of the basic competency program are substantial. The Trial Court noted an impressively increasing passing rate for which Florida teachers and students are to be commended. We hold, however, that the State may not deprive its high school seniors of the economic and educational benefits of a high school diploma until it has

Figure 4.7
Failure Rate in *Debra P.*

Date	% Fail—Black Students	% Fail—White Students
Fall 1977	78	25
Fall 1978	74	25
Fall 1979	60	36

demonstrated that the SAT II is a fair test of that which is taught in its classrooms and that the racially discriminatory impact is not due to the educational deprivation in the "dual school" years. (*Debra P. v. Turlington,* 1981, p. 408)

In 1984, this case returned to the courts to resolve the remanded issue of test fairness (*Debra P. by Irene P. v. Turlington,* 1984). The state presented evidence that it had completed a four-part study of the competency examination, including a teacher survey, a district survey, a series of site visits to verify the information provided by the districts, and a student survey conducted in randomly selected schools within each district. The results of this survey indicated that the test was instructionally valid and that there was an extensive remedial program in place for those students who initially failed the test. The Court did not agree with the claim that the MCT would increase the state's segregation of Black students but that "even if there were a causal connection, the state had proven that the test will help remedy these effects" (*Debra P. by Irene P. v. Turlington,* 1984, p. 1415). Subsequently, in its holding, the Court stated that

> We affirm the district court's findings (1) that students were actually taught test skills, (2) that vestiges of past intentional segregation do not cause the SAT-II's disproportionate impact on blacks, and (3) that use of the SAT-II as a diploma sanction will help remedy the vestiges of past segregation. Therefore, the State of Florida may deny diplomas to students (beginning with the Class of 1983) who have not yet passed the SAT-II. (*Debra P. by Irene P. v. Turlington,* 1984, p. 1416)

A similar case (*Brookhart v. Illinois State Board of Education,* 1983) focused on the denial of high school diplomas to certain exceptional students because they failed to pass minimal competency tests. This case was brought by 14 students with disabilities, including one with physical disabilities, one with multiple disabilities, four with mental retardation, and eight with learning disabilities. The students claimed that the denial of high school diplomas based on the passage of an MCT violated their FAPE rights under EAHCA because the evaluation component mandates (a) that no single procedure can be used to determine an appropriate educational program for a child with a disability, (b) that tests used to evaluate students with disabilities must be validated for such a purpose, and (c) that inadequate notice of the change in graduation requirements deprived them of their property interest without due process of law (*Brookhart v. Illinois State Board of Education,* 1982). The court held that the student rights under EAHCA were not violated and that they had not been denied FAPE. However, the Court did agree that the plaintiffs had not been provided adequate notice of the change in requirements, thus depriving them of a protected interest without due process. The Court, therefore, ordered that those students who had completed high school but received no diploma as a result of failure on the MCT be given the option to receive a diploma without completion of the MCT, if they had completed the other graduation requirements.

Specialized Medical Assessments.   IDEA 2004 states, "a State educational agency, other State agency, or local educational agency shall conduct a full and individual initial evaluation." With the increase in the number of students with physical and other health impairments entering the public school system, the issue of what assessment tools and strategies should be used to ensure the child's eligibility for special education and related services, and also provide the necessary information for the development of an appropriate IEP has become a concern. IDEA Regulations require that the evaluation be not only individualized, but also comprehensive. Also, the evaluations are to include, where appropriate, assessment in all areas of suspected need. In conjunction with this need, the school must include on the IEP team a member who is knowledgeable in the area being evaluated. Thus, if the child is in need of a medical evaluation, such as a neurological evaluation, the question may arise as to who should pay for this service? Is it a medical service that is not covered under IDEA, or is it a requisite component of a comprehensive evaluation and, thus, would be included as it is for diagnostic and evaluation purposes?

State- and Districtwide Assessments.   The inclusion of students with disabilities in state- and districtwide standardized assessments has also resulted in controversy. Prior to the enactment of IDEA Amendments of 1997, most school districts did not include students with disabilities in state accountability efforts. If students did complete the examinations, often their scores were not reported. This was considered to be a problem because the omission of students with disabilities from these assessments continued to support low educational expectations based on stereotypes. These stereotypes had previously been shown to be of concern in evaluation procedures because of the bias that resulted in misclassification. This concern was addressed with changes in IDEA 2004 (see Figure 4.8) that require states to include students in statewide assessments or provide them with alternative assessments and report their scores, where feasible.

No Child Left Behind Annual Testing.   One of the four principles of NCLB (2001) is accountability for results where it

> focuses on (a) increasing the academic performance of all public schools students, and improving the performance of low-performing schools. It does this by requiring states and school districts to identify each child and group of children and to measure their progress every year . . . [T]hese assessments are also used to hold schools accountable for the achievement of all students. (Yell & Drasgow, 2005, p. 13)

Figure 4.8
IDEA Requirements for Participation in Assessments

(A) IN GENERAL.—All children with disabilities are included in all general State and district-wide assessments, including assessment described under § 1111 of the Elementary and Secondary Education Act of 1965, with appropriate accommodations, and alternate assessments where necessary and as indicated in their respective individualized education programs.

(B) ACCOMMODATION GUIDELINES.—The State (or, in the case of a districtwide assessment, the local educational agency) has developed guidelines for the provision of appropriate accommodations.

(C) (i) IN GENERAL.—The State (or, in the case of a districtwide assessment, the local educational agency) has developed and implemented guidelines for the participation of children with disabilities in alternate assessments for those children who cannot participate in regular assessments . . . with accommodations as indicated in their respective individualized education programs.

(ii) REQUIREMENTS FOR ALTERNATE ASSESSMENTS.—The guidelines . . . shall provide for alternate assessments that—

(I) are aligned with the State's challenging academic content standards and challenging student academic achievement standards; and

(II) if the State has adopted alternate academic achievement standards to . . . measure the achievement of children with disabilities against those standards.

(D) The State educational agency (or, in the case of a districtwide assessment, the local educational agency) makes available to the public, and reports to the public with the same frequency and in the same detail as it reports on the assessment of nondisabled children, the following:

(i) The number of children with disabilities participating in regular assessments

(ii) and the number of those children who were provided accommodations in order to participate in those assessments.

(iii) The number of children participating in alternate assessments. . . .

(iv) The performance of children with disabilities on regular assessments and on alternate assessments if the number of children with disabilities participating in those assessments is sufficient to yield statistically reliable information and reporting that information will not reveal personally identifiable information about an individual student, compared with the achievement of all children, including children with disabilities, on those assessments. (IDEA of 2004, P.L. 108–446, § 612 [16], 118 Stat. 2647 [2005])

The statewide assessment includes students with disabilities, holds them to the standards for the grade in which they are enrolled, and requires that access to appropriate accommodations be provided for them. For these accommodations to be provided, the student must meet IDEA or Section 504 guidelines with the need for accommodation listed in his or her IEP or Section 504 plan. Students with severe cognitive disabilities may be allowed to take an alternative state-developed assessment, but no more than 1% of all students taking the assessments can be given an alternative examination. Although the concept of yearly assessments ties in with the yearly IEP evaluations, there is concern that the strong emphasis on yearly achievement and each student making substantial yearly progress will negatively impact students who may not be able to reach those goals, even with the provision of assessment accommodations (Wright, Wright, & Heath, 2004).

Summary

In the *Board of Education of the Hendrick Hudson Central School District v. Rowley* (1982), the Supreme Court indicated an educational plan is inappropriate if it is not developed according to the Act's protection in evaluation procedures and the requirements for nonbiased assessment. The major underpinning of the educational plan is the evaluation of the strengths and weaknesses of the individual child. The evaluation procedures included in IDEA and their clarification in the regulations and subsequent litigation provide school districts with the guidelines for completing a nondiscriminatory evaluation, while providing parents with protection in the form of parental consent and the availability of independent educational evaluations. The importance of nondiscriminatory evaluations cannot be discounted because it is the foundation for an FAPE.

Questions for Discussion

1. On what is the principle of nondiscriminatory evaluation based?
2. Compare and contrast the evaluation requirements in IDEA, Section 504, and ADA.
3. Why was specific protection in evaluation procedures included in IDEA?
4. What are some of the unintended results of the annual testing requirement of the NCLB?

Websites for Further Exploration

Basis for Principle of Nondiscriminatory Evaluation
www.nichcy.org/Trainpkg/toctext.htm
www.teachspecialed.com/coursesEval/ocada7011_norm2/1.html
www2.boisestate.edu/iassess/PSY%20421/chapter%2016.ppt
www.tourolaw.edu/patch/Mills/
www.arches.uga.edu/~jneigh/Laws_and_Legislation.html

Legislative Basis
www.fape.org/newsline/english/fwn_jan1999.html
www.geocities.com/~cpheart/edu6.htm
www.reedmartin.com/specialeducationstatutes.htm
www.reedmartin.com

Protection in Evaluation Procedures
www.kidsource.com/kidsource/content3/ada.idea.html

www.thearc.org/faqs/qa-idea-rights.html
ericec.org/digests/e606.html
www.ideapractices.org/

Independent Educational Evaluations
www.naspcenter.org/
www.ucp.org/ucp_channeldoc.cfm/1/12/69/69-69/705
www.ldonline.org/ld_indepth/assessment/iee_assessment.html
www.specialchild.com/archives/lf-001.html

Issues (Minimum Competency Testing, State-Districtwide Assessment, Specialized Medical Assessment, NCLB Annual Testing)
www.ecs.org/clearinghouse/32/67/3267.htm
www.findarticles.com/p/articles/mi_m0HDF/is_3_34/ai_76157521/pg_4
www.advocacyinstitute.org/LDA2004/IDEAvsNCLB-CEP.pdf
www.asha.org/about/legislation-advocacy/federal/nclb/nclb-facts.htm
www.nasponline.org/publications/cq321nclbprimer.html
resultsforamerica.org/education/toolkit_critique.php
www.ldonline.org/ld_indepth/special_education/peer_accommodations.html
www.nea.org/specialed/ideabrief2.html
www.ecs.org/clearinghouse/40/11/4011.htm

ILLUSTRATING THE LAW

Briefing of:
Larry P., by his Guardian ad litem, Lucille P., et al. v. Wilson Riles,
Superintendent for Public Instruction
United States Court of Appeals,
Ninth Circuit 793 F.2d 969 (9th Cir. 1984)

FACTS: A class action lawsuit was brought in District Court to prohibit the use of IQ testing for placing Black children in classes for the EMR in California public schools. The District Court found that, from 1968 until the trial in 1977, Black children were significantly overrepresented in EMR classes. The EMR classes were designed for children who were deemed incapable of learning in regular classes, and were not designed to help students learn the skills necessary to return to the regular instructional program. The Court characterized the EMR classes as "dead-end classes," and found that misplacement in EMR caused stigma and irreparable injury to the student. The Court also found that the IQ testing, which was the basis for EMR placements, had not been validated for such a purpose and that the tests had not been designed to eliminate cultural biases against Black children. Based on these findings, the Trial Court found the defendants guilty of intentional discrimination in violation of the equal protection clause of the California and U.S. Constitutions, violation of the Rehabilitation Act of 1973 and EAHCA of 1975, and violation of Title VI of the Civil Rights Act of 1964.

ISSUES: Whether the evidence supported the findings that (a) IQ tests were used to place students in EMR classes, (b) the tests had not been validated for that purpose, (c) use of the tests violated the Rehabilitation Act and EAHCA, (d) use of the tests had a discriminatory effect on Black children, (e) use of the tests violated Title VI, and (f) the facts constituted a violation of the equal protection clause of the Fourteenth Amendment.

HOLDING: The U.S. Court of Appeals for the Ninth Circuit affirmed the District Court's decision on the statutory violations, and reversed the decision on the equal protection issue, finding that the evidence did not support the finding that the superintendent exercised any discriminatory motive.

RATIONALE: The Court commended the detailed findings of the Trial Court and affirmed the holding that IQ testing was used for EMR placement, that the IQ tests had not been validated for that purpose, and that the use of the tests had a discriminatory impact on Black children that could not be statistically justified. The Court of Appeals agreed that the EMR placements violated EAHCA provisions on racially or culturally discriminatory testing for children with disabilities, and therefore subjected the children to discrimination in violation of the Rehabilitation Act. The Court cited congressional concern about the misclassification of the mentally retarded based on racial and ethnic factors, and agreed with the Trial Court that the tests were not validated and that the schools did not use the variety of statutorily mandated evaluation tools. The Court of Appeals also agreed that the placements violated Title VI of the Civil Rights Act of 1964 because the EMR placements had a discriminatory impact on Black school children. The Court rejected arguments that the higher placement rate of Black children in EMR classes could be justified by the lower socioeconomic status of Black children. Finally, the Court of Appeals disagreed with the Trial Court on the equal protection issue. The Court ruled that Superintendent Riles, who did not hold that position during the early stages of the litigation, was not guilty of any intentional discrimination under the Fourteenth Amendment.

EFFECTS: The narrow holding of this case forced California public schools to quit relying on IQ tests for placing Black children in EMR classes. It also required the state to report to the Court on the statistical progress of the number of Black children placed in EMR classes in future years. The broader impact may encourage school districts to rethink their EMR classes in general, as well as encourages multifaceted testing and evaluation so as not to unduly rely on a biased test for important placement decisions.

ILLUSTRATING THE LAW THROUGH DISCUSSION

The 1984 case, *Larry P. v. Riles*, significantly altered the procedures used to identify children with disabilities. Discuss the methods used to reduce bias in the assessment process, including test validation and test selection.

References

Americans with Disabilities Act, 42 U.S.C. § 12101 *et seq.* (1990).

Andress v. Cleveland Independent School District, 64 F.3d 176 (5th Cir. 1995), *reh. denied,* (no cite), *cert. denied,* 519 U.S. 812 (1996).

Baer v. Klagholz, 771 A.2d 603 (2001).

Bailey, D. B., Jr., & Harbin, G. L. (1980). Nondiscriminatory evaluation. *Exceptional Children, 46*(8), 590–596.

Bersoff, D. N. (1980). P. v. Riles: A legal perspective. *School Psychology Review, 9*(2), 112–122.

Board of Education of the Hendrick Hudson Central School District v. Rowley, 458 U.S. 176, 102 S.Ct. 3034, 73 L.Ed. 2d 690 (1982).

Bonadonna v. Cooperman, 619 F. Supp. 401 (D.C.N.J. 1985).

Brookhart v. Illinois State Board of Education, 697 F.2d 179 (7th Cir. 1983).

Brown v. Board of Education of Topeka, Kansas, 347 U.S. 483, 74 S.Ct. 686, 98 L.Ed. 873, 38 A.L.R. 2d 1180 (1954).

Carroll v. Capalbo, 563 F. Supp. 1053 (D.R.I. 1983).

Debra P. v. Turlington, 644 F.2d 397 (1981).

Debra P. by Irene P. v. Turlington, 730 F.2d 1405 (1984).

Doe v. Phillips, 20 IDELR 1150 (N.D. Cal. 1994).

Education for All Handicapped Children Act, 20 U.S.C. § 1400 *et seq.* (1975).

Gerstmyer v. Howard County Public Schools, 850 F. Supp. 361 (D. Md. 1994).

Great Valley School District v. Douglas and Barbara M. *ex rel* Sean M., 807 A.2d 315 (2001).

Hobson v. Hansen, 269 F. Supp. 401 (D.C. Cir. 1967), *dismissed,* 393 U.S. 801 (1968), *aff'd sub nom.,* Smuck v. Hobson, 408 F.2d 175, 132 D.C. 372 (D.C. Cir. 1969).

Holland v. District of Columbia Public Schools, 71 F.3d 417, 315 D.C. 158 (D.C. Cir. 1995).

Individuals with Disabilities Education Act, 20 U.S.C. § 1400 *et seq.* (1990).

Individuals with Disabilities Education Act Amendments, 20 U.S.C. § 1400 *et seq.* (1997).

Individuals with Disabilities Education Improvement Act of 2004, P.L. 108–446, § 601 *et seq.,* 118 Stat. 2647, (2005).

Larry P. v. Riles, 343 F. Supp. 1306 (N.D. Cal. 1972), *aff'd,* 502 F.2d 963 (9th Cir. 1974), *further proceedings,* 495 F. Supp. 926 (N.D. Cal. 1979), *aff'd,* 793 F.2d 969 (9th Cir. 1984).

Merriam-Webster's Collegiate Dictionary (10th ed.). (1995). Springfield, MA: Merriam-Webster.

No Child Left Behind Act, 20 U.S.C. § 6301 *et seq.* (2001).

Parents in Action on Special Education (PASE) v. Hannon, 506 F. Supp. 831 (N.D. Ill. 1980).

Quackenbush v. Johnson City School District, 716 F.2d 141 (2nd Cir. 1983), *cert. denied,* 465 U.S. 1071, 104 S.Ct. 1426 (1984).

Raymond S. v. Ramirez, 918 F. Supp. 1280 (N.D. Iowa 1996).

Rehabilitation Act, 29 U.S.C. § 794 *et seq.* (1973).

Seals v. Loftis, 614 F. Supp. 302 (D.C. Tenn. 1985).

Section 504 of the Rehabilitation Act, 34 C.F.R. § 104.35(b) (1977).

Turnbull, H. R., & Turnbull, A. P. (1979). *Free appropriate public education: Law and implementation.* Denver: Love.

W. B. v. Matula, 67 F.3d 484 (3rd Cir. 1995).

Wright, W. D., Wright, P. D., & Heath, S. W. (2004). *No child left behind.* Hartfield, VA: Harbor House Law Press.

Yell, M. L. (1998). *The law and special education.* Upper Saddle River, NJ: Merrill/Prentice Hall.

Yell, M. L., & Drasgow, E. (2005). *No child left behind: A guide for professionals.* Upper Saddle River, NJ: Merrill/Prentice Hall.

CHAPTER FIVE

Program Development

GUIDING QUESTIONS

1. How are the Right to Treatment cases and the Right to Education cases similar?

2. Under IDEA, what are the eight essential components of the IEP?

3. Who are the members of the IEP team, and what are their roles in the education of a student with disabilities?

4. Under IDEA, what is an IFSP?

5. Under IDEA, what is an ITP?

Basis for Individualized Program Development

When enacting IDEA in 1975, Congress stated that the educational needs of children with disabilities in the United States were not being met. Specifically, it stated "more than half of the children with disabilities in the U.S. do not receive appropriate educational services and are thus denied full equality of opportunity" (20 U.S.C. § 1401[b][2] and [3]).

Prior to the enactment of IDEA, there were two sets of cases that guaranteed the right to education. The first set, known as the Right to Treatment cases, involved the issue of educational programming and appropriate treatment in the institutional setting. In the area of Right to Treatment, two of the most influential cases are *Wyatt v. Stickney* (1971, 1974) (see chapter 1 for a discussion of this case) and *Halderman v. Pennhurst* (1979). *Halderman* is considered to be one of the most important of the Right to Treatment cases. In *Halderman,* the plaintiffs contended that conditions at Pennhurst State School and Hospital were so poor as to preclude the possibility of habilitation. The crucial finding of the Court was that "minimally adequate habilitation cannot be provided in an institution such as Pennhurst" (*Halderman v. Pennhurst,* 1979, p. 113). However, the Third Circuit Court of Appeals found the Trial Court's determination of the inappropriateness for the class *as a whole* to be in error. The Appeals Court held that each patient must be assessed and an individual determination made "as to the appropriateness of an improved Pennhurst for each such patient" (*Halderman v. Pennhurst,* 1979, p. 114). The Court recognized the focus of *individual* needs that required an individualized approach.

The second set, known as the Right to Education cases, involves the issue of appropriate educational programming in a public school setting. Litigation in the area of the Right to Education cases alluded to the issue of inequality by examining both the presence of educational programming and its appropriateness for the individual with disabilities. In *PARC v. Pennsylvania* (1972) and *Mills v. Board of Education of District of Columbia* (1972), the issue was not only exclusion from the publicly supported school system for children with disabilities, but also the issues of the individualization and appropriateness of that education. In each case, the courts examined the appropriateness of education and provided guidelines used by other courts. There are similarities in these two cases. First, both cases were brought on behalf of students with disabilities who were denied access to public schools based on their disability. Second, the courts in both cases supported the plaintiffs and ordered the school districts to provide an individualized education for each child identified.

Standards and the Law

CEC Standard 1: Foundations
INTASC Standard 1: Subject Matter
PRAXIS Standard: Legal and Societal Issues

The focus on individual needs noted in both the Right to Education and the Right to Treatment cases was included in the 1975 legislation in the form of the IEP requirements. The IEP became the means by which the FAPE was to be implemented. In fact, Gorn (1997) stated that "the IEP is the translation of Congress' idealistic vision of children with disabilities receiving meaningful education . . ." (p. 1:2). This vision was expanded in 1986 with the inclusion of an IFSP in the EHA Amendments (P.L. 99-456) to address the individualized needs of infants and toddlers with disabilities and their families. In 1990, it was expanded again with the inclusion of an individualized transition plan (ITP) in IDEA (P.L. 101-476) to address the individualized needs of secondary-age students who will be transitioning from the school to the community. These two additions were to ensure *all* individuals with disabilities, regardless of age receive the "appropriate" educational program.

Individualized Education Program

There are two precepts involved in the implementation of an IEP. The first precept is that the IEP is a document resulting from a collaborative effort of the parents, the school personnel, and other service providers. This group, known as the IEP team, may be providing support or services to the child and the child's family in establishing educational goals and objectives for the child. The IEP describes both the abilities and the needs of the child, and based on these specified needs, goals are developed that prescribe the services to be provided and the least restrictive educational setting in which they are to be delivered. Programming through an IEP differs significantly from the traditional method of programming. These differences include the requirements that

(a) Procedural safeguards be in place and followed

(b) The parents be included as established members of the educational team

(c) The educational team includes school personnel and other persons as needed or as invited to membership

(d) The educational goals be based on the current performance of the child with disabilities

Standards and the Law

CEC Standard 1: Foundations
CEC Standard 7: Instructional Planning
INTASC Standard 7: Planning Instruction
PRAXIS Standard: Delivery of Services to Students with Disabilities

The second precept is that the IEP is the culmination of a process outlined in both legislation and subsequent regulation.

The IEP team is responsible for the development of the IEP. The responsibility for providing the individualized education lies with the SEA, and, in most cases, with the local school district in which the parent resides. The IEP team consists of a group of individuals, including

#1 final exam

(i)   the parents of the child with a disability;

(ii) not less than one regular education teacher of such child (if the child is, or may be, participating in the regular education environment);

(iii) not less than one special education teacher, or where appropriate, at least one special education provider of such child;

(iv) a representative of the local educational agency who—

    (I)   is qualified to provide, or supervise the provision of, specially designed instruction to meet the unique needs of children with disabilities;

    (II) is knowledgeable about the general education curriculum; and

    (III) is knowledgeable about the availability of resources of the local education agency;

(v)   an individual who can interpret the instructional implications of evaluation results, who may be a member of the team . . .

(vi) at the discretion of the parent or the agency, other individuals who have knowledge or special expertise regarding the child, including related services personnel as appropriate; and

(vii) whenever appropriate, the child with a disability. (IDEA of 2004, P.L. 108–446, § 614 [d][1][B], 118 Stat. 2647 [2005])

The role of the regular education teacher as a member of the IEP team increased in importance with the 1997 Amendments to IDEA and continues with the 2004 reauthorization. The legislation requires that a regular education teacher participate in the "determination of the appropriate positive behavioral interventions and supports, and other strategies, and the determination of supplementary aids and services, program modifications, and support for school personnel" (IDEA of 2004, P.L. 108–446, § 614 [d][3][C], 118 Stat. 2647 [2005]). In addition, a regular education

Standards and the Law

CEC Standard 10: Collaboration
INTASC Standard 10: Collaboration, Ethics, and Relationships
PRAXIS Standard: Delivery of Services to Students with Disabilities

teacher is also required to participate in the review and revision of the IEP of the child (IDEA of 2004, P.L. 108–446, § 614 [d][4][B], 118 Stat. 2647 [2005]).

The multidisciplinary team must consider five special factors that may significantly impact the development of an appropriate IEP. The first is the behavior of the child, which may impede "the child's learning or that of others"; therefore, the team must consider "the use of positive behavioral interventions, and supports, and other strategies, to address that behavior" (IDEA of 2004, P.L. 108–446, § 614 [d][3][B], 118 Stat. 2647 [2005]). The second factor is the language needs of the child who may have limited English proficiency. Third, children who are blind or visually impaired must have their need for instruction in the use of Braille considered, unless it is deemed unnecessary by the IEP team. The fourth factor for consideration is the communication needs of the child who is deaf or hard of hearing because direct instruction to meet the child's communication needs is required. The fifth factor is determining whether the child needs assistive technology devices and services. An assistive technology device is

> Any item, piece of equipment, or product system, whether acquired commercially off the shelf, modified, or customized, that is used to increase, maintain, or improve functional capabilities of a child with a disability. . . . The term does not include a medical device that is surgically implanted, or the replacement of such device. (IDEA of 2004, P.L. 108–446, § 602 [1], 118 Stat. 2647 [2005])

In addition, an assistive technology service is defined in IDEA as

> any service that directly assists a child with a disability in the selection, acquisition, or use of an assistive technology device. Such term includes—
>
> (A) the evaluation of the needs of such child, including a functional evaluation of the child in the child's customary environment;
> (B) purchasing, leasing, or otherwise providing for the acquisition of assistive technology devices by such child;
> (C) selecting, designing, fitting, customizing, adapting, applying, maintaining, repairing, or replacing assistive technology devices;
> (D) coordinating and using other therapies, interventions, or services with assistive technology devices, such as those associated with existing education and rehabilitation plans and programs;

(E) training or technical assistance for such child, or, where appropriate, the family of such child; and

(F) training or technical assistance for professionals (including individuals providing education and rehabilitation services), employers, or other individuals who provide services to, employ, or are otherwise substantially involved in the major life functions of such child. (IDEA of 2004, P.L. 108–446, § 602 [2], 118 Stat. 2647 [2005])

As a result of this expanded focus, the identification and acquisition of assistive technology devices and services has become a major issue of concern for the IEP team. Prior to the inclusion of assistive technology in the IEP, school districts often did not consider the need for assistive technology services and devices for all children. In most cases, assistive technology was only considered for those students with significant physical and/or communication needs. Now, with the requirement in IDEA, the possible use of assistive technology is to be addressed by each IEP team.

After examining these five factors, the IEP team should develop an IEP for each eligible child. The team should consider

(i)   the strengths of the child;

(ii) the concerns of the parents for enhancing the education of their child;

(iii) the results of the initial evaluation or most recent evaluation of the child; and

(iv) the academic, developmental, and functional needs of the child. (IDEA of 2004, P.L. 108–446, § 614 [d][3][A], 118 Stat. 2647 [2005])

Under IDEA 2004 (P.L. 108–446, § 614 [d][1][A], 118 Stat. 2647 [2005]), the IEP document must be written to include 10 components:

1. A statement of the present levels of academic achievement and functional performance

2. A statement of measurable annual goals, including academic and functional goals

3. A description of how the child's progress toward meeting the annual goals will be measured

4. A statement of the specific educational services, related services, and program modifications or supports for school personnel that will be provided

5. An explanation of the extent to which the child will not participate with nondisabled children in regular class and activities

6. The extent to which the child will participate in state- or districtwide assessments, appropriate necessary accommodations, or alternative assessments that might be implemented

7. The projected date for the beginning of services and modifications with the anticipated frequency, location, and duration specified

8. Beginning at age 16, and updated annually, a statement of transition services

Figure 5.1
Individualized Education Program

... a written statement for each child with a disability that is developed, reviewed, and revised ... and that includes—

(I)   a statement of the child's present levels of academic achievement and functional performance, including—

(aa)   how the child's disability affects the child's involvement and progress in the general education curriculum;

(bb)   for preschool children, as appropriate, how the disability affects the child's participation in appropriate activities; and

(cc)   for children with disabilities who take alternate assessments aligned to alternate achievement standards, a description of benchmark or short-term objectives;

(II)   a statement of measurable annual goals, including academic and functional goals, designed to—

(aa)   meet the child's needs that result from the child's disability to enable the child to be involved in and make progress in the general education curriculum; and

(bb)   meet each of the child's other educational needs that result from the child's disability;

(III)   a description of how the child's progress toward meeting the annual goals ... will be measured and when periodic reports on the progress the child is making toward meeting the annual goals (such as through the use of quarterly or other periodic reports, concurrent with the issuance of report cards) will be provided;

(IV)   a statement of the special education and related services and supplementary aids and services, based on peer-reviewed research to the extent practicable, to be provided to the child, or on behalf of the child, and a statement of the program modifications or supports for school personnel that will be provided for the child—

(aa)   to advance appropriately toward attaining the annual goals;

(bb)   to be involved in and make progress in the general curriculum ... and to participate in extracurricular and other nonacademic activities; and

(cc)   to be educated and participate with other children with disabilities and nondisabled children in the activities described in this subparagraph;

(V)   an explanation of the extent, if any, to which the child will not participate with nondisabled children in the regular class and in the activities described ... ;

(VI)   (aa)   a statement of any individual appropriate accommodations that are necessary to measure the academic achievement and functional performance of the child on State and districtwide assessments ... ; and

(bb)   if the IEP Team determines that the child shall take an alternate assessment on a particular State or districtwide assessment of student achievement, a statement of why—

(AA)   the child cannot participate in the regular assessment; and

(BB)   the particular alternate assessment selected is appropriate for the child;

(VII)   the projected date for the beginning of the services and modifications ... and the anticipated frequency, location, and duration of those services and modifications; and

Figure 5.1 (*Continued*)

> (VIII) beginning not later than the first IEP to be in effect when the child is 16, and updated annually thereafter;
>
> (AA) appropriate measurable postsecondary goals based upon age appropriate transition assessments related to training, education, employment, and, where appropriate, independent living skills;
>
> (BB) the transition services (including courses of study) needed to assist the child in reaching these goals; and
>
> (CC) beginning not later than one year before the child reaches the age of majority under State law, a statement that the child has been informed of the child's rights under this title, if any, that will transfer to the child on reaching the age of majority. (IDEA of 2004, P.L. 108–446, § 614 [d][1][A], 118 Stat. 2647 [2005])

9. Beginning no later than 1 year before the child's age of majority, a statement of the child's rights to be transferred to him or her at the age of majority

10. How the progress toward the annual goals will be measured; how the parents will be informed of the child's progress, including whether the child's progress is adequate to meet the annual goals established by the IEP team; and with a frequency no less than that of parents of nondisabled children (see Figure 5.1)

is often as reg. kids get grades (includes midterms, if sent)

The IEP team's mandate also includes the responsibility to review the child's IEP periodically, no less frequently than annually. The purpose of an IEP review is to (a) determine if the IEP goals are being met; (b) revise the IEP if there is any lack of progress toward the annual goals and the general education curriculum; and (c) address the results of any reevaluation, any special factors or anticipated needs of the child, or any matters that may impact the child (IDEA of 2004, P.L. 108–446, § 614 [d][4][A], 118 Stat. 2647 [2005]).

Individualized Family Service Plan

Instead of an IEP, children who are infants and toddlers (birth to age 2) have an IFSP. The IFSP closely parallels the IEP (see Figure 5.2) and provides the requisite process and documentation for an individualized program that has a family focus.

> ### *Standards and the Law*
>
> **CEC Standard 7:** Instructional Planning
> **INTASC Standard 7:** Planning Instruction
> **PRAXIS Standard:** Delivery of Services to Students with Disabilities

Figure 5.2
Individualized Family Service Plan

The individualized family service plan shall be in writing and contain—

(1) a statement of the infant's or toddler's present levels of physical development, cognitive development, communication development, social or emotional development, and adaptive development, based on objective criteria;

(2) a statement of the family's resources, priorities, and concerns relating to enhancing the development of the family's infant or toddler with a disability;

(3) a statement of the measurable results or outcomes expected to be achieved for the infant or toddler and the family, including pre-literacy and language skills, as developmentally appropriate for the child, and the criteria, procedures, and timelines used to determine the degree to which progress toward achieving the results or outcomes is being made and whether modifications or revisions of the results or outcomes or services are necessary;

(4) a statement of specific early intervention services based on peer-reviewed research, to the extent practicable, necessary to meet the unique needs of the infant or toddler and the family, including the frequency, intensity, and method of delivering services;

(5) a statement of the natural environments in which early intervention services will appropriately be provided, including a justification of the extent, if any, to which the services will not be provided in a natural environment;

(6) the projected dates for initiation of services and the anticipated length, duration, and frequency of the services;

(7) the identification of the service coordinator from the profession most immediately relevant to the infant's or toddler's or family's needs (or who is otherwise qualified to carry out all applicable responsibilities under this part) who will be responsible for the implementation of the plan and coordination with other agencies and persons, including transition services; and

(8) the steps to be taken to support the transition of the toddler with a disability to preschool or other appropriate services. (IDEA of 2004, P.L. 108–446, § 636 [d], 118 Stat. 2647 [2005])

IDEA requires that the multidisciplinary team develop the IFSP that includes the parents, which is to meet the unique needs of the family and the child. A new component to be included in the IFSP is a description of the appropriate transition services for the infant or toddler. Children who are ages 3 to 5 may have an IFSP or an IEP developed, depending on their individual needs.

Individualized Transition Plan

Wright and Wright (2000) stated that

Although preparation for adult life is a key component of FAPE throughout the educational experiences of students with disabilities, Part B sets forth specific requirements related to transition planning and transition services that must be implemented no later than ages 14 and 16, respectively, and which require an intensified focus on that preparation as these students begin and prepare to complete their secondary education. (p. 215)

Thus, for those individuals 14 years or older, IDEA 1997 added a significant component to the IEP, known as the ITP. This transition plan addresses the needs of the students as he or she "transitions" into the community from the school setting. It more intensely focuses the attention of the school, the family, and the child on how the IEP can be expanded to ensure a successful transition to life after secondary school. Therefore, when planning for transition, the student, when possible, should be included as a member of the planning team.

Although IDEA 2004 retained the transition focus, significant changes were included. The earlier requirement that at age 14 (or younger if needed) the IEP must include a statement of transition needs, including the course of study that the student should follow to meet his or her future goals, was removed. Instead, IDEA 2004 states that transition needs should be considered beginning no later than the first IEP in effect when the child is age 16 and should be updated annually. This IEP must include

(1) a list of appropriate measurable postsecondary goals that have been developed based upon age appropriate transition assessments related to training, education, employment, and, where appropriate, independent living skills;

(2) a list of the transition services (including courses of study) needed to assist the child in reaching the identified goals; and

(3) a statement that the child has been informed of his/her rights transferring at the age of majority. (IDEA of 2004, P.L. 108–446, § 614 [d][1], 118 Stat. 2647 [2005])

The ITP is therefore considered to be a results-oriented process that focuses the IEP team on the student's postsecondary future.

In a New Jersey case (*Baer v. Klagholz*, 2001), parents challenged changes in New Jersey's special education law and regulations pertaining to the development of transition plans. At issue was a reduction in the assessment requirements included in transition planning in which assessments focusing on post-secondary outcomes were not required. The plaintiffs charged that

by eliminating the requirement that evaluations include assessments to determine appropriate post-secondary outcomes for students with disabilities, DOE's regulations violate the right of students to receive "outcome-oriented" transition services based on appropriate assessments, as required by IDEA, are arbitrary and capricious and violate state special education law. (*Baer v. Klagholz,* 2001)

The previous New Jersey legislation included a statement that "initial evaluation or reevaluation shall include assessment(s) to determine appropriate post-secondary outcomes," which was removed as a result of a belief that this statement was redundant and covered by IDEA's requirement that the assessments must include "assessment tools and strategies that provide relevant information that directly assists persons in determining the educational needs of the child." The New Jersey Appellate Court held for the plaintiffs and agreed that the change in "the Department's regulations violate the IDEA by failing to include the federal requirement that students receive assessments to determine appropriate post-secondary outcomes and a statement

Figure 5.3
Free Appropriate Public Education

The term "free appropriate public education" means special education and related services that—

(A) have been provided at public expense, under public supervision and direction, and without charge;

(B) meet the standards of the State educational agency;

(C) include an appropriate preschool, elementary school, or secondary school education in the State involved; and

(D) are provided in conformity with the individualized education program required under section 614(d). (IDEA of 2004, P.L. 108–446, § 602 [9], 118 Stat. 2647 [2005])

of needed services." With the current federal emphasis on reducing the amount of paperwork required in the development of IEPs and allowing SEAs and LEAs more latitude in developing and implementing special education regulations, this case may be a marker for future issues.

The IEP, IFSP, and ITP are the methods by which an FAPE is to be ensured for children with disabilities at all ages. Without this provision, a child might be included physically in the public schools but still be denied an education through functional exclusion. Functional exclusion occurs when a child is physically included in classes, but the education provided lacks meaning or significance to the pupil, resulting in no education at all. Hence, Congress instituted the requirement in IDEA that every student with a disability be provided a "free appropriate public education" in conformity with the IEP (see Figure 5.3). In addition, the vision of Congress was that individuals with disabilities would not only be successful in the school setting, but also that they would strive for and reach the goal of self-sufficiency in the community as adults. The individualized program plans developed for the different age groups are the means by which this is to occur.

IEP Litigation

Since 1975, a number of cases have been brought to the courts addressing the interpretation of the term "appropriate" within the context of an IEP. The appropriateness of the IEP has been specifically examined as it relates to the methods and procedures used by the school districts to provide individualized education. Litigation has occurred in the following areas:

(a) The provision of sign language interpreters (*Board of Education of the Hendrick Hudson Central School District v. Rowley,* 1982)

(b) The selection of teaching methods for children who are deaf (*Springdale v. Grace,* 1980)

(c) The decision on who is the final authority on the selection of methods to be used (*Deal v. Hamilton County Department of Education,* 2003)

(d) Parental disagreement with the appropriateness of the school's IEP and rejection of the proposed IEP

(e) The subsequent nonreimbursement for parental placement in a private school setting (*Burlington School Committee v. Department of Education of Massachusetts,* 1985).

Two other significant areas of litigation have also developed. The first concerns the appropriateness of the IEP when related services are required (e.g., *Felter v. Cape Girardeau School District,* 1993; *Tatro v. State of Texas,* 1979; *Macomb County Intermediate School District v. Joshua S.,* 1989; *Hurry v. Jones,* 1984; *Gary B. v. Cronin,* 1980; *Papacoda v. Connecticut,* 1981; *Taylor v. Board of Education,* 1986; *Espino v. Besteiro,* 1981; *Northville Public School,* 1990). The second focuses on the IEP's appropriateness when the length of the school year is mandated to no longer than 9 months, known as the ESY issue (*Armstrong v. Kline,* 1979; *Georgia Association for Retarded Citizens [GARC] v. McDaniel,* 1983; *M. M. v. School District of Greenville County,* 2001).

Appropriateness of the IEP

Issue Appropriate

In the case of the *Board of Education v. Rowley* (1982), the issue of appropriateness of the IEP transcended the issue of accessing education to that of maximizing the potential of the child with a disability. In *Rowley,* the Supreme Court found that Congress had provided assistance to states to carry out their duties of providing a free public education to all children in their jurisdiction, but that the states were not required to guarantee more than the "open door" (*Board of Education v. Rowley,* 1982, p. 476). *Rowley* addressed the issue of the appropriate methodology for implementing an IEP for a child who was deaf. The Court decided that, for the IEP to be appropriate, it must only be developed following the procedures outlined in the legislation and accompanying regulations. The *Rowley* Court defined appropriateness of an IEP as

> Such instruction and services must be provided at public expense, must meet the State's educational standards, must approximate the grade levels used in the State's regular education, and must comport with the child's IEP. In addition, the IEP, and therefore the personalized instruction, should be formulated in accordance with the requirements of the Act and, if the child is being educated in the regular classrooms of the public education system, should be reasonably calculated to enable the child to achieve passing marks and advance from grade to grade. (*Board of Education v. Rowley,* 1982, p. 475)

Additional cases have provided further clarification to the concept of "appropriateness" of the IEP. The first was *Springdale v. Grace* (1982). Sherry Grace was an 11-year-old female who was identified as profoundly and prelingually deaf. Since the age of 3, she had been enrolled in programs for students who were deaf. The first 2 years she attended a school program that emphasized the oral teaching method. As a result of Sherry's serious hearing loss, this method was inadequate to meet her educational and communication needs. From ages 6 to 11, she attended the Arkansas School for the Deaf, which employs the total communication method and where she progressed significantly. When her parents moved to Springdale, Arkansas, the IEP team suggested that the "Arkansas School for the Deaf was the proper school to meet Sherry's unique needs" (*Springdale v. Grace,* 1982, p. 303). The parents disagreed and began the review process. The Eighth Court of Appeals reviewed the District Court's discussion of "best" versus "appropriate" education using the *Rowley* standard and agreed that

> The district court, although convinced that the best place for Sherry is the School for the Deaf, correctly followed the Act's requirements when it determined that it was not the State's duty to provide the *best* education, but instead states are required to provide an *appropriate* education. (*Springdale v. Grace,* 1982, p. 304)

Although the IEP is required to provide an individualized program to meet the child's unique needs, it is to provide only such opportunity as is "commensurate with the opportunity granted to non-handicapped in the same system" (*Springdale v. Grace,* 1982, p. 305).

The issue of the "best" versus "appropriate" program was further reviewed in the case of *Steinberg v. Weast* (2001). In this case, the parents and school district disagreed on the program and placement for Cassie, a 17-year-old student with significant learning disabilities. The parents wanted Cassie to continue to attend a private school where she would be in a general education program working toward completion of a high school diploma. The school district disagreed and proposed a public school self-contained program with a Functional Life Skills curriculum, wherein Cassie would receive a certificate of completion as opposed to a diploma. The Court in this case reviewed the *Rowley* standard to determine whether the program being proposed would provide Cassie with an FAPE. Their decision corroborated the decisions in *Rowley* and *Grace* by stating that "there is no requirement that state educators must maximize the potential of the child," but that IDEA requires only "that the child receive some form of specialized education that is sufficient to confer some educational benefit." The Court's decision in this case was also supported by other cases at the Circuit Court level in which

> the Fourth Circuit has made it clear that the IDEA does not require that state or local authorities provide a child with the best education, public or private, that money can buy, or that the child's potential be maximized—it is enough if the disabled child benefits educationally from the proposed plan. (see *Burke County Board of Education v. Denton,* 1990; *Hessler v. State Board of Education,* 1983; *King v. Board of Education of Allegany County,* 1998; *M. M. v. School District of Greenville County,* 2001)

Another facet of preparing an IEP that meets the legislative mandate is present in *Burlington School Committee v. Department of Education of Massachusetts* (1985). Michael Panico was a child experiencing serious difficulties in school that were attributed to specific learning disabilities. For 8 years, the school district and the parents were involved in "negotiations and other proceedings . . . too involved to relate in full detail . . . " (*Burlington v. Department of Education,* 1985, p. 460). After rejecting the placement suggested by the public school as inappropriate, the parents enrolled Michael in a private school at their expense. Several hearings resulted in an order for the school district to reimburse the parents for Michael's schooling. The U.S. Supreme Court granted *certiorari* to consider the issue of reimbursement for parental placement in a private school after a rejection of a proposed IEP.

After reviewing the facts of this case, the Court concluded that reimbursement was useful and allowable "where a court determines that a private placement desired by the parents was proper under the Act and that an IEP calling for placement in a public school was inappropriate . . . " (*Burlington v. Department of Education,* 1985, p. 465). The courts discussed the problem that disagreements between parents and schools may continue for a significant amount of time. The quandary for the parent is what to do if the school offers an IEP that they do not believe is appropriate. In fact, the Supreme Court stated that

> parents who disagree with the proposed IEP are faced with a choice: go along with the IEP to the detriment of their child if it turns out to be inappropriate or pay for what they consider to be the appropriate placement. (*Burlington v. Department of Education,* 1985, p. 465)

If parents decide on the second course, then it would be an empty victory if they were vindicated and the schools were not required to reimburse them for what should have been the school's costs originally. The decision, therefore, that the school district must reimburse the parents was upheld.

As new methods for teaching students with disabilities become available, the question has arisen concerning who is the final authority on the selection of teaching techniques and methods to be used in the classroom. In the case of *Deal v. Hamilton* (2003), the parents of Zachary, a young child with Autism Spectrum Disorder, brought suit against the public schools of Knox County, Tennessee, requesting that the district implement a specific educational methodology, a Lovaas-style applied behavioral analysis (ABA) program prepared by the Center for Autism and Related Disorders (CARD). When Zachary was 3 years old, the parents and the school district began meeting to develop an appropriate IEP as Zachary transitioned into the public school system. Numerous meetings were held with the parents and the school personnel to discuss appropriate programming for Zachary and to consider the parents' concerns related to the type of educational methodologies that would be most appropriate to ensure Zachary's success in school.

According to the record, the school district proposed an extensive program that included a combination of special and regular kindergarten placement, discrete trial teaching, picture cues, incidental teaching, functional communication techniques with physical and visual prompting, activity-based instruction, and picture exchange communication system, as well as speech-language therapy, occupational therapy, and physical therapy. The parents disagreed and insisted that the school district implement the CARD program that had been used with Zachary in a program outside school. When the school district refused to implement the specific educational methodology requested by the parents, they requested due process and unilaterally placed Zachary in a private placement, where he would receive the aforementioned educational training. The ALJ decided for the parents with the school district, appealing the decision to the Eastern District Court of Tennessee. The Court held for the school district basing its decision on two authorities. The first was the intent of Congress in IDEA in which it stated "Congress did not intend for the federal courts to overturn a school district's choice of appropriate educational methods for a disabled child," and the second was the Supreme Court decision in *Rowley* where it stated that

> the primary responsibility for formulating the education to be accorded to a handicapped child, and for choosing the educational method most suitable to the child's needs, was left by the [IDEA] to state and local educational agencies in cooperation with the parents or guardian of the child. (*Deal v. Hamilton,* 2003)

The District Court also reviewed recent Circuit Court decisions such as *Cleveland Heights-University Heights City School District v. Boss* (1989) and *Burilovich v. Board of Education of Lincoln* (2000), where the courts agreed that the decision on educational issues should be left to those with expertise because the "state and local administrative agencies are deemed to have expertise in education policy and practice."

Related Services and the IEP

The main question involved in litigation surrounding the provision of related services concerns the question of whether school districts are obligated under IDEA to provide for the noneducational needs (e.g., catheterization services, psychotherapy services, transportation needs) of children with disabilities. According to IDEA, related services must be provided, at no cost, if they are essential for the child with a disability to "benefit" from the special education program developed in the IEP (see IDEA of 2004, P.L. 108–446, § 602 [26], 118 Stat. 2647 [2005]). To assist in the identification of related services that may be required, a nonexhaustive listing is provided in the legislation (IDEA of 2004, P.L. 108–446, § 602 [26], 118 Stat. 2647 [2005]). The IEP team should designate the type and amount of related services to be provided by the school district. According to Yell (1998), this listing of related services and the amount of services is "required so that the commitment of needed resources will be clear to the parents and other IEP team members" (p. 196).

Two important restrictions concerning related services are delineated in the legislation and its accompanying regulations. The first is that any identified related service must be a supportive service. Thus, related services cannot stand alone but are needed to support the special education program that has been developed for the child. In addition, the identified services must be necessary for the student to benefit from the IEP. Without the provision of the related service, it is assumed that the child will have difficulty benefiting from the educational services. Therefore, it is critical that when the IEP team prepares the IEP it considers two questions. First, will the service assist a child to benefit from an IEP? Then, does the child require that particular service to benefit from the special education program? The answer to these questions will vary according to the individual needs of the child, but both must be in the affirmative if the related services are to be provided.

Litigation can occur in any of the areas listed in IDEA because related services, including transportation; speech-language pathology and audiology services; interpreting services; psychological services; physical and occupational therapy; recreation, including therapeutic recreation; social work services; school nurse services; counseling services, including rehabilitation counseling; orientation and mobility services; and medical services. However, disputes most frequently occur in areas where the provision of services is expensive or where there is greater difficulty in providing the service. Examples of these areas include medical services, transportation, counseling and psychological services, and health-related services (e.g., air conditioning).

Medical Services.   The most controversial area of litigation concerning related services has arisen as a result of the "unclear" definition of medical services that, according to IDEA, are to be for diagnostic and evaluation purposes only. Thus, the courts have had to address what constitutes a medical service, defined by regulation as services provided by a licensed physician and, therefore, not included under the umbrella of related services. They have also had to address what constitutes a school health service, defined by regulation as services provided by a qualified school nurse or other qualified person. The case of *Irving Independent School District v. Tatro* (1984) (see *Tatro v. State of Texas,* 1979) is the major case in this area. Amber Tatro was a child born with spina bifida and a neurogenic bladder that required the performance of a procedure known as CIC every 3 to 4 hours. The parents had requested that CIC be provided at school as a related service, but the school district refused based on its view of CIC as a medical service. The Court of Appeals affirmed the lower court's conclusion that

> under Texas law a nurse or other qualified person may administer CIC without engaging in the unauthorized practice of medicine, provided that a doctor prescribes and supervises the procedure. The District Court then held that, because a doctor was not needed to administer CIC, provision of the procedure was not a "medical service" for purposes of the Education of the Handicapped Act. (*Irving Independent School District v. Tatro,* 1984, p. 670)

The Court based its decision on the fact that without the provision of CIC, Amber would be unable to benefit from the special education services to which she is entitled under IDEA. Thus, CIC becomes a support for the special education program, without which Amber could not attend school. Therefore, it meets the guidelines provided for a related service as put forth in legislation and regulation. As a result of this decision, the school district requested *certiorari,* and the U.S. Supreme Court heard the case in 1984. The Court addressed the issue of what constitutes a related service in its context as a means by which public education is to be made available to children with disabilities. The Court upheld the lower court's decision and clarification stating that "a service that enables a handicapped child to remain at school during the day is an important means of providing the child with the meaningful access to education that Congress envisioned" (*Irving Independent School District v. Tatro,* 1984, p. 3377).

Transportation.   Transportation services are those services that provide the means for the child with disabilities to travel to and from school, between schools, or within the school. Transportation services can also include specialized equipment such as ramps or lifts, and specially adapted buses, if required to transport the child (34 C.F.R. § 300.24 [b][15]). In *Macomb County Intermediate School District v. Joshua S.* (1989), the Court expanded the interpretation of transportation services. These services were expanded to include the provision of necessary care to a student who was determined to be medically fragile, who required positioning in his wheelchair, and who might require suctioning of his tracheotomy tube during transit. The Court found that there was no evidence that a licensed physician was needed to perform the services and that, although transportation was necessary for the student to attend school, these services could be performed as part of the transportation service. Therefore, the Court concluded that transportation was essential as a supportive service and should be provided.

In *Hurry v. Jones* (1984), the Court found that the school district failed to provide door-to-door transportation to George Hurry, violating both Section 504 of the Rehabilitation Act of 1973 and EAHCA of 1975. George Hurry weighed 160 lb; he used a wheelchair because of cerebral palsy and spastic quadriplegia. When the bus driver decided that it was unsafe to carry him up and down the steep concrete steps from his home to the bus, the school district stopped providing transportation services. The Court ordered the district to compensate the parents for the time and effort spent in transporting the child, as well as for other related expenses. In a later decision (*Kanawha County [WV] Public School,* 1989), the OCR found that the school district's busses were inaccessible to children with physical disabilities. It was unacceptable under Section 504 of the Rehabilitation Act to use a bus that required school staff to lift the student with disabilities on and off the bus. The Office of Special Education Programs (OSEP) also addressed the issue of transportation in an *OSEP Policy Letter* (1992), stating that Part B of IDEA requires that transportation services agreed on in an IEP meeting be provided for free as specified by the team in the IEP.

Although IDEA does not address the issue of time in transit, the length of time on the bus has been an issue examined by both OCR and OSEP. OCR has examined the issue of travel time for students with disabilities. They considered whether travel time that is in excess of travel time for nondisabled students results in the school district being in violation of Section 504 of the Rehabilitation Act (*Atlanta, GA Public Schools,* 1989; *San Bernardino, CA Unified School District,* 1990). The *OSEP Policy Letter* (1992) stated that IDEA regulations should be followed, and that issues of cost to parents and excessive travel time could be violations of both IDEA and Section 504 of the Rehabilitation Act.

Another concern was the provision of transportation services to children with disabilities enrolled in a parochial school but needing to be transported to a public school for special education. Sarah Felter (*Felter v. Cape Girardeau School District,*

1993) was enrolled in a private parochial school but also received special education services at the local public school because of a visual impairment and a lack of mobility. The Court ordered the school district to provide transportation from the sidewalk of the parochial school to her special education class at the public school as a related service. The Court found that a child's enrollment in a religious school does not prohibit the provision of special education services. This decision was supportive of a decision in an earlier case that considered a similar issue for a student who was deaf (*Zobrest v. Catalina Foothills School District,* 1993).

Counseling Services.   Counseling as a related service is an area of much litigation. In general, the courts have held that counseling when considered a related service is fundable when it allows the student with disabilities to benefit from special education. Indeed, the counseling services may be linked to the provision of psychological services in a residential placement, which must be provided by the school district at no cost to the child's parents. In *Gary B. v. Cronin* (1980), children who were emotionally disturbed were forced to attend private residential schools because Illinois public schools would not provide counseling or therapeutic services. An injunction was granted against the Illinois public schools from excluding counseling and therapeutic services as special education or related services because of its lack of compliance with IDEA.

In *Papacoda v. Connecticut* (1981), the Court stated that when the IEP calls for a therapy program coordinated with the education program in a residential setting, the school district is responsible for the cost of the residential program. This decision was also supported in *Kruelle v. New Castle County School District* (1981) and in *Gladys J. v. Pearland Independent School District* (1981), wherein the Court affirmed that when a child needs programming beyond that available in a day school, the school district is responsible for the residential placement. The Court reiterated that IDEA requires schools to provide a comprehensive range of services to meet the needs of children with disabilities.

The question of the school district's obligation to students who are addicted to drugs and in need of services in a residential placement has also been posed to OSEP (*OSEP Policy Letter,* 1988). The response from OSEP indicated that drug addiction alone is not a disabling condition under IDEA. However, if the addiction results in a disabling condition, then a determination may be made that the child is eligible for special education and related services. Therefore, if a residential program is deemed necessary in the IEP, it should be provided at no cost to the student or the student's family.

Physical Therapy.   Another area of potential controversy is that of physical therapy services because its availability is one of the factors used by the courts in determining the appropriateness of the placement. In *Taylor by Holbrook v. Board of Education* (1986), the Court upheld the placement of a child with cerebral palsy because the special school had access to physical therapy. Adrian Taylor was a 7-year-old boy with severe multiple disabilities who was receiving educational programming and related services from a private placement. His IEP called for him to receive physical therapy five times per day and frequent repositioning. His parents opposed the school district's proposed change of placement on the basis that the necessary related services (e.g., physical therapy, occupational therapy, medical services) would be unavailable. The Court found that the private placement provided the appropriate education in the least restrictive setting because of the availability of the related services.

In *Polk v. Central Susquehanna Intermediate Care Unit 16* (1988), the Court again held that the placement offered by the school district was inappropriate because of the lack of physical therapy services. Subsequently, in *Rapid City School District 51/4 v. Vahle* (1990) and *Das v. McHenry School District No. 15* (1994), the respective courts ordered the district to provide the necessary physical therapy services. Finally, in *Holmes v. Sobol* (1988), the Court ordered physical therapy services be included in the summer-extended school year as part of the 12-month IEP.

Related Services: Other Therapies and Services

Air Conditioning. In *Espino v. Besteiro* (1981), the Court held that a school district should provide a fully air-conditioned classroom for Raul Besteiro, a student who was unable to regulate his body temperature. This decision was in opposition to the air-conditioned Plexiglas cubicle that had been originally proposed. The Court determined that the use of the cubicle within the regular classroom was a violation of the LRE provision of IDEA. It also affirmed that air conditioning can be a related service, which, in this case, Raul needed in order to attend school.

SIBIS. Self-Injurious Behavior Inhibiting System (SIBIS) is a device that emits an electrical stimulus or shock and is frequently used as part of a behavioral management program employed in the education of persons engaging in behaviors that cause tissue damage. In *Northville Public School* (1990), the hearing officer found that the use of SIBIS would be covered under related services. However, the officer did not order its use because all educational and functional approaches had not been previously used. Likewise, in *Salinas Union High School District* (1995), the hearing officer acknowledged that SIBIS could be provided as a related service, but chose not to order its provision because the student was making significant academic and social progress under the current behavioral management plan.

Extended School Year

Another development in what constitutes an appropriate education has arisen in litigation with the concept of ESY. ESY can be defined as the provision of education services beyond the "regular" school year, in other words, for longer than the traditional 180 days. This service is to be provided at no additional expense to the child and must continue the programming developed in the IEP.

The issue in this area is whether an appropriate education means simply access to the same services as those that are offered to students without disabilities, or whether it is an equal opportunity to benefit from an education. The courts favor the latter. Thus, an equal opportunity to become educated requires that different services be provided for different students based on their individual needs. Two types of litigation have been heard concerning the denial of ESY programming. The first type of litigation concerns the review of state policies that deny the provision of ESY to children with disabilities. These policies are known as *de jure* policies (i.e., by law) and relate to state or school district statutes or regulations that limit the school year to a specified number of days. The other type of cases has reviewed the ESY issue of *de facto* policies (i.e., in fact) that result in a denial of ESY. In these instances, there was no written limitation on the number of days the school district may provide an education, but the school actually never provided children with other than the stated number of days of schooling.

The issue of ESY was brought before the courts in a combined class action lawsuit under the name of *Armstrong v. Kline* (1979). The suit was a combination of the cases of *Armstrong v. Kline, Battle v. Commonwealth of Pennsylvania,* and *Bernard v. Commonwealth of Pennsylvania.* The plaintiffs in this case were five individuals who had been labeled as SPI (severely and profoundly impaired, with IQs below 30) or SED (severely emotionally disturbed, including autism, symbiosis, and schizophrenia). The school districts had denied the parental requests for an individualized special education program in excess of the 180-day school year. This denial occurred even though the severity of the students' disabilities required a continuous program to prevent skill regression.

The issues in this case were ". . . what is an appropriate education, under the Act and does the 180 day rule interfere with its provision" (*Armstrong v. Kline,* 1979, p. 603). In reviewing these issues, the Court identified a syndrome based on the research that all children regress in skill development during a break in educational programming. However, in the case of some children, the recoupment of these lost skills is so lengthy that it renders it impossible, or unlikely, that they will attain a state of self-sufficiency they otherwise could be expected to reach. Thus, the syndrome is known as the Regression-Recoupment Syndrome. The Court, using the requirements for the IEP and considering it in light of the Regression-Recoupment Syndrome, held that inflexible state policies that support the refusal of more than 180 days of educational programming for certain children are incompatible with the Act's emphasis on the individualization of programming. In effect, the Court stated that these policies would implement programming restrictions that might be totally incompatible with the success of the child's goals. This holding was appealed to, and upheld by, the Third Circuit Court (*Battle v. Commonwealth,* 1980), and then appealed to the Supreme Court. At that time, the Court refused to hear the case, that is, *denied cert.* (see *Scanlon v. Battle,* 1981). Thus, *de jure* policies concerning the length of the required school year have not been upheld when they run counter to the appropriateness of the IEP.

Another class action suit that addressed the issue of *de facto* ESY policies was heard in 1984 (*GARC v. McDaniel,* 1984). The plaintiffs in this case were all children with mental retardation in the state of Georgia who required more than 180 days of schooling. The case began with the request by the parents of Russell Caine, a student with profound mental retardation. They requested that the school district provide summer school programming as part of Russell's IEP, and the school district refused. The district alleged in the litigation that they did not have a written policy limiting school programming and thus were not in violation of the Act's requirements. In deciding the case, the Court used the *Rowley* standard and also reviewed IDEA's concept of appropriate education as it pertains to the IEP. In its holding, the Court described a new concept, the *de facto* policy of limiting ESY. The Court stated that even though the research indicates that children with profound mental retardation usually regress significantly during breaks in programming, no child in this district had *ever* been provided with summer school. Therefore, according to the Court, the school district actually had a policy "in fact," even if it was not written down. The case was appealed to the Supreme Court, and it granted *certiorari*. The Supreme Court vacated the judgment and remanded it to the lower court for review. On remand, the Circuit Court affirmed the original decision that held that Georgia's policy of not considering or providing more than 180 days of education for children with profound mental retardation was in violation of the Act.

Another case (*M. M. v. School District of Greenville County*, 2001) addressed the issue of when ESY services should be included in a child's IEP. In this case, M. M. was an 11-year-old child with myotonic dystrophy and moderate autism who required extensive educational services. M. M. had been receiving services since she was 3 years old. Her parents and the school district disagreed over the educational methodologies to be used with M. M., especially regarding the use of the "Lovaas" method. As a result of these controversies, the IEPs that were developed were either not signed or not implemented, and the parents placed M. M. in a private school setting for her kindergarten program with participation in an in-home Lovaas program. Parents requested due process to review the program and placement for M. M., to request reimbursement for the private school placement, and to consider whether M. M.'s opportunity for FAPE had been denied by the school district not offering to provide ESY services. The Court stated that in the Fourth Circuit no standard had as yet been determined for when ESY services were appropriate, but that

> the Fifth and Tenth Circuits have concluded that ESY Services are appropriate when the benefits accrued to a disabled child during a regular school year will be significantly jeopardized if he is not provided with an educational program during the summer months (see *Alamo Heights Independent School District v. State Board of Education*, 1986, and *Johnson v. Independent School District No. 4*, 1990)

and that the Sixth Circuit had held that "ESY services are warranted when they prevent significant regression of skills or knowledge that would seriously affect a disabled child's progress toward self-sufficiency" (see *Cordrey v. Euckert*, 1990).

Thus, the courts continue to view the question of ESY services as an integral part of the delivery of appropriate individualized programming for a child with a disability. The view as to whether to provide such services must be made on an individual basis with consideration given as to the child's continued successful educational progress. The determination of educational progress must be based on a review of past educational progress and subsequent regression over times when the child has not received services, such as summer vacations.

Annual Testing for NCLB

In developing an appropriate education that meets the FAPE requirements of IDEA, the team must consider the more recent NCLB legislation. NCLB requires schools to prepare and distribute Adequate Yearly Progress (AYP) reports that include the overall progress of the school and their progress in educating several specific groups, including students with disabilities. Schools are to test at least 95% of the student population; however, schools are instructed to provide reasonable adaptations and accommodations for students with disabilities.

When standardized tests are being used, then the testing accommodations must be those specified within the testing protocol. NCLB requires accommodations, guidelines, and alternate assessments also be provided. Students with severe cognitive disabilities may be allowed to take an alternative state-developed assessment, but no more than 1% of all students taking the assessments can be given an alternative examination (Wright, Wright, & Heath, 2004).

State regulations often specify allowable accommodations, but accommodations are not necessarily limited to the listed examples (see Figure 5.4). Therefore, during the IEP meeting, the IEP team must address the need for testing adaptations or accommodations for general testing, and also whether accommodations for NCLB testing are also to be provided.

If the student has been identified as disabled under Section 504 of the Rehabilitation Act, the testing modifications and accommodations are to be provided based on the student's Section 504 plan. Testing accommodations may also be made for students identified as Limited English Proficiency (LEP) as indicated in the Language Assessment Plan. The importance of addressing the need for testing modification on a case-by-case basis during the educational program development cannot be overemphasized because it is necessary to accurately measure a student's progress relative to state academic standards.

Standards and the Law

CEC Standard 8: Assessment

INTASC Standard 7: Assessment

PRAXIS Standard: Delivery of Services to Students with Disabilities

Figure 5.4
Possible NCLB Assessment Accommodations

- Test administrator transfers answers from the student's test booklet to an answer sheet.
- Test administrator records student's verbal response.
- Translator signs directions for the student.
- Test administrator provides student with preferential seating.
- Test administrator provides student with small group testing.
- Test administrator provides student with individual testing.
- Test administrator reads the math test or writing test for the student; however, no portion of the reading test is read.
- Test administrator allows the use of magnifying devices.
- Test administrator allows the use of noise buffers.
- Test administrator allows extended time.
- Test administrator allows the use of large-print testing documents.
- Test administrator allows the use of Braille testing documents.
- Test administrator allows the use of testing documents in languages other than English.
- Test administrator allows the use of English/Native Language Word-to-Word dictionary that contains no definitions or pictures.

Summary

The cornerstone of IDEA and its legislative predecessors have been the development of individualized plans for children who need special education and related services. The first plan included in the legislation to circumvent the problems of functional exclusion that had often occurred after the holding in *Brown* and the enactment of early educational legislation was known as the IEP. In later IDEA amendments, the concept of individualized planning was expanded to include the IFSP for infants and toddlers and the ITP for secondary-age students. To provide the educational programming essential for a child to succeed in the world today, the multidisciplinary team must develop an "appropriate" individualized plan. The concept of "appropriate" and its definition has been the central focus of litigation in this area. Each piece of litigation has provided a further clarification of what constitutes an "appropriate" education for a child with a disability. The litigation supports the precept that an appropriate individualized plan leads to educational progress for students with disabilities. The development of this plan by a multidisciplinary team that includes the parents allows both parents and educators to monitor the student's progress toward the individualized goals. In essence, the development of an "appropriate" individualized plan ensures accountability for all involved in the process. Without this accountability, the philosophical underpinning of individualized programming would be useless.

Questions for Discussion

1. What is the basis for the principle of individualized planning included in IDEA?
2. Why was the IEP expanded to include two additional forms of individualized planning, the IFSP and the ITP?
3. How has the concept of "appropriate" education been addressed in litigation?
4. What types of related services have resulted in litigation and why?

Websites for Further Exploration

Basis for Individualized Program Development
www.ed.gov/parents/needs/speced/iepguide/index.html
www.disabilityinfo.gov/digov-public/public/DisplayPage.do?parentFolderId=102

Individualized Education Program
www.ldonline.org/ld_indepth/iep/legallycorrect_ieps.html
www.kidstogether.org/ieplist.htm
ericec.org/digests/e578.html
www.slc.sevier.org/iepv504.htm
www.reedmartin.com

Individualized Family Service Plan
ericec.org/digests/e605.html
www.ldanatl.org/aboutld/professionals/guidelines.asp
www.kidneeds.com/diagnostic_categories/articles/indivfamilyserviceplan.htm

Individualized Transition Plan
www.transitioncoalition.org/cg.wrap/tcas/new/resources/publications/index.php
www.parenttoparentofga.org/roadmap/education/educationtransitionhighiep.htm

Related Services (Medical Services, Transportation, Counseling Services, Physical Therapy, Air Conditioning, SIBIS)
www.kidsource.com/NICHCY/services.disab.k12.2.1.html
www.spedlaw.com/html/opnews/V7n5ja94.htm
www.whittedclearylaw.com/CM/Publications/publications7.asp
www.teach-nology.com/teachers/special_ed/pt/
ericec.org/faq/services.html
www.drm.com/newstand/publications/EDU_MedicalServices&IDEA.asp
www.cec.sped.org/law_res/doc/law/index.php

Extended School Year
www.kidsource.com/kidsource/content3/extended.school.k12.2.html
www.ldonline.org/ld_indepth/legal_legislative/extended_school_year.html
www.wpic.org/PDFs/Extended%20School%20Year.pdf

ILLUSTRATING THE LAW

Briefing of:
Burlington School Committee v.
Department of Education of Massachusetts
471 U.S. 359 (1985)

FACTS: Michael Panico was a first-grader in the town of Burlington, Massachusetts, when he began experiencing learning difficulties. As a result, an IEP was established whereby Michael attended the Memorial Public School and received 1 hour of special tutoring per day. Michael continued to have difficulties, and several discussions between his parents and the school district ensued. The parties agreed that Michael was of above average intelligence but that he had special educational needs that could not be met at Memorial.

The school district presented the Panicos with a proposed IEP that would place Michael in a small, structured class at the Pine Glen Public School. The Panicos rejected this IEP and sought review by the Massachusetts Department of Education's Bureau of Special Education Appeals (BSEA).

During the pendency of the appeal to BSEA, the Panicos enrolled Michael in the Carroll School, a private school, at their own expense. The BSEA decided that the district's proposed IEP was inappropriate and that the Carroll School was the "least restrictive adequate program" for Michael's needs. BSEA also ordered the school district to pay for Michael's tuition and transportation to Carroll for the 1979–1980 school year, including reimbursement to the Panicos for their expenses to date. The school district sought review in the U.S. District Court. Before the District Court heard the case, the school district agreed to pay some of the Carroll School expenses but refused to reimburse the Panicos for the expenses of the 1979–1980 school year.

After the District Court's decision, appeal was once again taken to the U.S. Court of Appeals for the First Circuit. The Court of Appeals remanded the case to the District Court, where a trial was held. The District Court overturned the BSEA decision, holding that the proposed IEP was appropriate and that the school district was "not responsible for the cost of Michael's education at the Carroll School for the academic years 1979–80 through 1981–82."

The case was once again appealed to the First Circuit Court of Appeals. The Court held that Section 1415(e)(3), which states that during the pendency of any review proceedings the child shall remain in the then current educational placement of such child, barred the Panicos from any reimbursement relief because they unilaterally changed Michael's placement to the Carroll School. As a result of unrelated unfavorable findings by the Court, the school district appealed the First Circuit's decision. The Supreme Court granted *certiorari* to answer two questions.

ISSUES: Does the potential relief available under Section 1415(e)(2) include reimbursement to parents for private school tuition and expenses?

Does Section 1415(e)(3) bar such reimbursement to parents who reject a proposed IEP and place a child in a private school without the consent of the local school authorities?

HOLDING: Section 1415(e)(2) directs a reviewing court to "grant such relief as [it] deems appropriate." The Supreme Court held that Section 1415(e)(2) gives the reviewing court broad discretion to fashion a remedy, that equitable considerations are relevant, and that ordering reimbursement is proper under the Act.

The Court further held that a parental violation of Section 1415(e)(3) did not constitute a waiver of reimbursement. However, the Court noted that reimbursement would ultimately depend on whether the challenged IEP was deemed appropriate. If the courts determine that the proposed IEP was appropriate, the parents would be barred from obtaining reimbursement for any interim period in which their child's placement violated Section 1415(e)(3).

RATIONALE: In support of the holding, the Court reasoned that the reimbursement remedy was in consonance with the child's right to an FAPE. The Court noted that IEP reviews can take several years; in the meantime, parents who disagree are faced with either going along with the IEP or paying for what they consider appropriate placement. If parents chose the latter course, it would be an empty victory to have a Court tell them several years later that they were right but that these expenditures cannot be reimbursed by the school district. If that were the case, the child's right to an FAPE, the parents' right to participate in developing a proper IEP, and all procedural safeguards would be less than complete. Because Congress undoubtedly did not intend such a result, the Court was confident that Congress meant to include reimbursement as "appropriate" relief.

A similar rationale was employed in deciding that a change in placement during the appeal process did not amount to a waiver of reimbursement. The Court noted that such a finding would defeat the principle purposes of the Act. Under the school district's reading of Section 1415(e)(3), parents would be forced to either leave their child in what might turn out to be an inappropriate placement or obtain the appropriate placement only by sacrificing any claim for reimbursement. The Court held that the Act was intended to give children with disabilities both an appropriate education and a free one, and that it should not be interpreted to defeat one or the other of those objectives.

ILLUSTRATING THE LAW THROUGH DISCUSSION

In light of the fact that school systems sometimes act without regard for the law or in the best interest of the student, discuss why the *Burlington* case was so important to children with disabilities.

References

Alamo Heights Independent School District v. State Board of Education, 790 F.2d 1153, 1158 (5th Cir. 1986).

Armstrong v. Kline, 476 F. Supp. 583 (E.D. Pa. 1979), *modified and remanded sub nom.,* Battle v. Commonwealth of Pennsylvania, 629 F.2d 259 (3rd Cir. 1980), *on remand,* 513 F. Supp. 425 (E.D. Pa. 1980), *cert. denied sub nom.,* Scanlon v. Battle, 101 S.Ct. 3123 (1981).

Atlanta, GA Public Schools, OCR, Region IV, 16 EHLR 19 (1989).

Baer v. Klagholz, 771 A.2d 603 (2001).

Board of Education of the Hendrick Hudson Central School District v. Rowley, 458 U.S. 176, 102 S.Ct. 3034, 73 L.Ed. 2d 690 (1982).

Burilovich *ex rel* Burilovich v. Board of Education of the Lincoln Consolidated School, 208 F.3d 560, 565 (6th Cir. 2000).

Burke County Board of Education v. Denton, 895 F.2d 973, 982 (4th Cir. 1990).

Burlington School Committee v. Department of Education of Massachusetts, 471 U.S. 359, 105 S.Ct. 1996, 85 L.Ed. 2d 385 (1985).

Cleveland Heights-University Heights City School District v. Boss *ex rel* Boss, 144 F.3d 391, 398–99 (6th Cir. 1998).

Cordrey v. Euckert, 917 F.2d 1460, 1474 (6th Cir. 1990).

Das v. McHenry School District No. 15, 41 F.3d 1510 (unpublished opinion) (7th Cir. 1994).

Deal *ex rel* Deal v. Hamilton County Department of Education, 295 F. Supp. 2d 687 (E.D. Tenn. 2003).

Espino v. Besteiro, 520 F. Supp. 905 (S.D. Tex. 1981).

Felter v. Cape Girardeau School District, 830 F. Supp. 1279 (E.D. Mo. 1993).

Georgia Association for Retarded Citizens (GARC) v. McDaniel, 716 F.2d 1565 (1983), *cert. granted,* 469 U.S. 1228, 105 S.Ct. 1228 (1983), 740 F.2d 902 (1984), *vacated,* 468 U.S. 1213 (1984).

Gary B. v. Cronin, 542 F. Supp. 102 (N.D. Ill. 1980).

Gladys J. v. Pearland Independent School District, 520 F. Supp. 869 (S.D. Tex. 1981).

Gorn, S. (1997). *What do I do when . . . The answer book on individualized education programs.* Horsham, PA: LRP.

Halderman v. Pennhurst, 612 F.2d 84, 124–129 (3rd Cir. 1979).

Hessler v. State Board of Education, 700 F.2d 134, 139 (4th Cir. 1983).

Holmes v. Sobol, 690 F. Supp. 154 (W.D. N.Y. 1988).

Hurry v. Jones, 734 F.2d 879 (1st Cir. 1984).

Individuals with Disabilities Education Act, 20 U.S.C. § 1400 *et seq.* (1997).

Individuals with Disabilities Education Improvement Act of 2004, P.L. 108–446, § 602 *et seq.,* 118 Stat. 2647 (2005).

Johnson v. Independent School District No. 4, 921 F.2d 1022, 1028 (10th Cir. 1990).

Kanawha Co. (WV) Public School, OCR, Region III, 16 EHLR 450 (1989).

King v. Board of Education of Allegany County, 999 F. Supp. 750, 764 (D. Md. 1998).

Kruelle v. New Castle County School District, 642 F.2d 687 (1981).

Macomb County Intermediate School District v. Joshua S., 715 F. Supp. 824 (E.D. Mich. 1989).

Mills v. Board of Education of District of Columbia, 348 F. Supp. 866 (D.D.C. 1972).

M. M. by D. M. and E. M. v. School District of Greenville County, 303 F.3d 523 (4th Cir. 2001).

No Child Left Behind Act, 20 U.S.C. § 6301 *et seq.* (2000).

Northville Public School, SEA, 16 EHLR 847 (1990).

OSEP Policy Letter, 213 EHLR 133 (OSEP 1988).

OSEP Policy Letter, 20 IDELR 1155 (OSEP 1992).

Papacoda v. Connecticut, 528 F. Supp. 279 (D. Conn. 1981).

PARC (Pennsylvania Association for Retarded Citizens) v. Pennsylvania, 343 F. Supp. 297 (E.D. Pa. 1972).

Polk v. Central Susquehanna Intermediate Care Unit 16, 853 F.2d 171 (3rd Cir. 1988), *cert. denied,* 488 U.S. 1030 (1989).

Rapid City School District 51/4 v. Vahle, 922 F.2d 476 (8th Cir. 1990).

Salinas Union High School District, 22 IDELR 301 (SEA Cal. 1995).

San Bernardino, CA Unified School District, OCR, Region IX, 16 EHLR 656 (1990).

Springdale v. Grace, 494 F. Supp. 266 (W.D. Ark. 1980), *aff'd,* 656 F.2d 300, *on remand,* 693 F.2d

41 (8th Cir. 1982), *cert. denied,* 461 U.S. 927, 103 S.Ct. 2086 (1983).

Steinberg v. Weast, 132 F. Supp. 2d 343 (D. Md. 2001).

Tatro v. State of Texas, 481 F. Supp. 1224 (N.D. Tex. 1979), *vacated,* 625 F.2d 557 (5th Cir. 1980), *on remand,* 516 F. Supp. 968, *aff'd,* 703 F.2d 823 (5th Cir. 1983), *aff'd sub nom.,* Irving Independent School District v. Tatro, 468 U.S. 883, 104 S.Ct. 3371, 82 L.Ed. 2d 664 (1984).

Taylor by Holbrook v. Board of Education, 649 F. Supp. 1253 (N.D. N.Y. 1986).

Wright, P. W. D., & Wright, P. D. (2000). *Wrightslaw: Special education law.* Hartfield, VA: Harbor House Law Press.

Wright, P. W. D., Wright, P. D., & Heath, S. W. (2004). *Wrightslaw: No Child Left Behind.* Hartfield, VA: Harbor House Law Press.

Wyatt v. Stickney, 325 F. Supp. 781 (M.D. Ala. 1971, 1974).

Yell, M. (1998). *The law and special education.* Upper Saddle River, NJ: Merrill/Prentice Hall.

Zobrest v. Catalina Foothills School District, 963 F.2d 1190 (9th Cir. 1992), *rev'd,* 509 U.S. 1, 113 S.Ct. 2462, 125 L.Ed. 1 (1993).

CHAPTER SIX

Least Restrictive Environment

GUIDING QUESTIONS

1. How did the process of deinstitutionalization lead to the principles of LRE being included in IDEA?

2. Explain the legislative basis for the principle of LRE.

3. How have the courts interpreted the implementation of the principle of LRE?

4. What are the major areas of controversy that have arisen as a result of the legal implementation of LRE?

A basic belief held by the founding fathers, as well as by citizens today, is that when the state undertakes to provide services to its citizens, the services must be provided in the least restrictive, or least oppressive, manner possible. One of these services for which all 50 states have accepted responsibility is education. In *Brown v. Board of Education of Topeka, Kansas* (1954) plaintiffs espoused the view that compulsory education provided in a segregated manner was too restrictive and oppressive, and that the result of this segregation was a denial of opportunity and equality. The U.S. Supreme Court upheld the plaintiffs' argument when it articulated the "separate is never equal" doctrine (as discussed in Chapters 1, 3, and 4). Subsequent litigation expanded the belief that the concept of segregation of individuals based on inalterable characteristics (i.e., gender, disability) was also a denial of opportunity and equality. This belief has been infused into educational legislation for individuals with disabilities by mandating the provision of services in nonsegregated educational settings where children can be with their peers. Litigation concerning what is an appropriate educational placement for children of different races (*Brown*) and also children with disabilities (*Mattie T.*) has supported the concept of "integration" versus "segregation." In this chapter, the genesis of the principle of education in the LRE is presented, and the resulting legislation and litigation are discussed.

Genesis of Least Restrictive Environment Principle: Deinstitutionalization

The origin of the principle of LRE can be traced to the "separate is never equal" doctrine of *Brown* (see discussion of *Brown* in Chapters 1, 3, and 4). In *Brown*, it was found that the plaintiffs had been denied the opportunity for an education based solely on the inalterable characteristic of race. Later, in deinstitutionalization cases (e.g., *Mattie T. v. Holladay,* 1979; *Wyatt v. Stickney,* 1971), educational opportunity was denied to those individuals with disabilities because of a different inalterable characteristic, that of disability. In both examples, the segregation of individuals was a result of their removal from others who did not possess the characteristic of disability, their placement in institutions, and the subsequent denial of the opportunity to receive an education while in the institution.

In *Wyatt v. Stickney* (1971), the guardians of residents committed to Bryce Hospital, a state hospital in Alabama's mental health system, initiated a class action lawsuit alleging the denial of a right to treatment. Bryce Hospital, at the

Standards and the Law

CEC Standard 1: Foundations
INTASC Standard 1: Subject Matter
PRAXIS Standard: Legal and Societal Issues

time of the court action, had approximately 5,000 patients. Of the 5,000 patients, approximately 1,500 to 1,600 geriatric patients and approximately 1,000 "mental retardates" received custodial care. The Court in its decision noted that

> The patients of Bryce Hospital, for the most part, were involuntarily committed through noncriminal procedures and without the constitutional protections that are afforded defendants in criminal proceedings. When patients are so committed for treatment purposes they unquestionably have a constitutional right to receive such individual treatment as will give each of them a realistic opportunity to be cured or to improve his or her mental condition . . .
>
> The purpose of involuntary hospitalization for treatment purposes is *treatment* and not mere custodial care or punishment . . .
>
> The failure to provide suitable and adequate treatment to the mentally ill cannot be justified by lack of staff or facilities. (*Wyatt v. Stickney,* 1971, p. 784)

Thus, the Court established the necessity of providing those persons involuntarily committed to the institution not only custodial care, but also individualized educational and habilitation treatment. If such treatment is not provided, then the patient who is involuntarily committed should not remain in the custody of the institution and should be released because the only justification for their removal from society is for the provision of treatment.

In the state of Mississippi, a class action lawsuit (*Mattie T. v. Holladay,* 1979) was filed on behalf of children who had disabilities or who were seen by the state as having disabilities. The plaintiffs alleged that the state was denying these children the opportunity to an education. The Court agreed and found that the plaintiffs were denied access to "educational programs which are in normal school settings with non-handicapped children . . ." (*Mattie T. v. Holladay,* 1979). In a comprehensive order, the Court required the state to monitor the districts to ensure children with disabilities were being educated in the LRE and not placed in institutions (i.e., segregated facilities). The Court stated that instruction of children with disabilities should be within the LRE. In its order, the Court emphasized the LRE by prohibiting (a) the removal of children with disabilities from the regular educational environment unless the severity or nature of the disability prohibited their education in that setting, (b) the placement in an educational setting that does not allow for participation in activities with nondisabled children, and (c) the educational placement in structures that are separate from regular public school buildings (e.g., state hospitals). Therefore, in *Mattie T.,* the Court interpreted and applied the language in IDEA as preventing state and individual school districts from separating children from their peers for educational purposes based solely on disability. It is clear from the order that the Court intended to enforce the integration of children with disabilities into regular educational environments.

In summary, the litigation surrounding deinstitutionalization began in the state hospitals and institutions by challenging involuntary placements where neither educational nor habilitative treatment was provided. The results of this litigation were subsequently included as a component of legislation (IDEA) supporting the integration of students with disabilities into regular educational programs. The combination of this piece of legislation and subsequent litigation resulted in schools being compelled to provide placement that would meet educational needs in a LRE.

Legislative Basis for Least Restrictive Environment

In 1975, legislation known as EAHCA was enacted. This legislation included as one of its purposes the assurance that children with disabilities were receiving an FAPE in the LRE. The principle of LRE was based on the litigation that had occurred in the early 1970s (e.g., *Wyatt* and *Mattie T.*). The principle was codified in EAHCA. Therefore, in 2004 IDEA, the definition of LRE is that

> To the maximum extent appropriate, children with disabilities, including children in public or private institutions or other care facilities, are educated with children who are not disabled, and special classes, separate schooling, or other removal of children with disabilities from the regular educational environment occurs only when the nature or severity of the disability of a child is such that education in regular classes with the use of supplementary aids and services cannot be achieved satisfactorily. (IDEA of 2004, P.L. 108–446, § 612 [a][5][A], 118 Stat. 2647 [2005])

The LRE requirement was expanded by the clarification of the additional requirement to the LRE section. This requirement is that any funding mechanism developed by a state must not result in placements that are in violation of the LRE provisions in IDEA. In addition, the state must not develop nor implement a funding method by which it

> distributes funds on the basis of the type of setting in which a child is served that will result in the failure to provide a child with a disability a free appropriate public education according to the unique needs of the child as described in the child's IEP. (IDEA of 2004, P.L. 108–446, § 612 [a][5][B], 118 Stat. 2647 [2005])

Standards and the Law

CEC Standard 3: Individual Learning Differences

INTASC Standard 3: Diverse Learners

PRAXIS Standard: Delivery of Services to Students with Disabilities

Professionals and parents often use the phrase "least restrictive environment" synonymously with the terms "mainstreaming" and "inclusion." This usage is erroneous because the terms "mainstreaming" and "inclusion" refer to the educational practice of placing students with disabilities into the general education classroom. However, the term "least restrictive environment" refers to IDEA's mandate that

1. Children with disabilities be educated with children who are not disabled whenever possible
2. Educational placement be based on the child's educational needs and be as close to the child's home as possible
3. Children with disabilities be provided access to nonacademic and extracurricular activities
4. Each public agency provides a continuum of alternative placements with increasing levels of educational supports

The intent of IDEA is for all children to be educated in the regular classroom to the greatest extent possible. According to the DOE, the continuum of alternative placements required by IDEA is the method by which this is to occur (Letter to Copenhaver, 1997).

Continuum of Alternative Placements

To clarify the goal of placement in the LRE for children with disabilities, the Secretary of Education has promulgated regulations that require a continuum of alternative placements (CAP) to be developed and implemented in each school district. This continuum is to be available at all levels of education from elementary through secondary school. The regulations describing CAP state that

(a) Each public agency shall ensure that a continuum of alternative placements is available to meet the needs of children with disabilities for special education and related services.
(b) The continuum . . . must—
  (1) Include the alternative placements listed in the definition of special education . . . (instruction in regular classes, special classes, special schools, home instruction, and instruction in hospitals and institutions); and

---

Standards and the Law

CEC Standard 5: Learning Environments and Social Interactions
INTASC Standard 5: Learning Environments
PRAXIS Standard: Delivery of Services to Students with Disabilities

Figure 6.1
Instruction and Supplementary Services Occurring in a Continuum of Alternate Placements

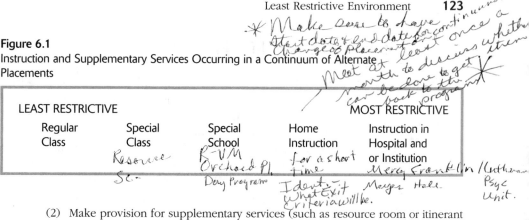

(2) Make provision for supplementary services (such as resource room or itinerant instruction) to be provided in conjunction with regular class placement. (34 C.F.R. § 300.551[b])

As can be seen in the regulations, the more severe the child's needs, the more the educational environment may become restrictive or segregated. The converse is also true. The fewer the needs, the less segregation can be tolerated. In other words, the needs of the child are to dictate where on the continuum the child will be served (see Figure 6.1). However, based on the IDEA mandate, inclusion in the regular classroom accomplished through the use of supplemental aids and services is the preferred placement. The child may be removed from the regular classroom and segregated, only if segregation is necessary to meet the goals of the child's IEP. In a Letter to Anonymous (1996), the Office of Special Education Programs stated that

> The options on this continuum include "instruction in regular classes, special classes, special schools, home instruction, and instruction in hospitals and institutions." . . . The options on this continuum must be available to the extent necessary to implement each disabled student's IEP. . . . Thus, placement of an individual disabled student in a separate school can occur only if an individual placement determination is made that the student's IEP cannot be implemented satisfactorily in a less restrictive placement, and that placement of the student in the separate school is needed to implement the student's IEP. (p. 3)

The IEP, as the force that moves the child along the continuum, must identify the setting from the continuum where the child will be educated. In considering the LRE for the child along the CAP, the IEP team must consider the educational setting and evaluate it either in terms of the "harmful effects on the child or on the quality of services that he needs" (SEA, School District of Beloit, 1996, p. 6). If the team decision is that the student's least restrictive placement is outside the regular classroom, then opportunities for interactions with peers who are nondisabled must be identified and maximized. As the Office of Special Education Programs (Letter to LaHodd, 1995) stated "any alternative placement, outside of the regular educational environment must maximize opportunities for the disabled student to interact with nondisabled peers, to the extent appropriate to the needs of the students" (p. 4). The legislative intent to retain children in the regular educational program as much as possible has resulted in significant amounts of litigation. This litigation has attempted to interpret the principle of LRE and its various components.

Judicial Interpretations of LRE Principle

IDEA clearly established the guidelines by which states were to provide education to children with disabilities but did not, and could not, define what was the LRE for every child. The LRE must be selected on its own merits as required by the IEP. Litigation can only provide guidance as to what has been found acceptable and what has been found unacceptable and, therefore, establish minimum standards.

For example, in *Roncker v. Walter* (1983), a suit was brought against a school district alleging violations of EAHCA's LRE requirement. The mother of Neil Roncker, a 9-year-old boy who was severely mentally retarded, alleged that the placement of her son in a county school where he would have contact only with students with disabilities was a violation of his right to an education in the LRE. The school district argued that the county school could provide a higher quality of instruction than could be provided in a regular classroom. The parents disagreed, asked for a due process hearing, and subsequently initiated litigation. During this process, they transferred Neil to another school that served children with and without disabilities. At that school, Neil had contact with children who were not disabled during lunch, gym, and recess.

In its decision, the Sixth Circuit Court of Appeals noted a "very strong preference" that children with disabilities be educated with children without disabilities. However, the most difficult question answered by the Court was whether a child with disabilities should be segregated from his or her nondisabled peers when he or she would receive a superior education by doing so. In its analysis, the Court stated that

> In a case where the segregated facility is considered superior, the court should determine whether the services which make that placement superior could be feasibly provided in a non-segregated setting. If they can, the placement in the segregated school would be inappropriate under the Act. (*Roncker v. Walter,* 1983, p. 1063)

The Court, therefore, required the school district to determine if the same benefits that were available in the segregated facility could *feasibly* be provided in the public school. The Court also noted that a school district could consider the cost of providing the service as a factor. Other factors to be considered included the student's physical and emotional needs. This balancing test, now known as the *Roncker* test, is intended to optimize the educational benefits to be conferred to the

Standards and the Law

CEC Standard 1: Foundations

PRAXIS Standard: Legal and Societal Issues

child with disabilities, while also allowing the school districts to provide funds so an appropriate education can be provided to all children.

In a subsequent case (*A. W. v. Northwest R-1 School District,* 1987), the Eighth Circuit Court of Appeals used the *Roncker* test for guidance in the identification of the LRE. A. W. was an elementary school-age child with Down syndrome. He required close supervision at all times, and his behavior was occasionally severely disruptive. The school district recommended that A. W. attend State School No. 2, a school exclusively for children with disabilities. The parents disagreed with the school district's recommendation and began the process that lead to the review by the Eighth Circuit Court of Appeals.

In its decision, the Eighth Circuit Court first looked to the case of *Board of Education v. Rowley* (1982) to determine if the Supreme Court had addressed the issue of appropriate education in the LRE for children with disabilities. The Court did find that the school district was providing A. W. with a free appropriate education. The Court then turned to the question of whether the education was satisfactorily provided in an environment with nondisabled students "to the maximum extent appropriate" (*A. W. v. Northwest R-1 School District,* 1987, p. 161). Using the *Roncker* test, the Court found that placement of A. W. in the State School was appropriate because any marginal benefit to mainstreaming would be outweighed by the cost. Therefore, it was not "feasible" to place A. W. in a public school because it was not feasible to transport the child's IEP to the public school. Hence, the "portability" standard could not be met. In its analysis, the Court ". . . quoted . . . from *Roncker,* and modeled its ultimate conclusion—that the marginal benefit of A. W.'s mainstreaming was outweighed by the deprivation of benefit to other handicapped children—on this language" (*A. W. v. Northwest R-1 School District,* 1987, p. 163). Despite the Court's recognition of the legislative preference for the provision of educational services in an integrated setting, both *Roncker* and *A. W.* resulted in a segregated education for the child with disabilities. This placement was in lieu of modified educational placements in integrated settings where both education and intangible factors such as socialization with nondisabled students and typical school experiences could have been provided.

Both *Roncker* and *A. W.* stressed the local nature of education and that the selection of educational methods is best left to the educational professionals of each individual school district. In *Mark A. v. Grant Wood Educational Agency* (1986), the Eighth Circuit Court's opinion is even stronger in its suggestion that selection and delivery of educational services to children should be left with the local school districts.

Mark and Ruth A. had placed their daughter, Alleah, who had disabilities in a private nonprofit day care center for children ages 1 through 6. This center educated children with disabilities, along with children without disabilities, in an integrated private preschool program. The school district initially agreed to the preschool placement but then decided that Alleah should attend a preschool developmental class in the public school. The parents objected, and the case was subsequently appealed to the Eighth Circuit Court. The parents argued that Alleah should not be removed from the private placement because she was being educated in an integrated setting with children who did not have disabilities, whereas education in the public school environment would result in a segregated education in a classroom of children with disabilities. The Eighth Circuit noted that

> we recognize that the Act creates a clear preference for *public* educational placement when that placement is not inconsistent with the mainstreaming provisions of the Act. We reject the view that the mainstreaming provisions of the Act are satisfied only if a handicapped child is educated *in the same classroom* with nonhandicapped children . . . Alleah, at the very least, will be educated *in the same school* with nonhandicapped children. (*Mark A. v. Grant Wood Educational Agency,* 1986, p. 54)

The Circuit Court of Appeals upheld the District Court's decision in favor of the school district, again leaving the method of providing an education in the LRE to the discretion of the local school district.

Present in *Roncker, A. W.,* and *Mark A.* was the intent by the school districts to segregate the child with disabilities from nondisabled peers. This intent hardly appears to satisfy the mandate of IDEA to educate children in the LRE possible. Along with the controversy concerning actual placement and the selection of educational services as a factor in the placement, there have been a number of other areas related to the legal principle of LRE that have resulted in litigation. The following are briefly discussed: mainstreaming and inclusion, placement in neighborhood schools, placement in private schools, parental reimbursement for private school placement, religious schools, and funding limitations.

Areas of LRE Litigation

Mainstreaming

Even though Congress has mandated development of an IEP for each child receiving special education services, it has only expressed a strong preference for the LRE. The term "mainstreaming" is not identified in the legislation, although it is often used synonymously with the term "least restrictive environment." Mainstreaming is considered to be the educational practice of implementing the LRE requirement. Therefore, mainstreaming must only be considered as a means to implement an appropriate IEP and accomplish the goals identified for each child. Limitations in the practice of mainstreaming have been identified and include consideration of the safety of the child and other children, any harmful effects on the child if fully mainstreamed, and the financial cost of including the child in the regular classroom. It is logical to assume the IEP team would consider any harmful effects or dangers mainstreaming might cause for the child and for the other children in the situation, as well as the financial impact of providing these services.

In the case of *Beth B. v. Lake Bluff School District* (2002), the concept of "reverse mainstreaming" was addressed as a means of providing the student with opportunities to participate with nondisabled children. Reverse mainstreaming is a concept in which nondisabled students are included in programs for children with special needs as opposed to the "mainstreaming" or inclusion of students with special needs in the regular education program. This case revolved around the development of an appropriate education in the LRE for a student who has Rett syndrome and is severely mentally and physically challenged. Throughout her elementary school years, Beth was in regular classes in her neighborhood public school. When she reached seventh grade, the school district noted that Beth's educational needs could be better met in a program that focused on educational life skills (ELS) rather than academics because she was functioning on a preschool level at that time. The parents refused this placement, stating that IDEA required that Beth be placed in a "mainstream" classroom in her neighborhood school. In the ELS program that was suggested for Beth, students were "mainstreamed into regular education classrooms during music, library, art, computer, and certain social studies and science classes, and join other students at the school during lunch, recess, assemblies, and field trips." Reverse mainstreaming was also employed, wherein regular education students would come into the classroom to interact with the other students. The court agreed with the parents that the LRE requirement indicates a strong preference in favor of mainstreaming, but it disagreed with them that the LRE requirement indicates a regular education placement even when that program would result in an unsatisfactory education. Thus, the Court upheld the program developed by the school district, stating that

> the regular classroom would be a less restrictive environment than the ELS classroom. That point is not at issue, however, because the Lake Bluff school district is not required to educate Beth in such an environment unless doing so would be appropriate. (*Beth B. v. Lake Bluff School District,* 2002)

This case illustrates the point that IDEA has a presumption that the LRE is the regular education program and that whenever possible students with disabilities should be mainstreamed into such programs in order to benefit from interactions with their peers. However, this mainstreaming presumption does not override the primary focus of IDEA: the development of an appropriate education to meet the unique needs of the individual with a disability.

Inclusion

The concept of mainstreaming has evolved and been incorporated into a philosophical term known as "inclusion." Inclusion, according to Friend and Bursuck (1999), refers to "students' participation in general education settings as full members of the classroom learning community, with their special needs met there the vast majority of the time" (p. 4). A number of cases have been heard since the early 1990s that have provided a standard for usage of the inclusion philosophy within the legal standard of LRE.

Daniel R. R. v. State Board of Education (1989) dealt with the issue of the inclusion of a boy with Down syndrome who had been placed in a half-day prekindergarten class and a half-day preschool class at the request of the parents. After the district placed him in a regular classroom, the teacher tried to modify the teaching schedule and services for Daniel but discovered that he consumed most of her time and the time of her aide. When it became obvious that inclusion in the classroom was not successful, the district changed Daniel's placement. In the new placement, Daniel was in a special education class for academics. Provisions were made for him to have lunch with children without disabilities, but this was only to occur when one of his parents was available to supervise him. The parents disagreed with this change in placement and asked for a due process hearing. The decision in favor of the school district was eventually appealed to the Fifth Circuit Court of Appeals.

To determine if the district had provided an FAPE in the LRE, the court first looked to EAHCA for guidance. Because the Court disagreed with the previously used *Roncker* test as a method for evaluating the appropriateness of a placement, it developed its own two-part test, now known as the *Daniel R. R.* test. The first part is whether an appropriate education including supplemental aids and services can be provided in the regular education placement. In conjunction with this part, the second requires that the school district demonstrate that an attempt has been made to mainstream the child to the maximum extent possible and provide documentation as to the child's ability to succeed in the regular classroom. To respond to the second part of the test, the Court reviewed three determining factors: (a) the accommodations made by the district to assist the child in succeeding in the regular classroom, (b) the benefits of the regular class placement, and (c) the effect of the child's placement on the other children in the classroom. Based on its analysis of the responses to these parts, the decision of the Court, was that Daniel's placement in special education, as provided by the school district, was appropriate and met IDEA standards.

In 1991, the Eleventh Circuit Court of Appeals adopted the test established in *Daniel R. R.* to decide the case of *Greer v. Rome City School District* (1991). This case was similar in its facts with *Daniel R. R.* because the student had Down syndrome and the parents wanted the child placed in the regular classroom, not a segregated special education classroom. The Court, like the Court in *Daniel R. R.,* started its analysis with the Act's requirement that the district develop an IEP to ensure the child received a free appropriate education. Then, the Court noted that occasionally tension may occur between the child's IEP and the Act's mainstreaming preference. The Court went on to say that the IEP

> must include, among other things, statements of the child's present level of educational performance, annual goals for the child, the specific educational services to be provided the child, and the extent to which the child will be able to participate in regular education programs. . . . As this court has recognized, "the IEP is more than a mere exercise in public relations. It forms the basis for a handicapped child's entitlement to an individualized and appropriate education." Thus, the importance of the development of the IEP

to meet the individualized needs of the handicapped child cannot be underestimated. (*Greer v. Rome City School District,* 1991, p. 695)

Clearly, the Court reviewed the child's IEP to evaluate whether the child is receiving an FAPE before evaluating the mainstreaming provision of the Act. Although the Court balanced the two requirements, it did give deference to the IEP as the controlling document as opposed to the preference for mainstreaming. The Court in *Greer* went on to say that

> Although the Supreme Court has not articulated a test applicable to mainstreaming issues, the language of the Act itself provides guidance. The Fifth Circuit, adhering closely to the language of the Act, articulated a two-part test for determining compliance with the mainstreaming requirement. . . . Because this test adheres so closely to the language of the Act and, therefore, clearly reflects Congressional intent, we adopt it. Like the Fifth Circuit, we hold that no single factor will be dispositive under this test. "Rather, our analysis is an individualized, fact-specific inquiry that requires us to examine carefully the nature and severity of the child's handicapping condition, his needs and abilities, and the schools' response to the child's needs." (*Greer v. Rome City School District,* 1991, p. 696)

Therefore, the Eleventh Circuit applied the *Daniel* test to decide on the appropriate placement in the LRE as designated by the IEP, and as a result, ruled in favor of the district.

Then, the case that has provided the definitive decision in this area was heard (*Sacramento City Unified School District v. Rachel H.,* 1994). In this case, the District Court combined factors from the *Roncker* and *Daniel R. R.* tests to develop a new test, known as the *Rachel H.* test. Using this test, the Court examined the educational benefits to Rachel of placement in a regular classroom. They determined that all her IEP goals could be implemented in the regular classroom through curriculum modifications and the assistance of a part-time aide. Next, the Court examined the non-educational benefits and found that social and communication skills had increased, as had her self-confidence during her placement in the regular classroom. The question next addressed was one of detrimental effect on other members of the class, and it was found that the child was well behaved and not a distraction in the class. Finally, the Court examined the issue of cost and determined that the school district had inflated the cost estimates and failed to provide a true cost comparison of placement in regular class versus full-time special education. Because the answer to all four questions indicated no difficulty with inclusion in the regular class, the District Court concluded that the appropriate placement was in the full-time regular class with supplemental services.

The Court in its review cited the *Daniel R. R.* case as support for its proposition that the preference for mainstreaming rose to the level of a rebuttable presumption that if the child was not educated in the regular classroom, the burden of demonstrating why shifted to the school district. In other words, the strong preference for mainstreaming requires that the school rebut the presumption that any placement other than the regular classroom is not beneficial for the child and violates IDEA.

In the case of *Katherine G. by Cynthia G. v. Kentfield School District* (2003), the issue of inclusion was expanded to include a consideration of what the Court called "substantive appropriateness," basing their decision on "a balancing test" in which the four factors noted in the *Rowley* test were used to identify the most appropriate program in the LRE. In this case, the school district had provided services for Katherine, a child with a language disorder since she was 3 years old. They consistently developed IEPs that mandated her placement in programs for preschoolers that did not include inclusion in regular programs. Katherine's mother wanted her placed in a program that not only met her individual needs, but also was provided in a fully inclusive setting. When the school district continued to suggest a day school placement that was noninclusive, Katherine's mother placed her unilaterally in a private afterschool preschool program that did provide such services, and requested transportation and tuition reimbursement from the school. For her kindergarten year, the school district offered to place Katherine for a half-day in a special day program for students with disabilities and in an afternoon program in an inclusive setting, both of which her mother refused. The Court, in reviewing this case, considered whether Katherine would have received benefit from the suggested programs, whether the program was designed to meet her unique needs, and whether the program was in the LRE. The Court supported the school district when it stated that "the child would not have received any academic benefit from a full inclusion placement for kindergarten, and the non-academic benefits would have been minimal," (*Katherine G. v. Kentfield*, 2003) but it supported the parent when it refuted the school's concern that there would have been a detrimental effect on the teacher and other students as a result of Katherine's inclusion, and that the cost of the program would not have been significant. As a result, they concluded that any placement selected by the school district should include a partial inclusion component.

Neighborhood School

The issues of mainstreaming and inclusion have been further investigated because they impact the placement of the child, not only in the LRE, but also in the neighborhood school. The Eighth Circuit followed the decisions referred to in the previous section with that in *Schuldt v. Mankato Independent School District No. 77* (1991). The parents of Erika, a child with spina bifida, requested that the school district modify the elementary school that she would have attended if she did not have a disability (often referred to as the "neighborhood school") to make it accessible. The Court found that federal law did not require that the school district place a child with disabilities in the neighborhood school if, by bussing, the child could receive a "fully integrated public education" (*Schuldt v. Mankato Independent School District No. 77*, 1991, p. 1357). The Court stated that

> We interpret section 300.552 as directing the school district to locate Erika at a school where her teachers can fully implement her program. The phrase "as close as possible" is not a mandate that the school place Erika at Roosevelt. As we pointed out earlier, the district court concluded that even if the school district had followed the proper procedures, Erika's individualized education program team would not have chosen Roosevelt as the location of her placement, . . . and the record contains ample evidence to support this conclusion. (*Schuldt v. Mankato Independent School District No. 77*, 1991, p. 1361)

The Court also noted that it was allowable for a school district to consider both the cost of modifications and the benefit to the child with disabilities; however, it stated that in this case (*Schuldt*) the cost of modification was not a factor in its decision. In addition, the Court rejected the premise of the neighborhood school as the only appropriate setting for a child with disabilities to be in compliance with IDEA. Instead, the Court examined educational benefits available and determined that Erika was receiving an adequate educational program in a properly integrated setting, which, indeed, is the focus of the Act.

Four years later, in *Murray v. Montrose County School District RE-1J* (1995), the Tenth Circuit Court followed to a large extent the Eighth Circuit Court's decision. In this case, Tyler Murray, a 12-year-old student with severe multiple disabilities, was to be moved from a local elementary school offering programs for students with mild and moderate needs to another elementary school 10 miles away that offered programs for students with severe and profound needs. The parents objected, stating that IDEA created a presumption for a child with disabilities to be educated in the school closest to his or her home, commonly known as the neighborhood school. The Court disagreed

> A natural and logical reading of these two regulations is that a disabled child should be educated in the school he or she would attend if not disabled (i.e., the neighborhood school), unless the child's IEP requires placement elsewhere. If the IEP requires placement elsewhere, then, in deciding where the appropriate placement is, geographical proximity to home is relevant, and the child should be placed as close to home as possible. (*Murray v. Montrose County School District RE-1J,* 1995, p. 929)

Clearly, the Court interpreted IDEA as not encompassing a presumption of neighborhood schooling and, indeed, at the most, as only presenting a preference in favor of the neighborhood schools.

✕ Placement in a Private School

As the issue of mainstreaming has become more complex with the introduction of the controversy concerning neighborhood schools, a further concern has been introduced with parental requests for placement of children in private schools. According to IDEA, if placement in a private school or facility is necessary for the child to receive special education, then such placement by the district must be at no cost to the parents (IDEA of 2004, P.L. 108–446, § 612 [10][B], 118 Stat. 2647 [2005]).

Although placement in a private program is part of the CAP, it must be justified by the needs of the child as designated in the IEP. If parents disagree with the IEP team's decision on needs and subsequent educational placement, they may place their child in a private placement, but they do so at their own expense. In Letter to Miller (1997), the Office of Special Education and Rehabilitation Services summarized their response as follows:

> There are three situations in which a student with a disability may attend a private school, and the obligations of a local educational agency change with each of those circumstances. In the first situation, the public school places the student privately because it is the means

by which it determines the student can receive FAPE, and thus, the private placement comes at no cost to the parents. In situation two, the parents place the student at a private school because they believe that the public program has denied them FAPE. In this case, the public school will only be responsible for assuming the costs of the unilateral private placement if there is a finding by a due process hearing officer or a court of law that the district denied the student FAPE. In the third situation, the parent elects to place the child privately as a matter of personal preference, and seeks services from the district. The Department of Education has consistently interpreted the obligations in this area to mean that some, but not all, private school students with disabilities are entitled to receive the services that they would receive if attending public school, and that the requirement to ensure "equitable participation" for this group applies only to federal funds. (p. 1)

The case of *Clevenger v. Oakridge School Board* (1984) is illustrative of the issue of placement in a private program at school district cost. In this case, a high school student who was identified as having serious emotional disturbance, impulsivity, aggressiveness, and difficulties learning from his mistakes was in need of a residential placement where he could be provided with an education to meet his unique needs. The school district agreed with this and selected Riverbend, a residential school with psychiatric treatment available that is part of the Lakeshore Mental Health Institute in Knoxville, Tennessee. The mother disagreed with the school district's selection and requested that they place Richard in the Brown School in San Marcos, Texas. All mental health professionals consulted agreed that the school district's choice of Riverbend was not appropriate for Richard because (a) he needed a long-term placement of at least 2 years, which was not provided there; (b) he required a secure, locked facility, also not available at Riverbend; and (c) the staff at Riverbend did not want Richard to attend because they stated that he was not sufficiently cooperative to allow its program to work. In contrast, the Brown School met the requirements of long-term treatment, locked wards, and willingness to admit Richard into its program. The school supported its selection of a least restrictive appropriate placement by stating that (a) it only needed to address Richard's educational needs, (b) it did not need to take into account Richard's oppositional behavior and runaway tendencies, and (c) Richard could take advantage of the educational program if he was motivated to do so. The Court disagreed, stating that

> The Board's approach unfortunately ignores both reality and its obligations under the Act. As all the psychiatric testimony in this case clearly established, Richard's main learning problem is his INABILITY TO COOPERATE with authority. Accordingly, the only appropriate placement for Richard is one which specifically takes into account and provides for this lack of cooperation. The Act requires that all "special education" students be provided with "specially designed instruction, at no cost to parents or guardian, to meet the UNIQUE needs of a handicapped child." 20 U.S.C. 1401(16) (emphasis added where capitalized). It would be disingenuous at best for us to find that placing Richard in an institution that does not want him and which claims to be unsuitable for him will meet his unique educational needs.

The school district also brought up the issue of the cost of the placement. The Court, noted that consideration of cost is a legitimate concern but is

> only relevant when choosing between several options, all of which offer an "appropriate" education. When only one is appropriate, then there is no choice. . . . Given the

magnitude of the costs involved, it would be the wiser course to spend more on a program that has a chance to work rather than less on one that has no chance at all. (*Clevenger v. Oakridge School Board,* 1984)

IDEA, with support from court decisions, states that placement along the continuum of services must be based on the needs of the child and the LRE in which it is most likely that the child will be successful. The appropriateness of the program should be considered first and then the LRE in which it can be provided should be identified. The issue should not be the selection of the appropriate program and then the determination of the least "costly" environment selected as opposed to the "least restrictive" environment.

Parental Reimbursement

When parents decide to unilaterally place their child in a private school, the issue often arises as to who is responsible for the cost of this placement. In *Florence County School District Four v. Carter* (1993), the U.S. Supreme Court addressed this issue of reimbursement for unilateral placement of a child in a private school. In this case, the school district proposed an IEP that the parents believed was inadequate to meet the needs of their child, so they placed her at Trident Academy, a school that specialized in treating children with disabilities. Trident was not state approved but provided evidence that, although it did not comply with all procedures in IDEA, it had provided the child an "appropriate" education. Evidence of the appropriateness of the education included (a) quarterly evaluations, (b) low teacher–student ratios, (c) an educational plan that allowed her to receive passing marks and progressive movement from grade to grade, and (d) significant academic progress in which her reading comprehension had risen three grade levels in 3 years. Eventually, the District Court ruled in favor of the parents, and the school district appealed to the Supreme Court. The school district argued that because Trident Academy was not a state-approved school, it could not be ordered to reimburse the parents for the unilateral placement. The Supreme Court disagreed and stated:

> As the Court of Appeals noted, "it hardly seems consistent with the Act's goals to forbid parents from educating their child at a school that provides an appropriate education simply because that school lacks the stamp of approval of the same public school system that failed to meet the child's needs in the first place." (*Florence County School District Four v. Carter,* 1993, p. 356)
>
> Accordingly, we disagree with the Second Circuit's theory that "a parent may not obtain reimbursement for a unilateral placement if that placement was in a school that was not on [the State's] approved list of private" schools. . . . Parents' failure to select a program known to be approved by the State in favor of an unapproved option is not itself a bar to reimbursement. (*Florence County School District Four v. Carter,* 1993, p. 366)

The Supreme Court ordered reimbursement to the parents for the placement, stating that

> There is no doubt that Congress has imposed a significant financial burden on States and school districts that participate in IDEA. Yet public educational authorities who want to avoid reimbursing parents for the private education of a disabled child can do one of two

things: give the child a free appropriate public education in public setting, or place the child in an appropriate private setting of the State's choice. This is IDEA's mandate, and school officials who conform to it need not worry about reimbursement claims. (*Florence County School District Four v. Carter,* 1993, p. 366)

Two later cases support this decision (*Reese by Reese v. Board of Education of Bismarck R-V School District,* 2002; *Stockton by Stockton v. Barbour County Board of Education,* 1995). In *Stockton,* a high school student was unilaterally placed in a private residential placement. This placement occurred after numerous attempts by the student's family to encourage the school district to develop and provide an appropriate education for Blaise. In reviewing the decision as to the appropriateness of the private school setting and the parent's claim for reimbursement, the Court reviewed the hearing officer reports and the student's progress reports, including attendance records at both the private and public school settings. They found that Blaise made little to no progress in the public school and attended a minimal number of days, whereas at the private school he had appropriate attendance and was progressing at a rapid rate. In summary, the school district had not seriously considered the private school placement (based on their decision to request funding for services in the public school setting prior to a placement meeting occurring), and then had not provided services that were included in the hearing officer's order and on the IEP. All experts but one had concluded that Blaise would be harmed by inclusion in the general education program. As a result of these findings, the school board's claim that the parent should not receive reimbursement was not supported. In fact, the Court stated that

> In balancing the harms, the Court finds that there will be irreparable harm to Blaise if the injunction is not issued in that he will be removed from the first school setting where he has achieved and not failed, and that for the short term, at least, probably through the end of this school year, he would be back in an environment where, he told Dr. Johnston, he would "get his butt kicked" by his peers. He has difficulty adjusting to new situations and does not have the skills to succeed in a nonstructured setting.
>
> The harm to the Board is financial. It does not at this time have the grant money allotted to Blaise and will have to pull the funds from some other part of the budget. It is likely, however, that the State will eventually reimburse these funds, and it receives money from the Federal government to do so. Thus, any harm to the Barbour County Board of Education is not irreparable.

This same issue of unilateral placement in a private school was addressed in *Reese.* In *Reese,* an elementary-age child had been identified as having emotional and mental illness, and was hospitalized at Hawthorn Psychiatric Center during the summer before his first-grade year and again in the spring of that same year. The school district provided services during Spencer's second-grade year and promoted him to third grade. During Spencer's third-grade year, his parents again placed him at Hawthorn and, after his release, at Edgewood Children's Center, a residential school for children with emotional and behavioral problems with authorization from the Missouri Department of Mental Health (DMH). The DMH paid for the residential and transportation costs for Spencer's placement, while the school district paid for the educational portion of this placement.

The problems arose when Spencer returned to his home district after his 4-month stay at Edgewood. The school district developed an IEP that provided homebound services, and when this placement did not work, no further services were provided. When the parents filed for a due process hearing, the school district agreed to pay for "day treatment" services at Edgewood if the Missouri Department of Elementary and Secondary Education would fund the transportation and living expenses. When they did not receive a response from the state department, the school district notified the parents that Spencer would be placed in a day treatment center in an adjoining county. The parents rejected this placement, unilaterally placed Spencer in Edgewood Children's Center and filed for due process, including a request for reimbursement for costs involved in this private school placement.

In reviewing the issue of whether reimbursement for private education is appropriate, the Court noted that reimbursement for costs are appropriate only when (a) the school district has failed to provide the child with an FAPE, and (b) the private school could provide an appropriate placement. Following the guidelines, the Court found that

> The overwhelming evidence showed that Edgewood was clearly a more restrictive placement than necessary, failed to provide Spencer with the opportunity to interact with nondisabled peers and benefit from exposure to positive behaviors, emphasized improvement in social skills over academic progress, and removed Spencer from his home, family, and friends which bolstered Spencer's separation anxiety and manifested itself in an increase of aggressive and violent behavior by Spencer.

Thus, in this case, the school could provide an appropriate program for Spencer in the LRE. That being the case, the parents were not eligible for reimbursement for expenses and costs resulting from their unilateral placement.

As with earlier cases, the issue of reimbursement for parental unilateral placement in private school settings is a contested issue. In a time when school districts are seeing budget restrictions and concerns for identifying ample funding to provide services for all children, the issue of appropriate placements outside the public school is a subject of concern. For parents, the issue of appropriateness of the services offered by the school often vies with their view of the needs of their child. The resultant disagreement and unilateral placement over the school district's decision continues to place parents at risk of nonreimbursement.

Religious Groups

Another area of controversy is the development of a specific district to provide special education services for religious groups. The U.S. Supreme Court addressed this issue in *Board of Education of Kiryas Joel Village School District v. Grumet* (1994). In this situation, the Supreme Court struck down as unconstitutional a New York State act creating a special school district for a religious community, the village of Kiryas Joel, which is a community of Satmar Hasidic Jews. The Supreme Court noted that it was impossible under the statute passed for the state to stay neutral in the melding of state and religion, and it struck down the law as being unconstitutional. Thus, the LRE requirement as implemented through mainstreaming does not require that parents give up their constitutional right to practice their religion, nor does it allow the state to single out a particular religion for special treatment.

Funding Limitations

The Court's opinion in *A. W. v. Northwest R-1 School District* (1987), which was previously discussed, clearly recognized that there are financial factors to consider when determining the LRE. This position has been accepted and followed by other circuits with the same reasoning. In *Barnett v. Fairfax County School Board* (1991), the Fourth Circuit Court of Appeals was presented with the question of whether the school board could centralize special education services in light of limited funding. The child initiating this issue was a high school student with a hearing impairment who required a cued speech interpreter. The school district had centralized these services so they were provided away from the neighborhood school. The centralized services resulted in the child travelling a longer distance, and the parents objected to it. As a result, the parents sought damages and requested that the Court order the school to provide the same services in the neighborhood school. The Court stated in its opinion

> At the outset, we note that Congress made two deliberate legislative decisions in enacting the EHA. First, Congress chose to leave the section of educational policy and methods where they traditionally have resided—with state and local school officials. . . . In addition, Congress's goal was to bring handicapped children into the public school system and to provide them with an education tailored to meet their particular needs. . . . We believe that a congressional mandate that dictates the substance of educational programs, policies and methods would deprive school officials of the flexibility so important to their tasks. Ultimately, the Act mandates an education for each handicapped child that is responsive to his or her needs, but leaves the substance and the details of that education to state and local school officials. (*Barnett v. Fairfax County School Board*, 1991, pp. 151–152)

Therefore, funding, although an issue, cannot be the ultimate deciding factor in the selection of the LRE for a child with a disability, but it can be one of the factors weighed. In this case, the Court found that because an appropriate education was available and was provided in the LRE, it was not necessary to duplicate a costly and specialized program at the local high school when one was already available.

Summary

The origin of the principle of LRE can be traced to *Wyatt v. Stickney* (1971), where deinstitutionalization resulted because persons who were involuntarily committed for services did not receive those services and the institutions were ordered by the Court to release those persons being held. The result of this case was the IDEA principle that the preferred placement for children was the general education classroom unless their educational program could not be accomplished without their removal from that setting. Returning to *Brown v. Board of Education* (1954), the principle also reflected the belief in the "separate is never equal" doctrine.

EACHA of 1974 is considered the legislative basis for the LRE because it included as one of its purposes the assurance that children with disabilities were receiving an FAPE in the LRE. Subsequent reauthorizations continued to use the same language as the original legislation.

The courts noted the "very strong preference" in IDEA that children with disabilities be educated with children without disabilities. The courts also determined that IDEA requires the school district to determine if the same benefits that were available in the segregated facility could *feasibly* be provided in the public school. The courts determined that IDEA did not promise the best setting, but rather an educational setting where the student's needs could be met with the preference being the setting that occurs in the LRE.

Major areas of controversies concerning the LRE include placement issues and the selection of educational services as a factor in the placement, mainstreaming and inclusion, placement in neighborhood schools, placement in private schools, parental reimbursement for private school placement, obligations of religious schools, and funding limitations. Currently, the courts in a number of circuits, as well as the Supreme Court, have indicated that the LRE provisions of IDEA require full inclusion in the regular classroom with supplementary aids and services as the preferred site whenever possible. However, factors such as disruption of the education of other children, financial resources, and the expertise of the LEA personnel may be considered in the decision of the appropriateness of the placement.

In conclusion, there is a growing belief that the goal of IDEA is for the child with disabilities to be provided an education that includes not only academic instruction, but also interaction with his or her peers. The result of this belief is that there is a growing emphasis on the provision of a continuum of alternative placements so students might participate in the regular classroom, regardless of the severity of their disability.

Questions for Discussion

1. How did the concept of deinstitutionalization impact the delivery of special education services?

2. How is the LRE concept similar to, and different from, the concepts of mainstreaming and inclusion?

3. Explain the differences in the *Roncker* test, the *Daniel R. R.* test, and the *Rachel H.* test?

4. Discuss how the courts have reinforced Congress's preference for educating children in their "natural environment," meaning at home for children birth through age 3 and in general education classrooms for those children ages 3 and older.

Websites for Further Exploration

Continuum of Alternative Placements
www.specialchild.com/archives/ia-042.html
barrier-free.arch.gatech.edu/
www.fragilex.org/html/continuum.htm

Least Restrictive Environment Principle
www.lrecoalition.org/
ericec.org/digests/e629.html

Inclusion
www.bridges4kids.org/articles/9-03/TASH9-03.html#top
www.caselink.education.ucsb.edu/caselink/case1/partVI/principal/princ_full.html
ericec.org/faq/incluson.html
www.uni.edu/coe/inclusion/
www.circleofinclusion.org/english/formsarticles/Articles/articleindex.html

LRE Litigation
www.ed.gov/about/offices/list/oii/nonpublic/idea1.html
www.futureofchildren.org/usr_doc/vol7no3ART9.pdf
www.cec.sped.org/pp/idea-b.htm#15

ILLUSTRATING THE LAW

Briefing of:
Mattie T. v. Holladay,
No. DC-75-31-s (N. D. Miss. January 26, 1979)
(consent decree)

FACTS: A class action lawsuit was filed in 1975 against state officials charged with operating Mississippi's public schools (hereafter "the Department") on behalf of all school-age children with disabilities in the state. The suit challenged (a) the denial of special education services to children with disabilities who were either excluded from school, placed in inappropriate special education programs (SEPs), or neglected in regular education classes; (b) the existence of segregated and isolated SEPs; (c) the use of racially and culturally discriminatory procedures; and (d) the absence of procedural safeguards to review the decisions of school officials.

Plaintiffs filed a motion for summary judgment based on EHA (see 20 U.S.C. § 1401 *et seq.*). That motion was granted after the Court found that the plaintiffs were denied the following: (a) procedural safeguards, including prior notice and a due process hearing; (b) a program to locate and identify all children with disabilities in the state; (c) racially and culturally nondiscriminatory tests and procedures used to classify them as disabled and place them in SEPs; and

(d) educational programs that were in normal school settings with nondisabled children to the maximum extent appropriate. When the Court granted the plaintiffs' motion, it ordered the Department to submit an annual plan for fiscal year 1978. Plaintiffs took issue with that submitted plan and filed objections. The parties thereafter agreed to the entry of the instant consent decree.

ORDER: The Court ordered the Department to institute several new policies and written regulations for the benefit of children with disabilities. The two most significant issues are addressed here.

1. _"Child find" program_—The Department was required to create a program to make all relevant agencies aware of the district's children with disabilities. The Department was to appoint a director of the program and widely publicize the program's function. The director was to correspond to all agencies that might have knowledge of children with disabilities in need of services, make personal contacts with those agencies, and submit written reports of the program's progress.

The Department was also required to issue parent information booklets to parents of children in SEPs or being evaluated for special programs. Along with the information in the booklet, the Department was responsible for providing an oral explanation.

2. _Least restrictive environment_—The Department was required to collect information from all state agencies responsible for educating or caring for children with disabilities in order to determine whether all local school districts were placing children with disabilities in the LRE. The Court's consent decree provided several definitions to be used in the collection of this information:

a. "regular class with resource room services" was to mean those services that supplement, but do not replace, the basic core academic program received by students in a regular class. Resource room services were to include tutoring and special skill development.

b. "self-contained special classrooms with part-time instruction in a regular class" meant at least two class periods each day in programs with nondisabled children in the same age range, one of which was to be an academic subject (e.g., mathematics, science, reading, or social studies) and one of which was to be in such subjects as art, music, or physical education.

The Department was charged with monitoring local school districts to ensure child placement in the LRE. The Department was to take action when (a) the number of children with disabilities being educated with nondisabled children was too low, (b) special education was being provided in a segregated or isolated manner, or (c) special education was being provided away from the regular school building. If any of these conditions were discovered at a local school district, the district was to submit a written justification (e.g., based on IEPs) within 14 days. The following criteria were established to determine whether the prohibited practices were justified:

1. No special or separate classes, or removal of children with disabilities from regular classes, was to occur unless the nature or severity of the child's disability was such that education in regular classes could not be achieved.

2. No child was to be placed in a setting where he or she could not participate with nondisabled peers, unless the child's IEP specifically stated otherwise.

3. No children with disabilities were to be placed in a building separate from the regular school building unless certain specific conditions existed.

ILLUSTRATING THE LAW THROUGH DISCUSSION

If any local school district did not comply with the previous requirements, the SEP would not be approved by the State Department of Education and, therefore, would not receive funding. In 1975, the same year as the passage of P.L. 94–142, a class action suit was filed on behalf of 26 children who were disabled or who were allegedly disabled residing in seven school districts in Mississippi. One of the two most significant issues addressed in the consent decree was that related to LRE. What policies and procedures would you recommend that the state of Mississippi institute to meet the mandate of LRE and still protect the rights of children with disabilities?

References

A. W. v. Northwest R-1 School District, 813 F.2d 158 (8th Cir. 1987), *cert. denied,* 484 U.S. 874, 108 S.Ct. 144 (1987).

Barnett v. Fairfax County School Board, 927 F.2d 146 (4th Cir. 1991), *cert. denied,* 502 U.S. 859, 112 S.Ct. 175 (1991).

Beth B. v. Lake Bluff School District #65, 282 F.3d 493 (7th Cir. 2002).

Board of Education of the Hendrick Hudson Central School District v. Rowley, 458 U.S. 176, 102 S.Ct. 3034, 73 L.Ed. 2d 690 (1982).

Board of Education of Kiryas Joel Village School District v. Grumet, 512 U.S. 687, 129 L.Ed. 546, 114 S.Ct. 2481 (1994).

Brown v. Board of Education of Topeka, Kansas, 347 U.S. 483, 74 S.Ct. 686, 98 L.Ed. 873, 38 A.L.R. 2d 1180 (1954).

Clevenger v. Oakridge School Board, 744 F.2d 514 (6th Cir. 1984).

Daniel R. R. v. State Board of Education, 874 F.2d 1036 (5th Cir. 1989).

Education for All Handicapped Children Act, 20 U.S.C. § 1400 *et seq.* (1975).

Florence County School District Four v. Carter, 510 U.S. 7, 114 S.Ct. 361, 126 L.Ed. 2d 284 (1993).

Friend, M., & Bursuck, W. D. (1999). *Including students with special needs: A practical guide for classroom teachers* (2nd ed.). Boston: Allyn and Bacon.

Greer v. Rome City School District, 950 F.2d 688 (11th Cir. 1991), *withdrawn,* 956 F.2d 1025 (1992), *and reinstated,* 967 F.2d 470 (1992).

Individuals with Disabilities Education Act Amendments of 1997, 20 U.S.C. § 1400 *et seq.* (1997).

Individuals with Disabilities Education Improvement Act of 2004, P.L. 108–446, § 600 *et seq.,* 118 Stat. 2647 (2005).

Katherine G. by Cynthia G. v. Kentfield School District, 261 F. Supp. 2d 1159 (2003).

Letter to Anonymous, Office of Special Education Programs (Aug. 26, 1996).

Letter to Copenhaver, Office of Special Education Programs (Feb. 12, 1997).

Letter to LaHodd, Office of Special Education Programs (April 6, 1995).

Letter to Miller, Office of Special Education and Rehabilitation Services (Feb. 19, 1997).

Mark A. v. Grant Wood Area Education Agency, 795 F.2d 52 (8th Cir. 1986), *cert. denied,* 480 U.S. 936, 107 S.Ct. 1579 (1987).

Mattie T. v. Holladay, No. DC-75-31-S (N.D. Miss. Jan. 26, 1979).

Murray v. Montrose County School District RE-1J, 51 F.3d 921 (10th Cir. 1995), *cert. denied,* 516 U.S. 909, 116 S.Ct. 278, 133 L.Ed. 2d 198 (1995).

Reese by Reese v. Board of Education of Bismarck R-V School District, 222 F. Supp. 2d 1149 (E.D. Mo. 2002).

Roncker v. Walter, 700 F.2d 1058 (6th Cir. 1983), *cert. denied,* 464 U.S. 864, 104 S.Ct. 196 (1983).

Sacramento City Unified School District v. Rachel H., 14 F.3d 1398 (9th Cir. 1994), *cert. denied,* 129 L.Ed. 2d 813 (1994).

Schuldt v. Mankato Independent School District No. 77, 937 F.2d 1357 (8th Cir. 1991), *cert. denied,* 502 U.S. 1059, 112 S.Ct. 937, 117 L.Ed. 2d 108 (1992).

SEA, School District of Beloit, 25 IDELR 109 (Dec. 21, 1996).

Stockton by Stockton v. Barbour County Board of Education, 884 F. Supp. 201 (N.D. West Va. 1995).

Wyatt v. Stickney, 325 F. Supp. 781 (M.D. Ala. 1971).

CHAPTER SEVEN

Procedural Due Process

GUIDING QUESTIONS

1. How do the disciplinary actions of suspension and expulsion affect student rights under the Fourteenth Amendment?

2. How was the concept of fundamental fairness included in the EAHCA of 1975?

3. What issues have resulted from the interpretation and implementation of the concept of due process in EAHCA?

4. Why are the mediation and due process guidelines essential factors in the provision of rights for children with disabilities?

One of the basic tenets underpinning the democratic government in the United States is codified in the Fifth Amendment to the Constitution. This amendment guarantees that no citizen will have his or her rights to life, liberty, and property removed by the federal government without legal due process. This right to due process is expanded in the Fourteenth Amendment.

Amendment XIV

The Fourteenth Amendment to the Constitution of the United States asserts

> All persons born or naturalized in the United States, and subject to the jurisdiction thereof, are citizens of the United States and of the State wherein they reside. No State shall make or enforce any law which shall abridge the privileges or immunities of citizens of the United States; nor shall any state deprive any person of life, liberty or property, without due process of law; nor deny to any person within its jurisdiction the equal protection of the laws.

Most state constitutions contain provisions, similar to those in the Fourteenth Amendment, guaranteeing these rights, including the right to due process. Even though the due process clause may seem to be simple and straightforward, the question of what constitutes property and liberty interests has been subjected to extensive judicial review. Through legislative and judicial actions, these interests have been expanded to include nontangible rights such as employment, welfare, and education. The interpretation of educational rights continues to be of singular importance to disadvantaged classes such as those with disabilities. The development and expansion of the due process clause has more clearly defined the concepts of life, liberty, and property. It has also defined the minimum actions that are required before a resident of the United States can be deprived of any one of the basic freedoms contained in the Fourteenth Amendment.

Two types of due process are subsumed within the Fourteenth Amendment. The first type is substantive due process, that is, the individual's rights under the law. The second type is procedural due process, that is, a procedure to be used to enforce the rights that are given to the individual by state and federal statutes. Even though education has not been classified within the Constitution as a right, it became a right as a result of its inclusion in state statutes.

Because these rights have been guaranteed by legislation, individuals may bring claims against public entities such as schools for deprivation or denial of these rights. When a court begins to review the record to determine whether a party has a legitimate due process claim under the Fourteenth Amendment, a determination must be made of the occurrence of a deprivation or denial of the right to life, liberty, or property, or a violation of the regulations that defines required or prohibited conduct. In so doing, it is important for the courts to determine whether a violation of due process has occurred. Then, if so determined, the courts must identify the type of violation, either substantive (the actions denying a right guaranteed by law) or procedural (the required procedures protecting those rights).

Early Due Process Litigation

Early due process litigation in the field of education focused on two types of actions that implicated substantive due process. These issues that affected student rights under the Fourteenth Amendment were (a) suspension and/or expulsion from school, based on student behavior and being applied without notification; and (b) exclusion from public school based on disability.

Suspension and/or Expulsion

Suspension and expulsion are two forms of disciplinary action used by schools when students manifest severe behavior that violates school policies or creates danger for other students. Suspension is defined as a student's removal from school for a period of time not more than 10 days, or in some instances, removal from the regular class program to a special site within the school building, commonly known as In School Suspension (ISS). Students who are removed from school often do not receive educational services during the period of their suspension, whereas those assigned to ISS do receive some educational services.

Expulsion, or long-term suspension, is a more serious disciplinary procedure resulting in removal from school for longer than 10 days, often for an indefinite period of time. Generally, students who are expelled do not receive educational services. A subset of expulsion, known as serial suspension, occurs when a student is suspended numerous times consecutively, resulting in *de facto* (*de jure*) expulsion from educational services (Turnbull & Turnbull, 1998; Yell, 1998).

The courts have reviewed a number of cases focusing on both the issue of suspension and/or expulsion from educational placements and the due process procedures that must be used in order for the individual student's rights to be protected. The year 1975 produced the seminal case in educational due process, *Goss v. Lopez*. In *Goss*, the U.S. Supreme Court directly confronted the issue of whether short-term suspensions of students from school were subject to the protections of the due process clause. Several students were suspended from high school without a hearing. The students brought a class action lawsuit, alleging that the suspensions were in violation of the Fourteenth Amendment's due process clause. The majority of the Court held that the suspensions did, in fact, violate the due process clause. In reaching this decision, the Court first analyzed whether the students had a protected interest in education. The Court stated that

> Having chosen to extend the right to an education to people of appellees' class generally, Ohio may not withdraw that right on grounds of misconduct, absent fundamentally fair procedures to determine whether the misconduct has occurred. . . . Although Ohio may not be constitutionally obligated to establish and maintain a public school system, it has nevertheless done so and has required its children to attend. Those young people do not "shed their constitutional rights" at the schoolhouse door. (*Goss v. Lopez*, 1975, p. 736)

The Court clearly found that the students had both a property and liberty interest in education. As a property interest, education is described as one of the most important duties of a state to its residents because it can determine the socioeconomic status of an individual long after leaving the public school system. As a liberty interest, the suspension from school could result in the arbitrary deprivation of the student's "good name," although it was pointed out by the dissent in *Goss* that suspension may become a badge of honor. However, suspension may also attach a stigma to the person, thereby raising questions about, or causing damage to, the student's honor, reputation, and integrity. Therefore, the Court found that

> Students facing temporary suspensions have interests qualifying for protection of the Due Process Clause, and due process requires, . . . that the student be given oral or written notice of the charges against him and, if he denies them, an explanation of the evidence the authorities have and an opportunity to present his side of the story. The Clause requires at least these rudimentary precautions against unfair or mistaken findings of misconduct and arbitrary exclusion from school. (*Goss v. Lopez*, 1975, p. 740)

Exclusion

Another issue related to exclusion from school based on the due process clause focused on children with disabilities. In this situation, the rights guaranteed by *Goss* were meaningless for children with mental retardation, behavior disorders, and other disabilities because they were excluded from even enrolling in public schools where these rights could be accessed.

Two major cases had a significant impact in this area. The first, *PARC v. Pennsylvania,* was heard in 1972. In the case of *PARC* (more fully discussed in Chapters 1, 3, and 5), the Court considered the issue of both procedural and substantive due process as it related to children with disabilities. *PARC* presented the question of whether children with disabilities were denied due process when they were excluded from public education without a hearing. The plaintiffs in *PARC* alleged that they were denied the right to a free appropriate education without procedural due process because they did not receive notification that their children with disabilities would not be allowed to attend public school. Furthermore, the parents had no opportunity to contest the school's labeling of their child as disabled, mentally retarded, or having a behavior problem. The Attorney General of the Commonwealth admitted these allegations, and a stipulated agreement was reached through compromise and negotiations.

The Court exhaustively addressed the procedural requirements of the Fourteenth Amendment and its application to education. It is clear from the *PARC* decision that, in an educational context, the minimum due process requirements under the Fourteenth Amendment are (a) notice of the school's action resulting in a deprivation of a right given by state or federal law, and (b) the opportunity to present evidence in opposition to the proposed school action. The final order of the District Court resulted in a due process hearing procedure, far exceeding the requirements of the Constitution, but considered essential in protecting the rights of children with disabilities.

That same year, *Mills v. Board of Education of the District of Columbia* (1972) was handed down, expanding and supporting the *PARC* decision. In *Mills* (also discussed in Chapters 1, 3, and 5), the plaintiffs were seven Black children who had been identified as disabled. The plaintiffs alleged, and the Court found, that a substantial number of children with disabilities were excluded from public education or education supported by the District of Columbia, and furthermore, that these children were moved, expelled, suspended, and terminated without due process.

The question then was whether due process procedures must be followed in every case to protect the rights of children with disabilities. In attempting to answer this question, the Court stated that before a child is classified as a child with disabilities, he or she should first be evaluated by valid testing conducted by people appropriately trained in test administration. Second, the Court found that the child should not be categorized without considering the sociocultural background to determine if the testing is biased by the child's background. Furthermore, the Court held that no child who has been determined to be a child with a disability might be suspended or expelled for more than 10 days without a hearing to determine why the child was expelled or suspended. In the case of removal from the public school environment, the parents must be notified and given an opportunity to contest the proposed placement. These fundamental due process procedures, which protect the educational rights of children with disabilities, were clearly articulated in *Mills.* Subsequently, the procedural due process rights of parents and children with disabilities, established in *PARC* and *Mills,* were incorporated into EAHCA of 1975 and continued through its amendments, including IDEA of 2004.

Legislation and Due Process Procedures

Due process, as set forth under the Fourteenth Amendment, must be flexible enough to meet the fundamental fairness required of the adjudicatory process. This procedural "fairness" is an integral part of EAHCA and has the foundational purpose of "assur[ing] that the rights of handicapped children and their parents or guardians are protected." To accomplish this goal, an explicit set of procedures was included in the legislation. These due process procedures, based on previous case law and set forth in the Act itself, support and protect the concept of "fairness" and "equity" that permeates this legislation.

Specifically, in Section 615(a), the Act required that an SEA establish and maintain procedures to ensure procedural safeguards for the rights of parents and students. The rights to be protected include the right to be notified of a proposed change in placement for a student, to have specific information included in the notice, to have the notice written in the receiver's native language, to receive a copy of the procedural safeguards, and to have that copy provided to them at specified times (Turnbull, Rainbolt, & Buchele-Ash, 1997).

Section 615(b) outlines the required due process procedures (see Figure 7.1), including the rights given to parents and/or guardians of children when participating in a due process hearing (see Figure 7.2). These procedures go beyond the basic procedural due processes contemplated by the Supreme Court in *Goss* and, instead, embody those requirements expressed in *PARC* and *Mills.*

Figure 7.1
Due Process Procedures in IDEA

(1) An opportunity for the parents of a child with a disability to examine all records relating to such child and to participate in meetings with respect to the identification, evaluation, and educational placement of the child, and the provision of a free appropriate public education to such child, and to obtain an independent educational evaluation of the child;

(2) (A) Procedures to protect the rights of the child whenever the parents of the child are not known, the agency cannot, after reasonable efforts, locate the parents, or the child is a ward of the State, including the assignment of an individual to act as a surrogate for the parents. . . . In the case of—

(Continued)

Figure 7.1 *(Continued)*

     (i) a child who is a ward of the State, such surrogate may alternatively be appointed by the judge overseeing the child's care . . . ; and

     (ii) an unaccompanied homeless youth . . . , the local education agency shall appoint a surrogate. . . .

(B) The State shall make reasonable efforts to ensure the assignment of a surrogate not more than 30 days after there is a determination by the agency that the child needs a surrogate.

(3) Written prior notice to the parents of the child . . . , whenever local educational agency—

(A) proposes to initiate or change; or

(B) refuses to initiate or change; the identification, or educational placement of the child, or the provision of a free appropriate public education to the child;

(4) Procedures designed to assure that the notice . . . is in the native language of the parents, unless it clearly is not feasible to do so;

(5) An opportunity for mediation . . . ;

(6) An opportunity for any party to present a complaint—

(A) with respect to any matter relating to the identification, evaluation, or educational placement of the child, or the provision of a free appropriate public education to such child;

(B) which sets forth an alleged violation that occurred not more than 2 years before the date the parent or public agency knew or should have known about the alleged action that forms the basis for the complaint, or, if the State has an explicit time limitation for presenting such a complaint . . . , in such time as the State allows . . .

(7) (A) Procedures that require either party, or the attorney representing a party, to provide due process complaint notice . . . (which shall remain confidential)—

     (i) to the other party . . . and forward a copy of such notice to the State educational agency; and

     (ii) that shall include—

          (I) the name of the child, the address of the residence of the child (or available contact information in the case of a homeless child), and the name of the school the child is attending;

          (II) in the case of a homeless child or youth . . . , available contact information for the child and the name of the school the child is attending;

          (III) a description of the nature of the problem of the child relating to such proposed initiation or change, including facts relating to such problem; and

          (IV) a proposed resolution of the problem to the extent known and available to the party at the time;

(B) A requirement that a party may not have a due process hearing until the party, or attorney representing the party, files a notice . . .

(8) Procedures that require the State educational agency to develop a model form to assist parents in filing a complaint and due process complaint . . . (IDEA of 2004, P.L. 108–446, § 615[b], 118 Stat. 2647 [2005])

Figure 7.2
Parental Due Process Rights Under IDEA

Any party to any hearing conducted . . . shall be accorded—

(1) the right to be accompanied and advised by counsel and by individuals with special knowledge or training with respect to the problems of children with disabilities;

(2) the right to present evidence and confront, cross-examine, and compel the attendance of witnesses;

(3) the right to a written, or, at the option of the parent, electronic verbatim record of such hearing; and

(4) the right to written, or, at the option of the parents, electronic findings of fact and decisions which findings and decisions—

(A) shall be made available to the public . . . ; and

(B) shall be transmitted to the advisory panel . . . (IDEA of 2004, P.L. 108–446, § 615[h], 118 Stat. 2647 [2005])

Litigation After P.L. 94-142

After the passage of EAHCA, litigation moved from its original focus on substantive due process (clarifying the student's rights to due process) to the interpretation and implementation of procedural due process (the designated and required due process procedures). As a result, the issues forming the basis of more recent suits have revolved around determining the extent of mandatory due process procedures, that is, the requirement for notice to parents or guardians when students are to be evaluated, identified, and/or placed in special education services, the specific content to be included in the notice, the availability of due process hearing and mediation, parental access to the students' records, and the timeliness of the review of alleged violations, especially as it pertains to levels of review and court-ordered remands.

Providing Notice

The major issue addressed in earlier litigation (*Goss, PARC,* and *Mills*) was the provision of notice prior to a denial or abrogation of a student's rights. In addressing this issue, the ensuing legislation differentiates between two types of notice. The first type, written notice, is required for all children (not just those with disabilities) and must be provided to a student prior to any proposed change in the student's program or placement. The other type of notice is a description of the procedural safeguards available to a child with a disability. *In re Child with Disabilities* (1990) clearly illustrates this requirement. The child was a 9-year-old boy who had been initially diagnosed as having a severe speech/language impairment. The school district changed the disabling condition, identified on the IEP, to "mental retardation" without evidence of the parents having been notified of the change in eligibility label and against the belief and desires of the parents. According to the hearing officer's decision, this change should have triggered the prior written notice requirements. . . . However, no written notice of the proposed change was given. The March 17, 1986 I.E.P. itself, which embodies the certification change, cannot be deemed to satisfy the notice requirement. (*In re Child with Disabilities,* 1990, p. 4)

Similarly, in *Max M. v. Thompson* (1984), the issue of verbal versus written notice and the preparation of an IEP for a child without parental input as a result of a lack of notification was the focus. Max M. was a high school student with emotional problems who was in need of psychotherapy. The parents claimed that they were not informed of their right concerning the program and placement of their child until his senior year when it was time for him to graduate and no longer receive services. The school district stated that the parents were "told" about the requirements at an IEP meeting. The U.S. District Court, in deciding that a clear violation of procedural due process rights had occurred, stated the following:

Though numerous conferences took place both in person and over the telephone, the *written* notice requirements . . . were never met, insofar as the regulations required District 203 to inform Mr. and Mrs. M. of their right to a due process hearing and other procedural safeguards. The only possible exception to these violations was the conference prior to Max's junior year . . . attended by Max's private psychiatrist, the Ms, and Dr. Wolter. The testimony . . . concerning Dr. Wolter's comments on a due process hearing suggests that the gist of Wolter's message was unclear. In any case, the communication did not satisfy 34 C.F.R. § 300.504, 505 (1983) because it was oral. (*Max M. v. Thompson,* 1984, p. 1448)

This issue of parental notice was further considered in the case of *Oliver v. Dallas Independent School District* (2003). During Kortney's 4 years in high school, her mother had discussed with teachers and staff concerns about Kortney's difficulty in mathematics. After Kortney failed the Texas Assessment of Academic Skills seven times, she was diagnosed as having a learning disability and allowed to retake the test with modifications. After Kortney graduated, a due process hearing was filed noting that Kortney had never been referred for an assessment for possible learning disabilities even though her mother had expressed concerns about her progress. In addition, Kortney and her mother had never been informed of, or given any notice (written or verbal) of, their procedural rights under IDEA.

The school district requested that the complaint be dismissed because Kortney and her mother had not exhausted all administrative remedies prior to filing for due process and because Kortney had graduated with a regular high school diploma, she had no standing under IDEA. The Court disagreed, stating that the district had failed to inform Kortney of her procedural rights under IDEA; thus, the fact that she had received a general education diploma did not release the school from its obligation to have provided her with services under IDEA. In fact, the Court explained that

Congress could not have intended that the simple act of conferring a high school diploma on a student who was improperly denied services under IDEA could insulate the district from all responsibility for failure to provide [FAPE] or inform the student of her procedural rights under IDEA. (*Oliver v. Dallas Independent School District,* 2003)

When parents are divorced, the issue of written notification becomes somewhat confusing. In *Doe v. Anrig* (1987), the parents of a Brookline, Massachusetts, student (who was labeled as emotionally disturbed and "drug abusing") were divorced with the mother having legal custody of the child, while the father remained financially responsible for any educational expenses. Over a period of 2 years, Timothy lived some of the time with his father, some of the time with his mother, and part of the time in a private psychiatric hospital. In the fall of 1978, the school district reviewed Timothy's medical and psychological reports, and from this information, prepared an IEP signed by the mother. The father did not receive notice of this meeting, nor of the review meeting 2 months later.

After receiving joint custody of Timothy in 1980, the father rejected the IEPs prepared by the Brookline School District and initiated proceedings to recover his costs for private schooling during the years from 1977 to 1979. BSEA ruled that ". . . a non-custodial parent has no right to be involved in the IEP process" and ". . . the non-custodial parent is without legal authority to accept or reject an IEP, and . . . school districts ought not get caught in the middle of warring divorcees" (*Doe v. Anrig,* 1987, p. 428).

The issue of notice and divorced couples, regardless of whether they have joint custody, has not been addressed by federal and state legislation. The legislation speaks only of "parents or guardian" and does not address a situation such as that presented in *Anrig.* However, the U.S. District Court concluded that

> under the Education of the Handicapped Act, Brookline improperly excluded Peter Doe from participating in his son's educational planning . . . Peter Doe had a continuing financial responsibility for his son's educational expenses. It would be imprudent to permit an educational program to be devised without consulting the party responsible for a child's overall education. Because of its failure to notify Peter Doe, Brookline could not properly rely on Jane Doe's acceptance of the IEPs. (*Doe v. Anrig,* 1987, pp. 428–429)

School districts, therefore, must notify *all* individuals who may have a financial responsibility for a child when they plan to initiate or change a program or placement. To do otherwise would appear to violate the due process procedures of IDEA.

Required Content of Notice

Because notice is a required component of due process, school districts must ensure the content of the notice meets the requisite guidelines. According to IDEA 2004, the content of the prior written notice must include the following:

(A) a description of the action proposed or refused by the agency;

(B) an explanation of why the agency proposes or refuses to take the action; and a description of each evaluation procedure, assessment, record, or report the agency used as a basis for the proposed or refused action;

(C) a statement that the parents of a child with a disability have protection under the procedural safeguards . . . , and, if this notice is not an initial referral for evaluation, the means by which a copy of a description of the procedural safeguards can be obtained;

(D) sources for parents to contact to obtain assistance in understanding the provisions of this part;

(E) a description of other options considered by the IEP Team and the reason why those options were rejected; and

(F) a description of the factors that are relevant to the agency's proposal or refusal. (IDEA of 2004, P.L. 108–446, § 615 [c][1], 118 Stat. 2647 [2005])

In addition to the content of a required notice, courts have examined the issue of parental understanding of the information included in the notice. The courts have addressed two different aspects of this issue. The first, in *Tennessee Department of Mental Health & Mental Retardation v. Paul B.* (1996), addresses the ability of a parent to understand a notice clearly describing the requisite components. Paul B. was a child who had been identified as seriously emotionally disturbed and who had required hospitalization as a result of his disability. Paul had a history of negative behavior, which "included depression, stealing, running away, self-mutilation, and threats to kill family members" (*Tennessee Department of Mental Health & Mental Retardation v. Paul B.,* 1996, p. 1468). Paul's father was an active member of his IEP team (known as the M-Team) and received copies of the written notice describing his due process rights. He did not receive any information related to the "stay-put" provision of IDEA, prohibiting the school district from removing the child from the placement that had initiated the controversy. In 1991, the M-Team decided to change Paul's placement from that of residential treatment to day services with him living in his family home. Paul's father disagreed with the interpretation of the M-Team as to his son's placement, stating that he was not provided a clear description of the action. In fact, he understood the document to be in support of a recommendation for residential placement. As a result of the allegations by the father and the school district and the conflicting issues of material fact that would impact the decision, the Appeals Court remanded the case to the District Court for further review. The Court stated that

> we believe it does matter what Paul B.'s father deduced from the discussion with Pinebreeze staff at the M-Team meeting. . . . Under 34 C.F.R. §§ 300.504–505, a clear description of the action proposed or refused by the agency should have been given to Paul B.'s father. Whether or not this procedural requirement was fulfilled is contested. (*Tennessee Department of Mental Health & Mental Retardation v. Paul B.,* 1996, p. 1478)

The case of *Reusch v. Fountain* (1994) addresses the adequacy of the notice if it does not include a description of the ESY option. This case was brought by a group of Maryland children with disabilities who believed they had been denied their right to a consideration of an ESY because they had been provided an inadequate notice. In 1992, the Montgomery County Public Schools sent each parent of a child with a disability an "Invitation to the Annual Review Meeting," which not only indicated the time and place of the meeting and the participants, but also the list of issues to be addressed. Enclosed with this invitation was a copy of a brochure explaining parental rights in the process. Although Maryland law requires four determinations to be made at each annual review, only three were mentioned in the letter provided to the parents:

whether the student has achieved his IEP goals, whether the IEP need be modified, and whether a less restrictive environment can be found for the students. Conspicuous by its absence—in both the letter and the accompanying brochure—was any mention of whether ESY would be appropriate, the fourth determination specifically required under Maryland law. (*Reusch v. Fountain,* 1994, p. 1429)

The Court found the district to be in violation of the due process procedures mandated by IDEA because it failed to provide adequate notice regarding the availability of ESY. It is apparent from these cases that not only the provision of notice of changes in a student's program is essential, but also that the information provided must address all facets of possible programmatic change and be provided in a manner that can be understood by the parents. If this does not occur, parents have the option to challenge the change that the school suggests or refuses by using the mediation and due process hearing options of IDEA.

Parental Access to Records

For parents or guardians to be "true" participants in the development and implementation of their child's education program, as well as to be able to challenge a school's decisions, it is imperative that they have access to their child's education records. IDEA has always contained a requirement that parents be allowed the opportunity to examine *relevant* records concerning their child. This was expanded with the reauthorization in 1997 and again in 2004 to ensure parents have access and opportunity to review *all* records, not just what the school deems as *relevant* records (see IDEA of 2004, P.L. 108–446, § 615[b], 118 Stat. 2647 [2005]). The regulations furnish the schools with guidance in the following areas: type of records that can be accessed, timeliness of school response to request for records, reasonableness of parental request, ability of parents to copy records, provision of a list of individuals who can access student records, a list of the type and location of each record on parental request, and the option for parents to request amendments to the record. These rights guarantee that not only can parents be intimately involved in their child's education program, but also that schools are to be held accountable for what is included in the records kept on each child.

In *Amanda J. v. Clark County School District* (2001), the issue of parental participation being dependent on their ability to review all records to make an informed decision was considered. Amanda J. was a young child who was evaluated by a psychologist and a speech-language pathologist in order to develop an individualized program to meet her unique needs. Although the parents attended all evaluations, the report that was provided to them at the end of the process did not include all information needed for them to fully participate in the development of their child's program. Both evaluators noted the possibility of autism as a diagnosis for Amanda, but this information was neither verbally provided to the parents nor included in the written materials that they received. After the evaluations were completed, Amanda was identified as having difficulties in language, cognition, self-help, and social/emotional areas, and was eligible for special education services under IDEA.

Prior to the initial IEP development meeting, Amanda's mother requested copies of the evaluation results. No records were provided to her until after the IEP was developed, and at that time, she only received a summary of the observations of the psychologist, not the complete records that she requested. Amanda and her family moved to another state shortly after school began. In December of that year, Amanda was evaluated by an independent evaluator and was diagnosed with autism in January of that year. When the parents met with the school to review Amanda's placement for the coming year, they were provided with copies of the previous district's reports noting the possibility of autism. The parents filed for due process, stating that Amanda had been misdiagnosed and thus had been denied FAPE and that they had not been provided access to her records so they could be her advocates and truly participate in the special education process. The Court agreed with the parents, noting that

> The IEP team could not create an IEP that addressed Amanda's special needs as an autistic child without knowing that Amanda was autistic. Even worse, Amanda's parents were not informed of the possibility that their daughter suffered from autism—a disease that benefits from early intensive intervention—despite the fact that the district's records contained test results indicating as much. Not only were Amanda's parents prevented from participating fully, effectively, and in an informed manner in the development of Amanda's IEP, they were not even aware that an independent psychiatric evaluation was recommended, an evaluation that Amanda's mother testified she would have had performed immediately. These procedural violations, which prevented Amanda's parents from learning critical medical information about their child, rendered the accomplishment of the IDEA's goals—and the achievement of a FAPE—impossible. (*Amanda J. v. Clark County School District*, 2001)

Mediation

According to Turnbull and Turnbull (1998), due process is "the right of a citizen to protest before a government takes action with respect to him or her" and "the right to protest actions of the state education agency (SEA) or the local education agency (LEA)" (p. 227). Without this opportunity to challenge the actions of the school district, the purposes of the legislation and its focus on parental participation in the education of their children would be meaningless. This ability to challenge is not only given to the parents or surrogates, but is also given to the school districts. In EAHCA, this right was provided through the option to participate in a due process hearing (see IDEA of 2004, P.L. 108–446, § 615[f], 118 Stat. 2647 [2005]). In the 1997 Amendments to IDEA, an intermediate step was added to provide and to resolve disputes prior to the due process hearing. This provision stated that

> Any State educational agency or local educational agency that receives assistance under this part shall ensure that procedures are established and implemented to allow parties to disputes involving any matter, including matters arising prior to the filing of a complaint . . . to resolve such disputes through a mediation process. (IDEA of 2004, P.L. 108–446, § 615[e][1], 118 Stat. 2647 [2005])

States are required to establish procedures that meet the guidelines under the legislation, although participation in the mediation process is not required (see

Figure 7.3
Mediation Guidelines

> (2) Such procedures shall meet the following requirements:
>
>   (A)   The procedures shall ensure that the mediation process—
>
>   (i)   is voluntary on the part of the parties;
>
>   (ii) is not used to deny or delay a parent's right to a due process hearing . . . or to deny any other rights . . . ; and
>
>   (iii) is conducted by a qualified and impartial mediator who is trained in effective mediation techniques. (IDEA of 2004, P.L. 108–446, § 615[e][2], 118 Stat. 2647 [2005])

Figure 7.3). To expedite this process, states must develop and maintain a list of qualified mediators, bear the costs of all mediation, and establish procedures for times when parents refuse to participate in mediation. State procedures should also provide guidelines that support a timely conclusion of the mediation. Any agreement reached by the parties in the mediation process shall be prepared in a written format and is a legally binding document. All discussions occurring during this process shall be confidential, and neither they nor the written agreement can be used as evidence in any subsequent due process hearing or civil proceeding. Although mediation is a new procedure, parents and school districts participating in the mediation process recommended it as a positive process (Yell, 1998).

Impartial Due Process Hearings

If the disputed issues cannot be resolved during the mediation process, or if mediation is not selected, then a due process hearing may be requested by either the parents or the school district. According to IDEA,

> Whenever a complaint has been received . . . , the parents or local educational agency involved in such complaint shall have an opportunity for an impartial due process hearing, which shall be conducted by the State educational agency or by the local educational agency, as determined by State law or by the State educational agency. (IDEA of 2004, P.L. 108–446, § 615[f][1], 118 Stat. 2647 [2005])

Mandatory Resolution Session.   With the 2004 reauthorization of IDEA, an additional meeting has been added to the due process hearing procedures. This meeting, known as the mandatory resolution session, is required prior to the occurrence of a due process hearing. The resolution session is called by the LEA after either party has requested a due process hearing. This session allows parents and relevant members of the IEP team to meet, discuss the facts of the complaint, and attempt to resolve the issue(s) prior to a due process hearing. If resolution does occur, a written settlement agreement is developed and signed by both parties. If no resolution of the complaint can be made during this session, then the due process hearing may occur. Although the resolution session is mandatory, the parents and the LEA may agree in writing to waive this session or may agree to use the voluntary medication process instead (IDEA of 2004, P.L. 108–446, § 615[f][1][B], 118 Stat. 2647 [2005]).

As has been noted, either party may request a due process hearing, although the parents or guardians of a child with a disability have initiated most cases. In the case of *Yates v. Charles County Board of Education* (2002), the school district was the initiator of the process. Adam Yates, a child with autism, had attended school at a private school for children with autism at public expense. During an IEP review, the district proposed to place the child in a public school classroom. The parents refused this placement and unilaterally placed Adam in a private school and requested that the district pay transportation costs. When no agreement concerning placement and costs could be made, the district requested a due process hearing. The parents stated that the request was premature because they had not filed for costs and the ALJ stated that the school district did not have standing to request a due process hearing. The courts, in overturning the ALJ's decision, stated that

> Under the applicable regulations, CCPS's standing to request a hearing before an ALJ to resolve its dispute with the Yates' concerning the proper placement of Adam for the 2001–2002 year is clear. The regulations expressly provide that either "[a] parent or a public agency may initiate a hearing" before an ALJ when there is a dispute about a child's educational placement. (*Yates v. Charles County Board of Education*, 2002)

An essential ingredient in the procedures outlined by IDEA is the requirement that the hearing be conducted by an impartial hearing officer (or panel of hearing officers) and that there be some degree of finality to the proceedings notwithstanding the ability to appeal at every stage. Some states have a single tier of hearings, meaning that the appeal from the hearing officer is taken directly to the federal District Court. With the single-tiered system, the District Court will consider the findings of the hearing officer but is given the choice to reject or adopt them.

Other states have a two-tiered system. In the two-tiered system, the first appeal is to an appeals panel of the SEA. The District Court still reviews the case and also reviews the decision of the appeals panel. The appeals panel, to be consistent with procedural due process, should give deference to the first (or initial) tier's findings of fact. To do otherwise would in effect deny the parties of the right to a hearing where there is an impartial magistrate (the hearing officer) weighing the credibility of the witnesses and their evidence. The District Court still reviews the case by reviewing the decision of the appeals panel. In either situation, the Court may take additional evidence and decide the matter based on its findings. This was illustrated in the case of *Saucon Valley School District v. Robert and Darlene O.* (2001), in which the decision of the hearing officer was appealed to the appellate panel who

> concluded that Student's IEP was so procedurally and substantively flawed that it denied Student a free and appropriate public education (FAPE). Moreover, the Panel's opinion discussed "appropriate remedies," which included an award of compensatory education to Student, use of a third party to develop an IEP and remedial education for the District's employees. (*Saucon Valley School District v. Robert and Darlene O.*, 2001)

The school district appealed this decision to the Court, stating that the appellate panel exceeded its authority when it not only reviewed the hearing officer's decision, but also ordered its own remedies. The Court

> in reviewing this case on appeal agreed with the district and determined that the appellate panel lacked the authority to order several remedies after it determined the district violated its FAPE obligation. (*Saucon Valley School District v. Robert and Darlene O.*, 2001)

Timeliness of Process

*Final
6*

For a free appropriate education to be provided to a child with a disability, it is essential that any dispute arising from disagreements concerning the evaluation, identification, or placement of a child be completed in a timely manner. Without timelines, it is possible that the rights of the child to an FAPE would be hindered as a result of the length of the mediation and hearing process. Timelines have been established by IDEA Regulations (see Figure 7.4) and incorporated into state statutes, but with the inclusion of an additional required step in the hearing process, questions have been raised about when the timeline begins—prior to, or after, the resolution session (COPAA, 2004).

States have specified timelines, but in some cases these have been abrogated by remands either from the hearing officer or the federal courts. For example, in *Carlisle Area School District v. Scott P.* (1995), the Third Circuit Court of Appeals was presented the issue of whether a remand from the District Court to the appeals panel for clarification of an order under appeal denied the child and parents procedural due process. Scott P. was a 20-year-old young man who had sustained a serious brain injury in a 1980 swimming pool accident resulting in cortical blindness and other physical injuries. The dispute arose when Scott's parents rejected the IEP developed by the school district, stating that it was not

Figure 7.4
Timelines for Due Process Hearings

> (a) The public agency shall ensure that not later than 45 days after the receipt of a request for a hearing—
>
>   (1) A final decision is reached in the hearing; and
>
>   (2) A copy of the decision is mailed to each of the parties.
>
> (b) The SEA shall ensure that not later than 30 days after the receipt of a request for a review—
>
>   (1) A final decision is reached in the review; and
>
>   (2) A copy of the decision is mailed to each of the parties.
>
>   (c) A hearing or reviewing officer may grant specific extensions of time beyond the periods set out in paragraphs (a) and (b) of this section at the request of either party. (IDEA regulations)

appropriate because it resembled the previous year's IEP under which they believed that Scott had not progressed. An evaluation completed at the A. I. duPont Institute at the request of the parents resulted in a recommendation that Scott be placed in an intensive specialized educational program at the Maryland School for the Blind (MSB). The school district disagreed. The parents then requested a due process hearing contesting the district's suggested placement and requesting reimbursement for Scott's education at MSB. The hearing officer found that the school was required to provide residential programming for Scott and awarded him 6 months compensatory education past his twenty-first birthday. Both parties appealed the decision of the hearing officer. The Pennsylvania Special Education Appeals Panel reversed the part of the hearing decision requiring residential programming at MSB but upheld the award of compensatory education. The school district appealed the decision of the Appeals Panel by filing a complaint in the District Court. The District Court remanded the case to the Appeals Panel for clarification. The findings of the Appeals Panel after remand were considered by the District Court, and the Court remanded the case a second time for clarification. After the second clarification, the District Court affirmed the Appeals Panel decision. The parents then made the claim that the District Court violated their procedural right to a final order within 45 days of the parents' request because of the Court's action in remanding the case twice to the Appeals Panel for clarification. The Court of Appeals disagreed with the parents' contention that their rights had been violated and stated that

> To prohibit the court from remanding for clarification would impair the court's ability to review the decision fairly. . . . Thus, while the statute clearly proscribes remands within the state's administrative system, we see no basis for prohibiting judicial remands. (*Carlisle Area School District v. Scott P.*, 1995, p. 526)

Given earlier decisions of the courts regarding the review of administrative decisions (e.g., see *Muth v. Central Bucks School District,* 1988), it is not surprising that the Court in *Carlisle* held that there was no violation of the plaintiff's due process rights and remanded the case to the Appeals Panel for further clarification. As the Court proclaimed, it was for the benefit of the parties rather than to their detriment for the Court to have all information available for review.

Timeliness of a mediation or hearing is an essential component in ensuring the rights of a child with a disability. Even though these timelines may be extended based on hearing officer decisions or court-ordered remands, the legislation supports the completion of the process as *Brown* previously stated with "all deliberate speed."

Summary

When the rights of children with disabilities to receive educational services were examined by the judiciary, the courts uniformly found that the students have both a property and liberty interest in education. Therefore, it is essential that schools avoid unfair or mistaken findings of misconduct and arbitrary exclusion from school through the use of suspension or expulsion. Unfortunately, the Court found that a substantial number of children with disabilities were excluded from public education and that these children were moved, expelled, suspended, and terminated without due process. To protect against this denial of rights, at a minimum, the parents must be notified by the school and provided an opportunity to contest the proposed change of placement through due process procedures as outlined in IDEA.

The concept of fundamental fairness is articulated through the assurance of procedural safeguards, whereby no person can deny another constitutionally protected rights. Legislation was enacted that provided an explicit set of due process procedures based on case law that supports and protects the concepts of "fairness" and "equity" for persons with disabilities.

Following the enactment of EAHCA, the issues that emerged were (a) determining the extent of mandatory due process procedures, that is, the requirement for notice to parents or guardians when students are to be evaluated, identified, and/or placed in special education services; (b) the specific content to be included in the notice; (c) the availability of due process hearing and mediation; (d) parental access to the students' records; and (d) the timeliness of the review of alleged violations.

Without the legislative requirements for mediation and due process combined with the regulatory guidelines providing the opportunity for challenging the actions of both school districts and parents, the purposes of IDEA legislation and its focus on parental participation in the education of their children would be meaningless. Even though education is not considered a constitutional right, the courts have considered it a property and liberty interest created by state statutes. As stated many times before, the state need not provide a free public education, but when it undertakes to do so, it must be provided to all. Therefore, children with disabilities have a property interest in public education, which cannot be taken away without due process of law under the Fourteenth Amendment.

Children with disabilities also have a liberty interest in that the stigma that attaches to a child classified or labeled as disabled, mentally retarded, emotionally disturbed, or physically disabled can cause long-reaching and long-lasting harm. The Supreme Court in *Goss* believed the stigma constituted a deprivation of a liberty interest that could not be imposed without due process of the law. Therefore, the "due process" right was embedded in the legislative mandate for the provision of a free appropriate education for all children with disabilities. To the developers of this legislation, due process was an essential factor in the provision of rights for children with disabilities. This is apparent when one reads IDEA and finds that one of its purposes is ". . . to ensure that the rights of children with disabilities and parents of such children are protected . . ." (IDEA of 2004, P.L. 108–446, § 601 [d][B], 118 Stat. 2647 [2005]). This component of the legislation protects children with disabilities by providing a specific means to hold schools accountable and to allow for parental participation in the educational program. In fact, as Turnbull and Turnbull (1998) succinctly wrote, "without due process, the children would have found that their right to be included in an educational program and to be treated non-discriminatorily (to receive a free appropriate education) would have a hollow ring" (p. 227).

Questions for Discussion

1. How have the Fifth and Fourteenth amendments been used to support special education legislation?
2. Why were suspension and/or expulsion seen as violations of a student's legal due process rights?

Websites for Further Exploration

Due Process
www.usconstitution.net/consttop_duep.html
www.lectlaw.com/files/lws63.htm

Suspension and Expulsion
ideapractices.org/
www.garlikov.com/philosophy/expulsion.htm
www.nces.ed.gov/pubs2003/hispanics/Section2.asp

Exclusion
www.peoples-law.org/education/discipline-process.htm

Parental Rights (Notice, Access to Records)
www.ldonline.org/ld_indepth/parenting/parentsrights.html
www.childdevelopmentinfo.com/learning/rights_LD.shtml
www.fapeonline.org/Parental%20Rights.htm
www.kidsource.com/kidsource/content2/Parents_of_Children.html

Mediation and Impartial Due Process Hearings
www.bridges4kids.org/articles/10-02/Cadre10-02.html
www.harborhouselaw.com/beacon/2001.v1n1.htm
www.ldonline.org/ld_indepth/special_education/due.html
familyeducation.com/article/0,1120,23-8149,00.html
www.open.org/~people1/articles/edu_idea_safeguards.htm

ILLUSTRATING THE LAW

Briefing of:
Max M. and his Parents, Mr. and Mrs. M. v. James R. Thompson, et al.
U.S. District Court, Northern District of Illinois,
Eastern Division 592 F. Supp. 1437
August 13, 1984

FACTS: Max M. is a child with a disability. He attended the New Trier High School in Northfield, Illinois, for the years 1977–1981. The district department of special education referred Max M. for evaluation. Intensive psychotherapy was recommended by the department of special education but was never offered by the school. The following summer, the parents requested that the school provide the therapy. The parents never participated in the development of the IEP, and the IEP never provided for the therapy. The parents obtained and paid for private treatment.

The school district issued a diploma to Max M., and he was no longer eligible for services. The parents brought this action seeking compensatory reimbursement for their expenses relating to the psychiatric treatment.

ISSUE: The case presented three issues. First, whether psychiatric treatment is required to be provided as a related service; second, whether the school failed to comply with the procedural safeguards required by EAHCA; and third, whether the failure to provide procedural safeguards was so egregious as to constitute bad faith.

HELD: The Court held that psychotherapy may be a related service if it could be provided by someone other than a psychiatrist, such as a social worker. The amount paid by the parents that could be recovered would be the cost of providing the service by someone other than a doctor. The Court held that the school had clearly failed to comply with the procedural safeguards required by EAHCA by failing to provide notice to the parents of meetings and failing to include them in the conferences. The Court held that it was a question of fact as to whether the school's procedural violations were sufficient to constitute bad faith.

RATIONALE: In deciding that psychotherapy may be a related service, the Court looked at who actually provided the service and who could provide the service. If the school could have provided the therapy by a social worker, they are required to do so. Just because a doctor provides a service does not mean that someone other than a doctor could not provide the same service.

The Court found that the district had clearly violated the regulations by not giving *written* notice of the right to a due process hearing and other procedural safeguards. The written notice must include a full explanation of the procedural safeguards, even if the parents had attended conferences and been orally notified.

ILLUSTRATING THE LAW THROUGH DISCUSSION

1. What if the parents acknowledge receiving copies of their procedural due process rights from another source?

2. Or, what if the parents were represented by an attorney?

References

Amanda J. by Annette J. v. Clark County School District, 260 F.3d 1106 (9th Cir. 2001).

Carlisle Area School District v. Scott P., 62 F.3d 520 (3rd Cir. 1995).

COPAA (Council of Parent Attorneys and Advocates). (2004). H.R. 1350 Individuals with Disabilities Improvement Act of 2004 compared to IDEA '97. Warrenton, VA: Author.

Doe v. Anrig, 651 F. Supp. 424 (1987).

Education for All Handicapped Children Act, 20 U.S.C. § 1400 *et seq.* (1975).

Goss v. Lopez, 419 U.S. 565, 95 S.Ct. 729, 42 L.Ed. 2d 725 (1975).

In re Child with Disabilities, 16 EHLR 538 (SEA Tenn. 1990).

Individuals with Disabilities Education Act, 20 U.S.C. § 1400 *et seq.* (1997).

Individuals with Disabilities Education Improvement Act of 2004, P.L. 108–446, § 601 *et seq.*, 118 Stat. 2647 (2005).

Max M. v. Thompson, 592 F. Supp. 1437 (N.D. Ill. 1984).

Mills v. Board of Education of the District of Columbia, 348 F. Supp. 866 (D.D.C. 1972).

Muth v. Central Bucks School District, 839 F.2d 113 (3rd Cir. 1988), *rev'd sub nom.*, Dellmuth v. Muth,

491 U.S. 223, 109 S.Ct. 2397, 105 L.Ed. 2d 181 (1989).

Oliver ex rel. Oliver v. Dallas Independent School District, 40 IDELR 10 (N.D. Tex. 2003).

PARC (Pennsylvania Association for Retarded Children) v. Pennsylvania, 343 F. Supp. 279 (E.D. Pa. 1972).

Reusch v. Fountain, 872 F. Supp. 1421 (D. Md. 1994).

Saucon Valley School District v. Robert and Darlene O. ex rel. Jason O., 785 A.2d 1069 (2001).

Tennessee Department of Mental Health & Mental Retardation v. Paul B., 88 F.3d 1466 (6th Cir. 1996).

Turnbull, H. R., & Turnbull, A. P. (1998). *Free appropriate public education: The law and children with disabilities* (5th ed.). Denver: Love.

Turnbull, H. R., Rainbolt, K., & Buchele-Ash, A. (1997). *Individuals with Disabilities Education Act: Digest and significance of 1997 Amendments.* Lawrence: Beach Center on Families and Disability, The University of Kansas.

Yates v. Charles County Board of Education, 212 F. Supp. 2d 470 (D. Md. 2002).

Yell, M. L. (1998). *The law and special education.* Upper Saddle River, NJ: Merrill/Prentice Hall.

CHAPTER EIGHT

Parental Participation

GUIDING QUESTIONS

1. What roles did IDEA specify as parent roles?

2. Who is a parent?

3. Why does IDEA place a "high premium" on parental involvement?

The fight to obtain educational access for children with disabilities was initially begun by parents. Thus, attempts to redress the inequity in educational opportunities have long been the parental standard of action. Parents initially organized advocacy groups (e.g., The Arc) to assist them in obtaining educational benefits for their children. Then, the advocacy groups supported the parents as they initiated litigation on behalf of the children. Parents also acted as lobbyists in state and federal legislative arenas. Active parental advocacy led to the inclusion of parents as required members of the educational team for children with disabilities. Parental rights and procedural safeguards were also delineated in the 1975 enactment of EHA. These rights and responsibilities have been further expanded with each reauthorization of IDEA.

IDEA and Parental Participation

A parent, according to IDEA, is

(A) a natural, adoptive, or foster parent of a child (unless a foster parent is prohibited by State law from serving as a parent); (B) a guardian (but not the State if the child is a ward of the State); (C) an individual acting in the place of a natural or adoptive parent (including a grandparent, stepparent, or other relative) with whom the child lives, or an individual who is legally responsible for the child's welfare; or (D) . . . an individual assigned . . . to be a surrogate parent. (IDEA of 2004, P.L. 108–446, § 602[23], 118 Stat. 2647 [2005])

"Parent" has been interpreted in the federal regulations to include not only a natural parent, but also a guardian, a surrogate parent(s) appointed by the LEA, and anyone acting in the place of a parent such as a relative or anyone else with whom the child lives (34 C.F.R. § 300.19). A surrogate parent may be anyone who is not an employee of the SEA, the LEA, or any other agency that is involved in the education or care of the child (IDEA of 2004, P.L. 108–446, § 615[b][2], 118 Stat. 2647 [2005]). The state cannot be considered a surrogate parent, even if the child is a ward of the state. However, a child's foster parents may serve as surrogate parents if the following conditions are met:

(A) the natural parents' rights have been terminated;
(B) the foster parent has a long-term relationship with the child;
(C) the foster parent is willing to participate in the role of "parent"; and
(D) no conflict of interest occurs with the foster parent assuming that role. (34 C.F.R. § 300.20)

Standards and the Law

CEC Standard 1: Foundations
PRAXIS Standard: Legal and Societal Issues

It is through the vigilance of parents that the provisions of IDEA can be ensured. These rights are enumerated in IDEA and include parental participation in and consent for the evaluation and reevaluation (see Figures 8.1 and 8.2) of their child.

The parent is also a required member of the IEP team (IDEA of 2004, P.L. 108–446, § 614[d][1][B], 118 Stat. 2647 [2005]) and is essential in making decisions concerning programming and placement of his or her child with a disability. The legislation's clear intent to include parents is apparent when it states that

> Each local educational agency or State educational agency shall ensure that the parents of each child with a disability are members of any group that makes decisions on the educational placement of their child. (IDEA of 2004, P.L. 108–446, § 614[e], 118 Stat. 2647 [2005])

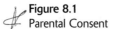

Figure 8.1
Parental Consent

> Consent for initial evaluation—The agency proposing to conduct an initial evaluation to determine if the child qualifies as a child with a disability . . . shall obtain informed consent from the parent of such child before conducting the evaluation. Parental consent for evaluation shall not be construed as consent for placement for receipt of special education and related services.
>
> Consent for services—An agency that is responsible for making a free appropriate public education available to a child with a disability . . . shall seek to obtain informed consent from the parent of such child before providing special education and related services to the child.
>
> Absence of consent for initial evaluation—If the parents of such child does not provide consent for an initial evaluation . . . , or the parent fails to respond to a request to provide the consent, the local educational agency may pursue the initial evaluation of the child by utilizing the procedures described . . . except to the extent inconsistent with State law relating to such parental consent.
>
> Absence of consent for services—If the parent of such child refuses to consent to services . . . , the local educational agency shall not provide special education and related services to the child by utilizing the procedures described in section 615. (IDEA of 2004, P.L. 108–446, § 614[a][1][D], 118 Stat. 2647 [2005])

Do not have to have parental consent for observations or screening; but, if you will use this info for placement then you must have consent (even for IRG programs)

Standards and the Law

CEC Standard 7: Instructional Planning
CEC Standard 8: Assessment
CEC Standard 10: Collaboration
PRAXIS Standard: Delivery of Services to Students with Disabilities

Figure 8.2
Parental Consent for Reevaluations

> (3) Parental consent—Each local educational agency shall obtain informed parental consent . . . prior to conducting any reevaluation of a child with a disability, except that such informed parental consent need not be obtained if the local educational agency can demonstrate that it had taken reasonable measures to obtain such consent and the child's parent has failed to respond. (IDEA of 2004, P.L. 108–446, § 614[c][3], 118 Stat. 2647 [2005])

Parental rights have also been outlined in legislation concerning due process and procedural safeguards. Parents have the right to examine all records and receive prior written notice of any proposed changes in their child's educational program or placement (see Figure 8.3).

To support parental participation in the IDEA process, parents have been given the right "to inspect and review any education records relating to their children that are collected, maintained, or used by the agency . . ." (34 C.F.R. § 399.562). In conjunction with this right, they may request explanations and interpretations of the records, request copies of records, and have a representative inspect and review the records. This legal support of parental records access is necessary to allow parents to fulfill their obligations to fully participate in the development and implementation of special programming for their child with a disability.

Confidentiality of Records

Parents have been concerned that when their child is included in the special education process that two areas of their lives are no longer under their control: their privacy and their claim to confidentiality of records (Turnbull, Beegle, & Stowe, 2001; Turnbull, Turnbull, Erwin, & Soodak, 2006). To address this issue, in 1974, Congress passed the Family Educational Rights and Privacy Act (FERPA), also known as the Buckley Amendment. This Act specifically deals with the companion issues of privacy and confidentiality (Wright & Wright, 2000).

Figure 8.3
Procedural Safeguards

The procedures required by this section shall include the following—

(1) An opportunity for the parents of a child with a disability to examine all records relating to such child and to participate in meetings with respect to the identification, evaluation, and educational placement of the child, and the provision of a free appropriate public education to such child, and to obtain an independent educational evaluation of the child;

(2) Procedures to protect the rights of the child whenever the parents of the child are not known, the agency cannot, after reasonable efforts, locate the parents, or the child is a ward of the State, including the assignment of an individual to act as a surrogate for the parents, which surrogate who shall not be an employee of the State educational agency, the local educational agency, or any other agency that is involved in the education or care of the child

In the case of—

(i) a child who is a ward of the State, such surrogate may alternatively be appointed by the judge overseeing the child's care provided that the surrogate meets the requirements of this paragraph; and

(ii) an unaccompanied homeless youth as defined in section 725(6) of the McKinney-Vento Homeless Assistance Act (42 U.S.C. 11434a(6)), the local educational agency shall appoint a surrogate . . .

(3) Written notice to the parents of the child. . . . whenever the local educational agency—

(A) proposes to initiate or change; or

(B) refuses to initiate or change, the identification, evaluation, or educational placement of the child, or the provision of a free appropriate public education to the child.

(4) Procedures designed to ensure that the notice required by paragraph (3) is in the native language of the parents, unless it clearly is not feasible to do so.

(5) An opportunity for mediation in accordance with subsection (e).

(6) An opportunity for any party to present a complaint—

(A) with respect to any matter relating to the identification, evaluation, or educational placement of the child, or the provision of a free appropriate public education to such child; and

(B) which sets forth an alleged violation that occurred not more than 2 years before the date the parent or public agency knew or should have known about the alleged action that forms the basis of the complaint, or, if the State has an explicit time limitation for presenting such a complaint . . . , in such time as the State allows . . .

(7) (A) Procedures that require either party, or the attorney representing a party, to provide due process complaint notice . . . (which shall remain confidential)—

(i) to the other party, . . . and forward a copy of such notice to the State educational agency; and

(ii) that shall include—

(I) the name of the child, the address of the residence of the child (or available contact information in the case of a homeless child), and the name of the school the child is attending;

(II) in the case of a homeless child or youth . . . available contact information for the child and the name of the school the child is attending;

(III) a description of the nature of the problem of the child relating to such proposed initiation or change, including facts relation to such problem; and

(IV) a proposed resolution of the problem to the extent known and available to the party at the time;

(B) A requirement that a party may not have a due process hearing until the party, or the attorney representing the party, files a notice that meets the procedures that require the State educational agency to develop a model form to assist parents in filing a complaint and due process complaint notice . . . (IDEA of 2004, P.L. 108–446, § 615[b], 118 Stat. 2647 [2005])

[handwritten margin note: Can Lose Fed Funds if released records w/o parental consent]

FERPA states that no educational agency or institution shall receive federal funds if they have a policy or practice of releasing educational records without written consent of the parents. The only exceptions are for (a) other school officials with a legitimate educational interest in the student, (b) officials of other school systems in which the student wants to enroll, (c) certain other authorized officers of state and federal government, and (d) certain judicial and law enforcement agencies.

It is important to determine what are considered educational records within the meaning of FERPA and IDEA. By regulation, the Secretary of Education has defined "education records" under FERPA as

(A) those records, files, documents, and other materials which—

  (i) contain information directly related to a student; and

  (ii) are maintained by an educational agency or institution or by a person acting for such agency or institution.

(B) The term "education records" does not include—

  (i) records of instructional, supervisory, and administrative personnel and educational personnel ancillary thereto which are in the sole possession of the maker

Standards and the Law

CEC Standard 8: Assessment
CEC Standard 9: Professional and Ethical Practice
INTASC Standard 10: Collaboration, Ethics, and Relationships
PRAXIS Standard: Legal and Societal Issues

> thereof and which are not accessible or revealed to any other person except a substitute;
>
> (ii) records maintained by a law enforcement unit of the educational agency or institution that were created by that law enforcement unit for the purpose of law enforcement;
>
> (iii) in the case of persons who are employed by an educational agency or institution but who are not in attendance at such agency or institution, records made and maintained in the normal course of business which relate exclusively to such person in that person's capacity as an employee and are not available for use for any other purpose; or
>
> (iv) records on a student who is eighteen years of age or older, or is attending an institution of post-secondary education, which are made or maintained by a physician, psychiatrist, psychologist, or other recognized professional or paraprofessional acting in his professional or paraprofessional capacity, or assisting in that capacity, and which are made, maintained, or used only in connection with the provision of treatment to the student, and are not available to anyone other than persons providing such treatment, except that such records can be personally reviewed by a physician or other appropriate professional of the student's choice. (34 C.F.R. § 99.3)

FERPA provides parents with the right to inspect, review, and copy all educational records pertaining to their child and to receive these copies within a maximum 45-day timeline. The school may charge a minimal fee for copying these records but may not charge parents for the time incurred in finding and copying the records. Parents may also challenge any information that they find in the records and request that the school district or other agency amend the records.

For parents whose children have medical involvement, an additional piece of legislation has been enacted to address the issue of confidentiality. This is the Health Insurance Portability and Accountability Act, known as HIPAA. This act, passed in 1996, was developed "to standardize the communication of electronic health information between health care providers and health insurers . . . [and] to protect the privacy and security of individually identifiable health information" (Moore & Wall, 2003). According to the OCR,

> While we strongly believe every individual should have the same level of privacy protection for his/her individually identifiable health information, Congress did not provide us with authority to disturb the scheme it had devised for records maintained by educational institution and agencies under FERPA. We do not believe Congress intended to amend or preempt FERPA when it enacted HIPAA. (Benitz, 2003)

There has been confusion whether school records are considered "protected health information" (PHI) per the HIPAA definition (*InFocus*, 2003) because health information may have been included in those records. If the child's records are considered to be educational records as defined by FERPA, then that information would not be considered as PHI and therefore not under the rules of HIPAA (Moore & Wall, 2003). An issue that has not been fully resolved concerns health-related information included in the educational records by a school nurse who may be considered a "health care provider" as defined by HIPAA (Engler, 2004; *InFocus*, 2002;

Levin & Lalley, 2002, 2003). When special education students are involved, the definition of what constitutes health information and educational records become more confusing. According to *InFocus* (2002), it is clear that

> School entities that provide special education almost certainly are providing "health care" as defined in the HIPAA regulations. When "related services" required under a student's individualized education plan (IEP) involve such things as occupational therapy, physically therapy or psychological counseling, for example, health care is being provided.

Regardless of whether a child's educational records are covered under FERPA or HIPAA, the parents continue to have the right to review this information until the child reaches the age of majority. The Department of Health and Human Services has stated that parents have additional rights under HIPAA because they are considered to be the "personal representatives of their minor children" when they have the legal right to make health care decisions (English & Ford, 2004). Thus, parents continue to have the right "to access and control information about their minor children" (*InFocus*, 2002), with the exception of instances when state laws provide minors access to specific health care without parental consent.

Legislation such as FERPA and HIPAA has been enacted to secure the privacy and confidentiality of information concerning the child with a disability and his or her parents. At the same time, this legislation allows those individuals who are participants in securing an appropriate educational program to review confidential records. State departments of education and local schools are both charged with the protection of the student's records. Both develop policies concerning the protection and destruction of school records. Both are responsible for informing parents of the policies concerning access, confidentiality, maintenance, and destruction of student records.

Special Situations

Surrogate Parents.   Under IDEA, parents have an essential role in the special education process. If the parents of the child are not known, or cannot be located, if the child is a ward of the state, or if the child is an unaccompanied homeless youth, a surrogate parent is to be appointed (IDEA of 2004, P.L. 108–446, § 615[b][2], 118 Stat. 2647 [2005]). The role of the surrogate is to safeguard the educational rights of the child and to perform the duties of a "parent" (IDEA of 2004, P.L. 108–446, § 602[23], 118 Stat. 2647 [2005]). The surrogate parent(s) cannot be an employee of any agency involved in the education or care of the child, have conflicts of interest with the interest of the child represented, and must have knowledge and skills that ensure the child is adequately represented (34 C.F.R. § 300.515[c–d]). The regulations also specify that a person paid by a public agency solely for the purpose of being a surrogate parent does not become an agency employee (34 C.F.R. § 300.515[d]) and may act on the child's behalf. The surrogate parent may represent the child in all actions involving identification, evaluation, placement, and rights to an FAPE (34 C.F.R. § 300.515[e]).

However, the appointment of a surrogate parent does not terminate parental rights under IDEA, even when the child reaches the age of majority. In *John H. v.*

MacDonald (1987), the Court reasoned that the appointment of a surrogate is to enforce the child's rights, not to displace the parents' rights. Therefore, parental rights under IDEA cannot be terminated by either the appointment of a surrogate parent or by the child reaching the age of majority.

Foster Parents.   The role of foster parents is not addressed in IDEA. The critical factor is whether the foster parents become "permanent" foster parents. In *Criswell v. State Department of Education* (1986), the state was prohibited from appointing surrogate parents for a student in permanent foster care. In *Converse County School District No. Two v. Pratt* (1997), the Court also held that IDEA allows foster parents to become surrogate parents, and that, under IDEA, when the foster parents were acting as the child's parents, the appointment of a surrogate parent was unnecessary. Therefore, decisions on the role of foster parents as "acting as parents" must be made on an individual basis.

Students at the Age of Majority.   As the child approaches the age of majority, and not later than 1 year before, the IEP must include a statement that the child has been informed of the rights, if any, that will transfer to him or her at the age of majority (IDEA of 2004, P.L. 108–446, § 614[d][1][A][VIII][cc], 118 Stat. 2647 [2005]). Thus, a state may allow a child with a disability, on reaching the age of majority and having not been ruled incompetent under state law, to receive the rights that under IDEA have been reserved for the parent. However, in some cases, it may be determined that the child does not have the ability to act with informed consent in respect to the parental requirements of IDEA. In that instance, the state shall be responsible for establishing procedures for appointing the parent of the child, or, if the parent is unavailable, another appropriate individual to represent the educational interests of the child (IDEA of 2004, P.L. 108–446, § 615[m][2], 118 Stat. 2647 [2005]).

Parental Participation Litigation

Litigation related to the parents' role is not extensive. When it does occur, it is usually in conjunction with other issues related to evaluation, programming, and placement of the child with a disability. The Supreme Court heard an early case that provides a foundation for parental decision-making involvement in the education of their child (*Meyer v. Nebraska,* 1923). In *Meyer,* the Court was presented with the issue of whether a state could prohibit the teaching of a foreign language because it infringed on the liberty interest guaranteed by the Fourteenth Amendment. Not only did the Court look at the liberty interest of the teacher in pursuing his or her profession, but also the right of the parents to control the education of their children. The Court stated "evidently, the legislature has attempted materially to interfere with the calling of modern language teachers, with the opportunity of pupils to acquire knowledge, and *with the power of parents to control the education of their own children*" (*Meyer v. Nebraska*, 1923, p. 401, italics added).

Two years later, the Supreme Court decided the case of *Pierce v. Society of Sisters* (1925) and, relying on the decision in *Meyer*, concluded that parents had a fundamental right under the Constitution to educate their children as they chose. In *Pierce*, the Court was presented with the issue of whether parents were required to send their children to public rather than private school. The Court stated "under the doctrine of *Meyer v. Nebraska* . . . we think it entirely plain that the Act of 1922 unreasonably interferes with the liberty of parents and guardians to direct the upbringing and education of children under their control" (*Pierce v. Society of Sisters*, 1925, p. 534).

Based on these cases, later attempts by school districts to prevent parental participation in the educational process of the child with disabilities have proven to be unsuccessful. More recently, in *Board of Education of Northfield Township High School District 225 v. Roy H. and Lynn H.* (1995), the Board of Education attempted to obtain an injunction against the parents to limit their participation in the educational decisions concerning their child. The Board of Education believed the parents were acting in bad faith and attempting to sabotage the process. The District Court had little difficulty in dealing with this issue. Citing the extreme importance that Congress placed on parental participation in the education of children with disabilities, the Court found that no action could be taken without the consent of the parents or at least without participation of the parents. The Court stated,

> The regulatory scheme of IDEA places a high premium on parental involvement in the placement process. . . . At no time may an agency regulated under IDEA proceed with respect to a child without making some effort to involve the child's parents. . . . Given that Congress has placed such extreme importance on the involvement of the parents in the education of their disabled child, plaintiff's request to enjoin Lisa's parents from any further involvement in her education is inappropriate. (*Board of Education v. Roy H.*, 1995, p. 52)

As can be seen in the *Roy H.* case, the Court was upholding rights bestowed by an act of Congress and rights established by previous case law.

Despite the fact that the right to an education is not a fundamental right (*Brown v. Board of Education of Topeka, Kansas*, 1954), parents do have the constitutional right to have their children educated and to make decisions concerning that education. This right to participation in the choice of education and the educational process is a fundamental right guaranteed by the Ninth Amendment, which states that rights guaranteed in the Constitution cannot be construed to deny or disparage other rights retained by the people. However, in ensuring parents the right to be significantly involved in the education of their child with a disability, IDEA is not ensuring them the right to select the educational methodology to be used by the classroom teacher.

In the case of *Deal v. Hamilton County Department of Education* (2003), the parents disagreed with the school's selection of teaching methodology for their child, Zachary, who had been identified as having autism. The parents requested that Zachary be taught using a program based on ABA therapy that had been developed by the CARD. The school elected to use multiple teaching methodologies, including one-on-one discreet trial teaching, picture cues, incidental teaching, functional communication techniques with physical prompting, activity-based instruction, and picture exchange communication system, among others.

In this case, the parents were active participants in the IEP process and did agree with some of the decisions made concerning Zachary's program. As a result, the courts disagreed with the parent's view that the school had not provided Zachary with an FAPE when they refused to incorporate the parent's selected methodology into the IEP. IDEA does not guarantee parents the right to choose the method of teaching their child, only the right to participate fully as a member of the team that is developing a program to meet the child's unique needs. As the Court stated in this case,

> The truth is, there are a number of effective ways to deal with autism. Methodologies are continually changing with the acquisition of more scientific knowledge. As the Supreme Court recognized in *Rowley*, courts must be mindful that they lack the "'specialized knowledge and experience' necessary to resolve 'persistent and difficult questions of educational policy.'" . . . Congress did not intend in the IDEA, to tie the hands of educators to any particular way of dealing with autism, or any other handicap. (*Deal v. Hamilton County Department of Education,* 2003)

The regulatory scheme of IDEA places a premium on parental involvement by requiring that the schools go to great lengths to involve the parents. Thus, when a school district fails to provide sufficient notification to parents of the types of educational programs available (e.g., ESY), the Court upheld the action as a violation of IDEA. The violation is seen as intentional misrepresentation and withholding from parents the information needed to make a meaningful decision regarding the education of children. This is demonstrated by the opinion in *Reusch v. Fountain* (1994). In this case, the Court found that the system for providing an ESY was flawed because it had provided inadequate and untimely notice regarding the opportunity for ESY services. The Court stated its conclusion as

> The IDEA requires that schools fully involve parents in the formulation, review, and revision of their child's IEP. As stated by the Court in *Rowley:* Congress sought to protect individual children by providing for parental involvement in the development of state plans and policies . . . and in the formulation of the child's individual education program. . . . The federal regulations state that "parents of a child with a disability are expected to be equal participants along with school personnel, in developing, reviewing, and revising the child's IEP." (*Reusch v. Fountain,* 1994, p. 1426)

The Court found that the school district had violated several sections of IDEA, including failure to notify parents of the ESY, and ordered immediate remediation. The Court noted that meaningful parental participation includes not only making decisions regarding the child, but also equal participation in the program planning process.

Standards and the Law

CEC Standard 9: Professional and Ethical Practice

INTASC Standard 10: Collaboration, Ethics, and Relationships

Parents must be encouraged to participate in order to safeguard the rights of the child and to make informed decisions concerning the options available. Failure of the school district to advise the parents of their legal rights and responsibilities, procedures available, and educational alternatives, in and of itself, constitutes a violation of IDEA. This concept has been upheld more recently in cases that noted that the failure of the school to provide parents with evaluation reports as they requested denied them the right to participate fully in the process (*Amanda J. v. Clark County School District,* 2001), that not providing copies of evaluation reports immediately after their preparation violated the parents rights to be involved in their child's education (*Baer v. Klagholz,* 2001), and a school district's refusal to read or review professional evaluation reports provided by the parents violated their rights to provide information and thus be involved in the decision-making process for their child (*DiBuo v. Board of Education of Worcester County,* 2002).

These cases indicate that the parent's role in the development of their child's program is essential for the development of an FAPE for the child. If parents cannot be involved because of a failure of the school to provide records in a timely manner or to review records provided from an outside source, an FAPE may have been denied.

Summary

Clearly, IDEA sets forth an important role for the parents of children with disabilities. Under federal regulations, a parent can be a natural parent, a guardian, a surrogate parent(s) appointed by the LEA, and anyone acting in the place of a parent such as a relative or anyone else with whom the child lives. Therefore, the persons who know the child best are made full and equal partners with the school. As a partner in the educational process, parents are given the power of advocate and decision maker to assist in the development of the IEP, to oversee the implementation of the plan, and to assist in the evaluation of its effectiveness.

Parents are viewed as having a fundamental right under the Constitution to educate their children as they chose. At no time may an agency regulated under IDEA proceed with respect to a child without making some effort to involve the child's parents. Therefore, parental involvement is essential both as a source of information and consent for programming and as an advocate for the student. Because of the importance of the role of parents, IDEA provides directions for those special situations wherein parents might be unable, or unwilling, to assume parental responsibilities. IDEA calls for the state to develop procedures for the appointment of surrogate parents, and further ensures the independence of the surrogates by prohibiting the appointment of a person who might have a conflict of interest and be unable to freely act on behalf of the child. Therefore, IDEA continues to strongly reaffirm the right of all parents to control the education of their children and establish the right of equal partnership in education for parents of children with disabilities.

Questions for Discussion

1. What are the important roles that parents play under the IDEA mandate?
2. The due process guarantees provide parents with a powerful tool in working with school. Explain how the parental participation requirement is just as powerful but less adversarial.

Websites for Further Exploration

Parental Participation and IDEA
ericec.org/digests/e611.html
www.thearc.org/faqs/qa-idea.html
www.transitioncoalition.org/egiwrap/teas/new/index.php
www.ed.gov/parents/needs/speced/iepguide/index.html
www.parentsmart.com/SpecialEd/IEP/
www.ld.org/advocacy/parent_involve.cfm
www.nichcy.org/Trainpkg/traintxt/9ohs.htm

FERPA and HIPAA
www.medicalprivacy.unc.edu/pdfs/
www.nasponline.org/publications/cq314hipaa.html
www.healthinschools.org/focus/2002/no4.htm
www.hhs.gov/ocr/hipaa
fetaweb.com/04/ferpa.Summary.htm
www.epic.org/privacy/education/ferpa.html
www.healthinschools.org/focus/2003/no1.htm

Surrogate Parents
www.ideapractices.org/
www.cleweb.org/Disabilities/QuestionAnswer/Q&Adecember.htm
www.edlaw.net/service/303sube.html

Foster Parents
parentpals.com/gossamer/pages/Detailed/923.html
www.ascd.org/publications/class_lead/200302/emerson_4.html
www.autism-pdd.net/guidep.html

Students at Age of Majority
www.ncset.org/publications/viewdesc.asp?id=318
www.transitioncoalition.org/egiwrap/teas/new/index.php

ILLUSTRATING THE LAW

Briefing of:
Christopher Reusch, et al. v.
Dr. Hiawatha Fountain, et al.
U.S. District Court of Maryland
872 F. Supp. 1421
December 29, 1994

FACTS: Children with disabilities in Montgomery County, Maryland, brought suit against the Montgomery County Public School (MCPS) District, alleging that the school district systematically violated IDEA by failing to provide them with an opportunity to have ESY services. The school had been aware of its obligation to provide ESY services to the children since 1979 but failed to provide it for at least 10 years. The court found that the parents of children with disabilities had to fight for ESY or send their children to a program that charged a fee. MCPS actually encouraged its personnel to direct children away from ESY to its tuition-based enrichment programs.

ISSUE: Whether the school district violated IDEA by discouraging ESY services to children with disabilities.

HOLDING: The school district violated IDEA by failing to provide adequate notice regarding ESY to parents of students with disabilities, by using procedures that delay decisions regarding ESY, by making decisions on ESY too late, by failing to document discussions about ESY and by failing to discuss the ESY options at annual reviews, by using the wrong standard to determine if a student should receive ESY, and by failing to comply with the IEP requirements.

RATIONALE: The court extensively evaluated the requirements of IDEA emphasizing the IEP, and directing the schools to fully involve the parents in the formulation, review, and revision of their child's IEP, making parents equal participants in developing the IEP. The court found that MCPS discouraged parental request for ESY and failed in its notice to the parents of the availability of ESY as a service and potential part of the IEP.

The court went on to find that the two-step process implemented by MCPS delayed the decision as to whether a child required the service of ESY and undercut the participants involved. Any roadblock to full realization of the benefits of IDEA must be terminated.

The procedural safeguards required by IDEA were consistently ignored by the school district, with the result that children with disabilities were denied the services of ESY to which they were entitled.

ILLUSTRATING THE LAW THROUGH DISCUSSION

IDEA requires that schools fully involve parents in the formation, review, and revision of their child's IEP. IEPs are not to be developed to fit existing placement decisions. What policies and procedures should be implemented to meet the mandates of IDEA?

References

Amanda J. by Annette J. v. Clark County School District, 260 F. 3d 1106 (9th Cir. 2001).

Baer v. Klagholz, 771 A. 2d 603 (2001).

Benitz, C. (2003). The relationship of HIPAA to special education. Retrieved November 29, 2004, from http://www.usu.edu/mprrc/infoserv/pubs/hipaaspeced.pdf.

Board of Education of Northfield Township High School District 225 v. Roy H. and Lynn H., 1021 IDELR 1173 (N.D. Ill. Jan. 12, 1995).

Brown v. Board of Education of Topeka, Kansas, 347 U.S. 483, 98 L.Ed. 873, 74 S.Ct. 686, 38 A.L.R. 2d 1180 (1954).

Converse County School District No. Two v. Pratt, C.D. and E. F., 993 F. Supp. 848 (D. Wyo. 1997).

Criswell v. State Department of Education, 558 EHLR 156 (M.D. Tenn. 1986).

Deal ex rel. Deal v. Hamilton County Department of Education, 259 F. Supp. 2d 687 (E.D. Tenn. 2003).

DiBuo by DiBuo v. Board of Education of Worcester County, 309 F.3d 184 (4th Cir. 2002).

Engler, K. (2004). HIPAA and the schools. Retrieved November 29, 2004, from http://www.mnmsba.org/Public/PublicationShow.cfm?PublicationsID=1413.

English, A., & Ford, C. A. (2004). The HIPAA privacy rule and adolescents: Legal questions and clinical challenges. *Perspectives on Sexual and Reproductive Health, 36*(2). Retrieved November 29, 2004, from http://www.agi-usa.org/pubs/journals/3608004.html.

Family Educational Rights and Privacy Act, 20 U.S.C. § 1232 *et seq.* (1990).

Health Insurance Portability and Accountability Act, 42 U.S.C. § 201 *et seq.* (1996).

Individuals with Disabilities Education Act Amendments of 1997, 20 U.S.C. § 1400 *et seq.* (1997).

Individuals with Disabilities Education Improvement Act of 2004, P.L. 108–446, § 600 *et seq.*, 118 Stat. 2647 (2005).

InFocus. (2002). Safeguarding individual health privacy: A review of HIPAA regulations. Retrieved November 7, 2004, from http://www.healthinschools.org/focus/2002/no4.htm#top.

InFocus. (2003). The other health privacy law: What FERPA requires of schools. Retrieved November 7, 2004, from http://www.healthinschools.org/focus/2003/no1.htm.

John H. v. MacDonald, 631 F. Supp. 208 (D.N.H. 1987).

Levin M., & Lalley, P. (2002). Is the HIPAA beast coming to your school district? Retrieved November 29, 2004, from http://www.nsba.org/site/docs/10900/10849.pdf.

Levin, M., & Lalley, P. (2003). What to do when the HIPAA beast is at your door. Retrieved November 29, 2004, from http://www.nsba.org/site/docs/10900/10850.pdf.

Meyer v. Nebraska, 262 U.S. 390, 43 S.Ct. 625, 667 L.Ed. 1042 (1923).

Moore, J., & Wall, A. (2003). Applicability of HIPAA to health information in schools. Retrieved November 29, 2004, from http://www.medicalprivacy.unc.edu/pdfs/schools.pdf.

Pierce v. Society of Sisters, 268 U.S. 510, 45 S.Ct. 571, 69 L.Ed. 1070, 39 A.L.R. 468 (1925).

Reusch v. Fountain, 872 F. Supp. 1421 (D. Md. 1994).

Turnbull, H. R., Beegle, G., & Stowe, M. J. (2001). The core concepts of disability policy affecting families who have children with disabilities. *Journal of Disability Policy Studies, 12*(3), 133–143.

Turnbull, A., Turnbull, R., Erwin, E., & Soodak, L. (2006). *Families, professionals, and exceptionality: Positive outcomes through partnerships and trust.* Merrill/Prentice Hall.

Wright, P. W. D., & Wright, P. D. (2000). *Wrightslaw: Special education law.* Hartfield, VA: Harbor House Law Press.

PART III

Remedies

CHAPTER NINE

Enforcement of Special Education Law

GUIDING QUESTIONS

1. Define the term "moot" and provide examples of the application of the mootness doctrine to special education cases and note possible exceptions.

2. List and explain the remedies specific to IDEA.

3. When are attorney fees available under IDEA, and when are they not permitted?

Early federal court decisions (e.g., *PARC v. Commonwealth of Pennsylvania* [1972], *Mills v. Board of Education of the District of Columbia* [1972]) stated that refusal to provide an education to students with disabilities violated the U.S. Constitution's provisions for equal protection and due process. These findings provided the foundation for the development of disability legislation. When state or local agencies did not comply with the requirements of this legislation, the courts have entered orders concerning the provision of education for students with disabilities. Prior to the enactment of IDEA, courts enforced their decrees through a number of judicial methods, including civil and criminal contempt proceedings, fines, injunctions, other traditional judicial remedies, and the appointment of special masters under Rule 53 of the Federal Rules of Civil Procedure.

Pre-EAHCA Judicial Methods of Enforcement

Cases brought before a court may contain both claims and remedies at law or equity (*Maldonado v. Benitez*, 1995). Claims and subsequent remedies of both claims at law and equity may be available under IDEA (see IDEA of 2004, P.L. 108–446, § 604(b) 118 Stat. 2647 [2005]). Money damages are usually reserved for claims at law. If the case is one of equity, courts may fashion a remedy suitable for the particular case it is deciding. Traditionally, courts have enforced compliance with its orders through the use of a variety of methods, such as monitoring of the school's implementation of the court's order, including compliance to court-established timelines, reallocating and withholding of funds, issuing contempt citations, and appointing special masters.

Court Citations for Contempt

When the court issues an order compelling or prohibiting a particular act, the expectation is that the party subjected to the order is to comply. When a party refuses to comply with an order, then the court may issue a citation of contempt against that party. Contempt is defined by the court as "an act or omission tending to obstruct or interfere with the orderly administration of justice, or to impair the dignity of the court or respect for its authority" (Gifis, 1996, p. 102). Because it is essential for the court to have its orders obeyed, the court will issue citations to force compliance with its orders (*Duane B. v. Chester-Upland School District*, 1994). Penalties for contempt range from fines to

Standards and the Law

CEC Standard 1: Foundations

CEC Standard 9: Professional and Ethical Practice

INTASC Standard 1: Subject Matter

PRAXIS Standard: Legal and Societal Issues

PRAXIS Standard: Delivery of Services to Students with Disabilities

imprisonment, depending on the circumstances of the case. In education cases, contempt of court typically results in a fine imposed by the court.

Court-Appointed Special Masters

When it is apparent that a fine would not achieve the desired compliance, the court may appoint an individual known as a court-appointed special master to oversee and, thus, to actually achieve compliance. District courts have employed a court-appointed special master in the area of special education because of the complexity of the litigation or because of the length of the litigation. Rule 53 of the Federal Rules of Civil Procedure allows the federal courts to appoint masters in limited circumstances; the rule provides in part that

> The Court in which any action is pending may appoint a special master therein. As used in these rules the word "master" includes a referee, an auditor, an examiner, and an assessor. . . . A reference to a master shall be the exception and not the rule . . . (p. 361)

The District Court may accept the special master's report, take additional evidence, or reject it entirely (*United States v. Merz,* 1964). The special master may be more than one person, and instead consist of a panel of persons knowledgeable about the subject matter of the litigation (*ARC of ND v. Schafer,* 1996). The special master may conduct evidentiary hearings and, in some cases, actually run the facility or enterprise under the direct supervision of the District Court. A difficulty with a special master administering parts of IDEA in an LEA is the possible impeding of the educational process itself. Furthermore, it may constitute unneeded federal interference with a purely local concern that should be avoided if possible. In addition, the school board pays the cost of the special master(s) and that can impact the educational budget of the system.

The overuse of special masters invalidates, to a certain extent, the judicial function of the court. A basic concept in American jurisprudence is that the parties are entitled to a hearing in front of an impartial tribunal. When the court relies on the special master to make judgments concerning the credibility of witnesses, it is delegating a function most often reserved solely for the court (*State of Connecticut v. Bruno,* 1996). Therefore, the court must appoint special master(s) only in situations where the appointment is essential for a fair and thorough hearing to occur.

Doctrine of Federal Abstention

In *Younger v. Harris* (1971), the Supreme Court explained the doctrine of federal abstention as a congressional "desire to permit state courts to try state cases free from interference by federal courts" (p. 43). Later, in *Colorado River Water Conservation District v. United States* (1976), the Supreme Court further explained abstention by categorizing the circumstances under which the use of abstention would be appropriate as where

(1) There is a federal constitutional issue which might be mooted or presented in a different posture by a state court determination of pertinent state law. . . .

(2) There have been presented difficult questions of state law bearing on policy problems of substantial public import whose importance transcends the result in the case then at bar. . . .

(3) Absent bad faith, harassment, or a patently invalid state statute, federal jurisdiction has been invoked for the purpose of restraining state criminal proceedings. (pp. 1244–1245)

The courts have further stated that the doctrine serves to preserve judicial economy and should only be used under exceptional circumstances (*Bills v. Homer Consolidated School District No. 33–C,* 1997). Similarly, federal courts have refused to exercise jurisdiction over matters that are purely local in nature, such as education and domestic relations cases (*Johnson v. Lancaster County Children and Youth Social Service Agency,* 1993). However, before the federal court will abstain from a case, it must be satisfied that the litigant has had the opportunity to fully and fairly litigate all his or her claims in state court (*Evans v. Evans,* 1993).

The Younger abstention doctrine (1971) originally dealt with the issue of enjoining a state criminal proceeding, a doctrine that was essential to faith in the state judiciary. The doctrine has been expanded and applied in several types of cases, including those brought under IDEA. The doctrine does not require that the federal court abstain from hearing all the claims, but allows the federal court to divide certain issues involved in a lawsuit and refer them to state court while retaining the other remaining issues (*Pennhurst State School and Hospital et al. v. Halderman,* 1984). Furthermore, the abstention doctrine does apply if the issue to be decided is a constitutional issue and a decision by the state supreme court would obviate the need for a decision on the issue. In determining if abstention is appropriate under the circumstances, the court must consider whether (a) there are ongoing state judicial proceedings, (b) the state proceedings implicate important state interests, and (c) the state proceedings afford an adequate opportunity to raise federal claims (*Baby Neal v. Casey,* 1993).

Grounds of Mootness

Another method used by the federal courts to preclude judicial review of an issue presented is to rule on grounds of the doctrine of mootness. The term "moot" means that the dispute in question is no longer a viable controversy. When a case has been deemed as being moot, then it does not need to be heard. Examples of where an issue has been declared as moot include when a student graduates prior to settlement of the issue, when parents continue to participate in educational program development even when they disagree and bring suit, or when the student dies before the issue is settled.

In *Rodricus L. by Betty H. v. Waukegan Community School District No. 60* (1998), the District Court explained the mootness doctrine and its application to a special education case. The plaintiff (Rodricus) was receiving educational services from the defendant school district before he was expelled. He subsequently brought an action claiming that the Waukegan Community School District had violated IDEA by not evaluating him for special education services. The student then moved from Illinois to Indiana while the suit was pending. The school district moved the District Court to dismiss the case because it had been rendered moot. In analyzing the issue, the District Court noted that it could only hear a case wherein there was an actual controversy. The fact that the plaintiff no longer resided in the defendant's school district resulted in a lack of controversy between the parties; thus, the case was moot.

In *Thomas R. W. by Pamela R. and Edward W. v. Massachusetts Department of Education* (1997), the District Court explained the rationale behind the mootness doctrine as being

> predicated on judicial economy—saving the use of the court's scarce resources for the resolution of real disputes. To avoid relitigation of an otherwise moot question, however, the mootness doctrine countenances an exception for issues "capable of repetition, yet evading review." (Citations omitted.) To preserve a case from mootness under this exception, two requirements must be met: "(1) the challenged action was in its duration too short to be fully litigated prior to its cessation or expiration, and (2) there was a reasonable expectation that the same complaining party would be subjected to the same action again." (pp. 479–480)

The Texas Court of Appeals stated this general rule for mootness and the exceptions in *University Interscholastic League v. Buchanan* (1993). At least 37 state courts have added an additional exception to the mootness doctrine that allows the court to hear the case if it involves an issue of significant public interest, yet evades review for some reason. Therefore, the fact that a child with disabilities is no longer enrolled in school, or has reached the age of majority and no longer has an IEP, does not require a decision of nonreview based on grounds of mootness. Nor does it preclude the child from having standing sufficient to constitute a case in controversy. Such was the case in *Heldman v. Sobol* (1992), when the Second Circuit Court, which agreed to hear the case, stated

> T. H. is currently nineteen years old and has not yet completed a high school education. Although he is not currently enrolled in the public schools and has no pending IEP review hearing, T. H. remains entitled to a free appropriate public education and an

impartial review of his IEP in New York state until he reaches age twenty-one. (Citations omitted.) Because the threat of future denial of an impartial hearing is sufficiently real and the right to contest an IEP is integral to active parental participation in the yearly process of determining what constitutes an appropriate education for their child, Heldman retains enough of a personal stake in the outcome for us to retain jurisdiction over this case. (p. 157)

Another exception to the mootness doctrine is where a member of a class remains when the named plaintiff no longer has a case in controversy. Thus, the issues may remain "live" in regard to the remaining members of the class. As stated in *Merrifield v. Lake Central School Corporation* (1991),

Exceptions do exist to the mootness doctrine. One exception is for class actions, where a controversy still exists between a named defendant and a member of a class represented by the named plaintiff, even though the claim of the named plaintiff has become moot. (p. 471)

To summarize, for a case to be heard by a court, it must present a controversy to the court in which the complaining party has standing (a stake in the outcome) to bring the action. The complaining party (plaintiff) must be eligible to derive some benefit (e.g., compensatory education, damages, or a new IEP) from a determination of the issues. The case is considered "live," or not moot. In other words, it is a situation in which the case is capable of repetition. That is, it could evade judicial review because of time limitations as in situations involving graduation or pregnancy (*Roe v. Wade,* 1973), significance to the public interest, or significant collateral effect.

Failure to Prosecute

A case may be dismissed if the plaintiff fails to prosecute the case. This dismissal by the court, which is equivalent to voiding the motion, may occur when the plaintiff fails to pursue his or her action. This is also known as *non prosequitur.* One example is the failure of the plaintiff to appear in court at the prescribed time.

In *Grun v. Pneumo Abex Corporation* (1999), the Seventh Circuit Court of Appeals described the doctrine of dismissal on the basis of failure to prosecute. The plaintiff in the *Grun* case brought suit against the defendants on an employment contract. The case was set for trial, but counsel for the plaintiff alleged that the notice of the trial setting had never been received. Neither party appeared for the scheduled date of trial; therefore, the Court dismissed the case.

After 3 months had elapsed, the attorney for the plaintiff filed a motion to advance the case for trial. Subsequently, the plaintiff learned the case had been dismissed. The plaintiff moved the Court to vacate the order of dismissal and to reinstate the case. The Court found that the order of dismissal should be vacated; however, it dismissed the case for failure of the plaintiff to prosecute the case under Rule 40 of the Federal Rules of Civil Procedure. The Seventh Circuit Court of Appeals reversed the District Court and stated

Also compelling is that the record is barren of any suggestion whatsoever that Grun was dilatory prior to the . . . dismissal. On the contrary, Grun had been vigorously prosecuting his case. The record demonstrates that Grun's counsel had appeared at all prior hearings, had timely propounded and answered written discovery, had filed a summary judgment motion which the magistrate judge had recommended be granted (in fact, the magistrate had recommended a sizable award to Grun), and had completed the submission of required pretrial materials and was prepared for trial. From Grun's perspective, he was simply awaiting a trial date. It is certainly not that unusual for a litigant to hear nothing from the courthouse for a period of five months. Obviously, defense counsel felt the same; he did not check the court docket or contact the court clerk to get a trial date either, as evidenced by the fact that he did not show up for trial. (*Grun v. Pneumo Abex Corporation,* 1999, p. 424)

Voluntary Dismissal

Either party in a lawsuit may also decide not to proceed with the case. When this decision is made, they may request the court to dismiss the suit against one or more of the defendants. This dismissal on its own motion, known as voluntary dismissal, is not commonly used. Rule 41 of the Federal Rules of Civil Procedure asserts that dismissal of a suit may occur by order of the court or by voluntary dismissal. It is clear from this rule that a plaintiff may dismiss the case without leave of court to do so if none of the parties have answered the complaint. The rule is equally clear that the plaintiff must obtain an order of the court to dismiss a complaint where the parties have been served and have responded.

However, if the plaintiff has already dismissed the complaint on a prior occasion, the dismissal is said to be with prejudice. "With prejudice" means that the case cannot be refiled and that the dismissal is the same as if the case had been tried on the merits and dismissed. When the court, at the request of the plaintiff, dismisses a case, the court may establish terms and conditions for the dismissal. Normally, unless the court notes otherwise, the case is dismissed without prejudice (*S–1 v. Spangler,* 1986).

In summary, a plaintiff may dismiss his or her case without prejudice if he or she does so before the parties respond to the lawsuit. If the named defendants have responded, then the plaintiff must get the approval of the court to take a voluntary dismissal, and the court may attach whatever terms and conditions it deems necessary to the dismissal. The court must consider whether the voluntary dismissal would result in prejudice to any other party. After a complaint is voluntarily dismissed, the court will allow a voluntary dismissal of the second complaint only with prejudice.

Post-EAHCA Compliance Techniques

When Congress passed the EAHCA, it was determined that the new requirements would place a severe financial strain on the LEAs and SEAs, so funds were made available for the education of students with disabilities. However, these funds were tied directly to compliance with the Act. Although these federal funds were to act as an inducement to compliance with IDEA, nonacceptance of the funds did not abrogate the constitutional rights of students with disabilities. Regardless of their acceptance or nonacceptance of IDEA funds, LEAs and SEAs were still required to provide an education to students with disabilities under the constitutional provisions for equal protection and due process. However, after Congress passed IDEA, the withholding of all federal funds in cases of noncompliance with the Act became one of the available enforcement methods.

Authorization and Appropriation of Monies

Under IDEA, the major statutory method to address noncompliance is the withholding of federal funds from states not in compliance with the regulations and legislation concerning the education of students with disabilities. According to IDEA,

final #8

> a State is eligible for assistance under this part for a fiscal year if the State submits a plan that provides assurances to the Secretary that the State has in effect policies and procedures to ensure that the State meets each of the following conditions:
>
> 1. free appropriate education;
> 2. full educational opportunity goal;
> 3. child find;
> 4. individualized education program;
> 5. least restrictive environment;
> 6. procedural safeguards;
> 7. evaluation;
> 8. confidentiality;
> 9. transition from Part C to preschool programs;
> 10. children in private schools;
> 11. state educational agency responsible for general supervision;
> 12. obligations related to and methods of ensuring services;
> 13. procedural requirements relating to local educational agency eligibility;
> 14. personnel qualifications;
> 15. performance goals and indicators;
> 16. participation in assessments;
> 17. supplementation of State, local, and other Federal funds;
> 18. maintenance of State financial support;
> 19. public participation;
> 20. rule of construction;
> 21. state advisory panel;
> 22. suspension and expulsion rates;
> 23. access to instructional materials;
> 24. overidentification and disproportionality; and
> 25. prohibition on mandatory medication. (IDEA of 2004, P.L. 108–446, § 612[a], 118 Stat. 2647 [2005])

Although the list of conditions is exhaustive, there still exist areas of controversy requiring interpretation from the federal courts.

When federal funds are conditioned on the performance of some duty by the state, that condition must be specifically set out in unambiguous terms in the statute. In fact, the statute must assert that Congress intended the receipt of funds to be predicated on the state's compliance with the Act. In addition, when the federal government does withhold funds, the state has the right to a hearing and an appeal. Thus, in *Virginia Department of Education v. Riley* (1997), the Fourth Circuit Court of Appeals found that the Secretary of Education could not withhold the state's Part B funding when the state did not offer educational services to students with disabilities who were expelled for reasons other than the disability.

Exhaustion of Remedies

IDEA requires that before a case under IDEA may go to a state or federal court, the plaintiff must exhaust the administrative due process procedures required in IDEA. In *Doe v. Smith* (1989), the Sixth Circuit Court held that parents were required to exhaust the IDEA due process procedures before seeking review in court. The Sixth Circuit in *Crocker v. Tennessee Secondary School Athletic Association* (1992), summarized the importance of an administrative review process, especially the fact-finding aspect, when it stated that

> The policies underlying this exhaustion requirement are both sound and important. States are given the power to place themselves in compliance with the law, and the incentive to develop a regular system for fairly resolving conflicts under the Act. Federal Courts—generalists with no expertise in the educational needs of handicapped students—are given the benefit of expert fact finding by a state agency devoted to this very purpose. (p. 935)

Thus, the federal courts will not hear a claim under IDEA until the state administrative procedures (i.e., mediation, resolution session, and/or due process hearing) have been exhausted, or the moving party demonstrates that an attempt to do so would be futile.

In *Peters by Peters v. Johnson* (1997), the Minnesota District Court also addressed the exhaustion argument. The plaintiffs claimed that their Section 1983 action did not require exhaustion of the state administrative remedies because it was a new action. The District Court agreed when it stated

> Notwithstanding the strong policies in favor of exhaustion, the IDEA's exhaustion requirement is not absolute. Courts, relying in part on legislative history, have recognized exceptions to IDEA's exhaustion requirement when "the pursuit of administrative remedies would be futile or inadequate; waste resources, and work severe or irreparable harm on the litigant; or when the issues raised involve purely legal questions." (p. 742)

In most circumstances, it is essential that these remedies be exhausted before the claimant may file in District Court. Generally, the court would not require exhaustion of state remedies where (a) it would be futile to do so, (b) the agency has engaged in a practice contrary to law, or (c) adequate relief could not be obtained through administrative remedies. In such cases, the claimant could file directly in federal court for resolution of the claims. Aside from these exceptions, however, failure to exhaust administrative remedies may be fatal to the case if and when it is filed in District Court.

Private Right of Action

As has been noted previously, IDEA does not create a private right of action for educational malpractice. However, there may be other state remedies available, depending on the nature of the harm caused to the child. In *Helbig v. City of New York* (1993), the plaintiffs alleged that the former principal had altered the answer sheets of certain individuals, including the answer sheet of the infant plaintiff. The plaintiffs sought recovery for negligence in failing to detect the infant's learning disability, and for fraud and intentional wrongdoing in altering the test scores. The District Court held that the state of New York did not recognize educational malpractice as a cause of action and dismissed the complaint of negligence. However, the Court recognized that the plaintiff's causes of action for fraud and intentional wrongdoing might be viable if correctly pleaded. The Court dismissed the case with leave to amend the pleadings.

In another case (*Deitsch v. Tillery,* 1992) cited by the lower court in *Helbig,* the Arkansas Supreme Court reversed the trial court's order granting the school district's motion to dismiss the complaint. The Supreme Court found that the pleadings established sufficient facts to state a cause of action for the tort of outrage. The elements of the tort of outrage, as defined by the Court are (a) the actor intended to inflict emotional distress or knew or should have known that emotional distress was the likely result; (b) the conduct was "extreme and outrageous," was "beyond all possible bounds of decency," and was "utterly intolerable in a civilized community" (p. 406); (c) the actions of the defendant were the cause of the plaintiff's distress; and (d) the emotional distress sustained by the plaintiff was so severe that no reasonable person could be expected to endure it. The Supreme Court concluded that the pleadings were sufficient to allege the elements of outrage. Although most jurisdictions do not recognize claims for educational malpractice as demonstrated by the *Helbig* and *Deitsch* cases, courts do recognize claims against school officials for their intentional wrongs such as intentional misrepresentation, intentional infliction of emotional distress, and outrage.

There is a definite trend toward liability for intentional acts of school officials that result in harm to the child with disabilities or to others. Attempts to hide a child's disability by misrepresenting the results of evaluations, fraudulently changing a child's test scores, or misrepresenting whether a child is qualified for special education could well be determined to be the basis for liability if it is determined that the result of the action is detrimental to the child.

Attorney Fees

When EAHCA was passed in 1975, it contained no provision for the awarding of attorney fees. In interpreting the Act in the case of *Smith v. Robinson* (1984), the Supreme Court found that because the granting of attorney fees was not contained in the Act, it was not allowed. In this case, the Court considered whether plaintiffs who sued to secure an FAPE for a child with disabilities under IDEA could recover attorney fees. The Court noted that IDEA is a comprehensive scheme and stated that a plaintiff may not "circumvent the requirements or supplement the remedies" (p. 1019) provided under IDEA. The Court held that IDEA is the exclusive avenue for a child asserting the right to an FAPE; therefore, plaintiffs could not recover attorney fees under any other legal theories that provided for such an award.

Soon after this decision, Congress amended the Act to allow for recovery of attorney fees. This amendment is known as the Handicapped Children's Protection Act of 1986 (HCPA). Attorney fees are now commonly awarded, and the trial court is charged with the responsibility of both assessing the attorney fees and determining what is allowable. HCPA sets forth what fees may be awarded and what restrictions apply, although IDEA 2004 has made some changes in who can receive attorney fees and when. Generally, the District Court, "in its discretion, may award reasonable attorneys' fees as part of the costs to a prevailing party who are the parents of a child with a disability who is the prevailing party" (IDEA of 2004, P.L. 108–446, § 615[i][3][B], 118 Stat. 2647 [2005]). This requires the Court to determine whether the fees are reasonable if the parents are the prevailing party. Essentially, the parents must prevail on most of their claim. An award of attorney fees may be made even though the school district has prevailed on one or more issues, as long as the parents substantially prevail in obtaining the desired relief. In deciding what fee is reasonable, the Court must determine what rates are prevailing in the community for the "kind and quality of services" furnished.

With the 2004 reauthorization of IDEA, two additions were added as to whom and when the courts may award attorney's fees. In addition to awards to the parent(s) who are the prevailing party, the courts may award attorney's fees to a SEA or LEA against

> (II) . . . the attorney of a parent who files a complaint . . . that is frivolous, unreasonable, or without foundation, or . . . the attorney of a parent who continued to litigate after the litigation clearly became frivolous, unreasonable, or without foundation; or
>
> (III) . . . the attorney of a parent, or . . . the parent, if the parent's complaint . . . was represented for any improper purpose, such as to harass, to cause unnecessary delay, or to needlessly increase the cost of litigation. (IDEA of 2004, P.L. 108–446, § 615[i][3][B], 118 Stat. 2647 [2005])

There are three instances when attorney fees may not be allowed under IDEA. First, attorney fees may not be awarded for attending a meeting with the IEP team unless the team was convened as a result of a judicial proceeding, administrative hearing, or, at the state's discretion, mediation. In addition, attorney fees are not awarded for attendance at the mandatory resolution session. It should be noted that this resolution meeting is not included in the judicial proceeding or administrative hearing exception described previously. Third, under the 2004 Amendments, attorney fees are not allowed after a written offer of settlement that is rejected by the parent within 10 days and the relief obtained is not more favorable to the parents than the settlement (IDEA of 2004, P.L. 108–446, § 615[i][3], 118 Stat. 2647 [2005]). However, an award of attorney fees may still be made if the parents are the prevailing party and are "substantially justified" in rejecting the settlement offer (IDEA of 2004, P.L. 108–446, § 615[i][3][E], 118 Stat. 2647 [2005]). This addition to the basic rule that attorney fees are allowed is intended to induce reasonable settlements and to prevent prolonged litigation when the results are likely to be the same as the offer of settlement.

Attorney fees that are otherwise allowable may be reduced by the court if the court finds that the parent or the parent's attorney unreasonably delayed the final resolution of the controversy; that the amount of attorney fees unreasonably exceeds the hourly rate in the community of other attorneys with comparable skills, reputation, and experience; that the time spent and legal services furnished considering the nature of the action was excessive; or that the attorney representing the parents did not provide the necessary information in the notice of the complaint (IDEA of 2004, P.L. 108–446, § 615[i][3][F], 118 Stat. 2647 [2005]). The reduction of attorney fees shall not apply if the SEA or LEA was the party who unreasonably protracted the final resolution of the proceedings (IDEA of 2004, P.L. 108–446, § 615[i][3][G], 118 Stat. 2647 [2005]). The addition of these factors was made to ensure neither party to the litigation prolongs the litigation more than necessary and imposes, although indirectly, a requirement that both parties deal fairly with one another to achieve the purpose of providing a free appropriate education to the child with disabilities.

In *Jason D. W. v. Houston Independent School District* (1998), the Fifth Circuit Court of Appeals applied the test for attorney fees established in *Hensley v. Eckerhart* (1983). In the *Hensley* case involving Section 1988 of the Civil Rights Act of 1964, the Supreme Court established the test to determine what constitutes reasonable attorney fees pursuant to the statute. The attorney claiming the attorney fees must submit evidence supporting the claim. The Court shall only award attorney fees in the amount that is supported by the evidence and shall not provide payment for hours that are excessive, redundant, or otherwise unnecessary. From the amount requested, the amount awarded may be adjusted upward or downward, depending on the successful results achieved through the litigation efforts. When determining success, the Court must make a two-part inquiry. First, the Court considers whether the plaintiff prevailed on part of his or her claims, and then it considers the relatedness of those claims on which he or she failed to prevail. Next, the Court considers whether the plaintiff achieved a level of success that makes the number of hours the attorney claims to have invested a satisfactory basis for the fee award. The Court should focus on the overall relief obtained in relation to the number of hours expended.

In the *Jason D. W.* case, the Fifth District Court reduced the determination of attorney fees to a checklist. First, the court determined a fee by multiplying the hours worked by the reasonable hourly rate. From that base figure, 12 factors were applied to adjust the amount of the award up or down (see Figure 9.1). In applying

Figure 9.1
Twelve Factors for Adjusting Attorney Fees

1. the time and labor required for the litigation;
2. the novelty and difficulty of the questions presented;
3. the skill required to perform the legal services properly;
4. the preclusion of other employment by the attorney due to acceptance of the case;
5. the customary fee;
6. whether the fee is fixed or contingent;
7. time limitations imposed by the client or the circumstances;
8. the amount involved and the result obtained;
9. the experience, reputation, and ability of the attorneys;
10. the "undesirability" of the case;
11. the nature and length of the professional relationship with the client; and
12. awards in similar cases. (*Jason D. W. v. Houston Independent School District*, 1998, p. 209)

these factors, the courts affirmed the reduction in attorney fees. The test established by the Fifth Circuit is a reasonable test and probably will be the guiding case for future cases.

Remedies for Violations of EAHCA

As the Supreme Court stated in *Burlington School Committee v. Department of Education of Massachusetts* (1985), the Court may fashion a remedy to achieve the purposes of the act pursuant to its equitable powers. The courts have considered several remedies, including permanent injunctions, compensatory education, monetary fines, punitive damages, and attorney fees.

Permanent Injunctions

Courts of equity have traditionally had the power to enter permanent injunctions to force the performance of an act or to prohibit the doing of a particular act. Violations of an injunction may result in contempt of court charges that may be punished accordingly. A permanent injunction may be enforced at any time after it is entered by one of the parties, regardless of the time that has passed. However, if there has been a change in the facts that gave rise to the injunction or there has been a change in the law, either party may petition the court to dissolve the injunction and enter an order consistent with the current facts or state of the law. In

Agostini v. Felton (1997), the Supreme Court was presented with an appeal from the order of the Trial Court that denied relief under Rule 60(b)(5) of the Federal Rules of Civil Procedure because of mistakes. In this case, the District Court had previously entered a permanent injunction against the New York City Board of Education, preventing it

> from using funds for any plan or program under [Title I] to the extent it requires, authorizes or permits public school teachers and guidance counselors to provide teaching and counseling services on the premises of sectarian schools within New York City. (*Agostini v. Felton,* 1997, p. 2005)

Ten years later, the parties working under the injunction requested that it be dissolved because of a change in both the facts and the law. The District Court denied relief and the decision was affirmed by the Court of Appeals for the Second Circuit. The case was appealed to the Supreme Court, which acknowledged that there had been a substantial change in the law and, therefore, reversed the Court of Appeals and District Court's order. In doing so, the Court overruled prior judgments and stated

> In *Rufo v. Inmates of Suffolk County Jail,* supra, at 384, we held that it is appropriate to grant a Rule 60(b)(5) motion when the party seeking relief from an injunction or consent decree can show "a significant change either in factual conditions or in law." A court may recognize subsequent changes in either statutory or decisional law. (Citations omitted.) A court errs when it refuses to modify an injunction or consent decree in light of such changes. (*Agostini v. Felton,* 1997, p. 215)

Thus, the Court may enter a permanent injunction and may modify or dissolve it as time passes, depending on the facts and the existing law.

Compensatory Education

Compensatory education is educational services provided to students with disabilities to remedy progress that may have been lost as the result of a denial of an FAPE. The provision of these educational services is above and beyond the "normal" services provided in a school setting. The availability of compensatory education as a viable form of relief under IDEA has been argued in the courts. Although early court cases did not support the provision of compensatory education, this changed with the holding in *Burlington School Committee v. Department of Education of Massachusetts* (1985). In the *Burlington* case, the Supreme Court held that the student had been denied an appropriate education and awarded retroactive reimbursement for private school placement by the parents. The Supreme Court concluded that the Act provides courts with the power and "broad discretion [to] grant such relief as the Court determines is appropriate" (*Burlington School Committee v. Department of Education of Massachusetts,* 1985, p. 459). According to the Court, this "means that equitable considerations are relevant in fashioning relief" (p. 468). From this broad statement concerning forms of relief, courts have held that compensatory education can be awarded in instances where students with disabilities have not been provided with an appropriate education.

For example, in the case of *Pihl v. Massachusetts Department of Education* (1993), the First Circuit Court of Appeals decided that compensatory education was an appropriate remedy. In this instance, the parents of a 27-year-old man with emotional problems and mental retardation sued the Massachusetts Department of Education for compensatory education because the Department had allegedly failed to provide an FAPE during his period of entitlement. The defendants responded to the lawsuit by contending that the case was moot because the plaintiff's IEP had expired 5 years earlier and that he was no longer entitled to the services because of his age. The First Circuit disagreed, stating that

> In order to give meaning to a disabled student's right to an education between the ages of three and twenty-one, compensatory education must be available beyond a student's twenty-first birthday. Otherwise, school districts simply could stop providing required services to older teenagers relying on the Act's time-consuming review process to protect them from further obligations. (*Pihl v. Massachusetts Department of Education,* 1993, p. 189)

Therefore, compensatory education is considered to be an appropriate remedy under the Act. In addition, this remedy can be awarded even if the individual with a disability is no longer entitled to educational services because of age.

Monetary Fines

Failure of any party to a lawsuit to obey the orders of the court may result in a finding of contempt and a subsequent fine. A finding of contempt is coercive in nature in that it is an attempt to obtain compliance with the order(s) of the court. Civil contempt may be found if the failure to comply does not demonstrate disrespect of the court or if there has been a substantial compliance with the order of the court (*Springer v. The Fairfax County School Board,* 1998). When the noncompliance is an act of disrespect or an obstruction of justice, it is treated as criminal contempt. Therefore, a party to an action under IDEA must comply with the orders of the court or run the risk of being fined for noncompliance.

Punitive Damages

The courts have been consistent in finding that IDEA does not authorize punitive damages (*Sellers v. School Board of City of Manassas, VA,* 1998). However, the circuits are divided on whether punitive damages are available when there has been a violation of IDEA or Section 504. In the case of *Ridgewood Board of Education v. N. E. for M. E.* (1999), the Third Circuit Court of Appeals found that a cause of action could exist under Section 1983 of the Civil Rights Act for a violation of IDEA. Section 1983 provides that

> Every person who, under color of any statute, ordinance, regulation, custom, or usage, of any State or Territory or the District of Columbia, subjects, or causes to be subjected,

any citizen of the United States or other person within the jurisdiction thereof to the deprivation of any rights, privileges, or immunities secured by the Constitution and laws, shall be liable to the party injured in an action at law, suit in equity, or other proper proceeding for redress, except that in any action brought against a judicial officer for an act or omission taken in such officer's judicial capacity, injunctive relief shall not be granted unless a declaratory decree was violated or declaratory relief was unavailable. (42 U.S.C. § 1983)

In the *Ridgewood* case, the plaintiffs brought an action seeking compensatory and punitive damages. They relied on an earlier case, *W. B. v. Matula* (1995), to reverse the lower court and remand the case back to the District Court to determine whether compensatory and punitive damages were available under Section 1983. The Third Circuit Court of Appeals did note in its opinion that the Fourth Circuit Court of Appeals had previously held that remedies under Section 1983 were not available for violations of IDEA, but held that relief could be requested under Section 1983.

In *Sellers v. School Board of City of Manassas, VA,* (1998), the Fourth Circuit Court of Appeals went into a lengthy discussion and analysis as to whether a person could bring an action under Section 1983 for a violation of IDEA. The court in the *Sellers* reasoned that compensatory and punitive damages available under Section 1983 were not an appropriate remedy under IDEA because of the remedial nature of IDEA and because it was intended to be the exclusive remedy for violations. The Court stated

> Tort-like damages are simply inconsistent with IDEA's statutory scheme. The touchstone of a traditional tort-like remedy is redress for a broad range of harms "associated with personal injury, such as pain and suffering, emotional distress, harm to reputation, or other consequential damages." (Citations omitted.) By contrast, the touchstone of IDEA is the actual provision of a free appropriate public education. To advance this goal, IDEA provides a panoply of procedural rights to parents to ensure their involvement in decisions about their disabled child's education. (*Sellers v. School Board of City of Manassas, VA,* 1998, p. 527)

The Court's reasoning in the *Sellers* case has been followed by other circuits. Nevertheless, until resolved by the Supreme Court, circuits may differ on the use of Section 1983 for IDEA claims.

Punitive damages are available in most circumstances when there is an intentional infliction of some form of harm, such as intentional infliction of emotional distress and intentional deprivation of a constitutional or statutory right such as in a Section 1983 action. It is not available for mere errors in judgment.

Summary

Schools are required to provide an FAPE to all students with disabilities. Failure to do so may result in the loss of federal funds for special education. The loss of these federal funds does not eliminate the constitutional obligation that the schools provide an FAPE to all students with disabilities. Since the adoption of IDEA and its predecessors, courts have fashioned a number of remedies for enforcement of the requirements of IDEA, as the statute authorizes the court to grant "appropriate" relief (IDEA of 2004, P.L. 108–446, § 615[i][2][c][iii], 118 Stat. 2647 [2005]). These remedies have included permanent injunctions (courts forcing an act to occur or prohibiting it from occurring with noncompliance resulting in fines), compensatory education (extra educational services provided at no cost to students with disabilities to remedy progress that may have been lost as the result of a denial of an FAPE), monetary fines (a finding of contempt and assessing monetary penalties when there is a failure to obey the orders of the court), and attorney fees (if the parents are the prevailing party may recover reasonable costs in specified situations). However, damages, as traditionally defined, have not been awarded.

More recently, there has been a trend to allow damages for intentional acts of school officials that result in some form of injury or harm to the child with disabilities. This is not pursuant to IDEA, but to a secondary cause of action such as Section 1983 of the Civil Rights Act, which has been used for intentional deprivation of a constitutional right or statutory right (*Ridgewood*), the intentional infliction of emotional distress (*Helbig*), or the tort of outrage (*Deitsch*).

In the past, have been hundreds of attempts to pursue an educational malpractice cause of action against school officials. Until more recently, the courts did not recognize a cause of action for educational malpractice. However, in *Helbig* (1993), the Court noted the growing distinction between intentional torts such as infliction of emotional distress versus negligence. In a footnote, the New York State Court made reference to an Arkansas case not dealing with educational malpractice, but with an issue of a separate cause of action for an intentional act that caused damage to a student and his or her parents. The Court stated

> In a recent Arkansas case not involving educational malpractice, but rather in a suit against a school district for failing to follow regulations over the removal of asbestos in the school, it was held that defendants were not immune from the intentional acts of school districts and their employees, only the negligent act. By alleging that defendants knowingly concealed a dangerous asbestos condition despite knowledge of the proper procedures under State and Federal law, plaintiffs stated a cognizable cause of action for the intentional infliction of emotional distress. (Citations omitted.) This case emphasizes the growing distinction developing in the case law between causes of action founded upon negligence and those founded upon some intentional tort. (*Helbig v. City of New York,* 1993, p. 588)

In summary, the pre-IDEA methods of enforcement remain and continue to be used by the federal courts. However, more recent court decisions may well offer options that were unavailable in the past. Along with these new options, the courts have provided us with a tantalizing hint that they may begin considering cases in special education that focus on issues related to professional responsibilities and expertise and the concurrent relationship with the concept of educational malpractice. This is an issue that bears close review as courts continue to hear cases based on special education statutes.

Questions for Discussion

1. Explain the differences in the methods used for enforcement pre- and post-IDEA.
2. Violations of IDEA have resulted in the provision of compensatory education for students. How has this been addressed when the student has aged out of the school system?
3. Why is there a controversy concerning the award of punitive damages when there is an IDEA violation?
4. How has Section 1983 of the Civil Rights Act been applied when violations of IDEA have occurred?

Websites for Further Exploration

Pre-EHA Methods of Enforcement (Contempt Citations, Special Masters, Federal Abstention, Mootness, Failure to Prosecute, Voluntary Dismissal)
www.nls.org/conf2002/special_ed_compliance_monitoring.htm
www.dredf.org/newsletters/f2001.html
www.uslegalforms.com/lawdigest/legal-definitions.php/US/US-CONTEMPT.htm
www.reedmartin.com/
www.lectlaw.com/files/exp09.htm
www.daubertontheweb.com/Special%20Masters.htm
www.law.cornell.edu/lexicon/moot.htm
www.fact-index.com/m/mo/mootness_ _law_.html

Post-EAHCA Compliance Techniques (Exhaustion of Remedies, Private Right of Action, Attorney Fees)
www.lectlaw.com/def/e077.htm
www.copaa.org/index.html
ojjdp.ncjrs.org/pubs/walls/appen-f.html
www.usdoj.gov/crt/ada/cguide.htm
www.reedmartin.com/
www.spedlaw.com/html/opnews2/parent%20gets2.95.htm
www.ideapractices.org/

Remedies for Violations of EAHCA (Permanent Injunctions, Compensatory Education, Monetary Fines, Punitive Damages)
www.spedlaw.com/html/opnews2/honig.3.96.htm
ericec.org/faq/spedhist.html
www.ldonline.org/ld_indepth/legal_legislative/attorney_manual.html
www.ed.gov/pubs/EdReformStudies/EdReforms/chap7a.html
www.raggededgemagazine.com/drn/10_01.shtml
www.wrightslaw.com/info/damag.index.htm

───────── **ILLUSTRATING THE LAW** ─────────

Briefing of:
Ridgewood Board of Education v. N. E.
172 F.3d 238 (3rd Cir. 1999)

FACTS: M. E. is a 17-year-old high school student whose learning disabilities qualify him as a "child with disabilities" under IDEA, 20 U.S.C. § 1400 *et seq.* M. E. experienced learning difficulties in both first and second grade, attended summer school on his teacher's recommendation without any appreciable success, and was transferred at his parents' request to another school in the district where his difficulties continued. During third grade, M. E. was evaluated by an independent learning disabilities teacher consultant and determined to be learning disabled with intelligence at the 95th percentile and reading skills at the 2nd percentile. The school district agreed with the general assessment but refused to classify M. E. as learning disabled because it concluded that he was not "perceptually impaired" within the meaning of New Jersey law.

In sixth grade, M. E. was reevaluated by the Child Study Team who maintained that M. E. showed no signs of perceptual deficits, again refused to classify him as perceptually impaired, and determined that he was not eligible for special education. M. E.'s academic difficulties continued throughout the remainder of elementary school. In seventh grade, after an evaluation by an independent child study team, the school district agreed to classify M. E. as perceptually impaired and developed an IEP.

At the end of eighth grade, the school district decided that M. E. should no longer be placed in regular classes. For the 1996–1997 school year, it proposed an IEP that provided for resource center instruction in all academic classes, two daily periods of supplementary instruction, and speech/language therapy once per week. M. E.'s parents disagreed with the IEP, stating it provided fewer services than the proven inadequate IEP of the previous year. In 1996, M. E.'s parents requested a due process hearing before the New Jersey Department of Education, contending the school district's proposed IEP for 1996–1997 failed to provide an FAPE within the meaning of IDEA and requesting that M. E. be placed in a private school at the school district's expense. The school district refused. The parents placed M. E. at a private school that specialized in educating students with learning disabilities. The school district also refused the parental request to pay for the private school's summer program. M. E. attended the summer school program at his parents' expense and made steady and considerable progress.

The ALJ held that the district's 1996–1997 IEP failed to provide M. E. with an FAPE. The ALJ then ordered the school district to pay M. E.'s tuition at the private school and reimburse the parents for the tuition costs of attending the private school's summer program in 1996.

In 1997, the school district filed a complaint in federal court under 20 U.S.C. § 1415(i)(2) (1998), and M. E. brought a counterclaim seeking compensatory education and the nontuition costs of attending the private school. He also filed a third-party complaint against various school district administrators and child study team members, alleging violations of IDEA, the Rehabilitation Act of 1973, New Jersey state law, and the U.S. Constitution. He requested compensatory and punitive damages under Section 1983.

In 1998, the District Court reversed the ALJ's decision that the school district had not provided M. E. an FAPE and reversed the decision that the school district pay M. E.'s tuition at the private school. The District Court also granted the school district summary judgment on M. E.'s third-party complaint seeking compensatory and punitive damages because M. E. had not been denied an education.

The District Court's decision was appealed to the Third Circuit Court of Appeals. M. E. remained at the private school at the school district's expense pursuant to an agreement between his parents and the school. After oral argument, the Circuit Court ordered the school district to comply with the District Court's order, enjoining the implementation of its earlier order, and to pay M. E.'s tuition and residential and transportation costs at the private school.

ISSUE: Provision of FAPE

HOLDING: The District Court held that an IEP need only provide "more than a trivial educational benefit" to be appropriate, equating this minimal amount of benefit with a "meaningful educational benefit." The standard set forth in the applicable case law requires "significant learning" and meaningful benefit. The provision of "more than a trivial educational benefit" did not meet these standards. The Circuit Court also found that the District Court failed to give adequate consideration to M. E.'s intellectual potential in its conclusion that the school district's IEP was appropriate. The District Court did not analyze the type and amount of learning of which M. E. was capable. The judgment of the District Court was vacated and remanded.

ISSUE: Placement at Landmark, a Private School

HOLDING: The District Court's holding that the school district was not required to pay M. E.'s tuition at the private school for the 1996–1997 school year because his IEP had

provided him with an FAPE was remanded for reconsideration.

ISSUE: Compensatory Education

HOLDING: The District Court erred when it dismissed M. E.'s claim for compensatory education for the years 1988–1996 on a finding that his 1996–1997 IEP was appropriate.

ISSUE: Costs and Fees at the Administrative Hearing

HOLDING: The decision to vacate the District Court's reversal required that the denial of fees and costs be vacated and remanded.

ISSUE: Third-Party Claims under 42 U.S.C. § 1983

HOLDING: The order of the District Court granting summary judgment was affirmed. To prevail on a Section 1983 suit brought against defendants in their official capacity, the plaintiff must establish that the deprivation of his or her rights was the result of an official policy or custom. The District Court held that M. E. provided no evidence that third-party defendants acted in such a manner. Indeed, the evidence presented indicated that the school district had failed to fulfill its responsibilities, not ignore them.

ISSUE: IDEA Claims

HOLDING: The grant of summary judgment on M. E.'s IDEA claims was vacated because it appeared that the District Court examined only the 1996–1997 school year.

ISSUE: Section 504 Claims

HOLDING: The District Court's grant of summary judgment on M. E.'s Section 504 claims was vacated and remanded because there was a genuine issue of fact concerning the school district's failure to satisfy its Section 504 responsibility.

ISSUE: Section 1983 and 1985 Conspiracy Claim

HOLDING: The Circuit Court agreed with the District Court's grant of summary judgment on M. E.'s 1985 claim because it found no evidence that suggested the alleged violation of M. E.'s rights was motivated by racial or "otherwise class-based" animus.

ISSUE: Qualified Immunity

HOLDING: The Circuit Court vacated and remanded the District Court's holding so that it could be reconsidered in light of *W. B. v. Matula* (1995).

ISSUE: State Law Claims

HOLDING: The District Court dismissed M. E.'s state law claims alleging violations of the New Jersey law against discrimination and the New Jersey constitution's guarantee of a thorough and efficient education because the third-party defendants had qualified immunity.

ILLUSTRATING THE LAW THROUGH DISCUSSION

For each identified issue, explain how the Circuit Court may have decided its holding. Base your answer on relevant sections of IDEA and case law.

ADDITIONAL PRACTICE

Select a case from the case list in Appendix D and research the facts and issues. Analyze and present the holdings of the court.

References

Agostini v. Felton, 521 U.S. 203, 117 S.Ct. 1997 (1997).

Arc of ND v. Schafer, 83 F.3d 1008 (8th Cir. 1996), *cert. denied,* 117 S.Ct. 482 (1996).

Baby Neal v. Casey, 821 F. Supp. 320 (E.D. Pa. 1993), *rev'd,* 43 F.3d 48 (1994).

Bills v. Homer Consolidated School District No. 33–C, 959 F. Supp. 507, 511 (N.D. Ill. 1997).

Burlington School Committee v. Department of Education of Massachusetts, 471 U.S. 359, 105 S.Ct. 1996, 85 L.Ed. 2d 385 (1985).

Civil Rights Act of 1964, 42 U.S.C. § 1983 (1981).

Colorado River Water Conservation District v. United States, 424 U.S. 800, 47 L.Ed. 2d 483, 96 S.Ct. 1236 (1976).

Crocker v. Tennessee Secondary School Athletic Association, 980 F.2d 382 (6th Cir. 1992).

Deitsch v. Tillery, 309 Ark. 401, 833 S.W. 2d 760 (1992).

Doe v. Smith, 879 F.2d 1340 (6th Cir. 1989), *cert. denied sub nom.,* Doe v. Sumner County Board of Education, 493 U.S. 1025 (1990).

Duane B. v. Chester-Upland School District, 21 IDELR 1050 (D.Ct. E.D. Penn. 1994).

Evans v. Evans, 818 F. Supp. 1215 (N.D. Ind. 1993).

Gifis, S. H. (1996). *Law dictionary.* Hauppage, NY: Barron's Educational Series.

Grun v. Pneumo Abex Corporation, 163 F.3d 411 (7th Cir. 1999), *cert. denied,* 119 S.Ct. 1496, 143 L.Ed. 2d 651 (1999).

The Handicapped Children's Protection Act, 20 U.S.C. § 1400 *et seq.* (1986).

Helbig v. City of New York, 597 N.Y.S. 2d 585 (Supp. 1993), *rev'd,* 622 N.Y.S. 2d 316 (1995).

Heldman v. Sobol, 962 F.2d 148 (2nd Cir. 1992).

Hensley v. Eckerhart, 461 U.S. 424, 103 S.Ct. 1933, 76 L.Ed. 2d 40 (1983).

Individuals with Disabilities Education Act, 20 U.S.C. § 1400 *et seq.* (1990).

Individuals with Disabilities Education Improvement Act of 2004, P.L. 108–446, § 601 *et seq.,* 118 Stat. 2647 (2005).

Jason D. W. v. Houston Independent School District, 158 F.3d 205 (5th Cir. 1998).

Johnson v. Lancaster County Children and Youth Social Services Agency, 19 IDELR 1094 (D.Ct. E.D. Penn. 1993).

Maldonado v. Benitez, 874 F. Supp. 491 (D. Puerto Rico 1995).

Merrifield v. Lake Central School Corporation, 770 F. Supp. 468 (N.D. Ind. 1991).

Mills v. Board of Education of the District of Columbia, 348 F. Supp. 866 (D.D.C. 1972).

PARC (Pennsylvania Association for Retarded Citizens) v. Commonwealth of Pennsylvania, 343 F. Supp. 297 (E.D. Pa. 1972).

Pennhurst State School and Hospital et al. v. Halderman, 465 U.S. 89, 104 S.Ct. 900, 70 L.Ed. 2d 67 (1984).

Peters by Peters v. Johnson, 25 IDELR 738 (D.Ct. Minn. 4th Div. 1997).

Pihl v. Massachusetts Department of Education, 9 F.3d 184 (1st Cir. 1993).

Ridgewood Board of Education v. N. E. for M. E., 172 F.3d 238 (3rd Cir. 1999).

Rodricus L. by Betty H. v. Waukegan Community School District No. 60, 28 IDELR 458 (D.Ct. N.D. Ill. E.Div. 1998).

Roe v. Wade, 410 U.S. 113, 93 S.Ct. 705, 35 L.Ed. 2d 147 (1973).

Rufo v. Inmates of Suffolk County Jail, 502 U.S. 367, 112 S.Ct. 748, 116 L.Ed. 2d 867 (1992).

S–1 v. Spangler, 650 F. Supp. 1427 (M.D. N.C. 1986), *cert. denied,* 115 S.Ct. 205, 130 L.Ed. 2d 135, *vacated as moot,* 832 F.2d 294 (4th Cir. 1987).

Sellers v. School Board of City of Manassas, VA, 141 F.3d 524 (4th Cir. 1998), *cert. denied,* 119 U.S. 168, 142 L.Ed. 2d 137 (1998).

Smith v. Robinson, 468 U.S. 992, 104 S.Ct. 3457, 82 L.Ed. 2d 746 (1984).

Springer v. The Fairfax County School Board, 134 F.3d 659 (4th Cir. 1998).

State of Connecticut v. Bruno, No. 14851 (1996).

Thomas R. W. by Pamela R. and Edward W. v. Massachusetts Department of Education, 130 F.3d 477 (1st Cir. 1997).

United States v. Merz, 376 U.S. 192, 84 S.Ct. 639, 11 L.Ed. 2d 629 (1964).

University Interscholastic League v. Buchanan, 848 S.W. 2d 298 (Tex. Ct. App. 1993).

Virginia Department of Education v. Riley, 106 F.3d 566 (1996), *superseded,* 106 F.3d 559 (4th Cir. 1997).

W. B. v. Matula, 67 F.3d 484 (3rd Cir. 1995).

Younger v. Harris, 401 U.S. 37, 91 S.Ct. 746, 27 L.Ed. 2d 669 (1971).

CHAPTER TEN

Discipline Issues

GUIDING QUESTIONS

1. How do zero tolerance rules relate to students with disabilities?

2. Under what circumstances should a manifestation determination occur?

In the classroom and in schools, many students, including those with disabilities, have behaviors that are inappropriate and may result in problems for themselves, other students, and teachers (Johns & Keenan, 1997; LaVigna & Donnellan, 1986; Meyer & Evans, 1989). Problems addressing student behaviors have been cited as one of the main reasons for teachers leaving the profession (Rose, Gallup, & Elam, 1997; Smith, Polloway, Patton, & Dowdy, 2004). In addition, these disruptive behaviors may result in children having difficulty being successful in school and possibly being identified as having an emotional/behavioral disorder. Parents are concerned for those same reasons but believe their children are the recipients more often of inappropriate disciplinary methods and excessive suspensions and/or expulsions from school. Such methods could be punitive in nature, while not providing the student with a means of addressing the underlying issues of the exhibited behavior.

Disciplinary Methods and Zero Tolerance Rules— Weapons, Drugs, and Serious Bodily Injury

Under state statutes, schools have been given the authority to develop policies (i.e., rules) that address student behavior in the school and/or on school property and identify the consequences for violations of this set of rules (Yell, 1998). However, these policies may not violate the student's constitutional rights. That means that the school must have a rationale for the action and that the rationale must have a school-related purpose. In other words, schools cannot prohibit or punish behavior that does not adversely affect the delivery of education. Rules must also be easily understood, meaning they must be both specific and clear. The courts examined these issues in *Cole v. Greenfield-Central Community Schools* (1986) and found that (a) the school district had acted reasonably and (b) a student with disabilities was not immune to a school's disciplinary procedures. According to Yell (1998),

> To determine reasonableness, the court analyzed four elements: (a) Did the teacher have the authority under state and local laws to discipline the student? (b) Was the rule violated within the scope of the educational function? (c) Was the rule violator the one who was disciplined? and (d) Was the discipline in proportion to the gravity of the offense? (p. 317)

Since the mid-1990s, there has been a strong movement to address the issues of violence, drugs, and safety in the schools. This has led to the development of

Standards and the Law

CEC Standard 1: Foundations
PRAXIS Standard: Legal and Societal Issues

school policies, known as zero tolerance policies, which include strict disciplinary consequences for students who bring weapons to school and/or who use or sell drugs at school or at school activities and often involve referral to law enforcement and judicial authorities (IDEA of 2004, P.L. 108–446, § 615 [K][1][C], 118 Stat. 2647 [2005]). IDEA defines illegal drugs, weapons, and serious bodily harm as

(A) CONTROLLED SUBSTANCE.—The term 'controlled substance' means a drug or other substance identified under schedules I, II, III, IV, or V in section 202(d) of the Controlled Substances Act [21 U.S.C. 812(c)].

(B) ILLEGAL DRUG.—The term 'illegal drug' means a controlled substance but does not include *a* controlled substance that is legally possessed or used under the supervision of a licensed health-care professional or that is legally possessed or used under any other authority under that Act or under any other provision of Federal law.

(C) WEAPON.—The term 'weapon' has the meaning given the term 'dangerous weapon' under section 930(g)(2) of title 18, United States Code.

(D) SERIOUS BODILY HARM.—The term 'serious bodily harm' has the meaning given the term 'serious bodily harm' under paragraph (3) of subsection (h) of section 1365 of title 18, United States Code. (IDEA of 2004, P.L. 108–446, § 615 [K][1][G][7], 118 Stat. 2647 [2005])

In schools, the consequences of such behavior are unilateral suspension from school for specified amounts of time. At issue is that students with disabilities and minority students may be more impacted by these policies than other students, and as a result, are prevented from receiving an FAPE (Zhang, Katsiyannis, & Herbst, 2004). In opposition to common thought, research indicates that there is little support for "the effectiveness of such policies in improving student behaviors specifically or in contributing to overall school safety in general" (p. 337).

Standards and the Law

CEC Standard 1: Foundations
PRAXIS Standard: Legal and Societal Issues

Idea Requirements for Discipline

There are few areas more contentious than the school's administration of discipline to children with disabilities. With one exception of where the child's behavior involves weapons, illegal drugs, or serious bodily harm, the 2004 Amendments to IDEA make it clear that the schools must deal with the behavior problems of children with disabilities within the educational context rather than removing them from school. Behavior that results in the discipline of a child at school is inappropriate behavior. In the context of schools, inappropriate behavior could be considered any behavior that violates a school rule or a criminal law. Before the school can take action, the school is charged with the responsibility of determining if the behavior is in any way related to the child's disability, even if the child has not been identified as being in need of special education.

Suspension/Expulsion

Suspension is defined as removal from school for a short period of time, usually less than 10 school days. Expulsion is removal from school for more than 10 school days. During this period of time, the student usually does not receive educational services. After implementation of IDEA in 1975, courts addressed the issue of suspension and whether it was a change in placement. Early court cases (*Stuart v. Nappi,* 1978; *S-1 v. Turlington,* 1981) supported the belief that indeed these removals from school were changes in placements, and as such, triggered the IDEA rules, including the principle of "stay-put." Under IDEA, stay-put is when the child remains in the current educational placement or, if applying for additional admission to the public school, stays in the public school program until all proceedings have taken place (IDEA of 2004, P.L. 108–446, § 615 [J], 118 Stat. 2647 [2005]).

Controversy continued over the use of suspension with students with disabilities until the 1988 Supreme Court decision, *Honig v. Doe,* and the 1994 decision, *Light v. Parkway C-2 School District.* The issue of suspension and the provision of an FAPE were discussed more fully in the previous chapters on FAPEs and procedural due process (see Chapters 3 and 7).

Interim Alternative Educational Setting

An alternative form of discipline that did not trigger the "stay-put" rule was that of an alternative placement within the school. This was known as Interim Alternative

---

Standards and the Law

CEC Standard 1: Foundations

PRAXIS Standard: Legal and Societal Issues

Educational Setting (IAES). If the time of suspension would exceed 10 school days, the student is removed from the general or special education classroom but continues to receive educational services through IAES as required by FAPE. The advantages of this form of discipline are that the student is supervised, is receiving educational services, is segregated from the student body, and is not in the community unsupervised during school hours. According to Yell (1998), most courts have upheld the use of such programs and have not considered them to be long-term suspensions that trigger "stay-put" considerations because (a) they are time limited and (b) the student is receiving educational services.

In the 2004 Amendments, several modifications to the preexisting regulations concerning a "change of placement" were included. The school personnel have been given the authority to remove a child with a disability who has violated the school's code of student conduct. This change of placement should be considered on a case-by-case basis and not used as a wholesale removal of any child with a disability whose behavior is a manifestation of his or her disability. When a decision is made to remove the child from the general education program, the removal may be to an appropriate IAES, or it may be a suspension from school for no more than 10 school days. The application of such a suspension should be no different than would be applied to a child without disabilities (IDEA of 2004, P.L. 108–446, § 615 [K][1], 118 Stat. 2647 [2005]).

If the child's behavior is not a manifestation of his or her disability, then the school may order a change in placement (i.e., a suspension from school that exceeds 10 school days as stated in the school's discipline procedures). This suspension may also be provided in an IAES at the discretion of the school personnel.

In the unique situation where the child's behavior involves weapons, illegal drugs, or serious bodily harm, the school may remove the student without consideration of whether the behavior is a manifestation of the student's disability. This removal to an IAES may not be for more than 45 school days (IDEA of 2004, P.L. 108–446, § 615 [K][1][G], 118 Stat. 2647 [2005]). When such a decision is made, the school must notify the student's parents no later than that day and provide them with information concerning their procedural rights.

If parents of the child with a disability disagree with the school's "decision regarding placement, or the manifestation determination . . . " or the LEA believes "maintaining the current placement of the child is substantially likely to result in injury to the child or to others," either party may request a hearing (IDEA of 2004, P.L. 108–446, § 615 [K][3][A], 118 Stat. 2647 [2005]). The hearing officer then hears the appeal and makes a decision concerning the placement of the child. This decision may be to return the child with a disability to the placement from which he or she was removed, or the decision may be to order a change in placement to an appropriate IAES for not more than 45 days if there is substantial evidence that the current placement is likely to result in injury to the child or to others (IDEA of 2004, P.L. 108–446, § 615 [K][3][B], 118 Stat. 2647 [2005]). An interim placement is to be selected so the child may continue to participate in the general education curriculum, although placed in another setting, and to continue to progress toward the goals set forth in the IEP. In addition, provisions should be made by the school for a functional behavioral assessment to occur and for the provision of behavioral intervention services and modifications so the behavior that resulted in removal from the general education curriculum does not reoccur (IDEA of 2004, P.L. 108–446, § 615 [1][D], 118 Stat. 2647 [2005]).

Manifestation Determination

[handwritten: You have to do this so you're not avoiding due Process & the stay—put provisions]

Assuming the child is a child with disabilities, the Act requires several steps to be taken by the school district before substantial disciplinary procedures may be imposed. One of the primary changes to the 1997 Amendments was the addition of the manifestation determination hearing. IDEA 2004 clarifies the manifestation process as

[handwritten: Final Exam ?]

   (i) IN GENERAL.—Except as provided in subparagraph (B), within 10 school days of any decision to change the placement of a child with a disability because of a violation of a code of student conduct, the local educational agency, the parent, and relevant members of the IEP Team (as determined by the parent and the local educational agency) shall review all relevant information in the student's file, including the child's IEP, any teacher observation, and any relevant information provided by the parents to determine—

      (I) if the conduct in question was caused by, or had a direct and substantial relationship to, the child's disability; or

      (II) if the conduct in question was the direct result of the local educational agency's failure to implement the IEP.

   (ii) MANIFESTATION.—If the local educational agency, the parent, and relevant members of the IEP Team determine that either subclause (I) or (II) of clause (i) is applicable for the child, the conduct shall be determined to be a manifestation of the child's disability. (IDEA of 2004, P.L. 108–446, § 615 [K][1][E], 118 Stat. 2647 [2005]).

The manifestation determination review is a procedure used to prevent the school from avoiding the due process procedures of the Act with its "stay-put" provisions by alleging that the offending acts of the student were not a result of the child's disability.

Functional Assessment of Behavior and Behavior Intervention Plans

After the manifestation determination review has been completed and the student's behavior has been identified as a manifestation of the student's disability, further

> **Standards and the Law**
>
> **CEC Standard 1:** Foundations
> **PRAXIS Standard:** Legal and Societal Issues

action by the school, parents, and other members of the IEP team is required. First, the IEP team shall conduct a functional behavioral assessment and implement a behavioral intervention plan to address the behavior that resulted in the disciplinary action. When the school is aware of the existence of a disability that may produce inappropriate or unacceptable behaviors, the school must take affirmative steps to deal with such behaviors by anticipating potential problems and then developing educational programs to deal with them. In each situation involving a child with a disability where behavior is a factor, IDEA requires the school to consider the functional assessment of behavior and base a behavioral intervention plan on its results. The plan must be evaluated periodically and modified according to the progress and needs of the child. In developing the plan, the IEP team must ". . . in the case of a child whose behavior impedes the child's learning or that of others, consider, the use of positive behavioral interventions, and supports, and other strategies, to address that behavior . . ." (IDEA of 2004, P.L. 108–446, § 614 [d][3][B][i], 118 Stat. 2647 [2005]).

If the child is subject to disciplinary action and a behavioral intervention plan is already in place, then the IEP team should

(ii) . . . review the behavioral intervention plan if the child already has such a behavioral intervention plan, and modify it, as necessary, to address the behavior; and

(iii) except as provided in subparagraph (G), return the child to the placement from which the child was removed, unless the parent and the local educational agency agree to a change of placement as part of the modification of the behavioral intervention plan (IDEA of 2004, P.L. 108–446, § 615 [K][1][F], 118 Stat. 2647 [2005])

As a result of these new requirements of the Act, a new era has begun wherein the school is responsible not just for the academic education of its children, but for the behavioral education.

"Stay-Put" Requirements

The South Carolina District Court interpreted these new provisions in *Horry County School District v. P. F.* (1998). In the *P. F.* case, the child was a 15-year-old female with mental retardation, severe brain injury, and behavioral problems. The school district filed a complaint seeking interim injunctive relief and a declaratory judgment that a proposed residential placement complied with IDEA. In a decision in favor of the school district, the District Court noted that the school district must provide evidence that the current placement could be harmful to the child or others and that the proposed placement would provide the child with the opportunity to participate in the general curriculum. It also stated that IDEA empowers

. . . a hearing officer to enjoin the "stay-put" provision of the IDEA in a manner similar to the courts. (Citations omitted.) In other words, § 1415(k) expands the powers of hearing officers to enable them to grant injunctive relief similar to that previously available only from courts under Honig. . . . Consequently, after the 1997 Amendments school districts may seek temporary injunctive relief at an administrative level in order to remove a dangerous child from his or her educational setting.

The "Honig injunction" is a tool to enjoining enforcement of the IDEA's "stay-put" provision pending administrative due process proceedings. Its purpose is to ensure that the Act's "stay-put" provision does not leave educators hamstrung when confronted with a dangerous or self-injurious student. (Citations omitted.) Similarly, the newly amended IDEA now authorizes hearing officers to enjoin operation of the "stay-put" provision. (*Horry County School District v. P. F.*, 1998, p. 364)

There does not appear to be any legitimate doubt that the practicality of these new procedures will result in more placements in an alternative setting than was previously the case, primarily because of the ease of obtaining relief from the *Honig* "stay-put" provision. However, just as important, the alternative educational setting gives the school personnel a "relief valve" for those children with disabilities who might injure other children.

Nonidentified Child with Disabilities

In some instances, a student whose behavior has resulted in disciplinary action by the school may state that he or she actually has a disability even though he or she has not been identified. For those children, the Act states that

A child who has not been determined to be eligible for special education and related services under this part and who has engaged in behavior that violated a code of student conduct may assert any of the protections provided for in this part if the local educational agency had knowledge . . . that the child was a child with a disability before the behavior that precipitated the disciplinary action occurred. (IDEA of 2004, P.L. 108–446, § 615 [K][5][A], 118 Stat. 2647 [2005]).

In other words, the schools cannot use the fact that a child has not yet been identified as having a disability to circumvent the legal procedures required otherwise. In fact, there are certain situations in which the school will have been considered to have known that the child may have been, or should have been, considered for special education services referral. The Act states that

A local educational agency shall be deemed to have knowledge that a child is a child with a disability if, before that precipitated the disciplinary action occurred—

(i) the parent of the child has expressed concern in writing to supervisory or administrative personnel of the appropriate educational agency, or a teacher of the child, that the child is in need of special education and related services;

(ii) the parent of the child has requested an evaluation of the child . . . ; or

(iii) the teacher of the child, or other personnel of the local educational agency, has expressed specific concerns about a pattern of behavior demonstrated by the child, directly to the director of special education of such agency or to other supervisory personnel of the agency (IDEA of 2004, P.L. 108–446, § 615 [K][5][B], 118 Stat. 2647 [2005])

Thus, the child may assert the protections of the Act if the school has had reason to believe the child may be in need of special education services. It would seem impossible for school personnel to assert that they were unaware of the behavior problems of a child, if the disciplinary action were to occur after beginning the first grade. In sum, if the child has behavior problems, school personnel are charged with the responsibility of knowing whether the child should be identified as a child with disabilities. If not identified, the child may still be under the protection of the Act until it is determined that the behaviors are not disability related.

Juvenile Authority Reports

Despite the increased accountability of schools in the area of behavioral education, IDEA has included a section delineating the school's role with law enforcement and judicial authorities regarding children with disabilities when the child with a disability allegedly commits a crime. The Act states that

(A) Nothing in this part shall be construed to prohibit an agency from reporting a crime committed by a child with a disability to appropriate authorities or to prevent State law enforcement and judicial authorities from exercising their responsibilities with regard to the application of Federal and State law to crimes committed by a child with a disability.

(B) An agency reporting a crime committed by a child with a disability shall ensure that copies of the special education and disciplinary records of the child are transmitted for consideration by the appropriate authorities to whom the agency reports the crime. (IDEA of 2004, P.L. 108–446, § 615 [k][6], 118 Stat. 2647 [2005])

Implicit in the foregoing statement is the fact that the schools may report any violation of the criminal law to law enforcement or judicial authorities. It is important to note that the section is limited only to criminal offenses and does not include status offenses such as truancy or child with behavior problems—behaviors typically under the jurisdiction of the Juvenile Court (see *In re Child with Disabilities,* 1993). Arguably, certain status offenses could be considered criminal offenses by a state, and the provisions of the Act would not prevent the school from reporting the crime to the authorities. However, such attempts to circumvent the system by converting status offenses to criminal offenses should not, and probably would not, meet with much success.

After the enactment of IDEA, several courts found that in certain circumstances when a school reported a child with disabilities to law enforcement or the

Standards and the Law

CEC Standard 1: Foundations
PRAXIS Standard: Legal and Societal Issues

Juvenile Court, it resulted in a change in placement, activating the procedural safeguards of the Act. Such was the case in *Morgan v. Chris L. by Mike L.* (1997). In the *Morgan* case, the child had Attention Deficit Hyperactivity Disorder and was in the process of being assessed for special education when he vandalized the school bathroom. The school filed a petition in Juvenile Court to have him declared a delinquent or unruly child. The parents requested a due process hearing, and the ALJ ordered the school to dismiss its petition in Juvenile Court. The District Court upheld the decision of the hearing officer, and the Sixth Circuit Court of Appeals affirmed the case. The Circuit Court held that the order requiring the school district to dismiss the Juvenile Court case was within the discretion of the District Court and the ALJ in fashioning a specific remedy to redress the school's failure to provide FAPE. The Amendments to the Act would seem to eliminate the *Morgan* decision and may allow the district to file any petition that recites a violation of the criminal code.

Considering the safeguards that close certain avenues previously available to school officials in expelling, suspending, or disciplining a child with disabilities, it is plausible that school officials will try to find some way to remove children with disabilities and behavior problems from their school systems. Some have done so in the past, and there is no reason to believe that the same thing will not occur in the future. The only avenue available to the school is to refer the child to the juvenile court system. As we have seen, a petition may be brought for delinquency or, alternatively, for a status offense. One may reasonably conclude that the juvenile justice system will see an increase in the number of children with disabilities who appear in court. This is especially true if the only avenue available to schools is to remove some children within the school system who consume more than their share of the financial resources and who may pose a challenge to school officials. This is at a time when the juvenile system is already overburdened. Thus, the child with disabilities who should have been provided services in the schools may be institutionalized as a result of the behavior. Even though the school would be required to pay the cost of the special education in the institution, the ultimate purpose of removing the child from the school system would be achieved. Only the Supreme Court can answer the question of whether the school may "dodge the bullet" by referring an increasing number of children with disabilities to the juvenile justice system.

Summary

The issue of disciplining students with disabilities has been one of the more contentious areas in more recent years, possibly in part because of the focus on school violence and zero tolerance. In disciplining students with disabilities, the court found in *Cole v. Greenfield-Central Community Schools* (1986) that, if the school district had acted reasonably, students with disabilities were not immune to a school's disciplinary procedures. To determine reasonableness, the court analyzed the four elements of (a) the teacher has legal authority, (b) the violation occurred within the scope of the educational function, (c) the target of the disciplinary action was the rule violator, and (d) the discipline was in proportion to the gravity of the offense. However, the 2004 Amendments to IDEA make it clear that the schools must deal with the behavior problems of children with disabilities within the educational context, rather than removing them from school, except when the child's behavior involves weapons, illegal drugs, or serious bodily harm. When the child's behavior involves weapons, illegal drugs, or serious bodily harm, the child may be removed to an IAES for not more than 45 school days. The school may remove the student to IAES without consideration of whether the behavior is a manifestation of the student's disability.

One of the primary changes to the 1997 Amendments was the addition of the manifestation determination hearing. IDEA 2004 clarifies the manifestation process by determining whether the conduct in question was caused by, or had a direct and substantial relationship to, the child's disability, or was the direct result failure to implement the IEP.

It must be noted that the 2004 Amendments contain substantial changes to IDEA in the arena of discipline—changes that will be interpreted by the courts as cases work their way through the system. The Amendments seem to embody the decisions resulting from cases reviewed by the courts that have restricted the ability of districts to eliminate students deemed undesirable due to the student's disability. An important change in previous restrictions concerns the release of information concerning discipline issues when a student with disabilities is referred to law enforcement agencies.

Indeed, if the past foretells the future, the education of children with disabilities continues to merge with that of children without disabilities within the general education setting. Congress through legislation continues to press the issue of full access within the community and to community services and facilities. In addition, the courts continue to underscore access as a constitutional right of all persons. However, in the educational arena, Congress is also grappling with the conflicting needs of schools and guaranteed rights. Schools are enjoined to protect the right of access to a free appropriate education for children with disabilities and to protect the personal safety of those within the public school. Therefore, Congress has prescribed, through the provision of the option of alternative interim educational settings, procedures for responding to those students feared to be a danger to themselves or others.

Congress also sought to clarify the school's role with law enforcement by balancing the school's need to act in concern with law enforcement with the rights and needs of students with disabilities through the requirement for a manifestation determination review. A manifestation determination review is an examination of the student's behavior to determine whether the behavior is a result of the child's disability. The result is an attempt to ensure a child with disabilities is not denied educational services and access to the public schools because of actions that are a result of disability. The future, as in the past, appears to be one where the actions of Congress and the courts continue to strive to improve the quality of life for individuals with disabilities and their families.

Questions for Discussion

1. Defend or attack the following statement: The manifestation determination is an essential component of the discipline process for students with disabilities and should not be eliminated as part of the paperwork reduction efforts.

2. What may be some of the unintended results of IDEA Amendments of 2004 in regard to students with disabilities and discipline?

Websites for Further Explanation

www.naspcenter.org/factsheets/zt_fs.html

www.buildingblocksforyouth.org/issues/zerotolerance/facts.html

www.whittedclearylaw.com/FSLSCS/Custom/TOCPublications.asp

www.causeonline.org/iep2.html

www.usd259.com/safeschools/Safe_&_Drug_Free_Schools/fact_sheets/1999–2000/4BenefitsIn-SchoolSuspension.pdf

www.disciplineassociates.com/tip10.htm

www.nasponline.org/futures/iaes.html

www.ideadata.org/docs/Discipline%20QA.doc

journals.sped.org/EC/Archive_Articles/VOLUME68NUMBER1FALL2001_EC_Maag.pdf

ILLUSTRATING THE LAW

Briefing #1 of:
Bill Honig, California Superintendent of Public Instruction v. John Doe and Jack Smith
Supreme Court of the United States

FACTS: This case grows out of the efforts of certain officials of the San Francisco Unified School District (SFUSD) to expel two emotionally disturbed children from school indefinitely for violent and disruptive conduct related to their disabilities. In November 1980, John Doe assaulted another student by choking him at a developmental center for children with disabilities. As a result, Doe was suspended for 5 days. Ultimately, a student placement committee recommended that Doe be expelled, and the committee extended Doe's suspension until expulsion proceedings were completed.

Doe brought this suit against a host of local school officials, alleging that the suspension and proposed expulsion violated EHA. Doe sought a temporary restraining order, canceling a local hearing and requiring school officials to convene an IEP meeting. The District Judge granted the requested injunctive relief and further ordered the school district to provide home tutoring for Doe on an interim basis; shortly thereafter, the judge issued a preliminary injunction directing the school district to return Doe to his current educational placement pending the completion of the IEP review process.

Upon learning of Doe's action, Jack Smith, an emotionally disturbed child who was enrolled in a California public middle school, obtained leave to intervene in the suit. Smith had been suspended for 5 days for stealing, extorting money from fellow students, and making sexual comments to female classmates. Ultimately, a student placement committee recommended that Smith be expelled, and the committee extended Smith's suspension until such time as expulsion proceedings were completed. Smith's counsel protested these actions on grounds essentially identical to those raised by Doe.

The District Court subsequently entered summary judgment in favor of Doe and Smith on their EHA claims and issued a permanent injunction enjoining the school district from taking any disciplinary action other than a 2- or 5-day suspension against a child with disabilities. The District Judge found that the proposed expulsions and indefinite suspensions for conduct attributable to disabilities deprived Doe and Smith of their mandated right to an FAPE. The judge also ordered the state to provide services directly to children with disabilities when, in any individual case, the state determined that the LEA was unable or unwilling to do so.

On appeal, the Court of Appeals for the Ninth Circuit affirmed the orders with slight modifications.

ISSUES: This case presented two issues. First, whether state or local school authorities may, in the face of a statutory proscription, nevertheless unilaterally exclude children with disabilities from the classroom for dangerous or disruptive conduct growing out of their disabilities? Second, whether a district court may, in the exercise of its equitable powers, order a state to provide educational services directly to a disabled child when the local agency fails to do so?

HELD: Congress intentionally omitted a "dangerousness" exception to the stay-put provision contained in U.S.C. § 1415(e)(3). The Court refused to accept Honig's invitation to rewrite the statute. U.S.C. § 1415(e)(3) does not operate to limit the equitable powers of district courts such that they cannot, in appropriate cases, temporarily enjoin a dangerous child with disabilities from attending school.

RATIONALE: In drafting the statutory language at issue, Congress meant to strip schools of the unilateral authority they had traditionally employed to exclude students with disabilities, particularly students with emotional disturbances, from school. Congress intended for the removal of students with disabilities from public schools to be accomplished through the permission of the parents, or as a last resort, the courts.

The evil that Congress sought to remedy was the unilateral exclusion of children with disabilities by schools, not courts. The stay-put provision in no way purports to limit or preempt the authority conferred on courts by § 1415(e)(2); indeed, it says nothing whatsoever about judicial power.

ILLUSTRATING THE LAW THROUGH DISCUSSION

1. Would this case have been moot if both Doe and Smith had been older than age 21 at the time the Court reviewed it?

2. Discuss Congress's most recent concern of returning decision making "power to local and state school districts" and how that differs from Congress's 1975 mistrust of local and state school districts' ability to place students with disabilities.

ILLUSTRATING THE LAW

Briefing #2 of:
Martin Light v. Parkway C-2 School District
United States Court of Appeals, Eighth Circuit

FACTS: Lauren Light is a 13-year-old child with multiple mental disabilities, including autism. Light often exhibits aggressive behaviors such as kicking, biting, hitting, and throwing objects. In 1993, Light was enrolled in a self-contained classroom for students with mental disabilities in a middle school in Missouri. Lauren's disability required that she be accompanied by two full-time staff personnel at all times, in addition to the classroom teacher assigned to her room. Light committed 11 to 19 aggressive acts per week, some of which required her attending staff personnel and other special education students to seek the attention of the school nurse. The record suggests that Light's aggressive behaviors had a negative effect on the educational progress of five other special education students in her program. As a result, Light's art teacher requested that Light be removed from the class. Light's parents protested any such change.

During art class, Light assaulted a student. Consequently, later that day, the principal held a meeting without Light's parents and imposed a 10-day suspension on Light for her behavior. Light's parents brought this action in District Court seeking to have the suspension lifted because Light was not afforded due process. The school district counterclaimed and invoked the court's equitable power to remove Light from the school pending the resolution of Light's administrative challenge to the proposed change in placement.

Initially, the District Court ruled that Light had been denied due process and granted Light's motion for a temporary restraining order. Later, the court vacated the temporary restraining order and granted the school district's motion for an injunction to remove Light from the middle school. The court found that "maintaining Lauren in her current placement is substantially likely to result in injury either to herself or to others." The court refused to inquire into the adequacy of the school district's efforts to accommodate Light's disabilities. The court further declined to make any assessment as to the best alternative placement for Light.

ISSUES: This case presented two issues. First, whether the Supreme Court's holding in *Honig v. Doe,* 484 U.S. 305 (1988), requires a district court to find that a child is not only "substantially likely to cause injury," but also "truly dangerous" before sanctioning a transfer? Second, whether a school district must make a reasonable accommodation of the child's disability before it can change her placement?

HELD: *Honig v. Doe* does not require a District Court to find that a child is "truly dangerous" before sanctioning a transfer. In this case, the District Court erred by refusing to consider whether Light's disabilities had been reasonably accommodated. Nevertheless, the Court of Appeals concluded that a reasonable accommodation was made and affirmed the District Court's order that Light be removed from her current placement.

RATIONALE: The test in *Honig v. Doe* looks only to the objective likelihood of injury. The Court of Appeals rejected Light's position that a child with disabilities must be shown to be "truly dangerous," as well as substantially likely to cause injury. A child's capacity for harmful intent plays no role in this analysis. The purpose of removal of a dangerous child with disabilities is not punishment but maintaining a safe learning environment for all.

The school district must show that it has made reasonable efforts to accommodate the child's disabilities so as to minimize the likelihood that the child would injure him- or herself or others. This second inquiry is necessary to ensure the school district fulfills its responsibility under IDEA to make available an FAPE for all children with disabilities. School districts should not seek to remove children with disabilities until reasonable steps have been taken to mitigate the threat of injury.

ILLUSTRATING THE LAW THROUGH DISCUSSION

1. What is the test for a district court to use in determining whether a transfer of a student with disabilities is appropriate under § 615(e), *Honig v. Doe*, and *Light v. Parkway C-2 School District*?

2. Attempt to predict the evolution of the interpretation of this case law and § 615(e).

References

Cole v. Greenfield-Central Community Schools, 657 F.Supp. 56 (S.D. Ind. 1986)

Honig v. Doe, 484 U.S. 305, 108 S.Ct. 592, 98 L.Ed. 2d 686 (1988).

Horry County School District v. P. F., 29 IDELR 354 (D.S.C. 1998).

In re Child with Disabilities, 20 IDELR 455 (SEA NH 1993).

Individuals with Disabilities Education Improvement Act of 2004, P.L. 108–446, § 600 *et seq.*, 118 Stat. 2647 (2005). 20 U.S.C. § 600 *et seq.* (2004).

Johns, B. H., & Keenan, J. P. (1997). *Techniques for managing a safe school.* Denver: Love.

LaVigna, G. W., & Donnellan, A. M. (1986). *Alternatives to punishment: Solving behavior problems with non-aversive strategies.* New York: Irvington.

Light v. Parkway C–2 School District, 41 F.3d 1223 (8th Cir. 1994), *cert. denied,* 115 S.Ct. 2557, 132 L.Ed. 2d 811 (1995).

Meyer, L. H., & Evans, L. M. (1989). *Nonaversive intervention for behavior problems: A manual for home and community.* Baltimore: Paul H. Brookes.

Morgan v. Chris L. by Mike L., 106 F.3d 401 (6th Cir. 1997).

Rose, L. C., Gallup, A. M., & Elam, S. M. (1997). The 29th annual Phi Delta Kappa/Gallup poll of the public's attitudes toward the public schools. *Phi Delta Kappan, 79,* 41–48.

Smith, T. E. C., Polloway, E. A., Patton, J. R., & Dowdy, C. A. (2004). *Teaching students with special needs in inclusive settings* (4th ed.). Boston: Pearson/Allyn and Bacon.

S-1 v. Turlington, 635 F.2d 342 (5th Cir. 1981), *cert. denied,* 454 U.S. 1030 (1981).

Stuart v. Nappi, 443 F. Supp. 1235 (D. Conn. 1978).

Yell, M. L. (1998). *The law and special education.* Upper Saddle River, NJ: Merrill/Prentice Hall.

Zhang, D., Katsiyannis, A., & Herbst, M. (2004). Disciplinary exclusions in special education: A 4-year analysis. *Behavior Disorders, 29*(4), 337–347.

CHAPTER ELEVEN

Mediation and Impartial Due Process Hearing

GUIDING QUESTIONS

1. Define "mediation" and explain the phases of the process.

2. Define "resolution session" and explain how it is different from mediation.

3. Define "impartial due process hearings" and explain the phases of the process.

4. How do the procedures of mediation, resolution session, and impartial due process hearings protect the parents' rights, the school's rights, and the educational rights of the child with disabilities?

According to IDEA, any state or local school district that receives federal funding is required to "establish and maintain procedures . . . to ensure that children with disabilities and their parents are guaranteed procedural safeguards with respect to the provision of a free appropriate public education by such agencies" (IDEA of 2004, P.L. 108–446, § 615 [a], 118 Stat. 2647 [2005]). According to the National Information Center for Children and Youth with Disabilities, this requirement was included in the legislation to provide parents and schools a venue wherein disputes concerning the education of students with disabilities could be resolved. IDEA 2004 changed the mandated two-part process for the resolution of disputes—mediation and impartial due process hearing—to include a third step—the resolution session.

Mediation

The 2004 Amendments to IDEA continued to include a requirement that provides parents with the opportunity to resolve disputes through mediation prior to the more adversarial due process hearing. Previously, the option for mediation could be made available to parents, but now the provision of this option is required. According to OSEP (2000), mediation is an impartial system that allows the proper parties who have a dispute to confidentially discuss the disputed issues with a neutral third party with the goal of resolving the disputes in a binding written agreement.

Requirements for Mediation Procedures

States must develop and implement a mediation process that is made available to parents whenever a complaint is filed (IDEA of 2004, P.L. 108–446, § 615 [e][1], 118 Stat. 2647 [2005]). The procedures for mediation developed by each state must be in accord with the requirements as outlined in IDEA and its regulations. The legislation states that

(A) The procedures shall ensure that the mediation process—
   (i)   is voluntary on the part of the parties;
   (ii) is not used to deny or delay a parent's right to a due process hearing . . . or to deny any other rights afforded under this part; and
   (iii) is conducted by a qualified and impartial mediator who is trained in effective mediation techniques. (IDEA of 2004, P.L. 108–446, § 615 [e][2], 118 Stat. 2647 [2005])

Standards and the Law

CEC Standard 9: Professional and Ethical Practice
INTASC Standard 10: Collaboration, Ethics, and Relationships
PRAXIS Standard: Legal and Societal Issues

Selection and Impartiality of Mediators

According to IDEA, a mediator is defined as "an impartial individual who conducts the mediation process" (OSEP, 2000). The issue of the impartiality of the mediator is essential because the success of mediation usually depends on the ability of the mediator to secure the trust of both parties in the mediation. Thus, the individual who serves in the role of mediator

> may not be employee of any LEA or any State agency . . . or an SEA that is providing direct services to a child who is the subject of the mediation process; and must not have a personal or professional conflict of interest. (Wright & Wright, 2000, p. 181)

Each state is required to develop guidelines for the selection and training of the mediators within its jurisdiction. According to IDEA a list of individuals who are qualified as mediators as well as knowledgeable concerning the laws and regulations relating to special education and related services must be maintained by each state (IDEA of 2004, P.L. 108–446, § 615 [e][2][C], 118 Stat. 2647 [2005]).

The 1999 Regulations also provide some guidance as to the selection of mediators when mediation is requested. The regulations state, "if a mediator is not selected on a random (e.g., a rotation) basis from the list described . . . both parties must be involved in selecting the mediator and agree with the selection of the individual who will mediate" (34 C.F.R. § 300.506 [b][2][ii]). The method selected by states in the development and maintenance of this list, as well as the selection process method, is to be incorporated into each state plan for IDEA implementation.

Parents Who Elect Not to Use Mediation

In some cases, parents may elect not to avail themselves of the opportunity for mediation but may prefer to take their dispute immediately to due process. Possible reasons for the decision by parents not to participate in this process may include (a) the knowledge they have the right to refuse; (b) the cost of the process in terms of time, money, and emotional stress; and (c) the anger and exasperation at the school personnel, resulting in the parents' wanting to present their argument in what they see as a stronger arena. The election to not use mediation is their right, but if they elect to do so, states and local school districts may establish procedures to offer parents and schools that choose not to use the mediation process, an opportunity to meet, at a time and location convenient to the parents, with a disinterested party who is under contract with—

(i)   a parent training and information center or community parent resource center in the State . . . ; or

(ii)   an appropriate alternative dispute resolution entity,

to encourage the use, and explain the benefits, of the mediation process to the parents. (IDEA of 2004, P.L. 108–446, § 615 [c][2][B], 118 Stat. 2647 [2005])

However, if a parent elects not to participate in mediation or to participate in meetings to encourage mediation, neither the state nor local school district may deny or delay their right to a due process hearing as a result of this refusal (34 C.F.R. § 300.506 [d][2]).

The Mediation Process

According to the Center for the Study of Dispute Resolution (1996), mediation is defined as "a process in which an impartial third party, the mediator, helps provide the parties to a dispute with an opportunity to seek a mutually satisfying resolution to the problem" (p. 6). In fact, this process has been labeled as "facilitated negotiation" (Riskin, 1996) or "facilitated communications for agreement" (Melamed, 1995). Each trained mediator has a process or method by which he or she coordinates and facilitates the mediation itself. Figure 11.1 summarizes the steps usually followed during mediation. A description of each step follows.

Premediation Caucus(es).   Prior to the actual mediation, the mediator may meet with the parties individually. These private sessions are called "caucuses" and may help the mediator and the parties clarify the concerns or provide the parties, if they are hesitant, with a nonthreatening area to first describe their issues of concern. In most

Figure 11.1
Steps in the Mediation Process

1.   Premediation Caucuses
2.   Introductory Mediation Meeting
3.   Mediation Meeting
        Phase One: Opening Statements
        Phase Two: Agenda Setting
        Phase Three: Resolution Option Generation
        Phase Four: Agreement Negotiation
        Phase Five: Written Agreement Preparation
4.   Agreement Document Provided to Parties

cases, though, it is best to begin the mediation with all parties involved. This will lessen the concerns of mediator bias that the parties may have if the mediator meets with each party individually.

Introductory Mediation Meeting.   When the first meeting of the parties involved in the mediation begins, it is essential that the mediator provides the parties with an understanding of the concept of mediation, assists the parties in identifying the areas of dispute, and provides a venue where they can decide whether mediation should continue. The mediator must also provide the parties with the ground rules for mediation (e.g., not interrupting the person speaking). At this time, an agreement to mediate may be verbalized with the understanding that either party may decide to halt the process, either for a short time or because they believe the issues cannot be solved. The mediator also has the right to terminate the process if it becomes apparent that the participants are misrepresenting the facts or are unable to amicably discuss the issues.

Mediation Meeting Phase One: Opening Statements.   Mediations are usually divided into five phases. The first segment is the explanation of the issues, generally begun by the parents. During this phase, each participant is provided with an opportunity to describe the controversial issues (i.e., an opening statement). Included in this opening statement is the hoped-for resolution of each issue. The mediator's role during this phase is to facilitate the uninterrupted presentation of the issues by each party and to attempt to identify the underlying interests and wants of each party.

Mediation Meeting Phase Two: Agenda Setting.   After the opening statements, the participants and the mediator generally review the issues and plan the most efficacious way to address them. This agenda setting may occur in joint session or in caucuses, depending on the amount of conflict present between the parties. The participants then discuss the issues and decide as a group the order in which the issues and proposed resolutions are to be reviewed. Although the mediator may have preferences concerning the order of the issue discussion, the parties involved have the final decision on this agenda. During this discussion, the parties should decide whether specific issues must be decided immediately, whether additional information may be required to fully address a specific issue, whether any witnesses may be needed, and whether all parties essential to the completion of an agreement are present (Riskin, 1996).

If it is essential to gather further information or to call witnesses, then the mediation may need to be postponed. When the mediation resumes, each party should be allowed the time to describe the additional information not previously included in their opening statement. This statement may be incorporated in the opening statement phase or in the agenda development phase. During this phase, the mediator's role is to assist the parties in (a) clarifying their positions; (b) identifying, where possible, the underlying interests of each party; (c) understanding the perceptions of the other party concerning this issue; and (d) moving beyond the initial disagreements and toward a solution.

Mediation Meeting Phase Three: Resolution Option Generation.   After the opening statements and expansion of issues and supporting facts have occurred, the parties meet to develop possible options that could be used to resolve the issues. During this part of the mediation, no decision on the options should occur. This is the brainstorming phase of the mediation and judging, selecting, or choosing specific options at this early phase in the mediation may hamper the final ability of the parties to reach an agreement. Depending on the adversarial nature of the issues and the length of time the adversarial status has continued, this may be the longest or the shortest phase of the mediation. The mediator's role during this phase is to assist the parties in generating options that are feasible ways to address the resolution of the issue(s) and to continue clarifying the positions of each party and the underlying interests and needs that may be driving the controversy. The mediator should encourage the parties to brainstorm and discourage any judgments concerning the feasibility or acceptability of any suggested options.

Mediation Meeting Phase Four: Agreement Negotiation.   The final step in the mediation process is the selection of options and the agreement of the parties of the viability of the options identified earlier. During this phase, the mediator may use a variety of methods to facilitate agreement on one or more options for resolution of the issues. According to the Center for the Study of Dispute Resolution (1996), there are nine different strategies that may be used to encourage the agreement (see Figure 11.2).

✝ *Mediation Meeting Phase Five: Written Agreement Preparation.*   Usually, it is essential for the negotiated agreement to be finalized in a written format. The mediator can draft this agreement at the end of the meeting and provide the parties with a final document at a later date or the document can be developed while the parties wait and copies provided to them immediately.

Figure 11.2
Nine Strategies Used in Negotiation

- identification of a single proposal that can be used as basis for negotiation,
- BATNA (Best Alternative to a Negotiated Agreement) decision by each party,
- creation of doubts about position of individual parties,
- evaluation of consequences of proposed options,
- explanation of each proposal to other party including that party's view of problem,
- identification of basis for making decision on which both parties can agree,
- negotiation of agreeable options, sometimes known as "logrolling,"
- emphasis of requisite deadlines in order to encourage decision making, and
- agreement of partial resolution and setting up of process to deal with other or future issues of concern. (Riskin, 1996, pp. 24–25)

Agreements reached through the less adversarial method known as mediation may be more appropriate in a school setting where parental and school collaboration is seen as a characteristic of school effectiveness. Professionals involved in the provision of appropriate educational programs for students with disabilities see the mediation process as one method by which parents and school districts may be able to reach a consensus on controversial issues. Others, though, raise concerns that the insertion of mediation into the dispute resolution process may not be advantageous to the needs of the child. They view mediation as an additional step that will neither reduce the adversarial relationship of the parties, nor reduce the number of due process hearings. Instead, it may prolong the timeline for resolution of the disputed issues because the parties may be unable to reach a resolution and ultimately "end up" in a due process hearing anyway.

Resolution Session

The 2004 IDEA reauthorization included a new component, the resolution session, in the dispute resolution process. After a parent has filed a complaint and request for due process, the LEA is required to convene a meeting with the parents and members of the IEP team knowledgeable of the facts noted in the complaint. This preliminary meeting must occur prior to the due process hearing and within 15 days of receipt of the complaint. In addition to the parents, and selected IEP team members, a representative of the LEA who has decision-making authority must attend this meeting. The LEA's attorney may not attend unless the parent's attorney is in attendance. The purpose of the resolution session is to provide the parents the opportunity to discuss their complaint, along with relevant facts that led to the complaint, and to provide the LEA with the opportunity to resolve the complaint prior to the occurrence of the more adversarial forum, the due process hearing.

The resolution session may be waived if both parties agree to do so or if a decision is made to use the mediation option. If resolution has not occurred to the satisfaction of the parents within 30 days of filing the complaint, the due process hearing is conducted. If resolution does occur, then a legally binding document, the written settlement agreement, is prepared and signed by the parents and the agency representation who has authority to make such an agreement. A 3-business day review period is also included, wherein the parents or other parties may void the agreement.

This new step was included to provide parents and LEA's one more opportunity to resolve their differences. Concerns have been voiced that this new step will not lessen but, in fact, may increase hostility between the complainants. In addition, clarification has not been provided concerning the timelines (i.e., when exactly does the due process timeline begin) (COPAA, 2004). These questions and others will be answered as this new aspect of the dispute resolution process is implemented.

Due Process Hearing

A due process hearing is an official forum that ". . . must be conducted by the SEA or the public agency directly responsible for the education of the child, as determined under State statute, State regulation, or a written policy of the SEA" (34 C.F.R. § 300.507 [b]). According to Yell (1998), the due process hearing allows an impartial third party, known as the due process hearing officer, to hear both sides of a dispute, examine the issues presented, and prepare a decision that is binding on both parties. A due process hearing may be initiated by the parents, guardians, or surrogate parents, or by the school district (34 C.F.R. § 300.507 [a][1]). This event may occur when issues arise related to the initiation and change, or refusal of a school to initiate or change, the identification, evaluation, or educational placement of a child in special education (34 C.F.R. § 300.507 [a][2]). Basically, a due process hearing may be requested if it is alleged that a child with a disability is not receiving an FAPE.

Due process hearings involve a number of persons, all of whom have different roles, rights, and responsibilities. Each believes the objective of the hearing is to reach a decision(s) that serves the best interests of the student with disabilities. According to the federal regulations, each party participating in a hearing has the following rights to

(1) Be accompanied and advised by counsel and by individuals with special knowledge or training with respect to the problems of children with disabilities;

(2) Present evidence and confront, cross-examine, and compel the attendance of witnesses;

(3) Prohibit the introduction of any evidence at the hearing that has not been disclosed to that party at least 5 business days before the hearing;

(4) Obtain a written, or, at the option of the parents, electronic, verbatim record of the hearing; and

(5) Obtain written, or, at the option of the parents, electronic findings of fact and decisions. (34 C.F.R. § 300.509 [a][1–5])

In addition, the parents have the right to have their child who is the subject of the hearing present, the right to elect to have the hearing open to the public, and the right to receive a record of the hearing and findings of fact at no cost to them (34 C.F.R. § 300.509 [c]).

Hearing Officer(s) Selection and Impartiality

To protect the integrity of the process, the hearing officer must be an impartial party in no way involved with the child, parent, or school system. IDEA 2004 stipulates that a hearing may not be conducted (a) by a person who is an employee of an SEA, (b) by the LEA involved in the education or care of the child, or (c) by a person who has a personal or professional interest that will conflict with objectivity (IDEA of 2004, P.L. 108–446, § 615 [f][3], 118 Stat, 2647 [2005]). An issue had been raised concerning whether hearing officers who received payment from the state for their services became state employees as a result and were then unable to serve in the capacity of a hearing officer. According to the 1999 Regulations "a person who otherwise qualifies to conduct a hearing . . . is not an employee of the agency solely because he or she is paid by the agency to serve as a hearing officer" (34 C.F.R. § 300.508 [b]). States must keep on file a list of those individuals who meet the guidelines to be a due process hearing officer. This list must include a statement of the qualifications of each person as specified by the state in its plan (34 C.F.R. § 300.508 [c]). Parents and schools may review this list to select an impartial hearing officer. Either party can file a complaint with the state, raising the issue of partiality of any hearing officer.

The Hearing Process

The hearing process has been outlined to "provide a legally constituted forum in which the contending parties have an opportunity to present their cases to an impartial hearing officer" (Yell, 1998, p. 284). This process provides an impartial arena in which disputes can be heard so a resolution (i.e., a ruling) can be made. This process, although legally binding, is less formal than that of a trial court. Following is a description of the activities and order usually included in the hearing process.

Prehearing Activities.   Before the hearing begins, a number of activities must be completed. In some states, the hearing officer is responsible for the coordination of the prehearing activities; however, in others, involvement of the hearing officer with the parties prior to the hearing is considered to be biasing so the prehearing activities may be assigned to another individual according to state regulations. While the hearing officer is preparing for the hearing, each party has specific activities that they should complete (see Figure 11.3).

School Prehearing Activities.   Prior to the hearing, the school should decide whether another attorney should be retained. Although most schools have an attorney on retainer to the school board, this individual may not be the most appropriate one to use during a due process hearing because school attorneys may be unfamiliar with special education law. An expert in special education law may need to be located.

It is essential that the key issues in the school's case relate to the instructional needs of the child. In addition, all those involved should understand and know the guidelines for due process hearings. The requirements and timelines for exchange of evidence should be reviewed and then adhered to closely. In most cases, the school should contact the state department compliance sector to ensure they are complying with the due process steps as required by state procedures.

In conjunction with the school's attorney, the district personnel should prepare their case. All issues, supporting information, and supporting documents should be understood fully by all school personnel involved. Testing procedures and placement recommendations should be reviewed and a defense prepared to support the school's decisions. If the school has witnesses, their testimony, along with answers to questions that may be asked by the parents' attorney during cross-examination, should be prepared. As with any good defense, the school should attempt to anticipate the case that the parents will present and prepare a rebuttal for each issue.

Figure 11.3
Activities to be Completed by Prehearing Coordinator

- Receipt of request for hearing and notation of date
- Determination of whether basic information about child has been received
- Development of list of persons who must receive all further information regarding hearing and/or whose presence will be required
- Arrangement for hearing dates and logistics (e.g., support services such as copying machines, telephones, mail services)
- Arrangement for verbatim record of hearing (by tape recorder or court stenographer)
- Determination of need for an interpreter
- Determination of whether parents will be seeking an independent educational evaluation for their child
- Determination of child's current educational placement and where placement will be during proceedings
- Ascertainment of child's current placement
- Provision of hearing information to parents
- Provision of information to parents of their rights to an open or closed hearing
- Obtainment of witness list from both sides and list of evidence that parties intend to submit
- Determination of appropriate means of compelling attendance of any witnesses who are reluctant to attend
- Provision for presenting a formal notice to participants at least 5 days prior to hearing

Generally, it is also the school district's responsibility to make the physical arrangements of the hearing. However, in some states, this responsibility has been given to the hearing officer. Preparation of the physical site of the hearing may include consideration of the following: size and temperature of the room, accessibility of restrooms, availability of refreshments, level of noise that will be present during the time of the hearing, availability of a smoking area, and availability of a copy machine. In most cases, the hearing is held in one of the school buildings; however, if the hearing is potentially adversarial, it may be better to select a more neutral site for the hearing. Examples of neutral sites include the conference room at the local school district central offices, conference rooms in city or county offices, church facilities, or conference rooms available at local banks or real estate offices.

Parent Prehearing Activities.   The parents also should be preparing for the hearing in conjunction with their attorney. According to Bateman (1980), "the first step in preparing for a hearing is to imagine the last step!" (p. 2). In other words, the parents should decide what decision they would like the hearing officer to make and then decide how to support that decision.

Because the parents will often be asked to describe the chronology of events leading up to the controversy, it is essential that a timeline with supporting documentation be prepared. This will help the parents and the attorney, as well as the hearing officer, in understanding how the issue(s) have become so adversarial. As the timeline of events is prepared, a tentative list of witnesses and requisite supporting documents can be identified. This list should also include possible "expert" witnesses who can provide a professional opinion supportive of the case.

After the timeline and issues have been prepared, questions for the witnesses should be developed. These questions should lead the witness to support the proposed decision that the parents identified at the beginning. Questions that might be asked in cross-examination should also be reviewed. Witnesses, including the parents, should be very comfortable with the answers to the questions and be knowledgeable about the documents and timeline.

In conjunction with this, the parents and their attorney should be cognizant of the school's case. They should identify the issues as the school district perceives them, the points of the law that may be supportive of the school, the witnesses the school plans to question, and the documentation that will be used in support of the argument. All documentation to be considered during the hearing must be disclosed by both parties no later than 5 days prior to the hearing. The parents should not waive this timeline without discussion with their attorney and provision of the waiver in writing.

Parents should decide prior to the hearing whether they want the hearing to be open or closed. An open hearing allows anyone to be present during the hearing. It is the parent's right to request a closed hearing if they believe that the presence of others may be detrimental to their case or that sensitive information may be discussed during the hearing.

Basic Order of a Due Process Hearing. Hearings usually follow the outline described, although each state may have different guidelines. IDEA does not provide specific directions for the presentation of a hearing. The first event in a hearing, after consideration of whether the court reporter and his or her equipment are ready, is an introduction by the hearing officer. This usually includes an introduction of the hearing officer(s) and a statement of the legal authority for the hearing. A clarification of the general purpose for due process hearings and an explanation of the specific purpose of the hearing in question are provided at this time. Along with this, the hearing officer explains the role and responsibilities of the hearing officer. Each person in the room, including attorneys, is acknowledged and asked to sign an attendance sheet that notes his or her name and reason for attending. The parents are informed of their due process rights and asked whether they want the hearing to be open or closed. Instructions on the proper behavior during a hearing are then stated.

When these preliminary items have been covered, the hearing officer asks for opening statements to be given. An opening statement is a brief, clear statement that explains the case in the view of the parent or the school. It should include a summary of the issues, the legal basis for the request for due process, and a broad overview of the facts leading up to the case. Usually, the school presents its opening statement followed by the parents, although this may differ with each hearing officer.

After the opening statements, the evidence in the form of witnesses is presented. Witnesses are sworn either in a group at the beginning of the hearing or individually as they are called. The witness states aloud his or her name and usually his or her title for the court record. At this time, the witness may identify documents that will be introduced as evidence. After the school has addressed the witness, the parents may cross-examine each witness. The school is then given an opportunity to reexamine the witness to clarify any points that have been raised by the parents. At this time, the hearing officer can question the witness. This process is followed for each school witness.

After the school's case has been heard, then the parents present their evidence through witness testimony and documentation. At the conclusion of each witness's testimony, the school may cross-examine. The parents may rebut that testimony, and the hearing officer then has an opportunity to examine each witness.

When all witnesses have been heard, then the school's attorney makes a closing statement. A closing statement should clearly summarize the case for the hearing officer. Points that have been raised that support the case should be emphasized as well as notice made of weak points in the other party's case. A closing statement should be short and to the point because all parties in the hearing are tired and ready for the hearing to be completed. Once the school has made its closing statement, then the parents follow the same procedure.

As the final step in the hearing, the hearing officer provides for the record a discussion of when written briefs, if any, must be submitted, and when the decision will be finalized. A reminder of the appeal process is also provided orally to the parties involved. Finally, the hearing officer thanks those present and announces the closing of the hearing.

Due Process Hearing Report

After completion of the hearing, it is the responsibility of the hearing officer to prepare a written decision concerning the issues raised in the hearing. This decision will be based on an examination of the information that has been heard, as well as the written or electronic record that has been prepared. The guidelines used by the hearing officer in making the decision are the (a) federal laws, (b) state statutes, (c) assessment procedures, (d) special education programming, and (e) evaluation of programs. The final decision must be limited to the issue(s) and based *only* on evidence presented at the hearing. Other peripheral information should not be used to make a decision concerning the issues that initiated the due process hearing.

A hearing report (i.e., the written decision) generally consists of the same components (see Figure 11.4). However, these components may be arranged in a different order based on the format used in each state or by each hearing officer.

The first component is a cover page that lists the parties involved, including the names of their attorneys. A description of the legal jurisdiction follows. The specific issues considered during the hearing and applicable laws are described.

Figure 11.4
Components of a Due Process Hearing Report

- Cover page listing parties involved
- Issue and purpose of hearing
- Legal jurisdiction
- Issue(s) considered
- Evidence list
- Summary and evaluation of evidence
- Findings of fact
- Conclusion(s) of law
- Order(s) issues (decision)
- Appeal procedure
- Signatures and date

A listing of the evidence considered is then usually included. This list may be incorporated into a summary and evaluation of the evidence in paragraph format instead of a list. The evidence is usually followed by a summation of the facts of the case, known as the findings of fact. Following this are the conclusions based on the relevant legislation and state statutes. The next section is the order(s), that may be provided in summary format or by individual issue. The final section is a description of the appeal procedure. The document is then signed and dated by the hearing officer(s) and submitted to each party involved and to the state department of education.

Due Process Hearing Decisions

Due process hearing decisions are considered the final authority until they are appealed. This appeal may be made to the SEA, which shall "conduct an impartial review of findings and decision." The individual who conducts the impartial review must

(i) examine the entire hearing record;

(ii) ensure that the procedures at the hearing were consistent with the requirements of due process;

(iii) seek additional evidence if necessary. If a hearing is held to receive additional evidence, the rights in § 300.509 apply;

(iv) afford the parties an opportunity for oral or written argument, or both, at the discretion of the reviewing official;

(v) make an independent decision on completion of the review; and

(vi) give a copy of the written, or, at the option of the parents, electronic findings of fact and decisions to the parties. (34 C.F.R. § 300.510 [b][2])

The decision made at this level is final, unless the parties decide to bring a civil action (IDEA of 2004, P.L. 108–446, § 615 [i][2], 118 Stat. 2647 [2005], 34 C.F.R. § 300.509 [2][d]). Either party may bring this action in any "State court of competent jurisdiction or in a district court of the United States without regard to the amount in controversy" (IDEA of 2004, P.L. 108–446, § 615 [i][2][A], 118 Stat. 2647 [2005]).

States outline a timeline for the completion of the due process hearing procedure, as well as completion and submission of the hearing report. This timeline must be in accordance with the guidelines outlined in both federal and state regulations. The federal regulations require that a final decision be reached and a copy of the decision mailed to each party within 45 days after the request for a hearing. If either party requests that the state complete a second-level review, then a final decision, with a copy sent to each party, must occur within 30 days of the request. At the request of either party, the hearing officer or the state review officer may grant an extension of the timeline (34 C.F.R. § 300.511). In addition, if either party decides to file a civil action, it must occur within 90 days of the decision made by the hearing officer unless the state has a different specified timeline (IDEA of 2004, P.L. 108–446, § 615 [i][2][B], 118 Stat. 2647 [2005]).

Expedited Due Process Hearings

To facilitate the implementation of the new discipline policies in a manner that is not harmful to children with disabilities, the option of an expedited due process hearing was included in the 1997 Amendments. When a child's parents disagree with any decision regarding placement, or with the school's determination that the child's behavior had no relationship to the disability, known as a manifestation determination, or the LEA believes maintaining the child in the current placement is likely to result in injury to the child or others, either party may request a hearing. When this appeal occurs, the child shall remain in the IAES until the hearing officer's decision or until the 10-day limit has been reached, whichever occurs first. In addition, the SEA or LEA shall convene an expedited hearing. This hearing must occur within 20 days of the appeal and must result in a decision no later than 10 days after the hearing (IDEA of 2004, P.L. 108–446, § 615 [k][4], 118 Stat. 2647 [2005]).

When the manifestation determination decision has been reviewed, then the due process hearing officer "shall determine whether the public agency has demonstrated that the child's behavior was not a manifestation of the child's disability consistent with the requirements of § 300.523 (d)" (34 C.F.R. § 300.525 [b]). The hearing officer may also review the decision to place the child in an IAES. In this review, the hearing officer

- determines that the public agency has demonstrated by substantial evidence that maintaining the current placement of the child is substantially likely to result in injury to the child or to others;
- considers the appropriateness of the child's current placement;

- considers whether the public agency has made reasonable efforts to minimize the risk of harm in the child's current placement, including the use of supplementary aids and services; and

- determines that the interim alternative educational setting that is proposed by school personnel who have consulted with the child's special education teacher, meets the requirements of § 300.522 (b). (34 C.F.R. § 300.521)

Summary

Mediation is an impartial system that brings together the parties who have a dispute to confidentially discuss the disputed issues with a neutral third party with the goal of resolving the dispute in a binding written agreement. The phases of the voluntary process include the introductory meeting, where ground rules are established; the opening statements; the agenda-setting phase; the resolution-option generation phase, where possible solutions are generated; the agreement negotiation; and the written agreement.

The resolution session is a mandatory meeting inserted into the due process hearing procedure. It is an additional method to resolve a dispute by allowing the parents and the SEA or LEA the opportunity to discuss the complaint, describe supporting facts, and decide on a resolution, if possible. A written settlement agreement is prepared when resolution occurs. This session may be waived if both parties agree either to use the mediation step or to move immediately to due process.

An impartial due process hearing is a method of settling a dispute by allowing an impartial third party, known as the due process hearing officer, to hear both sides of a dispute, examine the issues presented, and prepare a decision that is binding on both parties. The phases of the process include introduction, opening statements, presentation of evidence in the form of sworn witnesses, cross-examination, closing statements, discussion of written briefs, and conclusion of hearing and preparation of hearing report.

Through the provision of mediation, resolution session, and impartial due process hearing, IDEA protects parent rights, school rights, and the educational rights of the child with disabilities by providing them a venue wherein disputes concerning the education of students with disabilities could be resolved in an impartial setting. Without the guarantee of a procedural safeguard, then the guarantee of an FAPE is placed at risk.

Although mediation, resolution session, and due process hearing procedures are available to both parents and schools who are seeking resolution of concerns related to the programming and/or placement of the child with a disability, it is often in the best interest of all involved to avoid these adversarial situations. School districts and parents can avoid disputes by focusing on the child and his or her needs. Schools should remember that special education programs are required to be comprehensive and provide an FAPE for each student with a disability. When schools honestly attempt to provide appropriate programming for each child with a disability, they are less likely to be involved in disputes with parents concerning programming and placement.

The second focus is the "real" involvement of parents in the program provided by the school. Although parental involvement is required by IDEA, schools often provide only cursory attempts at true partnerships. Documentation should be kept of parents' involvement during all facets of the special education process. The school should send all correspondence by registered mail, and logs of telephone conversations and face-to-face conversations with parents and others involved in the development, implementation, and review of student programs should be kept.

When disputes arise, the school should support mediation as an option. When either party waits until a due process hearing has been requested, then adversarial positions have developed, mediated discussions are more difficult to attain, and the central focus of the needs of the student may be lost.

Questions for Discussion

1. Why was the mediation option made available for parents who have a dispute with the school district?

2. Explain the reason(s) why some parents choose not to participate in mediation. When a parent chooses not to participate, what might be the ramifications?

3. What is a resolution session, and why might it have been added to the dispute resolution procedures?

4. What is the difference between a due process hearing and an expedited due process hearing?

5. The goal of mediation is to reduce the adversarial nature of parent–school disagreements. Despite this, many individuals believe that both mediation and due process hearings are adversarial in nature and do more harm than good for the parent(s) and the child with a disability. Why would they believe this?

Websites for Further Exploration

Mediation (Requirements, Selection/Impartiality of Mediators, Nonelection by Parents, Mediation Process)

www.directionservice.org/cadre/implementing.cfm
ericec.org/faq/mediaton.html
www.nectac.org/topics/procsafe/procsafe.asp
www.ldonline.org/ld_indepth/legal_legislative/mediation.html
www.wrightslaw.com/info/mediate.idea.htm
www.cec.sped.org/pp/pp_docs/mediation01.doc
www.asha.org/about/legislation-advocacy/federal/idea/idea_summary.htm
www.edlaw.net/service/303sube.html

Due Process Hearing (H.O. Selection/Impartiality, Hearing Process, D.P. Hearing Report, Expedited D.P. Hearing)

www.ldonline.org/ld_indepth/special_education/due.html
www.ideapractices.org/
www.familyeducation.com/article/0,1120,23-8149,00.html
www.wrightslaw.com/info/dp.index.htm
www.ldonline.org/article.php?max=20&id=424&loc=15
www.cleweb.org/Disabilities/QuestionAnswer/Q&Aoctober.htm
www.spedlaw.com/html/opnews2/w-honig6.98.htm

ILLUSTRATING THE LAW

Due Process Hearing Decision
Before the Three-Member Due Process
Hearing Panel Empowered Pursuant to RSMo. 162.961

[_____]*, et al., Petitioners, and [_____] R-V School District, Respondent.

PERSONALLY IDENTIFIABLE INFORMATION: The parties to this hearing are:

Student:
Date of Birth:
Grade Level: 5
School District: [_____] R-V School District
c/o [_____], Superintendent of Schools
[_____]
Parents: [_____]
School District's Representative: [_____], Esq.
[_____]
Parent's Representative: [_____], Esq.
[_____]

ISSUE AND PURPOSE OF THE HEARING: Whether or not the annual goals and short-term objectives contained in the IEPs of August 14, 1997 and October 27, 1997 satisfy Respondent's obligation to devise and implement adaptations, strategies, and modifications including positive behavioral interventions and support?

INFORMATION TIME-LINE: The request for hearing was received by the Department of Education on or about October 2, 1998. A joint motion was received requesting an extension of the statutory time-lines and an order was entered, accordingly, on October 29, 1998 that the hearing be continued for trial to January 4, 1999 and that a final decision be submitted to the parties on or before 45 days after the conclusion of the hearing. On November 9, 1998 an order was entered pursuant to "Second Joint Motion Requesting an Extension of Statutory Time-Lines," continuing the hearing to the week of February 22, 1999 with a final decision to be rendered 45 days thereafter. Subsequently another joint motion was received, requesting an extension of the statutory time-lines in order to hear the case the week of May 3, 1999 with a final decision to be rendered 45 days thereafter. An order was so entered on January 13, 1999.
*Name and addresses of individuals have been omitted and replaced with [_____].

The due process hearing was held on May 3, 4, and 5, 1999 at the [_____] Middle School, [_____], Missouri before the Three-Member

Due Process Hearing Panel, including [_____]-Member, [_____]-Member, and [_____], Chairman. At the conclusion of the hearing, the Chairman requested that the parties submit proposed findings of fact and conclusions of law on or before May 28, 1999 and suggested that the opinion be submitted to the parties no later than June 30. Both parties agreed.

JURISDICTION AND ISSUES: The Individuals with Disabilities Education Act ("IDEA") codified at 20 U.S.C. 1400 *et seq.* entitles the parents of a child with a disability to "an impartial due process hearing" upon request, with respect to "any matter relating to the identification, evaluation, or educational placement of the child, or the provision of a Free Appropriate Public Education of such child" 20 U.S.C. 1415 (b) (1) (E) (2). In Missouri, the hearing authorized by 162.961, RSMo., is intended to be the impartial due process hearing mandated by the IDEA.

In Petitioner's Second Amended Statement of Issues, dated April 27, 1999, the final issues for determination were as follows:

1. Respondent failed to provide Petitioner with a free appropriate public education in that it failed to develop and implement an appropriate Behavior Management Plan for the 1997–98 school year, in violation of 20 U.S.C. 1400 *et seq.*

2. Respondent has failed to provide Petitioner with a free, appropriate public education, in that Respondent failed to develop appropriate Individualized Education Plan(s) for Petitioner, in violation of 20 U.S.C. 1400 *et seq.*

3. Respondent has failed to provide Petitioner with a free appropriate public education in that it failed to provide an appropriate educational placement for Petitioner for the 1997–98 school year, in violation of 20 U.S.C. 1400 *et seq.*

However, Petitioner in his opening statement narrowed the issues to one and confirmed same in his "Proposed Findings of Fact, Conclusions of Law and Decision" by stating: "The issues have now been refined to whether or not the annual goals and short term objectives contained in the IEPs of August 14, 1997 and October 27, 1997, satisfy Respondent's obligation to devise and implement adaptations, strategies and modifications including positive behavioral interventions and supports."

Therefore, the Panel's opinion will address that issue.

FINDINGS OF FACT: 1. The Petitioner is a [_____] year old male student who currently resides in the [_____] School District in [_____], Missouri and so resided during the 1997–98 school year.

2. The Respondent is a school district operating within the guidelines of the Missouri Department of Elementary and Secondary Education ("DESE"). The district receives federal financial assistance through DESE.

3. Petitioner was diagnosed as Learning Disabled by the Respondent prior to the start of the 1997–98 school year. Both prior to and subsequent to the Respondent's determination and diagnosis of Petitioner as Learning Disabled, Petitioner's parents obtained diagnoses of Autism-Asperger's Syndrome. Later in the 1997–98 school year Respondent evaluated Petitioner as having a behavior disorder.

4. Prior to June 16, 1997, Petitioner's parents initiated a due process proceeding in his behalf pursuant to the IDEA against the Respondent. On or about June 16, 1997, Petitioner and Respondent settled that proceeding. As part of that settlement it was agreed that Petitioner's educational placement for the 1997–98 school year would be changed to a self-contained setting

and that the Respondent would prepare an IEP to reflect that change in placement. In addition, the settlement agreement provided for a self-contained placement with mainstreaming in music, that the IEP team would convene every two weeks to determine if additional mainstreaming time should be added, provided for a full-time, one-on-one paraprofessional for Petitioner, as well as other provisions, all of which the Panel finds were carried out by the Respondent.

5. In addition, the Respondent agreed in the settlement agreement that: "The (IEP) plan will include a list of appropriate and inappropriate behaviors . . . interventions and strategies to be used in dealing with inappropriate behaviors."

6. Petitioner's challenging behaviors numbered as follows:

Month	Number of Challenging Behaviors
August	3
September	10
October	21
November	107
January	84
February	110
March	394

Although Petitioner's challenging behaviors were a serious issue, beginning early in the 1997–98 school year, and were the topic of discussion at virtually every IEP meeting which was held approximately every two weeks during that school year, the IEP team was never able to come to grips with the problem. The challenging behaviors steadily escalated throughout the year.

7. Although Petitioner's IEP plan dated August 14, 1997 and the one dated October 22, 1997 called for a behavior plan, none was attempted by the IEP team until April, 1998. A plan of sorts

had been developed during the prior school year for the Petitioner by an outside agency, [_____], whose representatives attended IEP meetings in support of Petitioner's parents and the Petitioner. That plan was used by Petitioner's special education teacher, [_____], as a behavior checklist, but this document was never adopted by the team, nor was it analyzed or deemed to be appropriate as a behavior management plan by the team.

8. Petitioner's IEPs contained certain short-term goals and objectives relative to behavior, but these "strategies" were clearly insufficient in order to prevent or substantially reduce Petitioner's challenging behaviors. The present level statements failed to give a definitive description of behaviors that needed to be extinguished and thus provide a basis for development of effective goals and objectives.

9. Petitioner produced an expert who testified that Petitioner's challenging behaviors required the adoption of a behavior management plan, which included a functional behavior assessment, which identified antecedent events, challenging behaviors and the development of consequences and reinforcements; a functional behavioral analysis; and a behavior management plan. The Panel finds that in this particular instance, such a behavior management plan should have been adopted in order that Petitioner's challenging behaviors could be appropriately reduced so that they would not substantially interfere with his ability to learn or to interfere substantially with other students' ability to learn.

10. Respondent made no attempt to identify antecedent events or devise appropriate consequences and reinforcements until March of 1998 and made no attempt to devise a formal behavior management plan for Petitioner until April of 1998. This plan was insufficiently tailored to meet Petitioner's needs.

11. Although Respondent made some effort to include Petitioner in non-academic activities with his non-disabled peers, his challenging behaviors precluded his being mainstreamed; that is, integrated into academic settings with his peers.

12. When Petitioner began the 1997–98 school year in August of 1997, he attended [_____]'s 5th grade special education classroom. During the first one to two weeks of school, Petitioner was the only student in [_____]'s class where he was accompanied by his paraprofessional, Mr. [_____]. Mr. [_____] continued to accompany Petitioner in all of his classes throughout the school year and indeed did an excellent job of attempting to cope with Petitioner's challenging behaviors, but Mr. [_____] did not have the professional training or experience to successfully prevent or substantially reduce those behaviors.

13. At the beginning of the school year, Petitioner generally was performing at the 3rd grade level. However, the only documented evidence of Petitioner's academic achievement indicates that on September 24, 1997, his midquarter grades were as follows: he was spelling at the 5th grade level, science at the 3rd grade level, math at the 4th grade level, reading at the 3rd grade level, social studies at the 4th grade level, English at the 3rd grade level, and writing at the 3rd grade level. This report card contained the following note: "A lot of help from Mr. [_____]" indicating that [_____] was assisting Petitioner in order for him to work at the levels indicated. There are report cards of some variety dated November 4, 1994 (sic) and November 18, 1997 (see Respondent's Exhibit R-252), which indicate that Petitioner received 100% in spelling, 90% in math, 98% in reading, 24% in social studies, 57% in science, 88% in English, and 71% in writing (November 4, 1994) (sic) and 100% in spelling, 79% in math, 81% in reading, 51% in social studies, 82% in science,

73% in English, and 88% in writing (November 18, 1997). Neither of these report cards indicates whether they were for a period of time or what level. Therefore, they are of little assistance to the Panel. Respondent's Exhibits R-337 and R-339 indicate grades as of April 22, 1998 but they appear to be grades for a particular lesson rather than work over a particular period of time. Moreover, Petitioner's special education teacher, [_____], testified that whenever the Petitioner was moved up from the 3rd grade level, he experienced great frustration in attempting to do the academic work and his behaviors increased dramatically. As a consequence, each time he was moved up, his teacher was required to subsequently move him back to 3rd grade level. There is no clear evidence from which the Panel can determine if or to what extent Petitioner progressed in his academic subjects. Various witnesses for the Respondent testified that in their opinion Petitioner made academic progress or received an educational benefit; however, in combination with the evidence that Petitioner became frustrated when he was advanced in his studies and had to be returned to the 3rd grade level, these expressions and generalizations of opinion are meaningless to the Panel.

14. Petitioner's mother insisted on Petitioner attending the IEP meetings. The Panel finds that his inappropriate behaviors increased at or near and after the IEP meetings. In the opinion of the Panel, Petitioner should be excused from attendance at IEP meetings.

15. Petitioner attended class in a combination classroom for self-contained and resource room students. During the school day, resource students were coming in and out of the class. This movement of students in and out of the classroom, together with the attendant noise and other disturbance had an adverse impact on the Petitioner's behaviors. Petitioner should be placed in a self-contained room (not a combination

room) where there are fewer distractions and less noise—at least until it can be determined that Petitioner can cope with greater inclusion.

16. The director of Special Education Services made little or no attempt to put together a behavior management plan or other effective behavior intervention strategies prior to April, 1998. He showed little leadership in addressing the behavior problems of the Petitioner. The Panel finds that the school district had no one on staff who was fully competent to devise a behavior management plan or other appropriate intervention strategies in order to significantly reduce Petitioner's behaviors. However, this is not to say that the Panel finds that certain members of the Respondent's staff did not make an honest effort to assist the Petitioner. Certainly, Petitioner's aide, Mr. [_____], and Petitioner's special education teacher, Ms. [_____], worked hard to help the Petitioner. They simply did not have the expertise to reduce his challenging behaviors substantially so that he could progress academically.

17. The Panel finds that there is no animosity towards Petitioner among those members of the Respondent's staff who will be employed during the next school year. Indeed, the Panel finds that from the principal down through the teaching staff, and the paraprofessionals who would be working with the Petitioner next year, that the past history of Petitioner's experience in the school district would have no adverse impact on the desire of the staff to assist the Petitioner academically, socially, and in his behavior. The Panel hopes that Petitioner's parents will show proper patience with Respondent in order to give Respondent time to devise and implement an appropriate behavior management plan. It will take time to reduce Petitioner's behaviors so that he can be successfully mainstreamed later. No one can predict how long it will take. Experience with an appropriate plan will be the proper determinant.

CONCLUSIONS OF LAW AND DECISION:

The Individuals with Disabilities Education Act ("IDEA") guarantees all public school children with disabilities an free appropriate public education ("FAPE") designed to meet their unique needs [20 U.S.C. 1412(a)(1)]. However, the IDEA does not prescribe any substantive standard regarding the level of education to be accorded to disabled children, *Board of Education v. Rowley,* 458 U. 176, 189, 195 (1982), *Fort Zumwalt School District v. Clynes,* 119 F.3d 607, 611-12 (8th Cir. 1997). Rather, a local educational agency ("LEA") fulfills the requirement of providing a free appropriate public education "by providing personalized instruction with sufficient support services to permit the child to benefit educationally from that instruction" (*Rowley,* 458 U.S. at 203; *Clynes,* 119 F.3d at 612). In determining the adequacy of the program provided by the public school, "Congress did not intend that school system could discharge its duty under the [IDEA] by providing a program that produces some minimal academic achievement, no matter how trivial." *Carter v. Florence County School District Four,* 950 F.2d 156, 160 (4th Cir. 1991), *aff'd.* U.S. , 114 S.Ct. 361, 126, L.Ed. 2d 284 (1993); compare *Doe by Doe v. Tullahoma City Schools,* 9 F.3d 455, 459 (6th Cir. 1993) (educational benefits must be more than D minus to be "appropriate"); *Oberti v. Board of Education,* 995 F.2d 1204, 1213 (3rd Cir. 1993); *Hall ex rel. Hall v. Vance County Board of Education,* 774 F.2d 629, 636 (4th Cir. 1985).

Thus, in the case of a student with a behavior disorder, the IDEA and the Missouri State Plan require that Respondent provide strategies, adaptations, and interventions calculated to allow that student to receive an educational benefit to successfully provide a FAPE to that student. In addition, the settlement agreement between Petitioner and Respondents (Respondent's Exhibit R-218) required an IEP, which included a list of appropriate and inappropriate behaviors and interventions and strategies to be used in dealing with inappropriate behaviors. By implication those interventions and strategies must be effective. Here, clearly they were not. Respondent not only failed to satisfy the requirements of IDEA with respect to the Petitioner, it failed to satisfy the requirements of the settlement agreement. That is, the Respondent failed to devise and put in place effective behavior management strategies calculated to meet the Petitioner's needs so that he could gain more than a D minus educational benefit. The Panel concludes that there is no credible evidence to establish that the Petitioner gained an educational benefit sufficient to satisfy *Rowley, Carter v. Board of Education,* or *Hall ex rel. Hall v. Vance County Board of Education, supra.* Consequently, Respondent failed to provide a FAPE for the Petitioner during the 1997–98 school year.

The IDEA also state Congress's preference for "mainstreaming," otherwise known as educating the child in the least restrictive environment ("LRE") [20 U.S.C. 1412(a)(5)]. However, federal law requires that states educate disabled and nondisabled children together only "to the maximum extent appropriate" [*Id.* See also *Oberti v. Board of Education of Clementon School District,* 995 F.2d 1204, 1207 (3rd Cir. 1993)]. The LRE determination is made in accordance with the child's abilities and needs [See OSEP Mem. 95-9, 21 IDELR 1152 (1994)]. The Supreme Court has recognized that "[d]espite this preference for mainstreaming handicapped children . . . congress recognized that regular classrooms simply would not be a suitable setting for the education of many handicapped children" (*Rowley,* 458 U.S. at 181 n. 4). Accordingly, the mainstreaming preference must be "balanced with the primary objective of providing handicapped children with an appropriate education." Thus, a more restrictive environment may be the least restrictive envi-

ronment for a particular child [*Carter v. Florence County School District Four,* 950 F.2d 156, 160 (4th Cir. 1991) ("where necessary for educational reasons, mainstreaming assumes a subordinate role in formulating an educational program")]. *See also* 34 C.F.R. 300.550 comment ("If the child's behavior in the regular classroom, even with the provision of appropriate behavioral supports, strategies or interventions, would significantly impair the learning of others, that placement would not meet his or her needs and would not be appropriate for that child.")

It is clear that the parties agreed in the settlement agreement that the Petitioner should be placed in a self-contained classroom at the beginning of the 1997–98 school year. His behaviors during the 1997–98 school year, which increased during the month of March to an astronomical number (394), established that he could not be mainstreamed. The Petitioner did not present any evidence with respect to his behaviors during the 1998–99 school year when he was placed in a private school that would indicate that he should be placed otherwise than in a self-contained setting. Therefore, Petitioner should not be mainstreamed until there is some evidence during the next school year that he can successfully participate in a regular classroom.

DECISION: It is the decision of this Panel that the Respondent immediately seek the expertise of a consultant or some qualified expert in order to devise a behavior management plan for the Petitioner which includes the following elements:

An ongoing functional behavior analysis which identifies causative factors and objectionable behaviors.

A behavior management plan that provides replacement behaviors and/or strategies for extinction of the cited objectionable behaviors calculated to substantially reduce the Petitioner's adverse behaviors which interfere with his and other students' ability to receive educational benefits. It is the further order of this Panel that Petitioner's teacher and other personnel of the Respondent who are assigned to implement the plan be provided ample staff development including strategies for working with students with Asperger's Syndrome and high functioning autistic students.

APPEAL PROCEDURE: *Please Take Notice that the Findings of Fact, Conclusions of Law, and Decision Constitute the Final Decision of the Department of Elementary and Secondary Education in This Matter*

PLEASE TAKE FURTHER NOTICE that you have a right to request review of this decision pursuant to the Missouri Administrative Procedure Act, Section 536.010 *et seq.* RSMo., specifically, Section 536.110 RSMo. which provides in pertinent part as follows:

1. Proceedings for review may be instituted by filing a petition in the Circuit Court of the county of proper venue within 30 days after the mailing or delivery of the notice of the agency's final decision. . . .

2. The venue of such cases shall, at the option of the plaintiff, be in the Circuit Court of [_____] or in the county of the plaintiff or of one of the plaintiff's residence. . . .

PLEASE TAKE FURTHER NOTICE that, alternatively, your appeal may be taken to the United States District Court for the [_____] District of Missouri in lieu of appeal to the state courts. 20 U.S.C. 1415.

SO ORDERED this 22nd day of June, 1999.
[_____], Chairperson
[_____], Member
[_____], Member
Copies of the foregoing mailed to:
[_____]

ILLUSTRATING THE LAW THROUGH DISCUSSION

1. What supports should have been provided to the teaching staff by the school system?

2. Which of these supports would have been essential to meet the FAPE requirements of IDEA?

References

Bateman, B. (1980). *So you're going to a hearing: Preparing for a P.L. 94-142 due process hearing.* Northbrook, IL: Hubbard.

Center for the Study of Dispute Resolution. (1996). *Missouri department of elementary & secondary education: Basic mediation skills training.* Columbia, MO: University of Missouri-Columbia School of Law.

COPAA (The Council of Parent Attorneys and Advocates). (2004). *H.R. 1350 Individuals with*

Disabilities Education Improvement Act of 2004 compared to IDEA '97. Warrenton, VA: Author.

Individuals with Disabilities Education Act, 20 U.S.C. § 1400 *et seq.* (1997).

Individuals with Disabilities Education Improvement Act, 20 U.S.C. § 600 *et seq.* (2004).

Melamed, J. C. (1995). *Bureau of Indian Affairs: Mediation training materials.* Eugene, OR: The Mediation Center.

Riskin, L. L. (1996). *Draft: Mediation training guide.* Columbia, MO: Center for the Study of Dispute Resolution.

Wright, P. W. D., & Wright, P. D. (2000). *Wrightslaw: Special education law.* Hartfield, VA: Harbor House Law Press.

Yell, M. L. (1998). *The law and special education.* Upper Saddle River, NJ: Merrill/Prentice Hall.

CHAPTER TWELVE

Ethics and the Special Education Professional

GUIDING QUESTIONS

1. Why is it important that the concept of ethics and ethical principles be included in the preparation of special education teachers?

2. Explain the ethic of care and how it relates to special education.

3. Discuss the four principles of IDEA, and give examples of where possible ethical questions may arise.

Professionals in various fields, such as medicine, law, and education, espouse the view that the practice should be "ethical" in its application. However, what is ethical practice? What are ethics? According to *Funk & Wagnalls New International Dictionary* (Smith, Voorhees, & Morris, 1997), ethics are "the basic principles of right action" (p. 436). Thus, Rosen (1968) stated that ethical principles, or ethical values, provide an answer to the question of "What is good?" "Good" is that which "resolves indeterminate situations in the best way possible" (p. 75). Such vagueness does little to assist professionals in the various disciplines in understanding and practicing their disciplines in an "ethical" manner.

Personnel Preparation

Special educators are considered by the public (i.e., parents and families of children with disabilities) to be a group of individuals from whom high moral actions and an adherence to a professional code of ethics are expected (Gartin & Murdick, 2000). The question though is, have special educators been trained to meet these ethical and moral requirements? Many in the field are concerned that ethical issues and how to address them in a legal manner are not a part of teacher training programs. For example, Edgar (1999) stated that he "neglected to consider ethical and moral principles to ground my work" (p. 366). Research by Gartin, Murdick, Thompson, and Dyches (2002) on the beliefs and experiences of special education teachers indicated that those teachers saw a need for training in the area of advocating for their students with disabilities, a place where ethics and legal issues often conflict. To ensure special education teachers receive training in ethical practice, the premier professional organization of special education personnel, the Council for Exceptional Children (CEC), has developed a book containing the essential professional knowledge base and a Code of Ethics to be used in the education of special education professionals.

CEC Code of Ethics

To provide assistance in determining what is ethical practice, each profession has devised a "code" of ethics. Typically, a code of ethics lists the principles that the professional practicing in that field should voluntarily follow. Thus, in 1983, the CEC, the main professional organization for educators in the field

Standards and the Law

CEC Standard 9: Professional and Ethical Practice
INTASC Standard 9: Reflection and Professional Development
INTASC Standard 10: Collaboration, Ethics, and Relationships
PRAXIS Standard: Legal and Societal Issues
PRAXIS Standard: Delivery of Services to Students with Disabilities

of special education, developed a Code of Ethics for Educators of Persons with Exceptionalities. This Code of Ethics was incorporated into the Professional Standards of Practice for the Preparation of Special Educators, which guides the training of beginning professionals. The Code of Ethics states that special educators

(A) Are committed to developing the highest educational and quality of life potential of individuals with exceptionalities.

(B) Promote and maintain a high level of competence and integrity in practicing their profession.

(C) Engage in professional activities which benefit individuals with exceptionalities, their families, other colleagues, students, or research subjects.

(D) Exercise objective professional judgment in the practice of their profession.

(E) Strive to advance their knowledge and skills regarding the education of individuals with exceptionalities.

(F) Work within the standards and policies of their profession.

(G) Seek to uphold and improve where necessary the laws, regulations, and policies governing the delivery of special education and related services and the practice of their profession.

(H) Do not condone or participate in unethical or illegal acts, nor violate professional standards adopted by the Delegate Assembly of CEC. (CEC, 1998, p. 1)

The implementation of these ethical principles, however, has become increasingly difficult in a profession that is regulated by state and federal legislation. In the past, ethics were seen as principle based, but now a growing number of persons interpret ethical behavior in the context of how a person who is virtuous might act within the context of human relationships (Howe & Miramontes, 1992). Thus, ethics can be viewed as highly context sensitive. The context of the situation becomes significant when questions of ethical behavior are examined because they pertain to an educational situation where the law provides the boundaries. Conflict between legal principles and ethical beliefs is of extreme importance to those in the field of education because the education of children with disabilities may be viewed and practiced as a moral endeavor. According to Howe and Miramontes (1992), ". . . in most cases, the legal thing to do will also be the ethical thing to do. But this will not always be so, since laws and regulations may be defective from an ethical point of view" (p. 9).

The Law and Ethical Practice

In the field of special education, dissension occurs when legal requirements and ethical principles appear incompatible. According to Pazey (1994), "individuals tend to rely on one of two value orientations: an ethic of justice or an ethic of care" (p. 19). The ethic of justice is a principle-based ethic, whereas the ethic of care is one of relationships and calls for a virtue-based ethic.

Principle-Based Ethic

Principle-based ethic arises from the philosophy of utilitarianism, or consequentialism. It is an abstract theory in which the individual who practices this form of ethics attempts to maximize the good. When faced with an ethical situation, the individual will first identify the principles involved, and then rationally evaluate his or her choices of action in terms of these principles. For the individual's actions to be a form of principle-based ethic, the actions must satisfy the requirements inherent in the concepts of impartiality and universality.

Virtue-Based Ethic

The ethic of care, in contrast, is considered to be a virtue-based ethic. This form of ethics is based on virtuous deliberation. In an ethical situation, the individual will first decide what actions a caring, virtuous person would take, and then evaluate the choices of possible action in terms of how the actions exemplify the behaviors of a virtuous person. The focus would be one of concern emphasizing personal connections with others and protecting others from harm. A virtue-based ethic is considered to be particularistic instead of abstract. In fact, the person espousing this form of ethical beliefs might abandon his or her ethical beliefs in certain situations. Three examples of where ethical abandonment might occur are when (a) practical wisdom dictates a different response, (b) shared community values conflict with the proposed action (a form of communitarian ethical theory), or (c) a caring relationship, such as friendship, love, or family, impacts the individual's proposed actions (Howe & Miramontes, 1992).

IDEA and Ethical Practice

IDEA can be interpreted as a compilation of principles set forth by Congress to guide educators in their interactions with children with disabilities and their families. As such, it is an example of a principle-based ethic that is impartial and legalistic. Five principles incorporated in IDEA that exemplify this view include

1. The belief in a free public education for all children based on the principle of zero reject

2. The belief that a separate education is inherently unequal, thus the principle of the LRE

3. The belief that appropriate education services are a requisite right through development of an IEP

4. The belief that full participation of parents in the education of their child is essential to the development of an appropriate education

5. The belief that due process protection for children with disabilities and their parents is essential to protect individual constitutional right of access to an appropriate educational program

Special education professionals draw from both these ethical orientations because of role-related obligations. Usually, actions based on either orientation are compatible. The problem arises, as Howe and Miramontes (1992) noted, when they are not. When such situations occur, educators could be asked to choose between their belief in the virtue-based ethic of care and the ethic of justice as interpreted through principles based on the legislative mandates of IDEA. These principles become issues when they are viewed in a context-specific situation and by a professional who has role-related responsibilities and espouses a view that includes virtue-based ethics. In such a situation, the CEC Code of Ethics may give only general direction.

Thus, a third type of ethical orientation appears to exist within the special education arena. Based on role-related obligations, this ethical orientation seems to be a combination of the virtue-based ethic and the principle-based ethic. This form of ethical action is apparent when one considers the litigation that has occurred as a result of IDEA and its predecessors. When viewed externally, much special education litigation appears to exemplify these types of situations. In some cases, it appears that special educators might have been faced with ethical dilemmas where a virtue-based ethic comes in conflict with the principle-based ethic of the legislation. Each principle comprising IDEA has been reviewed by the judicial system.

Principle One: Zero Reject.   Zero Reject is a belief in the availability of a free public education for all children. Prior to the enactment of IDEA, parents and advocates initiated litigation that addressed the individual's right of access to the public educational system. These cases (*Mills v. Board of Education of the District of Columbia,* 1972; *PARC v. Commonwealth of Pennsylvania,* 1972) based their argument for the provision of services to children with disabilities on the fact that the state had undertaken the responsibility to educate its citizenry. Because *all* citizens of a state include those with disabilities, the logic was that a policy that rejected the child's rights to an education that was free to others violated his or her constitutional rights. This concept, known as Zero Reject, was supported in principle through the FAPE and Child Find requirements in IDEA. Later cases further expanded the discussion of this principle, including *Goss v. Lopez* (1975), *Board of Education of the Hendrick Hudson Central School District v. Rowley* (1982), *Tatro v. State of Texas* (1984), *Honig v. Doe* (1988), *Timothy W. v. Rochester, New Hampshire School District* (1989), and *Light v. Parkway C-2 School District* (1994).

Principle Two: Least Restrictive Environment.   LRE is a belief that a segregated education is inherently unequal. Basing their argument on that described in the racial segregation case of *Brown v. Board of Education of Topeka, Kansas* (1954), advocates expanded the issue to include individuals with disabilities who were segregated from their peers by removal from the regular class to special "segregated" classes in the public school. This segregation was believed to lead to a view of differentness, which, in the past, has led to a potentially diminished view of the individual's worth. Numerous researchers have examined the ramifications of labeling and segregating students (Graham & Dwyer, 1987; Leitch & Sodhi, 1986; Stainback & Stainback, 1991). These researchers found that the labeling of children to provide services both perpetuated and reinforced the label and the behaviors it suggested. Researchers examined teacher reactions to disability labels (Aloia & MacMillan, 1983; Foster, Ysseldyke & Reese, 1975; Smith, Polloway, Patton, & Dowdy, 2004) and found that the labels generated negative expectations in the teachers. Therefore, an individual can be stigmatized through both the labeling process and the removal from the general education classroom. Decisions in a number of cases (*Mattie T. v. Holladay,* 1979; *A.W. v. Northwest R-1 School District,* 1987; *Daniel R. R. v. State Board of Education,* 1989; *Sacramento City School District v. Rachel H.,* 1994) supported the belief that all individuals should be treated with equal respect. The site where this is most likely to occur is believed to be the age-appropriate regular classrooms (the LRE).

Principle Three: Appropriate Individualized Programs.   Appropriate individualized programs is a belief that appropriate services is a requisite part of the right of access to an education. For an individual to "maximize the good" that is considered to be inherent in the first two beliefs, a child should be allowed to access *all* educational services without regard to disability. If not, it is believed that he or she will be unable to function successfully in the community. This belief expands the original concept—that access to an education is a right that the states have guaranteed—to include the fact that without access to education future success may not occur. Litigation expanded the issue of physical exclusion to one of programmatic exclusion by purporting that a child can be excluded even when he or she is allowed in the school, if no program is provided for him or her or the program is inappropriate and thus gives no benefit. Cases that support this idea include *Halderman v. Pennhurst State School* (1979), *Board of Education of the Hendrick Hudson Central School District v. Rowley* (1982), *Springdale v. Grace* (1983), *Tatro v. State of Texas* (1984), and especially, *Burlington School Committee v. Department of Education of Massachusetts* (1985).

Principle Four: Parental Participation.   Parental participation is a belief that the participation of parents in the education of their child with disabilities is essential for the development of an appropriate education for the child. Parental participation in the development and implementation of the educational program for their child was one of the original issues that led to the enactment of the original special education legislation, IDEA. Without full participation in their child's educational program, parents could not fully advocate for their child's unique needs. This belief supports the previous three principles and underscores the belief that full parental involvement will enhance the chances that a child with a disability will have an appropriate education that will lead to future success. Although not always fully implemented by the schools, this belief is accepted by most educators and therefore, litigation is not extensive. Litigation has mainly focused on the provision of a foundation for parental decision making (*Meyer v. Nebraska,* 1923; *Pierce v. Society of Sisters,* 1925), as well as and the definition of what is a parent, including surrogate parents (*John H. v. MacDonald,* 1987) and foster parents (*Criswell v. State Department of Education,* 1986; *Converse County School District No. Two v. Pratt,* 1997).

Principle Five: Procedural Due Process.   Procedural due process is a belief that protections for constitutional rights must be available to assure children with disabilities and their families the right of access to an appropriate educational program. The first four principles provide a framework for parents to advocate for the "good" of their child. Previously, parents did not have a vehicle for their advocacy concerning their child's needs, but through due process procedures such a vehicle was provided. However, the parental view of "what is good for my child" may not be consistent with the school district's view of what is good for all those in the school. To balance the parent's view with the school's view, the process includes numerous procedures that purport to ensure both parties that their rights under the constitution were not violated. Three cases (*Diana v. State Board of Education of California,* 1973; *Goss v. Lopez,* 1975; *Larry P. v. Riles,* 1984) provided the major litigative support and guidelines for this principle.

Summary

Ethics are defined as the basic principles of right action. In special education, issues of "what is the right action?" are often confounded because of the need for compliance to legislative and regulatory requirements. Because special education educators are seen as persons from whom ethical behavior is required, then it is important that ethical principles be addressed in their teacher preparation programs if they are to act ethically within the parameters of their profession. Indeed, knowledge of the ethics governing special educators is a requirement of the essential professional knowledge base for the beginning special educator. Because individuals tend to rely on one of two value orientations, an ethic of justice or an ethic of care, it is important that the person recognizes his or her ethical orientation because IDEA has four principles that might give rise to ethical questions. Following are some examples of conflicts that might arise. The first principle is Zero Reject, where a conflict might arise if a child has severe behavioral issues and is being educated in the neighborhood school. The second principle of LRE includes a potential area of conflict when children are provided educational placements based on the beliefs that segregation is inherently unequal, and that all children can learn and should be taught with their age peers. The third is that of Appropriate Educational Programs and expands the definition of accessible programs beyond the barrier of physical exclusion to that of programmatic exclusion. The fourth principle is that of Parental Participation, where parents have the right and the obligation to advocate for their child. The question becomes what is the ethical action when all principles align in opposition to the action that we fervently want to take.

In summary, special educators must be aware of the conflict that may arise in the performance of their duties. The issues surrounding the moral/ethical principles discussed are especially relevant as situations continue to occur where the ethics of justice and the ethics of care are in conflict. As such, each educator must seek an awareness and understanding of his or her own ethics and how it intersects with the professional code of ethics. According to Harris (1992),

> someone holding what she claims to be a moral principle must be prepared to justify that principle in moral terms. That is in terms which would refer to the way in which violating the principle causes harm to persons or otherwise adversely affects persons or their interests or violates their rights or causes injustice. (p. 42)

Questions for Discussion

1. How will special educators determine what is an ethical action if it is based only on the ethic of justice?
2. What is the difference between principle-based and virtue-based ethics? Give a classroom-based example of each.
3. How will special educators determine what is an ethical action if it is based on the ethic of care?
4. How do the role-related obligations of special educators impact their choice of ethical orientations? Give an example of how this choice of ethical orientation may bring about conflict with an administration.
5. Give an example of where special educators might be involved in decisions and issues that require an understanding of legal obligations and personal ethical belief systems. Give reasons why this might occur.

Websites for Further Exploration

Personnel Preparation in Special Education
www.edlaw.net/
www.ideapractices.org/
www.kidstogether.org/IDEA/d-673.htm

Codes of Ethics and Ethical-Based Practice (Principle-Based Ethic, Virtue-Based Ethic)
www.cec.sped.org/ps
www.naeyc.org/
www.aera.net/aboutaera/?id-717

www.use.hcn.com.au/subject.%60Principle-Based%20Ethics%60/home.html
www.seas.upenn.edu/~kfoster/definitions_ethics.htm
www.optimal.org/peter/rational_ethics.htm
www.kspope.com/ethcodes/index.php

IDEA and Ethical Practice (FAPE/Zero Reject, LRE, Appropriate Individualized Program, Parental Participation, Procedural Due Process)

Home.comcast.net/~erozycki/Triage.html

References

Aloia, G. F., & MacMillan, D. L. (1983). Influence of the EMR label on initial expectations of regular classroom teachers. *American Journal of Mental Deficiency, 88,* 255–262.

A. W. v. Northwest R-1 School District, 813 F.2d 158 (8th Cir. 1987), *cert. denied,* 484 U.S. 874, 108 S.Ct. 144 (1987).

Board of Education of the Hendrick Hudson Central School District v. Rowley, 458 U.S. 176, 102 S.Ct. 3034, 73 L.Ed. 2d 690 (1982).

Brown v. Board of Education of Topeka, Kansas, 347 U.S. 483, 74 S.Ct. 686, 98 L.Ed. 873, 38 A.L.R. 2d 1180 (1954).

Burlington School Committee v. Department of Education of Massachusetts, 471 U.S. 359, 105 S.Ct. 1996, 85 L.Ed. 2d 385 (1985).

Converse County School District No. Two v. Pratt, C. D. and E. F., 993 F. Supp. 848 (D. Wyo. 1997).

Council for Exceptional Children (CEC). (1998). *What every special educator must know: The international standards for the preparation and licensure of special educators* (3rd ed.). Reston, VA: Author.

Criswell v. State Department of Education, 558 EHLR 156 (M.D. Tenn. 1986).

Daniel R. R. v. State Board of Education, 874 F.2d 1036 (5th Cir. 1989).

Diana v. State Board of Education of California, Civ. Act. No. C-70-37 RFP (unpublished) (N.D. Cal. 1970, *further order,* 1973).

Edgar, E. (1999). A narrative for special education: A personal perspective. *ETMRDD, 34,* 366–372.

Foster, G. G., Ysseldyke, J. E., & Reese, J. H. (1975). I wouldn't have seen it if I hadn't believed it. *Exceptional Children, 41,* 469–473.

Gartin, B., & Murdick, N. (2000). Teaching ethics in special education programs. *Catalyst for Change, 30,* 17–19.

Gartin, B., Murdick, N., Thompson, J., & Dyches, T. (2002). Issues and challenges facing special educators who advocate for their students. *ETMRDD, 37,* 3–13.

Goss v. Lopez, 419 U.S. 565, 95 S.Ct. 729, 42 L.Ed. 2d 725 (1975).

Graham, S., & Dwyer, A. (1987). Effects of the learning disability label, quality of writing performance, and examiner's level of expertise on the evaluation of written products. *Journal of Learning Disabilities, 20,* 317–318.

Halderman v. Pennhurst State School, 612 F.2d 84, 124 (3rd Cir. 1979).

Harris, J. (1992). *Wonderwoman and superwoman: The ethics of human biotechnology.* New York: Oxford University Press.

Honig v. Doe, 484 U.S. 305, 108 S.Ct. 592, 98 L.Ed. 2d 686 (1988).

Howe, K. R., & Miramontes, O. B. (1992). *The ethics of special education.* New York: Teachers College, Columbia University.

John H. v. MacDonald, 631 F. Supp. 208 (D.N.H. 1987).

Larry P. v. Riles, 343 F. Supp. 1306 (N.D. Cal. 1972), *aff'd,* 502 F.2d 963 (9th Cir. 1974), *further proceedings,* 495 F. Supp. 926 (N.D. Cal. 1979), *aff'd in part, rev'd in part,* 793 F.2d 969 (9th Cir. 1984).

Leitch, D., & Sodhi, S. S. (1986). "Specialness" of special education. *British Columbia Journal of Special Education, 10,* 349–358.

Light v. Parkway C-2 School District, 41 F.3d 1223 (8th Cir. 1994), *cert. denied,* 115 S.Ct. 2557, 132 L.Ed. 2d 811 (1995).

Mattie T. v. Holladay, No. DC-75-31-S (N.D. Miss. Jan. 26, 1979).

Meyer v. Nebraska, 262 U.S. 390, 43 S.Ct. 625, 667 L.Ed. 1042 (1923).

Mills v. Board of Education of the District of Columbia, 348 F. Supp. 866 (D.D.C. 1972).

PARC (Pennsylvania Association for Retarded Citizens) v. Commonwealth of Pennsylvania, 343 F. Supp. 297 (E.D. Pa. 1972).

Pazey, B. (1994). Introducing the ethic of care into special education administration. *CEC Today, 1,* 19.

Pierce v. Society of Sisters, 268 U.S. 510, 45 S.Ct. 571, 69 L.Ed. 1070, 39 A.L.R. 468 (1925).

Rosen, F. B. (1968). *Philosophic systems and education.* Upper Saddle River, NJ: Merrill/Prentice Hall.

Sacramento City School District v. Rachel H., 14 F.3d 1398 (9th Cir. 1994), *cert. denied,* 129 L.Ed. 2d 813 (1994).

Smith, S. S., Voorhees, R. W., & Morris, W. (1997). *Funk & Wagnalls new international dictionary of the English language: Comprehensive edition.* Chicago: Ferguson.

Smith, T. E. C., Polloway, E., Patton, J. R., & Dowdy, C. A. (2004). *Teaching students with special needs in inclusive settings* (4th ed.). Boston: Pearson/Merrill.

Springdale v. Grace, 494 F. Supp. 266 (W.D. Ark. 1980), *aff'd,* 656 F.2d 300, *on remand,* 693 F.2d 41 (8th Cir. 1982), *cert. denied,* 461 U.S. 927, 103 S.Ct. 2086 (1983).

Stainback, W., & Stainback, S. (1991). Rationale for integration and restructuring: A synopsis. In J. W. Lloyd, N. N. Singh, & A. C. Repp (Eds.), *The regular education initiative: Alternative perspectives on concepts, issues, and models* (pp. 225–239). Sycamore, IL: Sycamore.

Tatro v. State of Texas, 481 F. Supp. 1224 (N.D. Tex. 1979), *vacated,* 625 F.2d 557 (5th Cir. 1980), *on remand,* 516 F. Supp. 968, *aff'd,* 703 F.2d 823 (5th Cir. 1983), *aff'd sub nom.,* Irving Independent School District v. Tatro, 468 U.S. 883, 104 S.Ct. 3371, 82 L.E. 2d 664 (1984).

Timothy W. v. Rochester, New Hampshire School District, 875 F.2d 954 (1st Cir. 1989), *cert. denied,* 493 U.S. 983, 110 S.Ct. 519 (1989).

The American Legal System

Governance of the United States of America

Government in the United States is based on a two-tiered system known as federalism. That is, the government is comprised of two levels that work as separate entities and as a group. The group of individual entities is known as states and has joined together to form a united governmental system. These states each have governing power, although a central, or "federal," government also governs each state. This central, or second-tier, government was envisioned as the protector of the rights and liberties guaranteed by the U.S. Constitution and as the purveyor of actions that are purported to provide for the "common good" of the people.

The U.S. Constitution does not address the provision of education to its citizenry. Because it is not addressed, it has been understood that it is under the governance power of the individual states. The federal government, though, has become involved in some situations, such as the provision of education to individuals with disabilities, where the government "stepped" in to provide for those citizens who it was believed were not being provided the rights and guarantees of the U.S. Constitution. The ability of the federal government to override the will of the states was seen as a power provided them in the general welfare clause of the Constitution. Therefore, the federal government has entered the educational arena, although indirectly, through the provision of monetary grants that states can accept or reject (acceptance meaning that they will follow the federal guidelines accompanying that grant), and, directly, through the enactment of legislation dictating educational policy. During the past few decades, the federal government's intervention has significantly increased using both methods. As a result, any professional involved with education and educational policy must understand the U.S. court system and the sources of law.

Sources of Law

The sources of law as they pertain to education can be found on three different levels: federal, state, and local. The sources differ at each level, as described.

Federal Level

At the federal level, the sources of law consist of the U.S. Constitution, statutes enacted by the legislative bodies of the federal government, regulations developed by agencies within the executive arm of the federal government, and case law decisions from the federal court system that interpret constitutional and federal law. Each has a parallel source at the state level.

Constitution. The U.S. Constitution is the primary source of law in the United States of America. Federal statutes developed from it are considered to take precedence over state or local statutes. The Constitution specifies the rules by which the federal system functions and allocates the powers and responsibilities of the different branches of the federal government (executive, legislative, judicial). The only way that changes can be made in the U.S. Constitution is by amendments that must be approved by the states. Only 26 amendments have been added to the Constitution, with the first 10 amendments known as the Bill of Rights.

Statutes. Laws, called statutes, are created in the U.S. Congress, under the authority of the U.S. Constitution. Legislation, in order to be enacted as law, follows a specific complicated process and may be promulgated by either the House of Representatives or the Senate. After reviewing the proposed legislation in committees and following the passage by both the House and the Senate, the bill is sent to the President for approval or veto. If a veto occurs, then the House and Senate may override it with a two-thirds vote of their membership.

When a bill is passed, it receives the letters, P.L., standing for public law with numbers that stand for the congressional session in which it was passed, and the number assigned to it has a hyphenated ending. Thus, P.L. 105–17 identifies the statute as a public law numbered 17 that was passed during the tenure of the 105th Congress.

Regulations. After passage of a bill, it is necessary to develop procedures to assist in implementation of the law. Depending on the area in which the bill is focused, the appropriate agency within the executive branch of the government is assigned to develop the procedures, known as regulations. Sometimes these regulations are referred to as rules or guidelines. However, when finalized, regulations have the force of the law, and therefore, violation of a regulation is comparable to a violation of the original law.

Case Law. When a complaint is heard by the judiciary system, an opinion is prepared by the sitting judge(s). These published opinions form a body of law known as case law. This information provides guidelines to decisions, that is, interpretation of the law for other courts. Bodies of these decisions when compiled provide information that sets precedent for later questions heard by the judiciary and may lead to further statutory enactment. An example of this was the case of *Smith v. Robinson,* which was reversed by the later passage of the Handicapped Children's Protection Act of 1986.

Executive Orders and Attorney General Opinions. An executive order is a statement by the U.S. president that when issued becomes a source of law. The attorney general may also provide an official opinion to a question concerning laws. The attorney general's opinion differs from that of the executive order in that it is only an advisory opinion and not as compelling as case law.

State Level

The sources of law at the state level mirror the federal level and are comprised of the same components.

State Constitutions.   Each state in the United States has a constitution that provides guidelines for the rights and responsibilities of its citizens. One major difference between the federal constitution and the state constitutions is that education is included in the state constitutions. With differing language, each state in the United States guarantees its citizens a free education for a proscribed length of time. In addition, each state requires that children residing within its borders attend school until a proscribed age, that is, compulsory education.

State Statutes.   Statutes, or laws, passed at the state level are the most significant laws for the citizens of that state. State statutes are particularly important in the area of education because in most situations these are the laws that govern the education of the children residing within the state. State statutes resemble statutes at the federal level and are designed to clarify and regulate governmental functions.

Regulations.   Similar to the federal government, state governments allot to various state agencies the task of developing regulations corresponding to the enacted statutes. These regulations provide more specific guidelines for the implementation of the statutes.

Case Law.   Litigation may also occur on the state level. Decisions from state litigation also provide assistance in the interpretation of statutes that may not have clear regulations. When numerous litigative decisions occur, they may be compiled into a significant body of case law that provides officials with legally approved guidelines.

State Board of Education, Chief State School Officer, and State Department of Education. Officials who guide education in the various states provide professionals at the local level with another source of law. Each state has identified a different title, duties, and responsibilities for its chief state school officer, state board of education, and state department of education. Any rule or regulation developed by these officials carries the weight of law as long as it does not conflict with the state and federal constitution.

Attorney General Opinions.   The attorney general at the state level functions in the same manner as the attorney general at the federal level. The opinions expressed by the attorney general concerning questions of law should be considered as advisory only. Attorney general opinions are guides, and the opinions are often tested with the courts.

Local Level

At the local level, the sources of education law consist of specific school board policies and regulations combined with the individual school's rules and procedures. Each district, even within the same state, may employ widely varying policies and regulations to meet the state statutes. These policies and regulations serve as sources of law for the specific district and have authority as long as they are in compliance with state and federal statutes and regulations.

United States Court System

The judiciary, or court, system in the United States is a two-tiered system that operates at the state and federal levels (see Figure A.1). This system has its basis in the federal and state constitutions. Generally, the courts hear different issues depending on the right or statute that has been violated. In some cases, though, the issues may overlap both levels. When that occurs, the individual bringing an issue to the court system may choose which one to hear the issue. In both the state and federal systems, the requirement is in place that administrative remedies, at the local and state levels, must be exhausted prior to initiating a court action under IDEA at the state or federal level.

Equity Law

There are specific areas of law, such as constitutional law, tort law, and others, that address different issues or suits pertaining to that specific legal area. However, education

Figure A.1
Geographic boundaries of the U.S. Courts of Appeals and the U.S. District Courts.

has no such specific body of law. As a result, education is heard within the body of civil law known as equity law. Equity law deals with issues related to due process and equal protection. When issues in equity law are heard, the courts must balance the individual's rights with the demands and rights of society as a whole.

State Court System

Each state has developed its own court system. As a result there is little uniformity among the levels and identifiers for the state courts. Although there is no consistent naming of the courts, they generally fall into three groups.

Courts of Original Jurisdiction.   The lowest level of court in each state is the level at which suits must be originally heard. Thus, it is known as the Court of Original Jurisdiction. Names identifying these courts include Circuit Courts, District Courts, Courts of Common Pleas, Superior Courts, and, in New York, Supreme Courts.

Intermediate Appellate Courts.   The second level in many of the state systems is an intermediate appellate court level. At this level, which approximately 25 of the states have, issues are reviewed based on the written record provided and issues specifically related to procedures are heard. These courts also have various names including Courts of Appeals, Appellate Divisions of the Superior Courts, Departments of the Superior Courts, Appeals Courts, and, in New York, Appellate Divisions of the Supreme Court.

State Supreme Court.   The highest level court in each state is generally known as the state supreme court. The purpose of this court is to review appeals from the decisions made at the lower courts level. The names for this court include the Court of Appeals, the Supreme Court of Appeals, and the Supreme Judicial Court. This court is the final level of decision for issues related to state matters. If an issue also relates to a federal question, then it may be appealed past the state supreme court to the federal court system.

Federal Court System

The federal system is three tiered. The judiciary system is designed and included in the U.S. Constitution as the judge reviewer of alleged violations of federal statutes or of the U.S. Constitution. At each level of the court system, the decisions made become sources of law, that is, are binding, for the portion of the state, or the circuit, in which the cases were heard. The decisions may be persuasive in other courts but are not binding.

District Courts.   The District Courts are the Courts of Original Jurisdiction at the federal level. Each state has at least one District Court, whereas some states have two, three, or four districts. The districts may be designated as the southern, northern, eastern, middle, or western districts within a state.

Courts of Appeal. The intermediate judiciary level for the federal court system is known as the Courts of Appeal. As on the state level, these courts review only written appeals of decisions made by the Court of Original Jurisdiction. At the present time, there are 13 federal judicial circuits, including the 11 geographic regions, the District of Columbia, and the Federal Circuit (see Figure A.1). The First Circuit includes Puerto Rico, Maine, New Hampshire, Massachusetts, and Rhode Island. New York, Vermont, and Connecticut comprise the Second Circuit. The Third Circuit includes Pennsylvania, New Jersey, Delaware, and the Virgin Islands. The Fourth Circuit includes West Virginia, Maryland, Virginia, North Carolina, and South Carolina. Texas, Louisiana, and Mississippi comprise the Fifth Circuit. In the Sixth Circuit are Ohio, Kentucky, Tennessee, and Michigan, whereas the Seventh Circuit includes Wisconsin, Indiana, and Illinois. The Eighth Circuit has North Dakota, South Dakota, Nebraska, Arkansas, Missouri, Iowa, and Minnesota. The Ninth Circuit includes Alaska, Washington, Oregon, California, Hawaii, Arizona, Nevada, Idaho, Montana, Northern Mariana Islands, and Guam. The Tenth Circuit is comprised of Wyoming, Utah, Colorado, Kansas, Oklahoma, and New Mexico, and the Eleventh Circuit includes Alabama, Georgia, and Florida. The District of Columbia Circuit hears cases for the District of Columbia only, whereas the Federal Circuit hears appeals related to patent and trade, as well as some claims brought against the federal government or its agencies.

Supreme Court. At the federal level, the Court of Final Jurisdiction, also known as the Court of Last Resort, is the U.S. Supreme Court. The authority to interpret federal issues was established in *Marbury v. Madison* (1803), and there is no appeal for a decision made by the U.S. Supreme Court. Supreme Court holdings (i.e., decisions) may be changed by a subsequent Supreme Court ruling or by amendment to the U.S. Constitution.

Generally, when an individual wants to appeal a lower court decision to the Supreme Court, a petition for a hearing must be made to the Court. This is known as a *writ of certiorari* or a *writ of cert.* This petition explains the reasons that the Court should hear the appeal. For an appeal to be heard, four of the nine Supreme Court justices must agree that the issue has merit and should be accepted for review, thus becoming known as the "rule of four." If the rule of four is not met, then the case is not heard and the decision of the lower court stands. The *denial of certiorari* or *denial of cert.* is neither a support nor a denial of the decision of the lower court, but rather it is a statement that at the present time there is no substantive reason for the Supreme Court to grant a hearing on the issue. A *denial of certiorari* is not as strong as a written decision by the Supreme Court but still provides assistance in the interpretation of statutes.

References

Handicapped Children's Protection Act of 1986, 20 U.S.C. § 1415 *et seq.* (West, 1990).

Marbury v. Madison, 5 U.S. 137 (1803).

Smith v. Robinson, 468 U.S. 992, 104 S.Ct. 3457 82 L.Ed. 2d 746 (1984).

APPENDIX B

Reading and Researching Case Law

Analysis or "Briefing" of Case Law

To collect succinct and significant information from case law, an orderly process known as "briefing" of a case is often used. "Briefing a case" is a legal term for a systematic method of obtaining information from a legal decision. By using this method, the researcher can identify the most relevant sections of a legal decision and glean information quickly and simply. The decision, as published in a legal reporter, includes information concerning the case title and citation, court type and level, facts of the case, disputed issues, and the holding (decision) of the court.

Case Title and Citation

First, the complete title of the case and all its citations should be listed. The title lists all litigants, with the plaintiff(s) named first. It also includes the court and year in which the case was decided. Other historical information may also be included. A more expanded discussion of citation rules is included later in this appendix.

Court Type and Level

Next, the level and type of court in which the decision was made should be listed. This provides the researcher with jurisdictional information that will provide information essential to the generalization and applicability of the court's decision to other states.

Facts

The section of the litigation entitled *Facts* should be read. The facts provide the reader with a description of the actual circumstances and events that are involved in the case. If there is not a section labeled "facts," then this information is usually provided in the first portion of the decision. From this information, a brief summary of the most relevant information can be prepared.

Issues

According to LaMorte (1993), "an issue is a disputed point or question of law upon which a legal action is based" (p. 417). Case law decisions usually result from disputes arising from two types of issues: substantive and procedural issues. Substantive issues are the broad legal questions or reasons on which the case has been brought to the court; that is, on what statute is this case based or what legal right has been violated? Procedural issues relate to disputes concerning the process of enforcing the rights that citizens are guaranteed. In other words, what steps in the process have been violated? These procedural issues thus become a reason for the case to be heard, as well as lead to its possible appeal. When reading a case, the researcher must clearly identify and understand the issues being litigated.

Court's Holding

The decision made by the court in a dispute is known as a holding(s). This decision when prepared in writing usually includes the specific decision(s), the reasons for the decision(s), the legal precedent for the argument, and applicable statutes. If there are concurring or dissenting opinions by individual judges, these may also be included with the holding. These additional opinions provide additional material to use when analyzing the case. Although these opinions have no bearing on the final results in the case, they may be used as precedent in other cases.

Legal Doctrine

Since case law decisions are based on specific legal doctrines, the researcher must identify the specific legal doctrine used to clarify what effect the holding(s) may have on other legal doctrines presently in effect. In other words, does this case affect the entire United States, or just a specific district or individual state, or how will it affect school policies?

Significance of the Decision

The final step in analyzing a case is to consider the significance this case may have for the field of special education and/or education in general. Although the decision on significance is one based on the personal opinion of the reviewer, it should be analyzed in regard to relevant legislation, other case law in the specific jurisdiction, and the professional knowledge particular to the reviewer.

Understanding Legal Citations

To identify cases and/or know where they can be found, one must become cognizant of the rules for legal citations. Cases are identified in a specific shorthand manner that the knowledgeable researcher can use to quickly find the correct reference book in which the case has been published.

A legal citation includes information in a specific order and manner. The first part of the citation is the title. This has three components: the name of the plaintiff(s); the letter "*v.*," which stands for the word *versus;* and the name of the defendant(s).

The party initiating the court proceeding is considered the plaintiff, and that name is listed first. If an appeal is heard, then the names are switched.

Following the title is the volume number of the book in which the case was published, the title of the reference book in which it was reported, known as a Reporter, and the page on which the decision begins. In parentheses immediately following this information is the level of court giving the decision and the year in which it was heard. For example, in the case of *Roncker v. Walters,* 700 F.2d 1058 (6th Cir. 1983), the parts would be identified as follows:

1. Title: *Roncker v. Walters,* with the plaintiff being named Roncker and the defendant named Walters
2. Volume: 700
3. Title of Reporter: F.2d (Federal Reporter, Second Series)
4. Page Number: 1053
5. Court: 6th Circuit (Federal Appeals Court)
6. Year: 1983

Parallel or Dual Citations

In some citations, other sources where the case has been reported are also listed. These are known as parallel or dual citations. In this situation, the official reporter or authoritative text is always listed first. In other words, the first citation listed is the one that has been approved by the state or circuit for publication. An example of this type of citation is as follows:

> *Abingdon School District v. Schempo,* 347 U.S. 203, 83 S.Ct. 1560, 10 L.Ed. 2d 844 (1963).

In this case the official reporter is the U.S. Reports (cited as U.S.), volume 347, with the case report beginning on page 203. This case is also reported in volume 83 of the Supreme Court Reporter (cited as S.Ct.), beginning on page 1560, and also in the U.S. Supreme Court Reports, Lawyers Edition (cited as L.Ed.), volume 10, beginning on page 844. The decision was made in 1963.

Explanation of Prior History

Sometimes explanatory words are included in the citation that provide the reviewer with the prior litigative history of the case. For example, in the case of *State v. Young,* the citation reads 234 GA 488, 216 S.E. 2d 586 (1975), *cert. denied,* 423 U.S. 1039 (1975). This indicates that this is a decision of the Georgia Supreme Court issued in 1975. It was reported in volume 234 of the Georgia Reports (cited as GA), beginning on page 488, and also reported in volume 216 of the Southeastern Reporter, 2nd Series (cited as S.E. 2d). Then, it also states that certiorari to the Supreme Court of the United States was denied (in other words, the Supreme Court declined to review the case). This action was reported beginning at page 1039 of volume 423 in the

U.S. Reports. Another example of an explanatory citation is that in the citation for *Alabama Civil Liberties Union v. Wallace,* 331 F. Supp. 966 (M.D. Ala. 1971), *aff'd* 456 F.2d 1069 (5th Cir. 1972). This is a 1971 decision of the federal District Court for the middle district of Alabama (cited as M.D. Ala.) that is reported in the Federal Supplement (cited as F. Supp.), beginning on page 966 in volume 331. This case also contained an action in which the U.S. Court of Appeals for the 5th Circuit affirmed the lower court's decision the following year. This was reported in the Federal Reporter, 2nd Series (cited as F. 2d) in volume 456, beginning at page 1069.

Introduction to Legal Research

According to Cohen and Olson (1996), "legal research is the process of finding the laws that govern most of our life activities and the materials which explain or analyze these laws" (p. 1). To complete legal research, it is necessary to become familiar with a variety of sources that can be consulted when researching an issue. These sources of information can be divided into three categories known as (a) primary sources, (b) secondary sources, and (c) finding aides.

Primary Sources

The first sources of information that should be searched are those considered primary sources of authority. These include the U.S. Constitution and the specific state constitutions, federal and state statutes, and relevant court decisions. Two other primary sources of authority are the state and federal attorney's general opinions and the policies and regulations of the state and local Boards of Education. Each piece of information is considered to include some form of binding authority in a specific legal area.

Secondary Sources

To further understand and/or search for relevant information about a specific issue, the researcher should consider the use of information known as secondary sources. Secondary sources do not have any authority but usually provide the researcher with discussions and analyses of legal issues. This material, although sometimes dated, can also provide the researcher with bibliographies related to the issues and lists of relevant cases. Secondary source materials include encyclopedias such as CJS (*Corpus Juris Secundum*) and AJ (*American Jurisprudence*), treatises and dissertations, periodicals and law review articles, and textbooks and casebooks in the field of law.

Finding Aids

To be effective in using the information identified through the aforementioned sources, the researcher must also review existing case law and the latest decisions available. Finding aids or tools provide the researcher with a method of accessing primary sources because finding aids do not have any authority. One finding aid is case digests, which are compilations of case references by topic. Another is loose-leaf services published by various groups throughout the United States that include case summaries and analysis of selected cases. Annotated codes and reporters are useful because they include an editorial discussion in conjunction with the publication of selected case decisions. An essential finding aid is a set of reporters known as Shephard's Citations. These citations provide the researcher with a method known as "Shephardizing" in which the current status of a case can be ascertained.

Using Computers for Legal Research

More recently, legal databases have been compiled on computer systems. These allow the researcher to access information in a rapid manner as well as the ability to access information when a law library is not convenient. The best known systems are Lexis, Westlaw, and Lois Law Library. A disadvantage to these databases is that they are generally only accessible to law students or lawyers. However, with the rapid expansion of the Internet, a significant amount of legal information is becoming available to anyone using a computer. According to Yell (1998), "the Internet is most useful for researching volatile areas of information, that is, areas in which information changes rapidly" (p. 39), such as the field of special education.

Examples of Internet sites referring to legal topics are

ABA's Lawlink: The Legal Research Jump Station
    www.abanet.org/lawlink/
American Law Sources On-line
    www.lawsource.com/also/
Commission on Mental and Physical Disability Law
    www.abanet.org/disability/
Council for Exceptional Children
    www.cec.sped.org
EDLaw
    www.edlaw.net
FindLaw: Internet Legal Resources
    www.findlaw.com/
'Lectric Law Library
    www.lectlaw.com
Special Ed Connection
    www.lrp.com/ed
The Law and Special Education
    www.ed.sc.edu/spedlaw/lawpage.htm

THOMAS: Legislative Information on the Internet
thomas.loc.gov/
U.S. Department of Education, Special Education & Rehabilitative Services
www.ed.gov/offices/OSERS/IDEA

References

Cohen, M. L., & Olson, K. C. (1996). *Legal research in a nutshell* (6th ed.). St. Paul, MN: West.

LaMorte, M. W. (1993). *School law: Cases and concepts* (4th ed.). Boston: Allyn & Bacon.

Yell, M. L. (1998). *The law and special education.* Upper Saddle River, NJ: Merrill/Prentice Hall.

APPENDIX C

Glossary of Legal Terms

A fortiori: Translation "from the most powerful reasoning." A conclusion that follows with even greater logical necessity than another already accepted in the argument.

Abstention doctrine: The principle that federal courts will not hear a case if it can be decided by state courts on the basis of state law alone.

Act: A law passed by a legislature. Synonym: statute.

Action: A proceeding in a court of law or equity, often referred to as a suit or lawsuit.

Ad litem: Translation "for the lawsuit." Designation of a person appointed by the court to represent a minor or an incompetent adult.

Advisory opinion: An opinion rendered by a court when no actual case is before it.

Affidavit: A written statement made or taken under oath before a person authorized to administer an oath.

Affirm (aff'd): To approve or uphold a lower court's judgment.

Amicus curiae: Translation "friend of the court." Generally, one who has an indirect interest in a case and offers or is requested to provide additional information to the court to clarify particular matters before the court.

Appeal: An application for review of a decision by a higher court to determine if the lower court committed an error.

Appellant: One who takes an appeal to a higher court. The appellant may have been the plaintiff or defendant in the lower court proceeding.

Appellate jurisdiction: The power vested in a superior court to correct legal errors and to revise the judgments of an inferior court.

Appellee: The party in an action against whom an appeal has been sought. Sometimes also called the respondent.

Bill: A formal written statement or complaint filed in a court of law.

Brief: A lawyer's written summary of facts and conclusion of law and facts involved in a particular case.

Capacity: The legal ability to sue or be sued based on a person's presumed ability to exercise his or her rights. For example, minors lack capacity to bring lawsuits on their own behalf. A *guardian ad litem* may be appointed by a court to represent a person lacking legal capacity to sue or be sued. "Capacity" also refers to legal or actual ability to make other kinds of decisions.

Case law: A body of law created by judicial decisions. By establishing precedents on which courts rely, the case law provides a primary source of legal authority.

Cause of action: The legal damage or injury on which a lawsuit is based. There must be a cause of action, or legal "wrong," for a court to consider a case. For instance, in several landmark lawsuits, such as the Willowbrook case (*NYSARC v. Carey*) and *Wyatt v. Stickney,* denial of treatment and maintenance of harmful conditions in institutions gave rise to causes of action for violation of constitutional rights.

Certiorari (cert.): Translation "to be informed of a means to gain appellate review." A judicial process whereby a case is moved from a lower court to a higher court for review. The record of the proceedings is transmitted to the higher court.

Civil action: A court action brought to gain or to recover individual or civil rights, or to obtain redress for an alleged noncriminal injustice.

Civil lawsuit: A noncriminal lawsuit filed to seek redress for an alleged wrong or injury.

Class action: A court action brought by one or more individuals on behalf of themselves and all others who have a similar interest in a particular issue.

Code: A systematic compilation of statutes (laws).

Commerce clause: The Constitution provides that Congress shall have power to regulate commerce, including federal regulations concerning business and industry.

Common law: A system of law in which authority is not derived expressly from statutes but from the traditional legal principles derived from usage and custom as a result of previous court decisions (precedent).

Compensatory damages: Damages or compensation awarded to reimburse the injured party only for the actual loss suffered.

Competing equities: A term describing a situation in which two or more people or groups of people have rights or privileges that cannot be fully satisfied without infringement on the right or privileges of the other.

Complaint: A formal pleading (document) to a court demanding relief and informing the defendant of the grounds of the lawsuit.

Conclusions of law: A judge's application of the law to the facts in a case.

Concurring opinion: An opinion written by a judge expressing agreement with the majority's holding. However, the concurring judge may disagree with the majority's reasoning or discuss additional principles or points of law and "concur in the result only."

Conflict of laws: An area of law dealing with the clarification of inconsistencies and differences in laws or jurisdictions as they apply to the rights of individuals in particular actions; a choice of which law to apply in any given case.

Consent (also *informed consent*): An intelligent, knowing, and voluntary agreement by someone to a given activity or procedure, such as a medical operation, a scientific experiment, or a commercial contract, that meets the following three conditions: (a) the person must be capable of understanding the circumstances and factors surrounding a particular consent decision, (b) information relevant to the decision must be forthrightly and intelligibly provided to the person, and (c) the person must be free to give or withhold consent voluntarily. Informed consent is a tool for safeguarding the rights of persons who may have difficulty understanding the implications of proposed activities or procedures—especially if activities or procedures are proposed that involve risk, may be irreversible or have an irreversible effect, or will be physically, psychologically, and socially intrusive.

Consent agreement (*consent judgment* or *consent decree*): An agreement of the parties made with the approval and sanction of the court.

Constitution: The supreme fundamental law of a nation or state that includes the authority to establish and organize the government and to distribute, limit, and prescribe the manner of the exercise of sovereign powers and that enumerates the basic principles and rights of the citizens.

Constitutional right: A right guaranteed by the U.S. Constitution or the constitution of the state in which a person resides, with the federal constitutional right superseding federal or state law or a state's constitution.

Contumacious conduct: Willful disobedience to the summons or orders of a court that may result in a finding of contempt of court; overt defiance of authority.

Court of record: A court whose actions are recorded, possessing the authority to prescribe sanctions.

Criminal action: A court action brought by the state against one charged with an offense against the state where the possible result can be the incarceration or fine of the defendant.

Cruel and unusual punishment (also the *Eighth Amendment*): A constitutional argument concerning the right of its citizenry to be free from punishment that is offensive to ordinary people; an argument that is often made in lawsuits regarding institutions for persons with mental illness and/or mental retardation, as well as prison cases and cases challenging the death penalty, because the residents were subjected to intellectual, emotional, social, and physical harm while in the custody of the state.

Damages: The monetary compensation or indemnity claimed by the plaintiff or allowed by the court for loss or injuries sustained as a result of a wrongful act or negligence of another.

De facto: Translation "in fact." A statement of affairs that must be accepted for all practical purposes but does not have the sanction of laws behind it; as distinguished from de jure.

De jure: Translation "by right, as a matter of law." A legitimate state of affairs with the force of law behind it; as distinguished from de facto.

De minimis: Translation "insignificant, minute." Trifling, or frivolous, matters with which the court will not concern itself.

De novo: Translation "new, afresh, a second time." A second trial of a case that on appeal has been sent back from a higher court to allow the lower court to decide the case on evidence without regard to prior procedures.

Decision: A conclusion or judgment of a court or a course of action decided on.

Declaratory judgment: A decision by the court that clarifies the law, proclaims the rights of parties, or declares an opinion without issuing an order for anything to be done.

Declaratory relief: A formal finding by the court of the parties' rights in a lawsuit that affirms the constitutional or statutory rights claimed by the plaintiffs and may be coupled with a court order granting injunctive relief.

Decree: A judicial decision.

Defendant: Party against whom the lawsuit is brought.

Defense: A denial, answer, or plea from the defendant as to why the accusation or lawsuit is without merit. Also, a defendant and his or her legal advisor(s).

Demurrer: A pleading claiming that although the facts may be accurate, the contentions submitted by the opposing party are insufficient in law to warrant justification in bringing action.

Discovery: A pretrial process for obtaining information possessed by the opposing party, which occurs after the lawsuit has been filed and prior to the trial; includes *depositions* to obtain oral testimony and *interrogatories* to obtain written answers to specific questions, requests for *documents* or *materials;* requests for *mental* or *physical examinations,* and requests for *admissions* (the opposing party admits the truth of certain statements or objective facts).

Dismiss: In the legal context, to terminate without a complete trial.

Dissenting opinion: An opinion written by a judge in disagreement with the rationale and/or decision of the majority of judges hearing the case on appeal.

Due process of law: A procedure where the powers of the government are exercised similarly in similar situations to protect individual rights; specifically required by the Fifth and Fourteenth Amendments when life, liberty, or property are involved. The right to a hearing with the opportunity to respond in a fair tribunal.

Eighth Amendment: The U.S. Constitutional Amendment that prohibits cruel and unusual punishment and excessive bails and fines.

Eleventh Amendment: The U.S. Constitutional Amendment that is rooted in the sovereign immunity doctrine and prohibits federal courts from hearing cases against a state unless the state consents to be sued. However, the amendment has been interpreted to allow suits against states for injunctive and declaratory relief based on federal law.

Enjoin: An individual, or institution, is required by a court of equity to cease or abstain from a particular action. See injunction.

Equal protection of the law: A particular branch of law that differs from the common law. Required by the Fourteenth Amendment of the U.S. Constitution. Primarily concerned with providing justice and fair treatment to all persons within its jurisdiction; it addresses issues that states are unable to consider.

Equity: Justice; fairness; neither inferior nor superior.

Et al.: Translation "and others." Indicates that unnamed parties are involved in the proceedings.

Et seq.: Translation "and following." Follows a noun and indicates that it includes the sections that follow.

Evidence: Documentation or proof, both physical and oral, that demonstrates the proof of a fact that is submitted to a court in support of the position in a suit. In court, the documentation submitted according to a complex set of rules that governs the admission of evidence in a court.

Ex parte: Translation "on behalf of, on the application of, one party, by or for one party." Proceeding made or done for the benefit of one party only and without notice to the adverse party.

Ex post facto: Translation "after the fact." A retrospective; after the action is taken; the

Constitution prohibits Congress and states from passing a law that makes earlier actions illegal.

Ex rel.:   Translation "upon relation or report." Legal proceedings initiated in the name of the state on information, or at the instigation, of a private individual with a private interest in the outcome. The individual on whose behalf the state is acting in a legal proceeding.

Exclusionary rule: A procedure used to suppress evidence that has been improperly obtained.

Exhaustion of administrative remedies: The doctrine that a person must attempt to resolve issues administratively before filing a lawsuit. A judge may decide not to hear a case unless administrative remedies have been exhausted. However, in most federal civil rights cases, including right to education and right to treatment suits, exhaustion of state administrative remedies is generally not required.

Expert witness: A professional who because of recognized competence or special knowledge of a subject is called to give evidence on matters related to the case within the professional's area of expertise and who is recognized by the court as having said knowledge.

Fifteenth Amendment: The U.S. Constitutional Amendment that guarantees citizens the right to vote, regardless of race, color, or previous condition of servitude.

Fifth Amendment: The U.S. Constitutional Amendment that provides for the protection of the citizenry by providing (a) that there must be an indictment from a grand jury before one stands for a capital or infamous crime; (b) that one cannot be placed in double jeopardy; (c) that one cannot be forced to testify against oneself; (d) that neither life, liberty, nor property may be taken without due process of law; and (e) that private property cannot be taken for public use without payment of just compensation.

Finding: A conclusion of a court, jury, or administrative body regarding a question of fact or law.

First Amendment: The U.S. Constitutional Amendment that limits the power of government, such as the rights of free speech, press, assembly, religion, and association.

Fourteenth Amendment: The U.S. Constitutional Amendment that guarantees that all persons born

within the United States are citizens of the United States and are guaranteed the privileges and immunities due to the citizens of the United States and to due process and equal protection of the laws.

Fourth Amendment: The U.S. Constitutional Amendment that guarantees the right of persons to be secure from unreasonable search and seizure and requires the authorities to seek a warrant (a) based on an oath (b) establishing probable cause from an (c) impartial magistrate, (d) which describes the place to be searched and (e) the items or persons to be seized.

Guardian: An individual who has the legal authority to make decisions on behalf of another. There are many types of guardians (also called conservators or committees), and guardianship rules vary by state.

Guardian ad litem: A person appointed by the court to represent the interests of a person lacking capacity (an incompetent) during legal proceedings. A *guardian ad litem* is sometimes referred to as *next friend* or *law guardian*.

Governmental immunity: See Sovereign immunity.

Habeas corpus: Translation "you have the body." The procedure for the judicial determination of the legality of an individual's custody. Also, an order (writ of habeas corpus) issued by a court to bring the person before the court to determine why the person is in custody and to release the person if unlawfully confined.

Hearing: A legal proceeding for the judicial determination of factual or legal issues.

Holding: The ruling of the court on the admissibility of evidence or other questions that apply to facts of the case.

In loco parentis: Translation "in the place of the parent." It includes the concept of assuming the obligations of the parent status, including discharging the duties and responsibilities.

In re: Translation "in the matter of." A method of entitling a judicial proceeding in which there are no adversaries.

Inalienable rights: Under the Bill of Rights, these are the fundamental rights that cannot be transferred to another or surrendered except by the person possessing them, such as the right to practice religion, freedom of speech, due process, and equal protection under the law.

Indemnity: The duty or obligation for one person to make good or compensate another for loss, damage, or injury sustained.

Infra: Translation "below or beneath." Included in a citation of a case and indicates that the same case is referred to in a later part of the same article, chapter, judicial opinion, etc.

Injunction: An order issued by a court of equity, which prohibits a person from committing a threatened act or continuing to perform an act that is injurious to the plaintiff.

Injunctive relief: An order from a court requiring or prohibiting the performance of specific acts; an order to remedy the violation of legally protected rights. Injunctive relief is often accompanied by *declaratory relief* or may be a *mandatory injunction.*

Inter alia: Translation "among other things."

Ipso facto: Translation "by the fact itself" or "in and of itself." As a necessary consequence.

Judgment: A decision rendered by a court that is effective when filed.

Jurisdiction: The power of a court to hear and determine a particular type of case.

Law: An act passed by a legislature. Synonym: statute.

Liability: A legal responsibility; an obligation to do or refrain from doing something.

Litigation: The formal contesting of a dispute in a court (lawsuit).

Majority opinion: The statement expressing the views of the majority of judges in a court decision.

Malfeasance: Commission of an unlawful or wrongful act.

Mandamus: A court order compelling a public official or institution to perform a particular nondiscretionary duty. Requiring someone to take action.

Mandate: A judicial command, order, or direction.

Mandatory authority: The supersession of rulings of higher courts over lower courts regarding legal interpretations. U.S. Supreme Court rulings are binding on all courts in regard to interpreta-

tions of federal statutes and the federal Constitution. A U.S. circuit court's ruling is authoritative for U.S. district courts within that circuit. State supreme court rulings are binding on all lower courts, as well as on federal courts concerning interpretations of that state's law.

Mediation: A process by which a neutral party attempts to negotiate a settlement in a dispute by persuading the parties to adjust their position.

Minority opinion: A statement expressing the views of a minority of judges in a court decision that may take the form of separate minority opinions. Normally occurs on appeal from a trial court.

Misfeasance: Wrongful or injurious performance of a legal act.

Money damages: Court-awarded financial payment for injuries suffered by one party due to the action or inaction of another. Damages are usually paid to the plaintiff by the defendant and may be either compensatory (to reimburse the plaintiff for loss or expenses) or punitive (to punish the defendant and deter future misconduct).

Moot: When a dispute no longer exists; the opposite of a "live" controversy.

Motion: A request to the court in the context of a specific case to take some action relating to the case.

Negligence: Failure to exercise ordinary prudence and foresight when such failure results in an injury to another.

Ninth Amendment: The U.S. Constitutional Amendment that guarantees that the rights enumerated in the Constitution shall not be construed to deny or disparage other rights retained by the people. These rights are so basic and fundamental that they must be considered essential rights.

Nolens volens: Translation "whether willing or unwilling."

Non Prosequitur: Translation "he has not proceeded." The plaintiff has not continued his or her action.

Nonfeasance: The total omission or failure to perform a required duty.

Notice: Actual communication of a fact to another.

Nuisance: Unreasonable interference with a right; continuous private or public use of property that results in injury, inconvenience, or damage.

On remand: To send back. Included in a citation of a case indicating that a lower court has entered a judgment, for at least the second time, when it received the case from a higher court with a judgment and order to act in a particular way.

Opinion: The reason given for a court's decision.

Order: A direction of the court or judge's ruling.

Ordinance: A local law, that is, a city, town, or county law.

Original jurisdiction: The jurisdiction of a court to entertain a case at its conception; the authority to consider and decide cases in the first instance as contrasted with appellate jurisdiction.

Parens patriae: Translation "the state is sovereign." Referring to the sovereign power of guardianship over persons such as minors.

Party: The litigant, either plaintiff or defendant, in a lawsuit.

Per curiam: Translation "by the court." An opinion of the majority rendered by an entire court, as opposed to an opinion of any one of several justices (compilation of thoughts of all justices).

Persuasive authority: A court's consideration of decisions from other jurisdictions in interpreting the law. For example, in *Welsch v. Likins,* the federal district court in Minnesota cited the Alabama federal court's ruling in *Wyatt v. Stickney,* and so did the Texas district court in *Morales v. Turman* as persuasive on the issue.

Petition: A formal written request to a court for the redress of a wrong or the grant of a privilege or license.

Petitioner: The party appealing a court's decision to a higher court. Synonym: appellant. Also sometimes used to identify the plaintiff in certain courts or types of cases.

P.L.:   Abbreviation for Public Law. The designation of a federal law with the numbers following "P.L." refer to the session of Congress during which the law was passed and the order in which the law was passed in that session, respectively. For example, P.L. 94-142 was the 142nd law passed during the 94th Congress.

Plaintiff: One who brings an action or files a complaint in a court.

Plea: A formal allegation filed by a defendant in an action in reply to the plaintiff's complaint or charges.

Pleadings: Formal documents filed in a court action, which may include the plaintiff's complaint, the defendant's reply, and relevant documents, indicating what is alleged by one party and denied or conceded by the other party.

Plenary: Full, entire, complete.

Prayer: A request by the plaintiff that the court of equity grant the particular relief sought.

Precedent: A prior court decision recognized as authority for the disposition of future cases and cited in the interpretation of a law or constitutional provision. A court may or may not accept a precedent as authoritative in interpreting the law in a specific case, depending on the factual similarities between the cases and the jurisdiction in which the precedent was decided.

Preliminary injunction: A form of injunctive relief that is a temporary order awarded to prevent a party from taking certain actions pending the court's final decision.

Prima facie: Translation "at first view." A fact presumed to be true unless disproved by some evidence to the contrary.

Private cause of action: An individual's ability to seek relief from a court for violation of a statutory or constitutional right (see Standing). A statute is said not to create a private right of action when it provides for remedies other than individual court proceedings and when there is no apparent legislative intent to allow individuals to sue when their rights under the statute are violated.

Pro se: Translation "on one's behalf." Generally refers to self-representation without the aid of counsel.

Procedural right: A right that relates to the process of enforcing substantive rights or to obtaining substantive relief.

Punitive damages: Compensation awarded that is over and above the actual loss suffered and designed to punish the opposing party for intentionally causing harm to another.

Quasi: Translation "as if, so to speak." Almost as it were, about, nearly, almost, like, analogous to.

Quid pro quo: Translation "what for what, something for something." A consideration, giving one valuable thing for another.

Relief: Legal redress or assistance awarded in court to the complainant, such as an injunction, but generally does not include damages.

Remand: To send back as for further deliberation. Following an appellate decision, a case may be sent back to the lower court from which it came for further proceedings.

Remedy: A court's enforcement of a right or the prevention of the violation of a right when the action is pending. The most common means to redress an injury is money damages.

Res ipso loquitur: Translation "the thing speaks for itself." A rule of evidence that contends that the occurrence of the injury or accident itself is evidence of negligence.

Res judicata: Translation "the thing has been decided." A matter that has been judicially decided and ends subsequent action on the same claim.

Respondent: The party against whom an appeal is taken in a higher court or the defendant at trial level in civil actions.

Restrain: To enjoin or prohibit.

Reversed (rev'd.): When present in a citation of a case, it indicates that a higher court has overturned the lower court's results and has entered a different judgment. May dismiss or send back to the lower court.

Review: A judicial reexamination of a lower court's decision by that same court or by an appeals court.

Second Amendment: The U.S. Constitutional Amendment that guarantees each state the right to maintain a well-regulated militia and the right for the people to keep and bear arms.

Settlement: An out-of-court agreement by the two parties considering a lawsuit. The settlement resolves some or all issues of the case.

Seventh Amendment: The U.S. Constitutional Amendment that guarantees the right to a jury trial in all civil cases before a federal court if the amount in the controversy exceeds a stated amount.

Shall/May: The term "shall" in a law, regulation, or court order is mandatory, whereas the term "may" is discretionary. The term "may" allows flexibility in a party's actions, including the flexibility not to act at all.

Sixth Amendment: The U.S. Constitutional Amendment that guarantees the accused in a criminal trial to a speedy trial by an impartial jury, to be informed of the charges, to be confronted with witnesses against him or her, to present witnesses on one's behalf, and to have effective assistance of counsel.

Sovereign immunity: A doctrine providing that a governmental body has absolute power and is immune to lawsuits unless the body itself consents.

Special master: A person appointed by a court to find fact, monitor, implement, or supervise the implementation of the court's order, or to provide reports to a court prior to a decision. The court in the *Pennhurst* case appointed a special master with the power and duty to plan, organize, direct, supervise, and monitor the implementation of its order. Appointment of a special master is usually on a defendant's presumed inability to implement a court's order.

Standing: An individual's right to bring suit before the court. The requirement that a plaintiff be an injured party or one in danger of being injured or, in other words, a direct interest in a suit.

Stare decisis: Translation "to stand by that which was decided." The doctrine whereby precedent assumes the authority of established law.

Status quo: Translation "the existing situation."

Statute: An act of the state or federal legislature; a law.

Statute of limitations: A statute that specifies the period of time within which a lawsuit must be brought after an alleged violation of rights. A person loses his or her right to sue after the time period has elapsed.

Statutory right: A right based on a statute, either federal, state, or local.

Stay: A judicial order forbidding or postponing the enforcement of a court ruling pending future legal action, such as an appeal to a higher court.

Stipulation: An agreement, admission, or concession between the parties in a lawsuit that certain facts are true.

Sub nomine (Sub nom.): Translation "under the name." Included in a citation and means that the title of the case was decided by another court under a different name.

Substantive right: A right, such as the right to an education, that has been granted by federal or state statutes or constitution.

Sui generis: Translation "of its own kind or class." Unique or in a class by itself.

Suit: A proceeding in a court of law brought by a plaintiff seeking a remedy.

Summary judgment: A preverdict judgment in response to a motion or pleading by defendant or plaintiff to settle a controversy or dispose of a case without conducting full legal proceedings.

Supra: Translation "above." In a citation indicating that the same case has been referred to previously in the same article, chapter, judicial opinion, etc.

Supremacy clause: Article VI of the U.S. Constitution. Under this clause, federal law is supreme when it conflicts with state and local law. Similarly, state law is supreme when it conflicts with local law.

Temporary restraining order: A form of emergency injunctive relief issued (often without a hearing) to preserve the status quo for a brief period pending a full hearing before the court. A party must show that immediate and irreparable harm will result if the order is not issued. For longer-term relief before the court's final decision, a preliminary injunction is necessary.

Tenth Amendment: The U.S. Constitutional Amendment that reserves to the states and the people any powers not specifically delegated to the United States or prohibited to the states.

Thirteenth Amendment: The U.S. Constitutional Amendment that prohibits involuntary servitude and peonage.

Tort: A private or civil wrong or injury.

Trial: A judicial examination of a civil or criminal case made by a judge or judges, with or without a jury.

Ultra vires: Translation "beyond, outside of, in excess of powers." Exceeding the power that is authorized by law.

Vacate: To cancel or rescind a court decision.

Verdict: A judge's or jury's decision on a question of fact.

Void: Without legal force or binding effect. Absolutely null.

Waive: To forego, renounce, or abandon a right. An intentional and voluntary giving up, surrendering, or relinquishing of a known right.

Writ: A written court order requiring performance of a specific act, such as a writ of injunction or mandamus.

Writ of certiorari (Writ of cert.): Translation "to be informed." A written request to the U.S. Supreme Court to review a lower court's ruling. The Supreme Court usually chooses to hear only those cases it considers important.

References

The definitions in this glossary were selected and revised from the following:

LaMorte, M. (1993). *School law: Cases and concepts*. Boston: Allyn and Bacon.

LaMorte, M. (1981). *School law: Cases and concepts*. Unpublished draft manuscript.

Taylor, S. J., & Biklen, D. (1980). *Understanding the law: An advocate's guide to the law and developmental disabilities*. Syracuse, NY: DD Rights Center of Mental Health Law Project and the Center on Human Policy.

Turnbull, H. R., III. (1990). *Free appropriate public education: The law and children with disabilities* (3rd ed.). Denver, CO: Love.

APPENDIX D

Case List

Abingdon School District. v. Schempo, 347 U.S. 203, 83 S.Ct. 1560, 10 L.Ed. 2d 844 (1963)

Age v. Bullitt County Public Schools, 701 F.2d 233 (1st Cir. 1982)

Agostini v. Felton, 521 U.S. 203, 117 S.Ct. 1997 (1997)

Alamo Heights Independent School District v. State Board of Education, 790 F.2d 1153, 1158 (5th Cir. 1986)

Amanda J. by Annette J. v. Clark County School District, 260 F.3d 1106 (9th Cir. 2001)

Andress v. Cleveland Independent School District, 64 F.3d 176 (5th Cir. 1995), *reh. denied* (no cite), *cert. denied,* 519 U.S. 812 (1996)

Arc of ND v. Schafer, 83 F.3d 1008 (8th Cir. 1996), *cert. denied,* 117 S.Ct. 482 (1996)

Armstrong v. Kline, 476 F. Supp. 583 (E.D. Pa. 1979), *modified and remanded sub nom.,* Battle v. Commonwealth of Pennsylvania, 629 F.2d 269 (3rd Cir. 1980), *on remand,* 513 F. Supp. 425 (E.D. Pa. 1980), *cert. denied sub nom.,* Scanlon v. Battle, 101 S.Ct. 3123 (1981)

Atlanta, GA Public Schools, OCR, Region IV, 16 EHLR 19 (1989).

A. W. v. Northwest R-1 School District, 813 F.2d 158 (8th Cir. 1987), *cert. denied,* 484 U.S. 874, 108 S.Ct. 144 (1987)

Baby Neal v. Casey, 821 F. Supp. 320 (E.D. Pa. 1993), *rev'd,* 43 F.3d 48 (1994)

Baer v. Klagholz, 771 A.2d 603 (2001)

Barnett v. Fairfax County School Board, 927 F.2d 146 (4th Cir. 1991), *cert. denied,* 502 U.S. 859, 112 S.Ct. 175 (1991)

Battle v. Commonwealth of Pennsylvania, 629 F.2d 259 (3rd Cir. 1980)

Beth B. v. School District #65, 282 F.3d 493 (7th Cir. 2002)

Bills v. Homer Consolidated School District No. 33-C, 959 F. Supp. 507, 511 (N.D. Ill., 1997)

Board of Education of the Hendrick Hudson Central School District v. Rowley, 458 U.S. 176, 102 S.Ct. 3034, 73 L.Ed. 2d 690 (1982)

Board of Education of Kiryas Joel Village School District v. Grumet, 512 U.S. 687, 129 L.Ed. 546, 114 S.Ct. 2481 (1994)

Board of Education of Northfield Township High School District 225 v. Roy H. and Lynn H., 1021 IDELR 1173 (N.D. Ill. Jan. 12, 1995)

Bonadonna v. Cooperman, 619 F. Supp. 401 (D.C. N.J. 1985)

Brookhart v. Illinois State Board of Education, 697 F.2d 179 (7th Cir. 1983)

Brown v. Board of Education of Topeka, Kansas, 347 U.S. 483, 74 S.Ct. 686, 98 L.Ed. 873, 38 A.L.R. 2d 1180 (1954)

Burilovich v. Board of Education. of Lincoln, 208 F.3d 560, 565 (6th Cir. 2000)

Burke County Board of Education v. Denton, 895 F.2d 973, 982 (4th Cir. 1990)

Burlington School Committee v. Department of Education of Massachusetts, 471 U.S. 359, 105 S.Ct. 1996, 85 L.Ed. 2d 385 (1985)

Carlisle Area School District v. Scott P., 62 F.3d 520 (3rd Cir. 1995)

Carroll v. Capalbo, 563 F. Supp. 1053 (D.R.I. 1983)

Chester County Intermediate Unit v. Pennsylvania Blue Shield, 896 F.2d 808 (3d Cir. 1990)

Cleburne v. Cleburne Living Center, Inc., 473 U.S. 432, 87 L.Ed. 2d 313, 105 S.Ct. 3249 (1985)

Cleveland Heights-University Heights City School District v. Boss, 144 F.3d 391, 398–99 (6th Cir. 1998)

Clevenger v. Oak Ridge School Board, 744 F.2d 516 (6th Cir. 1984).

Cole v. Greenfield-Central Community Schools, 657 F. Supp. 56 (S.D. Ind. 1986)

Colorado River Water Conservation District v. United States, 424 U.S. 800, 47 L.Ed. 2d 483, 96 S.Ct. 1236 (1976)

Converse County School District No. Two v. Pratt, C. D. and E. F., 993 F. Supp. 848 (D. Wyo. 1997)

Cordrey v. Euckert, 917 F.2d 1460, 1474 (6th Cir. 1990)

Criswell v. State Department of Education, 558 EHLR 156 (M.D. Tenn. 1986)

Crocker v. Tennessee Secondary School Athletic Association, 980 F.2d 382 (6th Cir. 1992)

Daniel R. R. v. State Board of Education, 874 F.2d 1036 (5th Cir. 1989)

Das v. McHenry School District No. 15, 41 F.3d 1510 (unpublished opinion) (7th Cir. 1994)

Deal *ex rel* Deal v. Hamilton County Department of Education, 259 F. Supp. 2d 687 (E.D. Tenn. 2003).

Debra P. v. Turlington, 644 F.2d 397 (5th Cir. 1981)

Debra P. v. Turlington, 730 F.2d 1405 (11th Cir. 1984)

Deitsch v. Tillery, 309 Ark. 401, 833 S.W. 2d 760 (1992)

Diana v. State Board of Education, Civ. Act. No. C-70-37 RFP (unpublished) (N.D. Cal. 1970, *further order,* 1973)

DiBuo by DiBuo v. Board of Education of Worcester County, 309 F.3d 184 (4th Cir. 2002)

Doe v. Anrig, 651 F. Supp. 424 (1987)

Doe v. Phillips, 20 IDELR 1150 (N.D. Cal. 1994)

Doe v. Smith, 879 F.2d 1340 (6th Cir. 1989), *cert. denied sub nom.,* Doe v. Sumner County Board of Education, 493 U.S. 1025 (1990)

Duane B. v. Chester-Upland School District, 21 IDELR 1050 (D. Ct. E.D. Penn. 1994)

Espino v. Besteiro, 520 F. Supp. 905 (S.D. Tex. 1981)

Evans v. Evans, 818 F. Supp. 1215 (N.D. Ind. 1993)

Felter v. Cape Girardeau School District, 830 F. Supp. 1279 (E.D. Mo. 1993)

Florence County School District Four v. Carter, 510 U.S. 7, 114 S.Ct. 361, 126 L.Ed. 2d 284 (1993)

Fullilove v. Klutznick, 448 U.S. 448, 100 S.Ct. 27, 65 L.Ed. 2d 902 (1980)

GARC v. McDaniel, 716 F.2d 1565 (1983), *cert. granted,* 469 U.S. 1228, 105 S.Ct. 1228 (1983), 740 F.2d 902 (1984), *vacated,* 468 U.S. 1213 (1984)

Gary B. v. Cronin, 542 F. Supp. 102 (N.D. Ill. 1980)

Gerstmyer v. Howard County Public Schools, 850 F. Supp. 361 (D. Md. 1994)

Gladys J. v. Pearland Independent School District, 520 F. Supp. 869 (S.D. Tex. 1981)

Goss v. Lopez, 419 U.S. 565, 95 S.Ct. 729, 42 L.Ed. 2d 725 (1975)

Great Valley School District v. Douglas and Barbara M. *ex rel* Sean M., 807 A.2d 315 (2001)

Greer v. Rome City School District, 950 F.2d 688 (11th Cir. 1991), *withdrawn,* 956 F.2d 1025 (1992), *and reinstated,* 967 F.2d 470 (1992)

Grun v. Pneumo Abex Corporation, 163 F.3d 411 (7th Cir. 1999), *cert. denied,* 119 S.Ct. 1496, 143 L.Ed. 2d 651 (1999)

Halderman v. Pennhurst State School, 612 F.2d 84, 124-129 (3rd Cir. 1979)

Helbig v. City of New York, 597 N.Y.S. 2d 585 (Sup. 1993), *rev'd,* 622 N.Y.S. 2d 316 (1995)

Heldman v. Sobol, 962 F.2d 148 (2nd Cir. 1992)

Hensley v. Eckerhart, 461 U.S. 424, 103 S.Ct. 1933, 76 L.Ed. 2d 40 (1983)

Hessler v. State Board of Education, 700 F.2d 134, 139 (4th Cir. 1983)

Hobson v. Hansen, 269 F. Supp. 401 (D.D.C. 1967), *dismissed,* 393 U.S. 801 (1968), *aff'd sub nom.,* Smuck v. Hobson, 408 F.2d 175, 132 D.C. 372 (D.C. Cir. 1969)

Holland v. District of Columbia Public Schools, 71 F.3d 417, 315 D.C. 158 (D.C. Cir. 1995)

Holmes v. Sobol, 690 F. Supp. 154 (W.D. N.Y. 1988)

Honig v. Doe, 484 U.S. 305, 108 S.Ct. 592, 98 L.Ed. 2d 686 (1988)

Horry County School District v. P. F., 29 IDELR 354 (D. S.C. 1998)

Hurry v. Jones, 734 F.2d 879 (1st Cir. 1984)

In re Child with Disabilities, 16 EHLR 538 (SEA Tenn. 1990)

In re Child with Disabilities, 20 IDELR 455 (SEA NH 1993)

Irving Independent School District v. Tatro, 468 U.S. 883, 104 S.Ct. 3371, 82 L.Ed. 2d 664 (1984)

Jason D. W. v. Houston Independent School District, 158 F.3d 205 (5th Cir. 1998)

John H. v. MacDonald, 631 F. Supp. 208 (D.N.H. 1986)

Johnson v. Independent School District No. 4, 921 F.2d 1022, 1028 (10th Cir. 1990)

Johnson v. Lancaster County Children and Youth Social Services Agency, 19 IDELR 1094 (D.Ct. E.D. Penn. 1993)

Kanawha County (WV) Public School, OCR, Region III, 16 EHLR 450 (1989)

Katherine G. by Cynthia G. v. Kentfield School District, 261 F. Supp. 2d 1159 (2003)

King v. Board of Education of Allegany County, 999 F. Supp. 750, 764 (D. Md. 1998)

Roncker v. Walter, 700 F.2d 1058 (6th Cir. 1983), *cert. denied,* 464 U.S. 864, 104 S.Ct. 196 (1983)

Rufo v. Inmates of Suffolk County Jail, 502 U.S. 367, 112 S.Ct. 748, 116 L.Ed. 2d 867 (1992)

S-1 v. Spangler, 650 F. Supp. 1427 (M.D. N.C. 1986), *cert. denied,* 115 S.Ct. 205, 130 L.Ed. 2d 135, *vacated as moot,* 832 F.2d 294 (4th Cir. 1987)

S-1 v. Turlington, 635 F.2d 342 (5th Cir. 1981), *cert. denied,* 454 U.S. 1030 (1981)

Sacramento City School District v. Rachel H., 14 F.3d 1398 (9th Cir. 1994), *cert. denied,* 129 L.Ed. 2d 813 (1994)

Salinas Union High School District, 22 IDELR 301 (SEA Cal. 1995)

San Antonio School District v. Rodriguez, 411 U.S. 1, 93 S.Ct. 1278, 36 L.Ed. 2d 16 (1973)

San Bernardino, CA Unified School District, OCR, Region IX, 16 EHLR 656 (1990)

Saucon Valley School District v. Robert and Darlene O. *ex rel* Jason O., 785 A.2d 1069 (2001)

School Board of Nassau County v. Arline, 480 U.S. 273, 107 S.Ct. 1123, 94 L.Ed. 2d 307 (1987)

Schuldt v. Mankato School District No. 77, 937 F.2d 1357 (8th Cir. 1991), *cert. denied,* 502 U.S. 1059, 112 S.Ct. 937, 117 L.Ed. 2d 108 (1992)

SEA, School District of Beloit, 25 IDELR 109 (Dec. 21, 1996)

Seals v. Loftis, 614 F. Supp. 302 (D.C. Tenn. 1985)

Sellers v. School Board of City of Manassas, Virginia, 141 F.3d 524 (4th Cir. 1998), *cert. denied,* 119 U.S. 168, 142 L.Ed. 2d 137 (1998)

Skinner v. Oklahoma, 316 U.S. 535, 62 S.Ct. 1110, 86 L.Ed. 1655 (1942)

Smith v. Robinson, 468 U.S. 992, 104 S.Ct. 3457, 82 L.Ed. 2d 746 (1984)

Southeast Community College v. Davis, 442 U.S. 397, 99 S.Ct. 2361, 60 L.Ed. 2d 980 (1979)

Springdale v. Grace, 494 F. Supp. 266 (W.D. Ark. 1980), *aff'd,* 656 F.2d 300, *on remand,* 693 F.2d 41 (8th Cir. 1982), *cert. denied,* 461 U.S. 927, 103 S.Ct. 2086 (1983)

Springer v. The Fairfax County School Board, 134 F.3d 659 (4th Cir. 1998)

St. Johnsbury v. D. H., 240 F.3d 163 (2nd Cir. 2001)

State *ex rel.* Beattie v. Board of Education of Antigo, 169 Wis. 231 (Wis. 1919)

State of Connecticut v. Bruno, No. 14851 (1996)

Steinberg v. Weast, 132 F. Supp. 2d 343 (D. Md. 2001)

Stockton by Stockton v. Barbour County Board of Education, 884 F. Supp. 201 (N.D. West Va. 1995)

Stuart v. Nappi, 443 F. Supp. 1235 (D. Conn. 1978)

Tatro v. State of Texas, 481 F. Supp. 1224 (N.D. Tex. 1979), *vacated,* 625 F.2d 557 (5th Cir. 1980), *on remand,* 516 F. Supp. 968, *aff'd,* 703 F.2d 823 (5th Cir. 1983), *aff'd sub nom.,* Irving Independent School District v. Tatro, 468 U.S. 883, 104 S.Ct. 3371, 82 L.Ed. 2d 664 (1984)

Taylor by Holbrook v. Board of Education, 649 F. Supp. 1253 (N.D. N.Y. 1986)

Tennessee Department of Mental Health & Mental Retardation v. Paul B., 88 F.3d 1466 (6th Cir. 1996)

Thomas R. W. by Pamela R. and Edward W. v. Massachusetts Department of Education, 130 F.3d 477 (1st Cir. 1997)

Timothy W. v. Rochester, New Hampshire School District, 875 F.2d 954 (1st Cir. 1989), *cert. denied,* 493 U.S. 983, 110 S.Ct. 519 (1989)

United States v. Merz, 376 U.S. 192, 84 S.Ct. 639, 11 L.Ed. 2d 629 (1964)

United States Railroad Retirement Board v. Fritz, 449 U.S. 166, 101 S.Ct. 453, 66 L.Ed. 2d 368 (1980)

University Interscholastic League v. Buchanan, 848 S.W. 2d 298 (Tex. Ct. App. 1993)

Virginia Department of Education v. Riley, 106 F.3d 566 (1996), *superseded,* 106 F.3d. 559 (4th Cir. 1997)

Watson v. City of Cambridge, 157 Mass. 561 (1893)

W. B. v. Matula, 67 F.3d 484 (3rd Cir. 1995)

Wilson Co. School System v. Clifton, 41 S.W.3d 645, 649 (Tenn. Ct. App. 2000)

Wisconsin v. Yoder, 406 U.S. 205, 92 S.Ct. 1526, 32 L.Ed. 2d 15 (1972)

Wyatt v. Stickney, 325 F. Supp. 781 (M.D. Ala. 1971, 1974)

Yates v. Charles County Board of Education, 212 F. Supp. 2d 470 (D. Md. 2002)

Yick Wo v. Hopkins, 118 U.S. 356, 6 S.Ct. 1064, 30 L.Ed. 220 (1886)

Younger v. Harris, 401 U.S. 37, 91 S.Ct. 746, 27 L.Ed. 2d 669 (1971)

Zobrest v. Catalina Foothills School District, 963 F.2d 1190 (9th Cir. 1992), *rev'd,* 509 U.S. 1, 113 S.Ct. 2462, 125 L.Ed. 1 (1993)

AUTHOR INDEX

This index contains author citations only. All citations of cases and laws appear in the subject index.

Note: Page numbers in *italics* indicate illustrations.